CROSSING THE AISLE

CROSSING THE AISLE

How Bipartisanship Brought

Tennessee to the Twenty-First Century

and Could Save America

by Keel Hunt

Vanderbilt University Press
Nashville

© 2018 by Vanderbilt University Press
Nashville, Tennessee 37235
All rights reserved
First printing 2018

This book is printed on acid-free paper.
Manufactured in the United States of America

Library of Congress Cataloging-in-Publication Data
LC control number 2018034571
LC classification number F440 .H863 2018
Dewey classification number 306.209768/0904
LC record available at *lccn.loc.gov/2018034571*

ISBN 978-0-8265-2239-9 (cloth)
ISBN 978-0-8265-2241-2 (ebook)

For Lewis

Politics is a beautiful word to me. Politics builds roads and bridges. Politics educates our children and helps handicapped children walk.
—State Senator Anna Belle Clement O'Brien 1984

And if we cannot be civil to one another, and if we stop dealing with those with whom we disagree, or that we don't like, we would soon stop functioning altogether.
—Senator Howard H. Baker Jr. 1998

While we yet hold and do not yield our opposing beliefs, there is a higher duty than the one we owe to political party. This is America and we put country before party.
—Vice President Al Gore 2000

This history is largely lost.
—Congressman Jim Cooper 2015

CONTENTS

FOREWORD

I GREW UP ON Missionary Ridge, the Civil War battlefield overlooking Chattanooga; in my childhood we could still find Minié balls from the battle in which a young Union soldier, Arthur MacArthur, the father of Douglas, received the Congressional Medal of Honor. The war's relics were real and tangible—I still have a few on my desk as I write—as was much of the complex American story. Braxton Bragg had been headquartered a few hundred yards from my house, and as children we would play baseball on the grounds of his camp. A few miles in the other direction sat the house of Chief John Ross of the Cherokee Nation. My contemporaries and I were sometimes taken to feed the ducks in a small pond there.

For Tennesseans, therefore, as for so many other Southerners, history is neither clinical nor remote, but real and present. And not just the ancient history: Chattanooga, like the state itself, reinvented itself in the twentieth and twenty-first centuries, building first an industrial economy and then, as the world changed, created an ethos that enabled it to thrive in the Information Age. Old times here may not be totally forgot, but they have also never been constricting.

How the Tennessee of today—a prosperous and congenial island of civility in a nation of division—came to be is the subject of the following pages. In this fascinating and constructive new study, Keel Hunt has given readers here and beyond an invaluable guidebook to confronting and overcoming the most difficult of civic challenges. Anyone interested in creating jobs, building communities, solving problems, and moving forward with what Franklin Roosevelt once called "strong and active faith" will find Hunt's thoughtful explanation of the Tennessee story illuminating and even inspirational.

Even more so than many of its neighbors in the perennially perplexing South, Tennessee is a study of contrasts. It's in our DNA. Taken as a whole, for instance, the state was always ambivalent about the Confederacy. In February 1861 a majority of the state's voters opposed a proposed secession convention. Union sentiment was particularly strong in the more mountainous eastern region of the state, with Confederate sympathy growing as one moved west, toward Memphis and the Mississippi.

Then came Fort Sumter, the federal call for militia to fight the secessionists, and Middle and West Tennessee carried the day at last, taking the state out of the Union.

By the end of the war, 120,000 Tennesseans had fought for the Confederacy, but a significant number, 31,000, took up arms for the Union. As historians have noted, that meant Tennessee alone provided the Federal forces with more soldiers than all other seceded states combined. Tennessee was the last state to secede and the first to rejoin the Union—a purplish state in the days before we spoke in terms of red and blue.

The state's complicated geography and politics has made it an intriguing case study in how to govern. And so Hunt's central theme is intriguing, too: the ways and means by which a series of transformative leaders have successfully transcended traditional political labels and divisions to create a place that welcomes pilgrims and strangers who quickly become neighbors and friends.

We make music and cars; we take care of the sick; we educate and we farm, even now. And we're able to do all of those things in no small measure because of the stories Hunt tells here—stories of political leaders from both sides of the aisle who kept their eye on the big picture, not the small fights. In 1978, when Lamar Alexander was running for governor (a biblical forty years ago, a fact I don't think he loves my mentioning, so I mention it a lot), he invited Tennesseans to "Come On Along"—along to a brighter future. Here's the story of that unfolding journey.

Jon Meacham
Nashville, 2018

INTRODUCTION

The In-Between Time

IN THE SPRING of 2014, after my book *Coup* had been out for ten months, I was still enjoying the interviews, lectures, and book talks that will come an author's way. One evening, near the end of one book club gathering in south Nashville, a gentleman in the rear of the room raised his hand and, referring to the decade of the 1970s, asked me this:

"So why was Tennessee so Democratic then and it's so Republican now?"

Good question. It had been a long day, and this particular event had already run well over an hour. The man's question was simple, but the answer was not. The truthful reply would take more time than any of us had to give on that waning evening.

THE GREAT TRANSITION IN southern politics, which changed the South from deep blue to crimson red, like most important trends in American history did not have a single cause. Many currents shaped the new shoreline.

What we may remember now as the modern turning point for Tennessee, and for much of the South, was gradual and occurred on many levels over the final third of the twentieth century. Political shifts, economic progress, policy reforms, racial tensions and political responses to them, the rising up of leaders and also of demagogues—all these influenced the internal story of this fraught period in Tennessee. Part of the turn was a seismic political shift that had manifestations in election results across the nation's broader politics. The change was brought on by personalities as well as events, both locally and nationally.

IN THE 1980s AND '90s, Tennesseans found ourselves smack in the middle of two political eras. The first was the one-party rule of Democrats, which had lasted until the 1960s. The other would be the one-party Republican dynasty, which was firmly in place by the year 2012.

It was a complicated period of transition, and I call it the In-Between Time. It was a time when intense political competition flourished. With each election, offices would swing back and forth between the political parties. As competition usually does in many realms, this vigorous political sporting attracted talent and produced excellence.

From these contests rose political figures of national stature that included a vice president of the United States (Al Gore Jr.), several presidential candidates (Howard Baker, Gore, Lamar Alexander, Fred Thompson), members of presidential cabinets (Alexander, Bill Brock), majority leaders of the United States Senate (Baker, Bill Frist), congressional committee chairmen (Jo Byrns, Kenneth McKellar, Joe L. Evins, Jim Sasser, Alexander, Bob Corker), and U.S. ambassadors (Prentice Cooper, Sasser, Baker, Victor Ashe). This phenomenon was noticed outside Tennessee. But more importantly for Tennessee's citizens, it sprang from and fed a rising competitiveness that attracted talented governors, mayors, and legislators who turned the political structure of the state upside down and inside out and began to chart a different, more ambitious course forward.

This book is about how this intense political competition and extraordinary infusion of political talent helped make the 1980s a turning point for Tennessee. Before the 1980s, Tennessee had the third-lowest family incomes of any state, almost no auto manufacturing jobs, sub-par education and road systems, and an inferiority complex left over from the financial realities of the poverty of mountain life, rural sharecropping, and the Civil War's legacy of devastation.

But beginning in the early 1980s, Tennesseans lifted our sights, thought bigger, and began to accomplish more. The state became the third-largest producer of cars and trucks, built the nation's best four-lane highway system, was the first state to pay teachers more for teaching well, and established "Centers of Excellence" and one hundred million-dollar-endowed faculty "Chairs of Excellence" at its public universities. Family incomes rose faster than in most states and so did the confidence of Tennesseans.

By 1986, astonishingly, *National Geographic* magazine put a big spotlight on this changing state, with the headline "Rising, Shining Tennessee" on its May cover.

❖

IT IS PROPER TO question whether too much credit can be given to the contemporary political leadership during that in-between time. Other factors were surely at play.

For one thing Americans more generally were now looking to the South and West as attractive places to live and work, and Tennessee captured its share of this economic migration. The state also took advantage of the economic rebound during the years of the Reagan presidency. The U.S. government was now using its power to force foreign automakers to make here what they sold here. Nissan and other important companies were therefore looking for the best environment in which to make their American products. They were attracted to the central location and "right-to-work" labor environment of Tennessee, as opposed to the Midwest where the auto industry and its union had become ossified and were producing noncompetitive products. (See *The Reckoning* by David Halberstam, whose own career began covering the civil rights movement for the *Tennessean* in Nashville.)

It made a difference that the 1980s were "in-between years" in other ways as well. This was before the internet, globalization, Amazon.com and Wal-Mart had so dramatically changed the workplace and eviscerated many small communities. There were only four national television networks delivering the news. The internet itself was not in common usage until the 1990s. No Facebook, no iPhone, generally no email or instant messaging as yet, and no social media device capable of transmitting and repeating millions of messages constantly questioning public officials. (It was not until 1988 that Rush Limbaugh began his national radio broadcasts, assaulting the political establishment on a daily basis.) In short, it was a time when governing was objectively easier.

For all these reasons, the turn that has made so much difference might to some extent have happened anyway or was at least easier to accomplish then than it might be today. But, as the following pages will also document, it is hard to escape the conclusion that it was the quality of Tennessee's political leadership that helped attract the auto plants and the sports franchises, that helped build the roads, challenge the education system, and renew citizen confidence.

Was it really competition that caused so many talented political leaders to spring from Tennessee during this decisive era? It had happened once before. As the nineteenth century began, when Tennessee *was* the western frontier of the United States (and its sixth most-populous state) there was rowdy political ferment. In that time it was Whigs versus Democrats. From that ferment sprang three presidents (Andrew Jackson, James K. Polk, Andrew Johnson), two speakers of the House (John Bell, Polk), and such characters as Governor Sam Houston and Congressman Davy Crockett.

Tennessee's nineteenth-century competition was arguably as fierce as that of the latter half of the twentieth century. In 1834, President Jackson became so enraged at Crockett's criticism of the administration's Indian removal policy that he recruited Adam Huntsman, a one-legged veteran of the

Mexican War, to run against the troublesome congressman. Huntsman won, leading Crockett to declare on the steps of the Madison County Courthouse what every defeated candidate has wanted to say to the voters: "You may all go to hell, and I will go to Texas." He departed for the Alamo, and there he died.

THE INTRIGUING QUESTION THAT the following set of stories now raises, but of course cannot answer, is how Tennessee's current one-party Republican rule might shape the future—and how long that particular majority might endure. This question may have broader significance beyond Tennessee; it has relevance today to much of the South and much of the nation.

In the 1960s, when Howard Baker and Bill Brock attracted a cadre of ambitious young Republicans to work toward a two-party state, Democrats held every state office and every federal office except for two congressional seats in East Tennessee. In 1965 only nine of the thirty-three state senators were Republicans. Today, the landscape is just reversed. All the federal office holders today are Republicans except for two urban Democratic congressmen—in Memphis and Nashville—and only six of the thirty-three state senators are Democrats. The supermajority has moved to the other side of the aisle.

Will today's relative lack of political competition produce for the Republican Party the same doldrums that existed before the 1960s when the Democrats' one-party rule was complete?

With only a few conspicuous exceptions (Cordell Hull's distinguished career, and the 1950s vice-presidential competition among Frank Clement, Albert Gore Sr., Kenneth McKellar, Prentice Cooper, and Estes Kefauver), there was no steady stream of unusually able political leaders issuing from Tennessee during the century between the Civil War, when the Democrat-Whig contests ended, and the 1960s, when Republicans began to challenge one-party Democratic rule.

I HOPE THESE NEW stories may provide lessons from a time not so long ago when politics worked better, when elected officials brought honor to the offices and the titles they held. They did not always agree, but on the major questions requiring speed and wisdom between elections, they found common ground and stood together upon it. They made things work and, together, achieved good results.

These are not chiefly stories about elections—which candidate won, who lost, by what margin—but of what happened between them, of the consequences of elections, with illustrations of why politics is ultimately important in our nation. These are true tales of how politics and public service are valuable, and how progress can be real in the public realm.

Growing up in a family of Democratic politicians who were local public officials, I learned from an early age about campaigns and electioneering. As a young reporter and editor at Nashville's morning newspaper, I observed politics and politicians at work, and how some of the victors were successful in their work in office and others were not. It does matter who wins.

History presents to each administration and each generation new issues and opportunities to transact. My hope is that these twenty-five stories provide some understanding of how the officials who won and served in the in-between time were able to work cooperatively with counterparts on the "other side of the aisle." They did not forget their own politics or parties— their own voter "bases" as we would say today—but wisely reached beyond narrow partisan interests in order to advance deeper purposes.

As Florida governor Bob Graham said to State Senator Anna Belle Clement O'Brien on that day in 1984—one Democrat to another Democrat— when he was urging her to vote for the pioneering education reform proposal from the Republican Alexander in spite of fierce opposition from the National Education Association:

"What I think we always need to consider is how best to use the time that we've been given to serve," Graham said. "We won't be here forever."

THESE ARE STORIES OF a time when Republicans and Democrats worked together to prepare Tennessee for the twenty-first century. It is about an earlier period in just one southern state not so long ago, but its lessons could be a handbook for anyone today in any state or community—and, yes, in Washington also—who is striving for results in our American system of government.

This story could be about other decades, even the current one, though stories about bipartisan cooperation today seem harder to locate. Governor Bill Haslam will tell you that Tennessee in 2018 has the lowest taxes, lowest debt, fastest-improving schools, and fastest-growing auto jobs of any state. Tennessee is also the first to grant free tuition for a two-year college degree. All this didn't happen by accident. It is the result of strong leadership, but its foundation is four decades of good, sometimes exceptional leadership by both Republicans and Democrats with similar goals working together to solve problems and get results.

The timeframe of this book is roughly the twenty-year period that closed the twentieth century, the decades of the 1980s and 1990s. It is worth noting that this time of progress closely followed the 1979 coup in Tennessee. I had concluded that the coup that ousted Governor Blanton was, ultimately, not a story of "bad guys doing wrong" but of "good guys doing right" in their rapid but unprecedented resolution of that crisis. The crisis was real enough, and indeed was brought on by corrupt people, but how the "good guys" stopped it was ultimately a leadership lesson—a story of statesmanship over partisanship. Likewise, in hindsight now, the bipartisan ouster of Blanton was the pivot point of crisis that got Tennessee's leaders of both parties—and thus the state itself—onto new, surer footing for the future. As in other southern states, Republicans by this time had become strong enough politically to end a century of one-party Democratic rule. Competitive campaigns attracted better candidates, and just before the decade of the '70s ended, in order to put an end to Blanton's power to pardon, it was Democratic legislative leaders who inaugurated a Republican three days ahead of schedule, ousting their own party's governor. Their secret negotiations over a climactic afternoon turned out to be a sort of boot camp for bipartisanship. In so doing, the key participants—senior leaders, both Democrat and Republican—came to know, trust, and rely upon one another to achieve results, and opened the door to a very different future.

Those boot camp lessons paid dividends, as the same leaders then worked together to help Tennessee win intensive national competitions for the Nissan and Saturn auto plants, and enacted four major road programs to build the nation's best four-lane highway system to carry auto parts from suppliers to the new assembly hubs. For the next forty years in Tennessee, Republicans and Democrats alternated as governor. They ran their races with ferocity, but once the campaigns ended each handed off to his successor in the other party more opportunities to make things work.

They made our system of government work in my time.

MY LONGTIME FRIEND AND colleague Lewis Lavine, whom I met in 1977, made a helpful comment to me one day: "In the South," he said, "the way we learn and make our points with each other is with stories." That reminded me of all the times I had heard Alexander recall the good advice of his friend Alex Haley, to wit: "If you would begin by saying, instead of making a speech, 'Let me tell a story' then somebody might actually listen to what you have to say."

This book is a collection of stories. It does not aim to be a history in the classical sense of that term. These are true tales that in the fullness of time have taken on significance for me, beyond the lives and careers of the immediate participants.

A final word about these stories and my own perspective during and after that time: At some places in the text, you will notice the pronoun "we" or an attribution that a principal character "told me" this fact or that personal memory. In cases of the former, it is because I was a participant myself; in the latter, the information came in one of the 384 interviews that have been so important to my research for this book. I was a young newspaper reporter when I met Lamar Alexander in Memphis in the summer of 1974, when he was running for governor the first time, the year he lost that race to Blanton. I left the newspaper staff in 1977 to join Alexander's second campaign as his research director and speechwriter. When he won, he asked me to join the governor's staff, where I worked as a policy advisor and speechwriter until the summer of 1986.

When Ned McWherter was elected governor that year, many of his key people had become my friends, and we threw a "transition" party at my house. So I acknowledge my subjectivity and, looking back over three decades, how my personal experiences have doubtless influenced which stories I have chosen to tell and how I have related them in these pages.

But I hope I have been fair in rendering them here, as illustrations of a special period of time and the lessons they offer us now. Especially now, when politics in America has become so angry.

Keel Hunt
Nashville, 2018

CHAPTER 1

Wild Ride to Washington

THE TWIN-PROP KING AIR bumped, shuddered, and careened its way through a frightening sky.

The VIP passengers were braced for nearly three hours of choppy air, from Nashville to Washington, DC. With every jolt of turbulence, the four elected officials who were on board would grip their arm rests for support, their eyes darting out the round cabin windows.

"If we still had the Lear jet, I guess we could have cut this trip in half," said the new senator, Lamar Alexander, a Republican and former governor, hoping to lighten the anxieties with a little humor. By this time the Lear was long gone.

"Well, I guess you're the one who sold it," Governor-elect Phil Bredesen, Democrat, replied in his own good humor. He would take the oath of his new office in just a few weeks.

The incumbent governor on this day, Republican Don Sundquist, nearing the end of his second four-year term, smiled slightly but otherwise did not respond. Eight years earlier, Sundquist had defeated Bredesen in a bitter 1994 race for governor.

In the fourth facing seat was Nashville Mayor Bill Purcell, Democrat. A former state legislative leader himself, he knew what they were talking about.

In the mid-1970s, an earlier Tennessee governor, Ray Blanton, had scandalized the jet, among other misuses of his office. He once took the Lear to Jamaica with his girlfriend, and then insisted to the reporters who quizzed him afterward that he had only used the jet to sell soybeans to the Chinese. The Lear thus became a campaign issue in the 1978 race for governor. Alexander, the winner that year, sold the controversial jet within a week after he took office.

"So, who did sell the Lear?" Purcell asked, knowing the answer. Alexander pointed to one of the rear seats, indicating Tom Ingram, his longtime chief of staff.

❖

NO ONE WAS ENJOYING this flight. As the King Air rocked forward, two other senior staffers were also in the shaking cabin: Tony Grande, Sundquist's economic development commissioner, and Tom Jurkovich, director of Purcell's economic development office.

"It was terrifying—the worst flight I was ever on," Jurkovich told me. "We hit this horrendous turbulence. The plane was shaking. Ingram and I were scrunched in the back two seats, and this ceiling panel fell down over our heads. I remember seeing it dangling by a wire."

Grande, seated forward, remembers vividly: "That plane was rocking and rolling. We were in a band of weather from Nashville all the way to Washington. At one point, I saw Don put his finger under his shirt collar, which I'd noticed he would sometimes do when he was nervous. When we landed at Andrews Air Force Base, I think we were all glad to get off the plane."

At Andrews, two Tennessee state troopers wearing street clothes met them and drove the group through driving rain to the Capital Hilton Hotel, one block north of the White House. Inside the lobby, Tennessee's senior senator met them: Republican Bill Frist, the former heart transplant surgeon. (Within weeks Frist would become the Senate's majority leader. As chairman of the Senatorial Campaign Committee, he was leader of the political and fundraising effort that kept the Republicans in the Senate majority, and his colleagues would soon reward him with their top leadership spot.) Frist walked with the group, in silence, to a private meeting room.

But the most important person inside that room was neither a senator nor a governor nor a mayor, but a man of Lebanese descent. This man—born in Brazil, resident of South Carolina, and fluent in four languages—was Carlos Ghosn, the chief executive officer of Renault and Nissan.

By this time, Ghosn was an international business celebrity. He was the man who had brought Nissan back from the brink of bankruptcy. In 1999, with an aggressive recovery plan he named "Nissan 180," Ghosn had pledged to revive the company, return it to profitability by the end of the next fiscal year, and by 2002 to a profit margin exceeding 4.5 percent with zero debt. He had also promised to resign if these goals were not met.

His goals were met. This is why Ghosn was now being called "Mr. Fix It" across the automobile industry. Confident and determined, he now presided over headquarters in both Tokyo and Paris, and devoted many of his working hours to air travel visiting his manufacturing plants around the world. These operations included the Nissan production facility southeast of Nashville, now twenty years old and the largest and most efficient auto and truck plant in North America.

For the Tennesseans in the room, this meeting had a simple purpose: To carefully hand off—from Republican governor Sundquist to his Democratic successor Bredesen—the state's pursuit of Nissan's new North American headquarters, including Tennessee's financial commitments that would make it possible. They were determined to assure Nissan's supreme leader that there would be a seamless transition of political support when Bredesen took office seven weeks later. In this ultra-private meeting, sitting around a square conference table, Commissioner Grande made a brief presentation, and the VIP discussion followed.

NISSAN HAD FIRST COME to Tennessee twenty-two years before this. In 1980, in Alexander's second year as governor, Nissan became the first Japanese automaker to place a major manufacturing facility in the southeastern U.S., initially producing small pickup trucks. Most other automakers had their leadership offices and production facilities in the Midwest. Now, two decades later, Tennessee was home to Nissan's largest and most successful auto manufacturing facility at Smyrna with engines made at Decherd and components from hundreds of other "just-in-time" suppliers.

This recruitment mission in Washington was a high-stakes bet. If these state leaders were successful, Tennessee would have the first-ever North American headquarters of any major automaker to be established in the Southeast. Sundquist had brokered this private meeting, having overseen the negotiations to date with top Nissan leaders, including Jim Morton, the former Michelin executive who rejoined Ghosn in 2000 and was now Nissan's vice chairman for North America.

"We'd been courting Nissan to move their headquarters here from California," Sundquist told me. "At that time Nissan had some problems, and I'd been talking to Carlos. He'd said to me that whenever he was ever able to straighten things out—he had been brought in to crack the problems at Nissan—that whenever they straightened those out, he was planning to move the headquarters. Earlier in 2002, I had a dinner at the governor's residence for Jim Morton and Carlos Ghosn, and we got a commitment from Carlos that, once he was able to do what he had to do at Nissan, he said, 'It's likely we will move our headquarters to Nashville.' So it was at that dinner that he committed to relocate in Tennessee. The deal was pretty well sealed when we went up to Washington, but the handoff to the next administration was obviously very important."

Bredesen, the Democrat, was elected governor on Tuesday, November 5, 2002, his second run at the office. That same night, Alexander, the Republican, was elected the state's junior senator. When the polls closed across Tennessee, it was already Wednesday morning for Sundquist, who was again in Tokyo on a separate recruiting mission with Commissioner Grande. When he learned who the new governor would be, Sundquist placed an international call to Bredesen to congratulate him.

Grande told me it was on this trans-Pacific call that Bredesen first learned from Sundquist of the ultra-secret Nissan headquarters project. The new governor-elect quickly became part of the state's Nissan HQ planning team. It was Bredesen who phoned Frist, asking him to attend the Washington meeting that would come only seven days after the election.

"I had received a phone call from Nashville from Bredesen about the significance of the meeting," Frist told me. "At the meeting, I sat next to Bredesen."

Frist, elected to the Senate in 1994, had taken a Senate delegation to Japan and, following the Washington meeting with Ghosn, visited with Howard Baker, the revered former Senate majority leader, now the U.S. ambassador there. At the ambassador's official Japanese residence, they discussed the effort to bring Nissan's U.S. headquarters to Tennessee.

Frist had authored the book *Transplant*, about his career as a cardiac surgeon. He gave Ghosn a copy of this book at the Washington meeting. "It had been translated into Japanese," he explained. "Because heart transplants were not done in Japan at the time—because of no recognition of brain death—it was viewed with fascination by readers there and was reasonably popular, maybe as science fiction!"

WHILE A MOVE FROM southern California to Middle Tennessee would certainly be Nissan's decision to make, Ghosn's Washington visit with Tennessee's top political leadership on November 12, 2002, was important to the company's decision-making process.

Sundquist and Bredesen, Frist and Alexander, together with Mayor Purcell, presented a stout bipartisan front. It demonstrated that as administrations changed in Tennessee there would be a smooth transition from the governor of one party to his successor in the other.

This was not the first such bipartisan handoff from one Tennessee governor to a successor of the other political party. Ned McWherter, the Democrat who followed Alexander as governor in 1987, had helped to welcome Nissan to Tennessee in the early eighties when he was speaker of the state house of representatives. In his turn, Governor McWherter took Sundquist with him to Louisville, Kentucky, in 1994 for a visit with top executives of the hospital company Columbia/HCA. The company's relocation to Nashville was announced in January 1995, ten days before Sundquist's inauguration.

And it would not be the last. Such a handoff between governors of different parties, and the private cooperation with decision makers in business that it enabled, has been going on now through five administrations over a quarter-century. During this period, in fact, the Tennessee governor's office has alternated between the political parties at regular intervals since 1970 when the Republican Winfield Dunn was elected. (Since 1977, Tennessee's governor has been limited to two consecutive terms.)

Alexander has suggested that by 2002 this practice of a smooth handoff between governors had become one of the reasons why so many businesses were choosing Tennessee—together with the state's central location in the U.S. market, right-to-work law, modern four-lane highways, and business-friendly environment. When Bredesen was asked many years later to name the most valuable accomplishments of his time in office, he cited two things: the upgrading of modern government, and this tradition of continuity between political leaders of different parties as administrations inevitably changed.

"You didn't have a bunch of governors trying to one-up each other, trying to keep each other from getting the credit for something," Bredesen told me. "That wasn't happening."

WHEN THE 1980S BEGAN, Tennessee had the third-lowest family incomes in America. Twenty years later, the practice of Tennessee governors making their end-of-term bipartisan handoffs—bringing new jobs, new capital, rising incomes, and national attention to a state by the turn of the century—had become an important tradition.

It was not always so.

In truth, all this began on a cold and dreary day in January of 1979, with a sudden coup at sundown.

CHAPTER 2

The Six-Hour Boot Camp

"The scene inside the court chamber struck me as something out of *All the King's Men*."
—Howell Raines

WINTER RAIN DRIPPED through a low fog as darkness fell on the old Supreme Court Building in downtown Nashville.

Deep inside, in the justices' private Robing Room, the state's leading Democrats and one lone Republican stood together solemnly. These men were acquainted but said little, acknowledging each other not with smiles and cordial handshakes but only with their eyes.

- The speaker of the House, Ned Ray McWherter, a man of such massive frame that when they first met, Governor Bill Clinton of Arkansas had declared, "My God, what a body. The Grand Ole Opry has its own Buddha!"
- Next stood the Lieutenant Governor, John Shelton Wilder, the speaker of the Senate, a genteel cotton ginner who seemed to conduct his legislative affairs in a mystical manner. He would receive constituents and lobbyists in his dimly lit office while sitting behind a desk raised so high that it seemed the visitor was peering upward toward a deity or an apparition.
- Gentry Crowell, the Secretary of State, a man of square build, medium height, and deeply partisan bent. Two days earlier he had formally attested to fifty-two pardons and clemencies that the incumbent governor, Ray Blanton, had granted to state prisoners by his own signature. The FBI believed some of those prisoners had paid cash for their release. "This takes guts," the governor had said, looking up to Crowell as he put his pen to a pardon for a particularly notorious inmate. The Secretary of State had replied in that moment, "Well, some people have more guts than brains."

- The tallest man in the room was the state attorney general, William Leech. He had been the busiest of them all on this dreary, fateful day. Two nights before, on the same Monday night Governor Blanton had signed those fifty-two clemencies, Leech was in Washington—preparing to appear before the Supreme Court of the United States on Tuesday morning. But then his hotel room phone rang, and he learned what was transpiring back home at the State Capitol: a young assistant attorney general had released an opinion saying Tennessee's state constitution would allow the new governor-elect to be sworn in sooner than Saturday's scheduled ceremony. That opinion would, in fact, have permitted an inauguration on this very Wednesday, January 17, 1979.
- The other senior Democrat standing in the Robing Room was Joe Henry, the Chief Justice of the Tennessee Supreme Court. A self-proclaimed "yellow dog Democrat," Henry had, eight years earlier, described the election of Winfield Dunn, Tennessee's first Republican governor in fifty years, as the return of "a plague of Republican locusts." On this afternoon he had left his downtown apartment, where he was recovering from a heart attack, to preside at the unusual and rushed ceremony—unprecedented in American history—where he would swear in a Republican.
- One important Democrat who was *not* in the Robing Room at this tense moment was the man who had initiated all of it at noon: the United States attorney, Hal Hardin. He had set the thing in motion with a phone call not to his superiors in Washington but to a Tennessee Republican, Governor-elect Lamar Alexander, insisting that he be sworn in immediately. Hardin and Alexander had agreed—knowing that the state constitution grants a governor unconditional power to empty the prisons if he chose to. But Hardin declined to attend. He thought it would be inappropriate for a federal official to be present at such an extraordinary function of a state government.
- Also standing in the quiet room, and joined by his young family, was the Republican Alexander. He had not intended for his new administration to begin this way.

FOR BILL LEECH, this had already been a stressful couple of days. His wife Donna was in Nashville's Baptist Hospital, expecting their new baby. But it was not the imminent birth of his son but a more sinister confluence of events that had him rushing home from Washington on Tuesday night. It was a swirl of scandal and constitutional crisis that would unfold in a five-hour marathon on Wednesday afternoon.

At midday on this Wednesday, in a hotel room across Broadway from the U.S. courthouse, he met secretly with Hardin, who persuaded him that the state's constitution did indeed allow an early swearing in. And also, given the bizarre conduct of the sitting governor, Blanton, that it must happen before the sun went down.

The two attorneys then began, by telephone, to persuade the speaker and the lieutenant governor of the same conclusion. Otherwise, more prisoners might be set free—some of them targets of a federal corruption investigation.

THE SIX DEMOCRATS WHO gathered in the Robing Room not only knew each other well and were veterans of political combat, but they were also culturally and politically bonded. All had political roots that ran deeply into rural small towns in West and Middle Tennessee, where voting patterns still traced the borderlines of the Old Confederacy. They presided over a state that for a century had been ruled by one political party only since the Civil War. By this time, the governor, the legislative majority, all members of the State Supreme Court, all the sitting constitutional officers, and therefore all the State Capitol lobbyists and assorted other hangers-on were all Democrats. In the congressional district from which McWherter and Wilder were regularly elected, the last congressman who had *not* been a Democrat was Davy Crockett.

Into this comfortable monopoly of Democrats had strolled an inconvenience: Alexander, a thirty-eight-year-old Republican who had walked over a thousand miles across the state to win the governor's race in 1978. The six did not know him well. This governor-elect was younger than any of them, had never been elected to political office, and his own cultural and political roots were at the other end of the state, in the mountains of East Tennessee. He had grown up in a congressional district that had never elected a Democrat to Congress since the time Abraham Lincoln was President. He was also fond of saying that his great-grandfather, John Alexander, when asked about his own politics, would proudly reply: "I'm a Republican. I fought to save the Union, and I vote like I shot."

At 5:45 p.m., thirty-eight-year-old Alexander entered the Robing Room with his pregnant thirty-three-year old wife and their three children, ages nine, seven, and 5. The governor-elect gave instructions about how the ceremony was to proceed. The somber group then formed a single file to walk into the adjacent courtroom. "A celebration has become more like a funeral," said his wife, Honey Alexander. But despite the upheaval and turmoil of the afternoon (this was also the day the Alexanders were moving into the governor's official residence) she had thought to bring along the family Bible.

Suddenly McWherter asked, "Wait a minute. Has anybody told Governor Blanton?"

The procession halted. McWherter's aide, Jim Kennedy, reached into his jacket pocket for his black book, picked up a black rotary telephone, and dialed the number at Governor Blanton's new private home in south Nashville. The governor came on the line.

BLANTON: "Hello, Ned."

McWHERTER: "Governor, Bill Leech is here and he has something to tell you."

LEECH: "Governor Blanton, I wanted to let you know that in a few minutes Lamar Alexander will take the oath of office, and he will be the new governor of Tennessee."

BLANTON: "The hell you say!"

The participants then continued filing out of the private room and through the narrow passage leading up three steps to the open court chamber. No one had walked this walk before for such a purpose. They moved in silence, and with great dignity, emerging into a glare of TV camera lights and flashes of still cameras.

A breathless anticipation descended on the room—the feel of something important about to happen, although most of the observers in the solemn room had no idea what was occurring or anything of the swift and silent way it had come about.

THE CEREMONY COMMENCED at 5:56 p.m., Nashville time. Six minutes later it was over and Tennessee had a new governor, three days early.

The local CBS television affiliate had new equipment with which to make remote live broadcasts. This ceremony became its first live broadcast, breaking startling news to local viewers and then within a few minutes to the nation on *The CBS Evening News with Walter Cronkite.*

Howell Raines, then a southern correspondent for the *New York Times,* had driven to Nashville and covered the strange event. "The scene inside the court room struck me as something out of *All the King's Men,*" he told me later. "With all the dramatic personae arrayed as if in a scene from a novel or stage play about southern politics. I remember being impressed with how McWherter and Alexander handled themselves."

In interviews after the swearing-in, Wilder called it "impeachment Tennessee-style." Chief Justice Henry said, "This is certainly unprecedented." No one could remember anything quite like it in United States history.

❖

THIS EPISODE WAS ALSO a lesson in trust.

Those five hours of secret negotiations, Alexander told me thirty-five years later, became "a sort of a boot camp for how we could work with each other and that started with one word: Trust."

Figuring out how to do it meant, first, trusting Hardin—a man Alexander barely knew on this day—to engineer the afternoon's coup with Leech and the other Democratic leaders whom he also barely knew. Alexander and Hardin trusted each other based on their reputations. On the other hand, Hardin and Leech, the lawyers who engineered the coup, already trusted each other based upon years of political, professional, and personal relationships. Most important was a lasting trust that developed, through the afternoon of the crisis, among the three principal actors: the young governor and the two senior legislative leaders.

These events forged a remarkable and unlikely union between the new Republican governor and the two veteran Democratic leaders, McWherter and Wilder. In spite of their substantial differences, the three men learned to trust each other. They agreed to the early swearing in. They agreed not only to make it happen and to do it together, but they also negotiated a joint statement that Alexander recited to the press and public.

There were no surprises. Each performed just as he promised to do. Alexander said later that perhaps most important was this proof: "When it was all over, there was no backsliding. No one announced, 'I won.'"

Years later, looking back, Alexander also said that extraordinary afternoon of cooperation had set the stage for eight following years of similar collaborations and agreements: these would involve highways, better schools, and attracting manufacturing plants, including the Japanese auto industry. It would provide an indispensable framework for moving Tennessee forward.

Fred D. Thompson, the former Republican Watergate counsel whom Alexander quickly summoned home to review the fifty-two pardons and paroles that Blanton had granted, said, "We only knew each other by reputation, although the reputations were good."

This level of trust permitted them not only to execute the coup but also to govern the Tennessee state government for eight years in a bipartisan and results-oriented way.

At least some ingredients for success were already there. Alexander had learned, from his years with Senator Howard Baker, the necessity of reaching across party lines, in order both to be elected and to govern. And soon after Alexander's election, a skeptical member of the Capitol Hill press corps had asked McWherter, "Mr. Speaker, what are you going to do with this new young Republican governor?"

"I'm going to help him," McWherter answered. "Because if he succeeds, the state succeeds."

The road forward would be full of sudden twists and unexpected turns. Even at this late date, there were more revelations to come from the Blanton administration. And Thompson, as Alexander's special counsel on the clemency mess, would work for another four months unraveling which of the former governor's final pardons were legitimate and which were not. Some of these cases, brought by convicts who claimed their releases were unlawfully held up by the new governor's people, would go to criminal court trials before the dust finally settled.

LONG BEFORE IT WAS publicly known that the Blanton corruption had extended well beyond the clemencies for state prisoners, engulfing several other state agencies, Alexander appointed Susan Simons of Nashville to be the new chairman of the Tennessee Alcoholic Beverage Commission. Simons recalled for me her first day on that job—the day she met Carl Jones, publisher of the *Johnson City Press Chronicle* and a Blanton appointee to the ABC.

Had it not been for the coup that ousted Blanton, Jones likely would have become the new board chairman himself. Simons remembered Jones was polite but seemed unhappy. She recalled, in particular, one comment that Jones made to her on her first day as chair of the ABC:

"Little lady," Jones said gruffly, "this ain't gonna be no bed of roses."

CHAPTER 3

Blue State Turning Red

"We went to every county seat in West Tennessee, and most of them had not seen a Republican candidate before."
—Judge Harry Wellford

"The national Democrat Party changed, and the south changed with it. The pro-life and the gun issues broke the back of the southern Democrats. It was guns and God."
—Chip Saltsman

AT THE BEGINNING OF the nineteenth century, Tennessee was the West.

When the Revolutionary War ended, in 1783, the longhunters and the other pioneers poured across the daunting Appalachian Range, a journey that had been forbidden since 1763 by England's King George. The easiest route was down wagon roads in Virginia's Shenandoah Valley and through mountain gaps into the Tennessee country. From there settlers headed north through the Cumberland Gap into the Kentucky wilderness or further west to Texas or faraway Oregon. Throughout East Tennessee, front doors of abandoned log cabins were marked with the rough letters *GTT*—Gone to Texas.

The rugged individualists who remained made Tennessee the sixth most populated state. From this ferment emerged new leaders of the American nation: three Presidents of the United States, a president of the Republic of Texas, a bear hunter with a coonskin cap who became the best-known U.S. congressman, a speaker of the U.S. House of Representatives, and many others. To the dismay of more refined Americans whose families had resided for two centuries on the eastern side of the mountains, America's new political leadership was moving from the genteel parlors of Massachusetts and Virginia and rising from the rowdy towns and backwoods of Tennessee.

Chief among the rowdies was Andrew Jackson, who was famous for fighting "Indians"—in fact, for offering to fight a duel with almost anyone who slighted him—and for stirring the populist fever of the expanding nation. Jackson's protégé, Sam Houston, came to Maryville with his mother and six brothers and sisters by way of the Virginia wagon roads in 1793. Houston became congressman, then governor of Tennessee before becoming president of the Republic of Texas. After Texas joined the Union, Houston became its governor and then senator from the new state. In 1859, he was prominently mentioned for president of the United States. Another Jackson protégé, James K. Polk of Tennessee, became speaker of the U.S. House and later president.

Jackson's politics was a determined populism and provoked a strong reaction. Another Whig, the 125-pound "Lean Jimmy" Jones, campaigned against the Democrat Polk for governor and twice defeated him. Polk, the well-educated Jackson disciple, nevertheless became president of the United States in 1845. In 1856, Whigs in East Tennessee nominated anti-Jackson Hugh Lawson White for president. Andrew Johnson, a tailor and Democrat from Greeneville, who supported the Union, became Abraham Lincoln's vice president—and later president himself following Lincoln's assassination. Not content with having held virtually every state and local office before he became president, Johnson ran three times for the U.S. Senate after he left the presidency, winning on the third try in 1874.

During this period, no state—not even Virginia and Massachusetts—produced more colorful and successful political leaders. Why was this true? "Competition," Alexander has suggested. "I have always thought competition between the Democrats and Whigs, between Jackson and Crockett, Polk and 'Lean Jimmy' Jones did what competition usually does: It attracts talent and brings out the best." Alexander's thesis is that the inverse was also true.

For about a hundred years, from the end of the Civil War in 1865 until the 1950s, Tennessee sent few distinguished men onto the national stage. There were notable exceptions, including Senator Kenneth McKellar, elected to the Senate in 1916, and Cordell Hull, who went to Congress in 1907 and became President Franklin Roosevelt's secretary of state in 1933, serving until 1944. But in the late 1940s and 1950s there was a burst of political talent in Tennessee. In that heady postwar period, the youthful Governor Frank Clement and Senators Estes Kefauver and Albert Gore Sr. all competed for the presidency, with Kefauver winning the Democratic vice presidential nomination in 1956 to run alongside the Democrats' presidential nominee, Adlai Stevenson of Illinois. This surge of reform Democrats destroyed the vestiges of Boss E. H. Crump's old-time machine dominance in Memphis—and with it his grip on statewide politics as well—and nearly a hundred years of two-party political competition ceased. Republican voters were either legacy unionists, mostly isolated in the hollows of the East Tennessee mountains, or they were blacks in the cities. Across the long state, there was only one political party—the Democratic Party—that held sway in statewide elections, ruling over both policy and patronage.

From the end of the Civil War until Howard Baker's election in 1966, there were no Republican U.S. senators from Tennessee and only two Republican governors. One of them, Ben Hooper, an orphan from Newport, split the Democrats over whisky and the temperance issue. He was elected governor in 1910 and 1912.

In post-Depression Tennessee, except for the two Republican majority districts in the eastern mountains, voters all but shunned the GOP in elections from the courthouse to the statehouse, unless the war hero Dwight Eisenhower was on a ballot. In 1948, following World War II, the Grand Ole Opry entertainer Roy Acuff waged an unexpectedly strong campaign as the Republican nominee for governor. Johnson City congressman B. Carroll Reece, then the Republican national chairman, wanted to be U.S. senator and recruited Acuff, believing that campaigning alongside the popular radio star might draw crowds large enough to elect them both. The crowds showed up—as many as 30,000 turned out for one rally—but once Acuff and his Smoky Mountain Boys finished singing and walked offstage the audience dispersed, just as Congressman Reece launched into his own speech. On their election day, Acuff received more votes than Reece, but neither won. "It was a good thing, too," Acuff reportedly said. "If I'd been elected, it would've ruined my career."

President Lyndon Johnson's crushing defeat of Senator Barry Goldwater in 1964 actually gave a glimmer of new hope to the nascent Republican Party in Tennessee. In that same year, Baker made his first run for statewide office, hoping to fill the unexpired term of Senator Estes Kefauver, who had died the previous August. Even in face of the Johnson landslide, Baker came within 30,000 votes of defeating his own Democratic opponent, Congressman Ross Bass of Pulaski. The closeness of Baker's loss that fall was an encouragement to him and his growing circle of supporters statewide. Two years later, in 1966, Baker ran again and won, defeating Clement in what would be the former governor's last campaign for a public office. In the Democratic primary of that year, the incumbent, Governor Buford Ellington, won his final term over John Jay Hooker Jr., who was running his first campaign.

In 1970 a Republican won the governorship for the first time in fifty years. Winfield Dunn, a personable dentist from Memphis who had never before held public office, successfully ran a campaign designed to save the state from Hooker, a flamboyant liberal Democrat who by this time had deeply divided his own party.

This was the beginning of a new era of intense political competition. Over the next forty years and more, Tennessee political leaders marched again onto the national stage, fueled by a return of two-party competition. Congressman Bill Brock of Chattanooga, a Navy veteran who in 1962 had become the first Republican from the Third District since the Civil War, became United Senate senator on the same night that Dunn won his race. (Both Brock and Baker would go on to other significant national leadership roles: Brock would become chairman of the Republican National Committee, and later President Reagan's U.S. trade representative and secretary of labor. Baker became the Senate majority leader, Reagan's White House chief of staff, and President George H. W. Bush's ambassador to Japan.)

In time, Democrats took their turn again, opening a period of alternating party victories. Congressman Albert Gore Jr. became U.S. senator (succeeding Baker who retired) and later President Bill Clinton's vice president, and in 2000 was the winner of the popular U.S. presidential vote. In 1994, the three-term incumbent Democrat Jim Sasser, who had defeated Brock in 1976, was about to become majority leader of the Senate when Bill Frist upset him in his re-election bid. Frist himself became the majority leader in 2003. In 1985, George Cranwell Montgomery, a Chattanooga native and former aide to Baker, became the U.S. ambassador to Oman, nominated by Reagan. Sasser became Clinton's U.S. ambassador to China. Fred D. Thompson parlayed his fame as Republican counsel to the Senate Watergate Committee—and later as a movie and television star—into the Senate seat previously held by Baker and then Gore. Alexander, who had walked across the state to become governor, later became President George H. W. Bush's secretary of education, and was a candidate for president twice before landing in the U.S. Senate himself for three terms after Thompson retired.

This remarkable deluge of Tennessee political leaders of both parties prompted Jonathan Martin, reporter for the *New York Times*, to ask Alexander one evening at a Nashville dinner party at the home of historian Jon Meacham: "Why is it that Tennessee has produced, and continues to produce, more outstanding political leaders than any other state?" Alexander replied that he had no answer except for competition—that the same vigorous competition that had produced the array of political stars in Tennessee's first century could be the reason for the rise of a new generation of national leaders in the present century.

FROM BAKER'S NARROW DEFEAT in the 1964 race, the candidate and his supporters drew encouragement and a belief in eventual victory. It would come two years later.

Baker's 1964 campaign, though unsuccessful, had been powered by a new east-west coalition of traditional Republicans in the east and the early stirrings of a new western GOP base in the Shelby County suburbs around Memphis. Baker's first run for the open Kefauver seat was, in fact, an impressive first field test for the coalition that Baker had brokered with the leaders of an emergent Republican apparatus in Tennessee's most populous county. Baker's plan established the framework for what soon emerged as a new statewide Republican alliance not seen in Tennessee since Reconstruction, but it would flourish over the next forty years with mounting Republican gains.

Baker's early law practice was based in rural Scott County, his ancestral home, and also in Knoxville. One of his early political allies, in the east, was the young Knoxville entrepreneur James Haslam II. Now in his twenties, "Jim" Haslam had been a prominent figure in Knoxville. In his college days, he had been a lineman on the University of Tennessee's 1951 national championship football team, and he was a team captain in the following season. After graduation, Haslam was commissioned a second lieutenant in the U.S. Army, served in Korea, and after discharge went to work for Fleet Oil, based in LaFollette, Tennessee, near the Kentucky state line. He incorporated his own business, calling it Pilot Oil Corp., in 1958 and opened his first gasoline station in Gate City, Virginia.

Haslam recalled his first meeting with Baker, in 1964, at the Knoxville office of the lawyer George Morton. "George called me one day, and he said he wanted me to meet Howard Baker," Haslam told me. "I asked George why Baker wanted to meet me. George said, 'He wants to run for the U.S. Senate.' I said, 'OK, but again why does he want to meet me.' Anyway, I went, and we kinda hit it off. I liked him."

In 1980, building on the original gasoline distribution and retail business, Haslam opened his first truck stop, called a Pilot Travel Center, in Corbin, Kentucky. By 2015 the Pilot chain would become the eighth-largest private company in America, with revenues of $31 billion. Haslam himself would become one of the Republican Party's most productive fundraisers as well. He was finance chairman for both of Alexander's campaigns for governor, and has been an important donor and fundraiser for many other Republican politicians. His younger son, Bill Haslam, became governor of Tennessee in 2010.

IN THE EARLY 1950S, in the suburbs of Memphis on the western end of the state, a group of former Eisenhower supporters were forming an upstart new GOP organization for Shelby County. They were ten couples—husbands and wives—who were ready to break with the past and the gridlocked local political machine that still clung to the remnants of its power.

"We started in '52 to try to revive the Republican Party," the attorney Lewis R. Donelson recalled. He served that year as chairman of "Tennesseans for Eisenhower." Already he and his wife Jan and the nine other founding couples were committing themselves to re-launching the Republican Party in the state. "There were actually about twenty of us—ten couples. In those days, most wives didn't work outside the home and these were very active in getting the party started. And we began to try to build the party."

"The first year we tried to have a primary," he said. "Even though it's provided for in the statute, Mr. Crump said, 'You can't have it. It would just confuse people.' We went to court. No judge said we couldn't have it, but no judge would say we could. 'I'll take this under advisement,' they said. That meant they were going to take it under advisement until after the election. Fortunately, the next time we tried to have an election, Mr. Crump had died, and we got 750 votes. That was in 1954, and it gradually built up, and in 1966 we had our first victory." That was the year Baker won his Senate seat.

DONELSON, AT ABOUT THIS same time, would also join with a cadre of lawyers in Nashville and Memphis in bringing the landmark *Baker v. Carr* lawsuit to court. They challenged a 1901 Tennessee statute governing the apportionment of legislative representation among rural and urban communities. The U.S. Supreme Court decided it in 1962, establishing the "one man, one vote" standard for state and local elections.

The high court agreed that the Tennessee legislature had failed, since 1901, to carry out the proper redistricting following the decennial U.S. Census. The result was that "these plaintiffs, and others similarly situated, are denied the equal protection of the laws accorded them by the Fourteenth Amendment to the Constitution of the United States by virtue of the debasement of their votes." In time, this had the effect of rebalancing voting strength and gave the state's large cities a new share of representation in the state's General Assembly.

Harry Wellford, also a lawyer, was another of the husbands in the original group of activist Shelby County couples. He, too, had supported Eisenhower and had deep family roots in Memphis politics. He was distantly related to Crump, on his grandmother Wellford's side (her family name was Hull).

"But then everybody said they knew Mr. Crump," he told me over lunch at the Memphis Country Club. "He made it his business to have a connection. When Mr. Crump was in his heyday, he had representation on—and I would say control of—every civic group and every community group that was Crump-representative. It was amazing. He was absolutely a control freak, and that is the fair thing to say. Mr. Crump was a very smart, shrewd, tough leader."

Wellford followed Winfield Dunn as the county Republican chairman.

"We were the county chairmen at the time the growth of the Republican Party really began. It came along, in my view, at a time that this was propitious because the longtime era of Boss Crump's domination of Shelby County had come to an end and the Republicans, strangely enough, were working to bring about a more representative government to replace the Crump 'commission' form of government, where the commissioners were elected at-large (countywide, not by smaller districts). That old commission system was done away with and there were a mixture of new Republicans, the non-Crump Democrats, and some of the old Crump holdovers."

What became significant for Baker, in his first race for U.S. Senate in 1964, was the new alliance between Wellford, Donelson, and their Shelby County circle with the rising group of East Tennesseans who were supporting Baker.

"The Crump setup," Wellford explained from his West Tennessee perspective, "was a combination of the Crump leadership here in Memphis and the East Tennessee Republicans. They, together, were able to do pretty well with the predominant Democrats across the state. The interesting thing was that now the new incoming black leadership and the Republicans were interested in district representation because each of them knew they would have a better chance of being elected in their home areas. In East Memphis, generally, and also in the adjacent area of the county the Republicans were strong. The blacks, of course, were strong in many areas, but had no representation. There were no blacks serving as elected officials during the time of the commission form of government. But the demographics were changing. Memphis was becoming more and more black, unlike any city in the state."

At about this time, Wellford was attending a Republican executive committee meeting in Knoxville. There he met Baker, and from that point a lifelong alliance developed between the two young lawyers. Baker and Wellford now traveled together throughout West Tennessee, traditionally Democratic territory, working with local allies at planning meetings and public events.

"We went to every county seat in West Tennessee," Wellford told me, "and most of them had not seen a Republican candidate before."

(In 1970, on Senator Baker's recommendation, Nixon appointed Wellford to a federal district judgeship for West Tennessee. Twelve years later, Reagan elevated him to the U.S. Court of Appeals for the Sixth Circuit.)

❖

THE MIDDLE AND LATE 1960s were already a volatile time across the nation. There was much churning, from national social policy to war and the draft, and these issues would help to turn the tide for Republican politics.

The faraway war in Vietnam was severely dividing Americans at home, and roiling campaigns and elections. The civil rights movement and school desegregation—and the partisan backlash that ensued—created racial turmoil in many of America's cities and deep divisions within the Democratic Party. All these forces were beginning to transform what was happening in the nation's elections, including Tennessee's. In the 1960 presidential election, a third of the African American voters in Memphis still supported the party of Lincoln in Nixon's narrow loss to Senator John F. Kennedy; this was a carryover from the historic black support dating to the Emancipation Proclamation. When Nixon won the White House in 1968, it was the most visible example of the new disruption, with his "southern strategy" of drawing to the GOP the angry white Democrats who had boosted George Wallace in his day. The result was to turn many traditional conservative Democrats into Republican voters, and the party of Nixon would ride this wave for the next fifty years.

While Baker was the first Republican to be elected statewide in this modern era, there was already a long tradition in the mountains of Republican officeholders serving in Tennessee's two easternmost congressional seats—Districts 1 and 2—which have remained in Republican hands since Reconstruction.

In the First District, Congressman Jimmy Quillen was elected to the House in 1962. He would continue in that office for thirty-four years and achieve an institutional status as the most influential Republican in his territory; Democrats running for statewide office, as well as Republicans, would regularly visit with Quillen and seek his blessing, some even his permission, to enter his congressional district.

The Second District, centering in Knoxville, has been represented since 1950 by members of just two families, both of them hailing from Scott County. Senator Baker's father, Howard H. Baker Sr., served six terms in the U.S. House. When he died in January 1964, his wife Irene Bailey Baker succeeded him. Later that year she was followed by John J. Duncan Sr., who had been a young field coordinator for the elder Baker and was now in his third term as mayor of Knoxville. Duncan served twenty-three years, until his death in 1988, and was followed by his son, Jimmy Duncan Jr. The father had won his seat in Congress at the same time Goldwater lost to Johnson, in November 1964. Duncan's son remembers that his father had enjoyed strong support among Knoxville's black voters in the nonpartisan mayoral elections, but that the black vote fell away when he declared as a Republican for the open congressional seat.

"I remember, when I was six years old, my dad taking me with him into black churches where he spoke," Duncan told me in our 2017 interview. "In three races for mayor, he got about 95 percent of the black vote, and we also had much more peaceful integration than many cities had at that time. When he started running as a Republican, in his first election for Congress, the black vote fell off to about 45 to 50 percent. That was in '64—the Goldwater year."

The Third District, centering in Chattanooga, was in the Democratic column for forty years until Republican businessman William E. Brock won the seat in 1962. Brock had been reared as a Democrat (his grandfather and namesake, William Emerson Brock I, was briefly a Democratic senator from Tennessee, from 1929 to 1931). The younger Brock's election moved Tennessee's Third District into the GOP column.

In West Tennessee, Republican Dan Kuykendall and his wife Jackie, another of the original ten founding couples (and later a co-chair) of the modern Shelby County Republican Party, mounted his own Senate campaign in 1964 to unseat the elder Gore. Kuykendall's vote fell short but statewide he polled an impressive 46 percent. Two years later, running in the Ninth District that encompassed Memphis, Kuykendall defeated Democrat George W. Grider, the incumbent, and went on to serve four terms in the House.

THIS MID-CENTURY PERIOD WAS also the time that Tennesseans of a certain age call the era of "leap-frog" government. The Democratic governors Frank G. Clement and E. Buford Ellington alternated terms in the office over a period of eighteen years, from 1953 until 1971. While members of the same party, Clement and Ellington were notably different in their training, policy aspirations, and attitudes about race. Ellington was a segregationist; Clement, a moderate on race, sent the Tennessee National Guard into Clinton, Tennessee, in 1956 to quell rioting sparked by court-ordered school integration.

The "leap-frog" period came to an end, as did the long uninterrupted tradition of Democratic governors in Tennessee, when Dunn was inaugurated in 1971, succeeding Ellington. (The state's constitution prohibited Ellington from succeeding himself; Clement, who might have sought a fourth term, had died in an automobile accident in 1968.) Dunn's victory in the Republican primary, in August 1970, stunned everyone but his most ardent fellow GOP organizers in Shelby County. Dunn was a Mississippi native, in fact the son of a Mississippi congressman, before he was a Memphian. He became a dentist and established his practice in suburban Shelby County. He soon joined the local county Republican organization. When he became its chairman, he took a prominent role with the early group of new party organizers who initially had formed around the Eisenhower campaign in 1952 and would support Goldwater a dozen years later.

Wellford became Dunn's campaign chairman in the early months of 1970. Soon after the August primary victory, Wellford recruited Lamar Alexander, then working in Washington on Nixon's White House staff, who agreed to return to Tennessee to manage Dunn's general election campaign. That November Dunn defeated Hooker, the Nashville Democrat. On the same night, Brock defeated the incumbent Senator Gore Sr., to join Baker in the upper chamber the following January.

Tennessee's three statewide elected officials—the governor and both U.S. senators—were now all Republicans for the first time since Reconstruction.

IT WAS JUST BEFORE this—during the latter years of the Clement-Ellington period—that Tennessee's Democratic legislature began to assert more independence relative to the executive branch.

Over most of the years of the long-running Democratic supermajority, legislative leaders were all but subservient to the sitting governor. While the governor served full-time, the state's constitution limited legislative sessions to a fixed number of days stretching over a two-year period. In other words, the governor was on duty all the time, while legislators could act as a body on a much more restricted schedule. This could cause tensions and resentments between the two branches, with a sitting governor sometimes inclined to dismiss prerogatives of legislative members. (William L. Barry, a top aide to Clement, recalled in a 2013 interview: "Clement used to say, 'Instead of the legislature meeting for seventy-five days every two years [as provided in the state's constitution], it should meet two days every seventy-five years.' This was said in jest, partly.")

M. Lee Smith was legal counsel to Dunn and remembered the preceding period when the governor and his advisers effectively dominated the government and the legislature had minimal power. Smith was later publisher of the *Tennessee Journal* and so had observed many of Tennessee's governors and legislatures in his career. "During the Clement-Ellington years, with the exception of the latter part of Ellington's last term, the governors ran everything at the State Capitol," he told me. The Legislature was almost a nonentity. The Legislature was a rubber stamp. The governors would send the state budgets to the Legislature, and the Legislature would let it sit around for a month or two. They'd pass the budget. They might hold a few hearings. They might make a few nickel and dime changes. But the governors ran the state at the State Capitol. Period, paragraph."

The transition to more legislative independence had also been aided by the historic redistricting shift—urban versus rural—that had been brought by the U.S. Supreme Court's seminal *Baker v. Carr* decision of 1962, in a case that originated in Tennessee. (Charles Baker, a Republican, had been the mayor of suburban Millington in Shelby County. Joe Carr was Tennessee's secretary of state.) A battery of lawyers, chiefly from Memphis and Nashville, argued that the state's legislative districts—which had not been redrawn since 1901—were seriously malapportioned after six decades of neglect, and the old district lines now significantly disadvantaged the larger cities. The high court's decision essentially found that legislative redistricting was not exclusively a political decision and, therefore, could and should be addressed by the court. (This led, within a few years, to a similar decision governing congressional elections.)

"Redistricting brought more representatives from the urban areas into the Legislature," said Smith, who also had been a law clerk to U.S. District Court Judge William Miller in Nashville. "It brought more minority representatives into the Legislature. It brought some more Republicans into the Legislature. And those legislators weren't nearly as inclined to be as much of a rubber stamp for the governor as had been the case in the past."

In this new environment of shifting demographics and representation, legislative independence began to accelerate during the earliest days of Dunn's governorship—both in policy positions and even in decisions about legislative office accommodations. The Democrats in the General Assembly quickly began to clash with Dunn on a range of issues, notably Dunn's proposal for a statewide kindergarten program. The combative House speaker, Representative Jim McKinney of Nashville, was a fierce partisan Democrat always looking for ways to embarrass Dunn and defeat his initiatives. It was Representative Ned Ray McWherter who ousted McKinney as speaker, in 1973, by a narrow one-vote margin in a bitter contest within the House Democratic caucus.

McWherter and his allies, especially among the West Tennessee legislators, had their own notions of what independence for the legislative branch should look like midway through the Republican Dunn administration. An early demonstration of this separation came with new speaker's changes to the design work for construction of new legislative offices in downtown Nashville.

The modern complex required the excavation of the old War Memorial Park. This was a modest green space established early in the century, just south of the capitol building across Charlotte Avenue between Sixth Avenue North and the War Memorial Building. Below ground, the new "Legislative Plaza" was taking shape on the drawing tables of the state architect. In the early concept this new installation would have provided legislative committee hearing rooms and offices for the General Assembly's support staff (called the Legislative Council), together with a new cafeteria and a more fashionable public entrance. But in this design there were to be no new offices for the thirty-three senators and ninety-nine representatives; they would continue to be relegated to spaces in the older War Memorial Building next door. That 1925 structure, elegant on the outside, was cramped in its office arrangements on the inside, which were accessible by a combination of elevator, escalator, and stairs.

Seeing this, the two speakers stepped in. McWherter and Wilder insisted the new facility be rearranged. At their behest, a new interior design scheme made room for office spaces for legislative committee chairmen, vice chairs, and other members with seniority. The two speakers themselves would now have proper office suites with conference rooms. In this way the new office plaza, which opened in 1975, became a showplace for the Tennessee legislature and its leaders.

Four years later, on the afternoon of January 17, 1979, it was in those new offices that McWherter and Wilder would coordinate by phone on the ultimate act of legislative independence: the bipartisan coup that ousted Governor Blanton.

THE 1980 PRESIDENTIAL CAMPAIGNS of Ronald Reagan and others on the right combined with the nation's economic turmoil and racial unrest into a special ferment across the South. Political allegiances were beginning to shift dramatically and historically, and the Democratic Party would be the loser.

This transition was most visible in the Deep South states of the old Confederacy—Mississippi, Alabama, Georgia—but it was also manifest in Tennessee, particularly in the western third of the state. There, traditional conservative Democrats embraced the message of Reagan and many of them emerged as new Republican voters.

Tennessee Republicans were deeply engaged in the national party's affairs by this time. In addition to Baker's role in the Senate, Brock had become the chairman of the Republican National Committee. Also, during this time three prominent Nashville businessmen—David K. Wilson, Joe M. Rodgers, and Ted Welch—served as chairs of the Republican National Finance Committee.

Democrats re-nominated President Carter at their August convention in New York City, putting down a challenge by Senator Ted Kennedy of Massachusetts. Two years before this, Republicans had been in high-level disagreement over where to hold their own convention in 1980. While some party leaders favored one of the prosperous sun-belt cities as a convention site, Brock preferred that the national TV audience see Republican delegates meeting in a city that was struggling with the current economy. Brock prevailed, Detroit was chosen, and there Reagan was nominated.

CHIP SALTSMAN, WHO WOULD become chairman of the state Republican Party in 1999, recalled the shift in national issues that drove many Tennessee Democrats to the GOP through the final decades of the 20th century.

"The national Democrat Party changed, and the South changed with it," he said. "It took awhile but for the longest time you'd see these 'yellow dog Democrats' vote for a Republican nationally, for president in Washington, but they voted for the hometown Democrat. They'd vote for Reagan but they'd also vote for John Tanner and Jimmy Naifeh, because they'd known them all their life. Then the pro-life and the gun issues broke the back of the southern Democrats—it was guns and God. That's an oversimplification, but it was pretty much true."

CHAPTER 4

Picking Up the Pieces

The coup was now four days old.

At this hour early on Sunday evening, after a long and tiring afternoon of moving into the State Capitol building, six of us on the new governor's staff found a quiet spot to rest on the lower steps of the grand staircase. The limestone treads lead upstairs to the vaulted second floor and Tennessee's legislative chambers. The steps are worn smooth by over a century of foot traffic. They have borne much history.

The ceremonial first and second floors of Tennessee's capitol, the oldest operating state capitol building in the United States, are a cavern of stone floors and walls. On the right-side handrail of the banister leading upstairs, there is a three-inch chip in the old Tennessee marble. Some say it was caused by a pistol shot in 1866, fired in anger from the flight above, by a sergeant-at-arms aiming at a pro-Union member of the Reconstruction-era legislature. Historians say this didn't actually happen, but tour guides point out the crack in the reddish stone. The legend, whatever its origin or veracity, makes this spot a mute reminder even now that politics sometimes will get out of hand.

On this Sunday evening, the six of us—Julia and Bill Gibbons, Marc and Lewis Lavine, Lisa Barnes, and me—sat there a few steps below that old damage, oblivious to it. Each of us had been involved in Alexander's 1978 campaign (and the Gibbonses and the Lavines went even further back, to the losing 1974 race). Now, we were tired from moving boxes and rearranging furniture in our newly assigned offices. In silence, we were doubtless all wondering what might happen when this building opened for business again the following morning.

The hour was not late, but outside the January sky was already dark. Combined with the subdued interior lighting typical of the capitol on a weekend, all of this gave the staircase where we sat an air of stillness that seemed now also to be heavy with history. As we rested, the sounds of footsteps echoed down the corridor as other new staffers moved about. Down the hall in both directions, Tom Ingram and Lewie Donelson and John M. Parish and Debby Patterson were getting settled in their new workspaces, too.

Alexander was not in the building as yet. The new governor had decided he should not occupy his new office, on the southeast corner of this floor, until Monday morning. In fact, Bill Koch had directed all the new cabinet members who would head the twenty-one departments, from Agriculture to Veterans Affairs, to refrain from taking any significant actions until Monday. The reason: it was possible there might be legal challenges to the early swearing-in, and the last thing this very young administration needed was for any of its first actions to be invalidated.

Now, in this darkened hour of Sunday evening, the question in each of our minds—hopeful yet anxious—was, "What now?"

THE EXTRAORDINARY NATURE OF the coup that removed Blanton set up a tricky transition period for virtually everyone it touched and everyone who became involved in the importance of moving forward.

Part of this, for Alexander and his team newly in office, was the prospect of divided government and the question of how to navigate through it. Since the legislature had been dominated by Democrats for decades—and still was—the path forward could likely be tangled in a hundred ways, making problematic any initiative that required approval of the General Assembly. The annual operating budget would be the earliest and most obvious opportunity for blockage and mischief, but in truth any policy initiative, no matter how great or humble, could be stymied or derailed outright in any one of dozens of different legislative committees and subcommittees—if the legislators who ruled them were inclined to do so. There was also the matter, now rather urgent, of restoring public confidence in the government itself.

Clearly this was uncharted territory, and it was fraught with political quicksand. There was no guidebook for a transition like this one, no manual for what to do, no instructions to be found in the state's constitution nor in history or tradition. Likewise, the traditional "honeymoon" period for a new governor did not seem to apply to Alexander in this wholly new circumstance.

On the plus side of the ledger, Alexander had won a decisive election after all. He had defeated Jake Butcher by a wide margin the previous November. In fact he had done so with a voting coalition that included support from prominent Democrats from the primary campaigns that Butcher had defeated (notably in the Bob Clement camp). The new governor had also just emerged from the maelstrom of the Blanton coup with a heightened luster of leadership, a glow of prestige that he shared with McWherter and Wilder for their courage in summarily ending Blanton's tenure and its corruption. All three were arguably heroes now, having guided Tennessee's government out of the wreckage of unprecedented national scandal. All this might have suggested smooth sailing for a period of unknown duration.

Yet for the two speakers especially, and also many in their respective Senate and House Democratic caucuses, the coup had been a grievous time of sad duty. When the facts of the clemency scandal became publicly known, Democrats in the legislature were largely resigned to the necessity of the sudden transfer of power, but a few bitter-enders even continued to insist that Blanton had not known of the crimes that occurred around him. (Secretary of State Crowell, whose office published the biannual *Tennessee Blue Book*, had attended Alexander's early oath-taking, but he refused to print *Tennessean* photographer Nancy Rhoda's iconic photo of the early swearing-in in the next edition.) In any case, the gathering sense of legislative independence, which had begun at least two decades before and accelerated among Democrats after Dunn's election in 1970, now seemed ready for a resurgence.

Soon enough, it seemed, the old fundamental partisanships could be expected to rise again. In this environment, nothing could be left to luck. Alexander sensed it would require a new strategy of several parts.

❖

THE FIRST PART OF Alexander's solution was a new concept that came to be called the "Leadership Breakfast." In time it became a lasting tradition observed by all future governors.

As soon as the full legislature reconvened in mid-January, Alexander hosted a breakfast meeting attended by eight people—all principals, no staff. This would become the new routine. The two speakers, McWherter and Wilder, had agreed to it.

The principals, in addition to Alexander, were the top six leaders of the legislature: the Senate and House speakers and the majority and minority leaders of both chambers. This included two senators in addition to Wilder, Democratic Majority Leader Milton Hamilton, and Senate Republican Leader Tom Garland—and two House members joining with McWherter, Democratic Leader Jimmy Naifeh and Republican Leader Jim Henry.

The eighth participant was Lewis Donelson, an exception in the room inasmuch as he was not an elected official but, as commissioner of the Department of Finance and Administration, he was in effect the governor's top cabinet officer. (Donelson was the first cabinet member Alexander had appointed, before Christmas. In our interview in his Memphis law office, Donelson described their understanding this way: "Lamar told me 'Lewie, you run the government, and I'll be the governor.'" Alexander told me he had suggested to Donelson that he would be the "chief operating officer" of state government. In any case, it would be the first time a Tennessee governor had designated a COO.) Donelson was also a longtime friend and confidante of both McWherter and Wilder; in years past, Donelson had been McWherter's personal tax attorney, and he had also advised Wilder on tax policy.

This group began to meet each Wednesday morning, gathering at 7:00 a.m. around Alexander's conference table. Such a meeting had not happened before. For the first time, the most senior leaders of the executive and legislative branches were able to meet and discuss pending issues of concern to either branch. No votes were taken in this setting, but partisan differences could be discussed and ironed out.

Henry, the top House Republican, remembers there were only two ground rules for these formative early meetings, and both were quickly agreed to at the very first session:

1. *No surprises:* If you or your caucus were planning to oppose an administration bill later in the week, that could be understood and forgiven, but at these Leadership Meetings you were to share that plan with the group.
2. *Speak only for yourself:* If you were confronted by a news reporter afterward, you could tell the reporter what you said in the Leadership Meeting, but do not speak for anyone else who attended. Each participant speaks only for himself.

The Wednesday morning meetings continued not only for the rest of that legislative session but also for every session throughout Alexander's years in office—whereupon McWherter continued the practice over his own eight years as governor. His successors did the same. Republican governor Don Sundquist, Democrat Phil Bredesen, and Republican Bill Haslam all told me they maintained the morning Leadership Meetings. Of course, participants changed as elections came and went, and over time the total number of attendees grew, but the core group at the table were the governor, his finance commissioner, and the six leaders of the legislature.

Jeff Wilson was one of the news reporters who covered state government during this period, first for the *Jackson Sun* and later the Associated Press. He recalled McWherter's practice, when he was speaker of the House, of letting him attend his Democratic leadership and caucus meetings. Wilson was the only reporter permitted to sit in, and on a background-only basis. (As the *Sun*'s Nashville correspondent, Wilson told me, McWherter favored him "because the *Sun* was basically his hometown newspaper.") These sessions were held after hours on each Tuesday at 5:00 p.m. in the speaker's suite at the Continental Inn, a mid-rise hotel on the east side of the Cumberland River.

Wilson credits Wilder's administrative aide Nelson Biddle with first suggesting a regular coordination meeting between Senate and House Democrats. Biddle had been Blanton's chief lobbyist and had shifted to a similar role in Wilder's office soon after Alexander won the governorship in November 1978.

"Biddle made the point to Wilder and to McWherter that coordination between the Senate and the House was weak—and how the Blanton administration had taken advantage of that, sometimes to play them off against each other," Wilson told me, "so he suggested that they have a weekly Leadership Meeting. And Ned agreed to host it, in his suite down at the Continental Inn. Every Tuesday evening after business, they'd go down to the Continental Inn, and it was the proverbial smoke-filled room."

McWherter's and Wilder's experience with this early type of legislative coordination meeting probably made them more amenable when Alexander suggested a comparable meeting be instituted when the 1979 session began that January. It was, among other things, a way to transition away from the period of Blanton's embarrassing scandals, and to add more structure and a willingness to move forward with the new Republican administration.

THIS SPIRIT OF COOPERATION largely prevailed through the immediate post-coup period. Both Democrats and Republicans were in need of showing constituents, as well as the wider world looking on, that Tennessee's state government was stable, sound, and moving responsibly past the Blanton troubles. This did not mean, however, that the sailing was smooth, nor that the very next election—the 1980 legislative races—would be free of partisan electioneering. They were not.

This, of course, would be the year of the Reagan sweep across the nation, defeating the incumbent Democrat, President Jimmy Carter. Not only would the former California governor win the White House, but the national Republican strategy targeted Tennessee and other southern states in hopes of winning or strengthening GOP majorities in those state legislatures. This added to the pressure on Alexander to further solidify the position of Tennessee Republicans in elective offices.

Tom Beasley, the state GOP chairman, remembers his office was already active in targeting incumbent Democrats for defeat in the legislative races. "We played hardball," he told me. "We had made a big push in '78 and had picked up some seats in the Senate and also in the House. We were aggressive in 1980, too, but it didn't turn out so well."

Wilder himself was up for re-election in 1980, along with other senior Democrats in the state Senate. One of Beasley's tactics was to seize any opportunity to link those incumbents to the former Blanton regime, including use of a doctored news photo that would picture selected senators together with their party's disgraced governor. One of the GOP targets was Carl Moore, Democrat of Johnson City, a former House member who was elected to the state Senate in 1976.

"It was a real vicious attack," he recalled. "They said we were letting murderers loose. [Republican senator] Victor Ashe had filed a resolution in 1978 to condemn Governor Blanton for the pardon mess. I thought Blanton had had a pretty good administration otherwise, so I voted against it."

At this time, Ronnie Greer was a young operative who had been Alexander's political director in his 1974 campaign for governor. At that time, Greer was student government president at East Tennessee State University. Another young campaign worker that same year was Tom Anderson of Lexington, who dropped out of the University of Memphis Law School in order to be Alexander's driver. Anderson's classmates told him that dropping out of law school would ruin his legal career; today he is the chief federal district judge of the western district of Tennessee. Greer is the chief judge in East Tennessee. Both were recommended by Senator Alexander to President George W. Bush. Greer had been Alexander's political director in the 1978 campaign. In his hometown of Greeneville, Tennessee, he had been a protégé of Judge Thomas Hull, who was now Alexander's chief legal counsel. (Greer left the governor's staff in 1981 to return to law school, served in the state Senate himself, and in 2003 became a U.S. District Court judge for East Tennessee.) For the 1980 legislative races, Greer worked with Beasley and his state GOP staff.

"Lamar had to work with the Democrats," Greer told me. "I watched him and that's where I got to know John Wilder and Milton Hamilton and Ned McWherter. But Lamar really wanted to take control of the state Senate. There were six races (with Democratic incumbents). Carl Moore blamed me for the negative ads."

On the night of that Reagan sweep across America, there was another kind of sweep across Tennessee: all six of the targeted Democrats were re-elected, from Memphis to Johnson City.

"We lost every one of those races," Greer remembers. "I also remember the morning after, sitting down to talk with Lamar about it. Not a good situation. We'd lost every one of them. I think Lamar learned something from those races—what he learned was that you couldn't necessarily beat them at the polls, so you had to work with them. And he did work with them. I think Lamar, after that, never made another effort to unseat an incumbent."

❖

FOR MANY OF THE winners that November, the hard feelings were not easily or quickly forgotten.

Paul Summers, who had been Wilder's campaign manager, recalled a tense Senate Democratic Caucus meeting in Nashville in early December. This was the caucus meeting where the Democratic majority would informally select their speaker, who would take office the following January. Wilder of course hoped to be re-elected, retaining the honorific title of lieutenant governor.

"I was thirty years old at the time," Summers told me years later. "I got a call from Wilder. He wanted me to go with him to a meeting in Nashville, and he said we'd fly over for the meeting and come home after. He said, 'I don't want you to say a word. Just sit there and take notes.' We flew to Nashville on his plane, *Jaybird*."

When they arrived in the suite at the Capital Park Inn, the emotions of the unpleasant campaign had not subsided.

"I remember the room was pretty full," Summers said. "I don't remember if I sat on the floor or in a chair. I remember Miss Anna Belle Clement was there, Ernest Crouch, Tommy Cutrer, John Rucker, Douglas Henry, Milton Hamilton, John Wilder, Ed Gillock, Carl Moore. At one point, I remember a few were out on the balcony—Henry was out there smoking a cigar, others were smoking cigarettes. There were a lot of comments, directed to Wilder, from the people in the room, about the campaigns some of them had just been through. I got the impression those negative ads that ran in some of the senators' districts, with pictures showing them with Blanton, that they had never seen anything like this before. They were surprised that their opponents would do this. Today, of course, this is a common practice."

He recalled the angry dialogue. At one point, Summers saw a senator approach Wilder and poke a finger in his chest.

"John, this is the kind of stuff they did to me, in my hometown!" one senator complained.

"No more!" said another.

"John, I hope you put them all (Republican senators) in the War Memorial Building," referring to the older office structure. "I hope you're not thinking about giving any of them chairmanships."

Wilder "just stood there and listened," Summers remembers. Then the lieutenant governor spoke, softly, referring to himself in the third-person, as he often did.

"I understand," he told the room full of colleagues. "You're mad. They did it to Wilder, too. I was attacked just like you were."

But he made no promises. On the flight home that night, Wilder didn't say much. He was in the pilot seat of *Jaybird*, with Summers in the right-hand seat. The noise level of the airplane's engines was loud, making any conversation hard to hear. About halfway back to Somerville, in the air somewhere over Jackson, this brief exchange took place:

SUMMERS: "Mr. Speaker, so what are you gonna do about what they said?"

WILDER: "Paul, I am the speaker of the Senate. I am not the speaker of the Democrats. We need to let the Senate be the Senate. They don't know what they want. They just know they ain't got it. And they don't know how to get it."

CHAPTER 5

Lamar and Ned

"I'm going to help him, because if he succeeds, the state succeeds."
—Speaker Ned Ray McWherter

ON THE COLD, gray afternoon of the coup—in January 1979—the unlikely conspirators McWherter and Alexander barely knew each other. This fact is surprising to many Tennesseans who knew both men in later years, having watched them work together on issues, in spite of their party differences, through stormy legislative sessions in Nashville.

The two men first met, but only for a few moments, during Alexander's 1974 campaign for governor, probably at the Naifeh "Coon Supper," an annual must-attend for Tennessee politicians held at the country club in Covington, in West Tennessee. It was Tom Beasley, a Dickson lawyer and later state GOP chairman, who introduced them that day.

Beasley was a native of Smith County, east of Nashville, in the Upper Cumberland region, and a 1966 graduate of the U.S. Military Academy at West Point. After his military service, and while a law student at Vanderbilt in Nashville, Beasley lived in a small apartment above the garage at Alexander's home on Golf Club Lane. Soon he was involved in the congressional campaign of the Republican Robin Beard, who won, and Beasley would himself go on to be a combative chairman of the state's Republican Party, from 1977 to 1981.

Despite their current partisan differences, Beasley and McWherter had both been brought up in Democratic politics of rural Tennessee counties. Beasley's mother, Margaret Elizabeth Wilson Beasley, was the first woman elected Trustee in Smith County, the birthplace of Democrat icons Albert Gore and Cordell Hull. McWherter was raised in Weakley County, a cotton county that had more boll weevils than Republicans, as the speaker was fond of saying. Both were accustomed to rough-and-tumble Democratic politics. McWherter was more comfortable with Beasley than with the new breed of buttoned-up suburban Republicans.

And the two men had at least one mutual business interest: they were in a group of four co-owners of the Capitol Park Inn in Nashville. In fact, it was situated prominently on the east side of Capitol Hill and became a regular watering hole for Democrats in the state legislature. (Another co-owner was state senator Carl Moore, Democrat of Bristol, in upper East Tennessee.) Moore and his Senate colleagues held many of their caucus meetings at the Capitol Park.

Beasley remembers the 1974 encounter when he introduced Alexander to McWherter. At that point, Blanton, who was McWherter's contemporary, had won the Democratic nomination for governor in August. In truth, he had only barely won it, polling just 23 percent of the vote in a large field of twelve contenders. Blanton and McWherter had been born in the same year (1930) less than a hundred miles apart and attended the same college (the University of Tennessee at Martin). But they rose from different strains of the state party's politics—McWherter with family connections to the Gores and early work with U.S. Representative Robert A. "Fats" Everett, then the eighth district congressman, while Blanton was from a more recent variant. The two men's experiences in the state legislature were also markedly different. Blanton never advanced from the back bench before he quit in 1972 to run for Congress, while McWherter quickly rose to speaker by building and nurturing his own power base, initially among other West Tennessee Democrats who knew him well.

In Beasley's telling, on the day Alexander met the speaker, McWherter told the young Republican: "I wish you were *our* nominee." Alexander told me he did not remember this scene, and two of McWherter's closest associates disputed the story when I asked them about it. One of these, J. W. Luna, who was a McWherter campaign manager in 1986, insisted that if his old boss had ever made such a comment, it was more likely he could have done so four years later, in 1978, when the Democratic nominee was the Knoxville banker Jake Butcher. McWherter and Butcher were never close.

LAMAR AND NED WERE together for a second time, in December of 1978, at Amon Evans's duck-hunting lodge in Henry County at the Springville Bottoms. This happened in the weeks following Alexander's election and only about a month before the two men would be thrust together in Nashville on the afternoon of the coup. That weekend at Springville Bottoms, on the Tennessee River east of Paris, they were in a large group at Evans's compound and did not socialize much directly at the time.

These gatherings in duck-hunting season were never so much about shooting waterfowl as about watching Evans, the publisher of the *Nashville Tennessean*, assemble his high-profile political friends, important advertisers, and sundry celebrity chums—with the host showing them all off to each other over weekends of red meat and fine wine. The publisher's guest list at Springville Bottoms routinely included leaders of both political parties, and for any of them an invitation to "Amon's duck blind" was a prized piece of mail.

Evans's own aide-de-camp was a jovial outdoorsman named Jimmy Holt. In his weekday job, Holt was a photographer and sportswriter for the *Tennessean*, but he served double-duty for his boss as weekend hunting guide and cook at the Tennessee River retreat.

"Every time you turned around Amon had people coming in there— politicians and all, even some out of Washington from time to time," Holt told me. "Lamar would go. 'Course he didn't care anything about hunting. Howard Baker, he was into photography and would shoot pictures all weekend. Over the years, Ray Blanton would come, Jim Sasser, Ned McWherter, Harlan Mathews, Jimmy Naifeh, Mario Ferrari (the Nashville restaurateur), Fate Thomas (the Davidson County Sheriff), Hal Hardin, John Seigenthaler, of course. John hated to go down there worse than anything in the world. He'd sit in the back of the blind, over in the corner, with John Jay (Hooker) and Bill Willis and that bunch. They never hunted, that bunch of lawyers from Nashville. All they did was sit in the back of the blind, drink coffee, and tell stories."

Alexander had come to Springville on this particular weekend for two reasons. First, Evans had invited him, and for a Republican governor coming into office in a still-Democratic state, accepting this invitation was a smart move politically. The governor-elect's more private purpose was to recruit his first press secretary.

John M. Parish, the veteran journalist at the *Jackson Sun* newspaper, had covered Capitol Hill in Nashville over three decades, and he was known and respected by a generation of ruling Democrats in the legislature, notably McWherter and his circle.

Alexander had known that his campaign manager, Tom Ingram, a top adviser dating back to the 1974 campaign, had been interested in the press secretary job. Ingram had also been a career journalist beginning with his part-time work as a "campus correspondent" while an undergraduate at David Lipscomb College in Nashville and later as a staff reporter for Seigenthaler's *Tennessean*.

"Tom and I had discussed his being the press secretary because of his journalism background," Alexander explained, "but Seigenthaler had told me it was important to get someone crusty and as independent as possible and give him the permission to walk into any meeting uninvited."

"Big John" Parish fit this prescription. He was older than Ingram by twenty-three years and had a stout frame and a journalist's reputation for toughness in dealing with elected officials. He had also become chairman of the Capitol Hill press corps in Nashville.

"I had advance warning that this was more than a hunting trip," Parish wrote in his memoirs years later. "A *Tennessean* reporter called me to ask if I was going to be Alexander's press secretary. I told him that I knew nothing of such plans but confirmed I was going to be with Alexander at Evans' hunting lodge. It was clear to me that the reporter knew something I didn't know, especially since it was coming from the *Tennessean*." In that meeting, Parish said he would need time to talk with his wife, Cile. Before Christmas came, he had accepted the job. Alexander, meanwhile, had offered Ingram the top staff position: deputy to the governor and chief of staff.

So, while Alexander and McWherter had shaken hands at least twice, and certainly knew of each other by political reputation, at this early point they were more acquaintances than friends. Their first serious private conversation came soon after the 1978 election when the new governor-elect invited both McWherter and Wilder to his home on Golf Club Lane to discuss the traditional inauguration planning. By this day, each was certainly aware of the other's politics. After this, they would not meet until January 17—on the fast-moving afternoon that toppled Blanton.

The truth was, they came from different worlds.

Place of birth, tradition of family, these are the strongest determinants of how most Tennessee Democrats and Republicans come to be what they are. Owing to their varied circumstances of birth, geography, and early tutelage, Ned naturally became a Democrat and Lamar a Republican. If somehow they had been switched at birth—if one had been born and raised in the other's hometown at such distant corners of the same state—the party identifications with which these two men would advance and become famous might well have been reversed from the cradle.

For two adult white males born in the same southern state, McWherter and Alexander were as different as two personalities could be. They were both reared by parents of modest means, and each was an athlete in his teens, but any parallels ended about there.

Their physical characteristics were, of course, the most obvious difference. Ned was a large man who weighed 250 pounds and wore size 52 suits and size XXXL shirts. He was the football team co-captain and also played basketball at Dresden High School. He was president of the Future Farmers of America, and his classmates voted him "Best Looking." He wanted a college degree on a football scholarship—he was enrolled at different times at

Murray State University, the University of Tennessee in Martin, and Memphis State University—but a recurrent knee injury kept that dream elusive.

Billy Stair, McWherter's longtime policy adviser and biographer, believes it was McWherter's physical stature that contributed to a genuine warmth he enjoyed among his constituents. "His size contributed to that. When he walked in a room, his physical size would dominate the room. In most cases his persona would not resonate with urban voters, but in rural counties, as soon as he opened his mouth, he sounded just like them. He got margins of 70 and 75 percent in county after county out there. Lamar was highly educated, went to Vanderbilt and NYU, and played classical piano. McWherter went to college but didn't finish. He dropped out and sold shoes."

Lamar, of medium height and weight, was also popular in high school. He was elected class president three times. In 1957, he was chosen for Boys State, the summer model government program then held at Castle Heights Military Academy in Lebanon, Tennessee. There he was elected governor of Boys State. At his inauguration, he remembers Tennessee Governor Frank Clement telling the assembled boys, "Someday one of you boys will grow up to be the real governor of Tennessee." At Vanderbilt University, Alexander was a sprinter and member of the track relay team; he and his teammates set a school relay record that still stands. He was also editor of the *Hustler*, the VU student newspaper.

Alexander was only ten years younger, but to friends who knew them both, McWherter always seemed older than just one decade might suggest. This had to do, in part, with Ned's lower-key public demeanor, the deeper timbre of his booming voice, and his kinship with farmers and fondness for rural courthouse squares that even now look and seem of an older time.

Alexander, through his early adulthood at least, was more identified with the cities—Nashville, New Orleans, and Washington, D.C. He had worked in each of those (as well as in New York and Los Angeles during law school), and over time his speech took on a more neutral accent. His adult voice contrasts sharply with the voice on a tape-recording of an early radio interview from his years at Maryville High School.

Politics cannot be separated from understanding the formative years of these two very different men. Before they found their respective political paths, each was shaped also by his own set of mentors, who likewise could not have been more different. And there was the matter of geography. They came from opposite ends of the state. Lowland and highland—differences in terrain and history, and how these contrasts mold their children, shape their souls, and remain touchstones on their paths forward.

Ned was the son of sharecroppers who later became the owner-operators of the City Café in the tiny township of Dresden. After high school, he came under Congressman Everett's early influence and was his driver, volunteer aide, and certainly his eager student of politics and campaigns.

Lamar was the son of teachers in Blount County in the east, next door to the Great Smoky Mountains National Park. Starting at age four he learned to play the piano and became good enough to win two statewide competitions as a teenager. He rose early to deliver newspapers. The first adult politician he remembers meeting was Congressman Howard Baker Sr., whose son was Senator Howard Baker Jr. In time, Baker the son would become the most important mentor of Alexander's life outside his own family.

Alexander got his own first taste of politics in 1966 as a campaign aide to the younger Baker, the year Baker defeated the former Democratic governor Frank Clement and became the first Republican U.S. Senator in the state's history. Alexander watched his mentor win that race by developing warm relations with many Middle and West Tennessee Democrats who had supported Senator Ross Bass, who had lost that party's primary to Clement. It was a lesson Alexander learned well.

After the election, Alexander joined Baker's youthful Senate staff in Washington, and after that he took a job as a staff aide in the Nixon White House. He returned to Tennessee in August 1970 to manage the general election campaign of Dunn, the Shelby County dentist who defeated Hooker three months later. In 1974 Alexander, at age thirty-four, won the Republican nomination for governor himself but lost to Blanton in the general election in the wake of the Watergate scandal. In that race, Blanton had dismissed Alexander, with ridicule, as "Nixon's choir boy."

Alexander ran again in 1978, after deciding to walk 1,022 miles across the state wearing a red-and-black flannel shirt. Traveling with this Vanderbilt graduate were four members of the University of Tennessee marching band. One of the student musicians drove a flatbed truck that provided a modest performance stage. Every few miles the truck would stop and the band would climb onto the back with their instruments and strike up the music. The candidate himself would join the band, playing trombone or sometimes the washboard (with a spoon), and then unburden himself of a speech about the evils of one-party government, at least until the crowd melted away.

CHIP SALTSMAN, WHO WOULD become chairman of Tennessee's state Republican party in 1999, remembers the day he met McWherter on a rural West Tennessee roadside in the early 1980s. Chip was working for his father, Bruce Saltsman, who would become Governor Sundquist's commissioner of transportation a decade later.

"We were knocking down bridges between Dresden and Jackson," he recalled. "They were all wooden bridges, and how we knocked them down was to burn them. My job was to watch 'em burn and make sure the fire didn't burn anything else. One day Ned McWherter drove up, and he spoke to me out his car window."

McWHERTER: "Are you Bruce Saltsman's boy?"
SALTSMAN: "Yes, sir."
McWHERTER: "What's your job out here?"
SALTSMAN: "I'm watching these bridges burn."
McWHERTER: "Well, you're doing a good job."

One who closely observed both Alexander and McWherter in their respective gubernatorial terms, and from a somewhat neutral vantage point, was W. J. Michael Cody, the Memphis lawyer and Democrat who was the state's twenty-second attorney general (1984–88).

Tennessee is the only state where the attorney general, the state government's top lawyer and chief legal authority, is selected by the state's Supreme Court rather than by popular election, and he serves a fixed term of eight years. Just after graduating from the University of Virgina Law School in 1968, Cody had served as Dr. Martin Luther King's lawyer during the Memphis sanitation workers' strike. Cody was seated in a front-row pew at the Mason Temple when King delivered his "I Have Been to the Mountaintop" speech the night before his assassination. Cody's appointment as attorney general began midway through Alexander's second term, and ran until the midpoint of McWherter's first term as governor. During this period, he counseled with them both, the Republican and the Democrat, on many legislative matters and also such long-running cases as the federal court lawsuits calling for desegregation of public higher education and the plan to upgrade Tennessee's prisons.

"Lamar and Ned tried hard to work together," Cody told me. "This also affected some of the people who were closest to them. I remember one day we went into Lamar's office for him to sign some bills. The secretary of state must also sign; that was Gentry Crowell, who was very close to Ned. After we finished Gentry and I were walking back out, onto the stone floor of the capitol corridor, and I remember Gentry said to me, referring to Lamar, 'I've tried so hard *not* to like that guy, but I just can't do it.'"

AFTER THE 1983 LEGISLATIVE session ended, at the contentious midpoint of the education reform battle, Alexander invited McWherter to his home in

Blount County, at the edge of the Great Smoky Mountains in East Tennessee. Joining them was Nashville lawyer Bill Willis, a prominent Democrat and lawyer for the *Tennessean* newspaper as well as a friend of Alexander's. (Alexander would later ask Willis to chair a key commission for building a teacher evaluation system for the Master Teacher program.)

The three men would have dinner and stay overnight at the Blackberry Farm resort, adjacent to property where the Alexander family owned a cabin. Blackberry Farm is on West Millers Cove Road, only a few miles from the Townsend entrance to the Great Smoky Mountains National Park.

When troopers ferrying McWherter reached West Millers Cove Road, Alexander was there to greet them at the intersection with U.S. Highway 321. The governor was sitting behind the wheel of his favorite weekend vehicle, a 1974 model Volkswagen product that was no longer in production, called the VW Thing. The Thing is an odd-looking, topless, Jeep-like conveyance that Alexander liked to drive on his own property with the windshield folded down. The speaker climbed in, settling himself into the front seat on the passenger side. As Alexander drove slowly up the winding country lane, he pointed out the modest residences they passed along the way.

"We were driving past small houses and trailers and farms and gardens, toward Blackberry Farm," Alexander remembers. "I'm sure we had troopers following us. It was the first time Ned had been there. "

Then, as they rode along the narrow two-lane, they exchanged these words:

ALEXANDER: "Ned, look left and right. All those people who live there, they're Republicans, and their families have been ever since they fought with the Union in the Civil War. This congressional district hasn't elected a Democrat to Congress since Lincoln was president."

McWHERTER: "Well, they look just like the homes of people where I come from. Except over my way, they're all Democrats."

ALEXANDER: "Yes, and that's the difference between us, but you and I—and the people where we live—have a lot more in common with each other than that."

McWHERTER: "You're right. I agree with you."

When the vehicles arrived at Blackberry Farm, Willis was already there. After dinner at the inn that evening, they moved to a row of rocking chairs on the stone terrace, just outside the dining room. From this vantage point, facing east, the Chilhowee Mountain range and Miller's Cove unfold to a scenic vista on the far horizon.

It was at this point that McWherter fell off the porch. He was standing too near the edge, with his back toward the mountain range, engaged in animated conversation with Willis and Alexander, who were seated in rocking chairs facing him. Then, while making a vigorous point, the 250-pound speaker took a half-step backward. Suddenly he disappeared, plunging three feet into the rhododendron bushes.

Horrified, Willis and Alexander jumped from their rocking chairs. (Alexander remembers thinking in the moment, "My gosh, I've killed the speaker! Now, we'll never pass the bill.") After an anxious few seconds, McWherter slowly rose from the shrubbery and gathered himself. Assuring his host that he was unharmed, the speaker then walked around to the end of the porch and climbed back up the steps, taking his seat in the third rocker.

The conversation resumed, chairs slowly rocking, and stretched into the late evening.

CHAPTER 6

Political Family Trees

"This history is largely lost."
  —Congressman Jim Cooper

UNLIKE THE ANGRY, HYPER-PARTISAN tone and divisions of the present day, in both state and national politics, in the in-between time there was more cordiality between elections. Campaign battles were no less combative than now but between election campaigns, broadly speaking, there was good government. This was because many of the victors understood the necessity of working with those from the other party who had also won.

To grasp why that was—how it was different then, how it changed later on—it is necessary to know how alliances were formed, how friendships were made and sustained, how the work was actually done, and how the environment of politics eventually changed.

BY THE TIME OF Baker's first re-election, in 1972, it was becoming clear that Tennessee's senior senator was inspiring a generation of new politicians, and recruiting and mentoring a new set of activists—and eventually candidates—to the state's deepening Republican Party. The best known of these in the period would be Alexander and Thompson.

From the middle 1960s onward, Baker was a pivotal mentor to Alexander, who throughout his life would acknowledge Baker as having been one of the most important influences on his own career. In 1972, Alexander recruited Thompson to be Baker's re-election campaign manager for Middle Tennessee.

The following year, Alexander helped Baker recruit Thompson to a much higher-profile role: minority counsel to the new Senate Committee on Presidential Campaign Activities (the "Watergate Committee"), which brought Thompson his own significant national exposure.

At this time there were only four television networks. As the committee dug into how much the Nixon White House knew about the Watergate break-in, the hearings were given gavel-to-gavel TV coverage on most weekdays over the summer of 1973. From May 17 to August 7, the committee members and staff and their administration witnesses would appear on TV screens across America, especially the chairman, Senator Sam Ervin of North Carolina; Baker, the vice chair; the majority counsel Sam Dash; and Thompson.

There were many others in Baker's political family tree. One of the young interns in Baker's 1972 campaign office was a young Bill Haslam, son of Jim Haslam of Knoxville, then a college student at Emory University in Atlanta. Bill would go on to join the family business, Pilot Oil Corp., and was elected mayor of Knoxville in 2003 and governor of Tennessee in 2010. Bill's older brother Jimmy Haslam, later the owner of the NFL's Cleveland Browns, attended the University of Tennessee in Knoxville, where he was a Sigma Chi fraternity brother and roommate to Bob Corker of Chattanooga, later mayor and U.S. senator.

Early in his Senate career, Baker began to hone a gift for fostering bipartisan cooperation on important policy issues. His success with this relied on a practiced respect for his colleagues, whether Republican or Democrat. He often quoted his father as saying, "Remember, the other fellow may be right." In time Baker became known as "The Great Conciliator" of the Senate, and his growing reputation for civility and capacity for finding common ground served him well.

When the 1980 elections put Ronald Reagan in the White House and gave Republicans a new Senate majority, Baker became the majority leader. The election result was a shock to the current majority leader, Democrat Robert Byrd of West Virginia. Baker went to see Byrd, who now would be the leader of the Democratic minority in the Senate, their roles were now reversed.

> BAKER: "Senator Byrd, I'll never know the rules as well as you do. I'll
>   make a deal with you: I won't surprise you, if you won't surprise me."
> BYRD: "I'll think about it."

The next day Byrd told Baker that he agreed. The two of them worked together from 1981 to 1985. Veteran Senate watchers say the Senate operated more effectively in that period than at any time since.

BAKER'S FINAL SENATE TERM overlapped with the first term of Tennessee Democrat Jim Sasser, the Nashville lawyer who had defeated the Republican Brock in 1976. Sasser remembers Baker as a cordial colleague, both on and off the Senate floor. I spoke with Sasser about this in December 2014.

"My father knew Howard's father," Sasser told me, "but I did not know Howard until we got to the Senate, and we always got along." The elder Sasser, in his day, was a federal agricultural official serving in West Tennessee, where he became politically close to the Democratic congressmen Fats Everett and Ed Jones. (His son first met Ned McWherter through Pauline LaFon, who later married Albert Gore Sr.)

"When Howard became majority leader, he would sort of look after a lot of national interests, and he was thinking about running for president. So I would sort of handle the Tennessee end of it and Howard would handle the national end of things. When something came up for Tennessee that we needed, we would work together and get it done."

Sasser remembers one cordial scene in particular. It was the private senators-only dining room on the first floor of the U.S. Capitol building. In this space—officially called the Styles Bridges Room but commonly referred to as the "inner sanctum"—it was routine practice for Republican senators to gather for lunch at one table and Democrats at another. But on this day, Senate business had run late so it was after the regular lunch hour when Sasser arrived, alone, and took a seat at the Democrats' table. Baker and several fellow Republicans were sitting at their table.

"That's when I heard Howard call out my name," Sasser remembers, "and he said, 'Jim, why don't you come over here and join us—and get some real old-time religion!' So I joined them for lunch.

"Howard was very nice to me. We worked very well together in Washington. I respected him. I never saw Howard get angry; he was always genial. We never took a cheap shot at each other, cooperated always on Tennessee projects. There was no hostility that I was aware of. Partisanship was there on the elections, but not on the day-to-day basis." Sasser recalled evenings when he and his wife Mary would dine out with Howard and Joy Baker.

"When I went to the Senate, in my first term Howard Baker was minority leader. He took the lead—and the heat—on getting President Jimmy Carter's Panama Canal treaty ratified. Can you see that happening in today's Senate? Could you see Mitch McConnell taking the heat on something that Obama wanted to do, even though he may think it's what's best for the country? So, times have just changed. Howard and I would get together and we might fly across the state together. Of course, at election time, I would go with the Democrats and he would go with the Republicans."

Nashville Democrat Jim Cooper, son of Tennessee governor (1939–45) and later U.S. ambassador to Peru Prentice Cooper, won his own seat in Congress in 1982 in a Fourth District race against Baker's daughter, Cissy. This was the same year that Don Sundquist, Republican, won the Eighth District seat by defeating Democrat Bob Clement. Neither Cooper (in spite of his father's long public service) nor Sundquist were expected to win, owing to their opponents' famous family names and presumed organizational strength.

Sundquist told me that Alexander, then governor, had actually counseled him against making the race, in view of the Clement family's statewide name recognition. Not only had Bob's father been governor for a total of ten years, but by this time Bob himself had served for ten years on the elected Tennessee Public Service Commission, regulator of utilities and railroads. The son had won his first PSC election, in 1972, by a 3-to-1 margin over the incumbent Hammond Fowler.

But both these district races turned the conventional political wisdom on its ear in 1982. Cissy Baker lost to Cooper in a 2-to-1 landslide (93,453 votes to 47,865). And Sundquist defeated Clement, though by only 1,476 votes in a race where 141,318 votes were cast. Clement and his people were stunned. Years later, Sundquist told me that the "concession" call from Clement—where the loser traditionally phones and bows graciously to the victor—never came.

In his 1986 book, *Steps Along the Way*, Alexander acknowledges urging Baker's daughter to run ("This district's made for you," he told her. "You can win it.") and also that he had privately counseled Sundquist to stand down in the other district ("Don, I hate to tell you this, but you'll never be able to win"). He called 1982 "The Year My Political Advice was One Hundred Percent Wrong," yet his political acumen wasn't totally incorrect. On the same November day that Cooper and Sundquist won their first terms in Congress, Alexander was re-elected governor.

IN MY JUNE 2015 interview with Cooper, he praised Senator Baker both for his durable civility and also his political courage, especially for his role in aiding the Carter administration in achieving Senate ratification of the Panama Canal treaty in 1978.

"I think the seminal event of the 1980s was Howard Baker's selfless decision to agree with Jimmy Carter to give away the Panama Canal," he said. "That was an astonishing act of statesmanship. It killed him (Baker) here in Tennessee—he could not run for public office after that—and then giving up his seat as Senate majority leader? You can't even imagine a Mitch McConnell today agreeing with a Barack Obama on something controversial. This history is largely lost. This would be an unheard of, unimaginable thing to do today. There could have been a 'clash of the titans' here in 1984 (had Baker not resigned and if Al Gore Jr. had run against him), and Al Gore would've been forced to oppose the Panama Canal and oppose Carter on that, but the right thing was done. To me, Baker gets credit for that. The right thing was done. That would be unthinkable today. . . . Baker came from that tradition. That's the tradition Lamar Alexander comes from."

Speaking of his own early years in Congress, Cooper recalled a time when party labels were not as supremely important in the day-to-day work as they are today. There was more collegiality, more cooperation across party lines on issues. Party labels were also less visible in Tennessee's statewide politics from the viewpoint of voters.

"I call that period 'friendly competition'—it really was not partisan. It was not ideological," Cooper said. "For example, John Waters from Sevier County, who used to be on the TVA Board, used to say the three most important influences in his life—and this guy was a strong Republican—were the TVA, Social Security, and the Smoky Mountains National Park. That's a pretty nice comment from a hard-shell Republican. You never see that today. If you asked the average voter whether Ned McWherter or Phil Bredesen was a Democrat or Republican, half of them would say 'Republican'—they were as business-like as any governor in American history."

This quality began to ebb with the rise of extreme gerrymandering, partisan zeal, and modern campaign financing. Those accelerating trends combined in the latter third of the twentieth century to chill many relationships between Democratic and Republican members, Cooper observed. And the modern conveniences of technology, air travel, and even air-conditioning also contributed to a diminution of the old routines of personal interactions across the aisle, cordiality, and socializing by members of Congress in the evenings and weekends in the capital.

"As recently as 1976," Cooper recalled, "we had Tennessee congressmen who would return to Tennessee only twice a year. Congressman Joe L. Evins hated to fly, so he would drive to Washington and back, and he only did it twice a year. That changed when Al Gore Jr. took Mr. Evins's seat; he was back home almost every weekend. But his father, Albert Gore Sr., would get a lot of credit because he would drive back to Nashville in the middle of the night so he could be on the Ralph Emery radio show early in the morning. The listening audience loved it, because here he'd made this superhuman effort to get there. Howard Baker used to say it was air-conditioning that ruined Washington. I think a much better case could be made that it was the airplanes that ruined Washington. There's nobody there on the weekends now. That's why we don't know each other's names. You never have time to eat together or socialize. An hour after the session, everybody's on a plane."

❖

IN HIS LATER YEARS, Baker himself would lament how modern air travel had hampered lawmakers from gathering socially on weekends. This was still on his mind long after he left public office.

It came up again in the summer of 2009, over a casual lunch with two of his law partners, Don Stansberry and Charles W. Bone, and the journalist Sam Hatcher of Lebanon, Tennessee. Hatcher shared his memory of the conversation that occurred (over "skillet-fried peanut butter and jelly sandwiches," Baker's favorite) in Huntsville, Tennessee. The retired senator and ambassador recalled his own working relationships across the Senate aisle.

"Baker said he could have a spirited disagreement on the floor of the Senate with a Democratic colleague, and later he and his wife and the senator with whom he had disagreed and his wife would join each other for dinner," Hatcher recalled. "Sure they were members of different political parties, had different ideas, but fundamentally they all wanted what was best for the country, and for the most part they were friends and could get along with each other despite their differences."

Baker had also singled out the Democratic House speaker, Representative Tip O'Neill of Massachusetts.

"He recalled that he and the speaker would often meet after a day on the Hill, share an adult beverage, and talk. He said they'd inquire about each other's family, about personal plans, vacations and such, and eventually they'd get around to talking about issues in Congress. While they wouldn't necessarily agree, Baker said they usually could find a way to compromise and move forward."

In twenty-first-century Washington, of course, such words—especially *compromise*—would be shunned as anathema to the republic.

THERE HAVE BEEN TENNESSEANS in the nation's capital city, of course, since Congress granted statehood in 1796. These have included not only those holding elected offices but also presidential appointees to the regulatory agencies and their staffs, cabinet officers, and a long line of lobbyists and trade association executives. In the mid-twentieth century, many of these from the Volunteer State would often socialize both privately and through formal organizations such as the Tennessee State Society that would involve both Democrats and Republicans through the in-between time.

On June 14, 1994, in the final year of McWherter's time in the governor's office, Jim and Ann Free threw a party in his honor at their Washington home in the Kalorama neighborhood. By this time Free, born in Columbia, Tennessee, had become established as a prominent lobbyist and was well known in Washington power circles. But he always acknowledged how his first boss, McWherter, had been his primary mentor. In 1973, when Free was only twenty-six years old, McWherter had made him his administrative assistant and also the Chief Clerk of the Tennessee House of Representatives. Two years later the speaker introduced his personable protégé to his Georgia friend Jimmy Carter, then running for president. Free worked in Carter's campaign for president and after the 1976 election he joined Carter's congressional liaison team with the title of special assistant to the president and with an office in the White House.

Free recalled that in his first days on the White House job, he had visited Baker at his Capitol office, and the Republican leader extended an extraordinary courtesy for a fellow Tennessean. Free says that after their private visit Baker escorted him over to the House side of the Capitol and introduced the young Tennessee Democrat to the Republican leaders of the House of Representatives. These were congressmen John Rhodes, the Republican House leader; Bob Michel, the Republican whip, and John Anderson, chairman of the GOP caucus. At each stop, Free remembers, Baker said to his GOP colleagues: "Jim's working in the White House now. He's our friend from back home. We know his people. We're lucky to have him down there. I hope you'll help him—if it's not partisan, work with him. If it's partisan, whip him!"

"Everybody laughed," Free told me. "At that time, very few issues were purely partisan in nature. I've reflected on those meetings for the past forty years. Can you imagine that happening today?"

At the 1994 reception for McWherter, the Frees' guests were a bipartisan crowd, though leaning to the Democratic. President Clinton was there. So was Vice President Al Gore Jr., and several members of Congress with Tennessee roots. These included both senators, the Democrats Jim Sasser and Harlan Mathews, and at least four House members, Republicans Quillen and Duncan, and the Democrats Bart Gordon and John Tanner. (Sundquist, a Republican who admired McWherter, had been invited but was back home campaigning for governor, a race he would win five months later to succeed McWherter.)

Quillen, of course, was the most senior. By this time he had been in Congress for thirty-two years, always re-elected from the state's reliably Republican First District in upper East Tennessee. A fixture in Tennessee's delegation, Quillen was also quietly influential in statewide elections back home, reminiscent of how Senator McKellar and Congressman Reece in their day had presence and political influence beyond their home territories. Two of the most prominent Democrats attending this reception had, in fact, enjoyed Quillen's support—or at least his helpful acquiescence—in their own races. Both McWherter and Gore had run, in different years, against Republican nominees who had displeased Mr. Quillen over the same issue.

Free remembers a moment in his entrance foyer when Gore—standing there with McWherter, Sasser, Mathews, Quillen, and Free—declared: "Everybody in this room has one thing in common: Jimmy Quillen got us all elected!" At this Quillen smiled knowingly, and the others laughed. What Gore was referring to had long been an unspoken truth of politics in Tennessee.

Gore himself, when he was first elected to the Senate in 1984, had enjoyed Quillen's quiet blessing across the aisle. The Republican nominee that year was State Senator Victor Ashe of Knoxville, who a decade earlier had opposed creation of a new medical school in Quillen's district. The state's Higher Education Commission had said it could not justify a second state-supported medical school at East Tennessee State University in Johnson City since the University of Tennessee had a longstanding medical school in Memphis. Ashe, who represented UT's headquarters city of Knoxville, voted against the new school in the 1974 legislative session. When it passed, with Speaker McWherter's support, and was brought to the governor's desk, Dunn vetoed it. McWherter then helped to engineer an override of the veto, and planning for the second medical school moved forward. (The school was eventually named for Quillen.)

Ten years later, in the same year as Reagan's re-election, the Democrat Gore came within 105 votes of beating Ashe in the reliable Republican stronghold of Quillen's district. This prevented Ashe from coming out of the First District with the kind of majority that had enabled other Republicans before him to win their statewide races. Statewide, Gore drew a million votes, 60 percent of the total votes cast, and he buried Ashe in a landslide.

Two years after that, when McWherter ran for governor in 1986, his Republican opposite was Dunn. At one point, Dunn met with Quillen in his East Tennessee district, hoping to patch over any residual hard feelings about the medical school affair. Afterward, Dunn would try to put a hopeful best face on how the meeting went. But a source close to Quillen remembers this exchange with the congressman days later:

"Did you two bury the hatchet?" a fellow Republican asked. "We did," Quillen replied, "but I know where it's buried."

Quillen never forgave Dunn for his veto. As the 1986 election approached, this knowledge became an important part of McWherter's campaign strategy throughout East Tennessee. For Dunn, as it had been for Ashe, Quillen's memory was long and payback was hard. On Election Day, November 4, McWherter carried Quillen's First District by a five-point margin. This time, Baker's old east-west coalition could not hold. The Memphian Dunn finished the night trailing by nine percentage points statewide, and his political career was over.

When Quillen left Congress in 1996, eleven Republicans ran for the party's nomination to fill his House seat. The winner was Bill Jenkins, a lawyer from Rogersville who served briefly (1969–71) as speaker of the Tennessee House of Representatives. Jenkins represented the First District for ten years, until 2007.

❖

IN THE SUMMER OF 1980, the Reagan presidential campaign was in full swing, and Tennessee politicos on both sides of the aisle were facing their first post-Blanton legislative elections in November.

Nationally, this would be Reagan's year, and Republican strategists saw opportunity with down-ballot elections, particularly in southern border states such as Arkansas, Tennessee, and North Carolina. The "Southern Strategy" of the national Republican Party that had helped Nixon win in 1968 and 1972 was in resurgence by this time and would likewise help advance the Reagan campaign.

This would also be a year of dramatic recovery and revival for the national party following the GOP disaster of Watergate. No one deserved more credit for that turnaround than the Tennessean Bill Brock, who was now chairman of the Republican National Committee. He had lost his Senate seat in 1976 to Sasser, who of course had missed no chance to link Brock to the recent Watergate scandals. One year later, the former U.S. senator became the party's chairman, inheriting the planning for the 1980 national convention. An early issue was where to convene that convention, with many party leaders favoring Dallas, Texas.

Brock insisted that the party's nationally televised gathering be held in Detroit, not Dallas. He said he wanted the TV networks to show his delegates and Republican candidates gathering not in the Sunbelt where times were more prosperous, but in a place more closely with the nation's deepening economic issues. It was this assortment of economic pains—particularly the so-called misery index, which added double-digit inflation with double-digit unemployment—that Reagan would use to lambast President Carter in the campaign to come.

❖

IN JUST SIXTEEN YEARS, from 1983 through 1998, Tennessee lost four daily newspapers across its four largest cities.

These particular four—the *Chattanooga Times*, *Knoxville Journal*, *Memphis Press-Scimitar*, and *Nashville Banner*—were arguably Tennessee's most colorful dailies, with respect to editorial positions in their respective towns and the way those editorial views occasionally seemed to bleed onto the news pages, too. The editorials and political cartoons in these broadsheets varied in stridency and partisan loyalties. With each of the four, local readers had come to expect sharp-edged editorials, original political cartoons, and news coverage that some days reflected the personality of a strong-minded publisher.

As it would with competition between candidates, competition between newspapers within each city would also make their work sharper. Reporters and their editors at each of these afternoon dailies scrambled in competition with the larger-circulation morning newspaper in town—in Chattanooga that was the *Free Press*, in Knoxville the *News Sentinel*, in Memphis the *Commercial Appeal*, and in Nashville *The Tennessean*. Savvy politicians over the years had grown accustomed to having a friendly ear, at one or the other, when pitching new policies and positive announcements, or when defending against new scandals.

In the end, the circumstances of their disappearance differed in the details, but one element they shared was the sobering reality of a changing economy for traditional print journalism, particularly for afternoon newspapers. They were lost through the trend of increasing consolidation of media ownership during a period of deep transformation. This was happening across the nation as consumer habits with the emergence of television and other forms of entertainment. Even more numerous were consolidations in the electronic media, as large commercial radio chains continued to make new acquisitions in local markets. Programming formats shifted in many cases, often bringing about reductions in news department staffs.

In Nashville, Lynette Easley had been a news reporter, editor, and news director at a number of radio stations. She recalled a period of rapid change in the early 1980s when the new Reagan administration declined to nominate new members to the Federal Communications Commission. The current FCC commissioners had been in a mood to expand FCC oversight to the emerging technologies of cable television, a new format (CNN was the only cable news provider at that early point). Commissioners favored an expanded mission, requiring new members, but the White House declined.

"That lead to the demise of radio news," Easley remembers. "The FCC would continue to regulate with respect to payola and so forth, but if you didn't want to do 'news' anymore, you didn't have to. It happened in a week. Station managers began to say they were interested in music, not words. We (news departments) never made any money for them. Radio news had been a rather stable market, but in Nashville in less than two weeks no station was doing news." In retirement, Easley teaches creative writing.

What would prove to be even more deeply disruptive for traditional politics and politicians across the nation was the rise of conservative "talk radio," best exemplified by Rush Limbaugh. The ABC Radio Network syndicated

Limbaugh's daily three-hour show in 1988, and his firebrand style became wildly popular among conservative political activists coast-to-coast. Like-minded elected officials clamored to appear on his program, and Limbaugh ascended as an influential new element in political theatre. His success—and flamboyant, combative on-air style—inspired a new generation of conservative radio personalities, not only in Washington but also in state capitals across the country.

In Tennessee, this new phenomenon would play out most dramatically when Republican governor Don Sundquist, in the late 1990s, proposed a new state income tax. Conservative radio personalities Steve Gill and Phil Valentine inflamed their audiences, encouraging citizen action against the new tax. Hundreds of the activists drove their automobiles around the State Capitol building, honking their horns to disrupt proceedings inside the building. The proposal failed.

More recently, the advent of social media—especially Twitter—has further dispersed the control of information in broad circulation, well beyond the traditional gatekeepers of news: the editors of newspapers and the news directors of local television and radio stations.

This rise of new media would, soon enough, help put an end to the relatively polite in-between time of government, and cordiality across the aisle would be its victim.

CHAPTER 7

Strange Bedfellows

"Politics is the best place in the world not to take yourself too seriously."
—Mayor Randy Tyree, Knoxville

MANY OF THE TENNESSEE politicians holding office through the in-between time made some of their most enduring friendships through a small number of networks, some formal and official but others informal.

In some cases these relationships dated back to college and law school days. Others developed or were reinforced through military service, or in early political campaigns, by working across the aisle in state government, or simply by chance encounter.

- In the 1960s, Lamar Alexander and Frank Hunger (who would later marry Al Gore's sister Nancy) were young law clerks together on the Fifth Circuit U.S. Court of Appeals in New Orleans.
- Jimmy Naifeh, who would become speaker of the Tennessee House in 1991, roomed with Jake Butcher, who would run for governor in 1974 and 1978, when they were undergraduates at the University of Tennessee in Knoxville.
- Eddie Sisk, who would serve later as Governor Ray Blanton's legal counsel, and Fred Thompson, future U.S. senator, once worked as assistant district attorneys in the same Middle Tennessee district.
- Hal Hardin, the future U.S. attorney who would trigger the coup that brought Blanton down, lived briefly with Sisk and a dozen other law students when they were all in law school in Knoxville.
- Bob Corker, the future senator, lived with Jimmy Haslam, brother of future governor Bill Haslam, when they were in college at Knoxville.
- Early in his career, Randy Tyree, later mayor of Knoxville and the 1982 Democratic nominee for governor, worked with the Law Enforcement Planning Agency in the office of Republican governor Winfield Dunn.

- The future Republican notables A. B. Culvahouse of Ten Mile near Chattanooga and Roger Kesley of Knoxville lived in the same off-campus house at UT with the future Democratic leaders J. Houston Gordon of Covington and Charles W. Bone of Gallatin. (Culvahouse and Gordon, from different ends of the state, are also cousins.)
- Democrat Ned McWherter and Republican state chairman Tom Beasley were once in business together, owning a downtown Nashville motel with two other investors.
- Jim Hall, who became a top lieutenant to McWherter in his campaigns and administration, first met Corker on a racquetball court in Chattanooga.
- Democrat Gordon Ball, the 2014 nominee for U.S. Senate, first met the Republican Lee Smith on a Nashville basketball court in 1977 when Ball was a delegate to the state's constitutional convention.
- Smith and Alexander were roommates in Washington in 1967–68, and they married roommates.

More formally, within the state government there were the legislative committees and other leadership structures. Members would work during the daytime, where they might either collaborate or argue or both, and then frequently find dinner and drinks together in the early evenings. In these informal settings, Democrats and Republicans would mix in friendship and good humor. The GOP leader in the House, Representative Jim Henry of Kingston, would regularly commute on the long drive to Nashville in the same car with three very senior ranking Democrats: Senator Anna Belle Clement O'Brien of Crossville; Representative Tommy Burnett, the Democratic majority leader from Jamestown; and Representative Peabody Ledford of Roane County. The most common after-hours venues during legislative sessions in Nashville were, for Democrats, a suite at the Capitol Park Inn, and for Republicans a comparable suite (affectionately called "the Kremlin") at the Hyatt Regency Hotel across Memorial Plaza. Yet these rooms were not politically exclusive; members of "the other party," both elected officials and staff members, were cordially welcomed at each of these.

At some point in the latter 1990s, these bipartisan social hours vanished. Whether they ended because of new ethics rules, or a rising level of partisan intolerance, legislative veterans remember them fondly. And in many cases the personal friendships persisted through the in-between time in spite of heated daytime policy debates, even as Tennessee's political composition evolved through the 1980s and 1990s in the Great Transition. Some of these longtime relationships began to wane through the decade of the nineties, as political offices changed hands and all the principals moved deeper into the Democrat-to-Republican transition that shifted the ruling majorities.

❖

ONE OF THE MOST enduring bipartisan networks through the in-between time—and probably the least visible to a given member's constituents—was service in the Tennessee National Guard, either the Army Guard or the Air Guard.

Across the U.S., the National Guard still serves as part of the reserve forces of the active military. Selected units can be deployed to active duty when either foreign or domestic emergencies occur. In the twentieth century, this deployment of additional manpower occurred most often in response to floods, hurricanes, and other natural disasters. For many draft-age young men during the Vietnam War, six years of Guard membership was an alternative route for discharging their military service obligation. Guard units were subject to mobilization to war zones, but customarily a guardsman could expect to be deployed with his unit. When the draft ended, Guard enlistments by young men declined across the nation.

When civil disturbances erupted in 1968 following the assassination of Dr. Martin Luther King Jr., Tennessee guardsmen were deployed as peacekeepers to Memphis and Nashville. During the Vietnam War, units of the Tennessee Air Guard flew frequent supply missions to Southeast Asia in the later 1960s and early 1970s, supporting the regular military. More recently, Tennessee guardsmen were deployed to Iraq in the 1990 Gulf War and later to both Iraq and Afghanistan as the war on terror escalated. Since 2001, an estimated 43 percent of total U.S. military forces were from Guard and Reserves in units across the U.S., with more than 780,000 individuals mobilized; guardsmen and reservists also accounted for about a fifth of all U.S. military fatalities in Iraq and Afghanistan.

Not all Tennessee Guard officers were politicians, but a notable number were, especially during this period. This tradition, both political and practical, dated back at least to the early 1950s, when the most famous of these was the flamboyant lawyer Joe W. Henry of Pulaski. He was a U.S. Army veteran of World War II, a post-war member of the state House of Representatives, a Guard member since 1947, and later a close adviser to Governor Frank Clement.

In 1953, Clement appointed Henry to the post of Tennessee adjutant general, top commander of the state's Military Department overseeing the National Guard. Three years later, when Clement ordered Guard troops into Clinton, Tennessee, to quell rioting over the court-ordered desegregation of Clinton High School, Major General Henry personally lead 171 troops of the Guard's 30th Armored Division into the town. He rode ahead of them in a military tank, wearing his combat uniform and helmet, and with pearl-handled pistols holstered on each hip.

Of the unruly crowd that he and his troops confronted in Clinton, Henry declared, "I've got as much guts as they have, and more men." The governor's show of force worked. The segregationist crowd dispersed and the high school opened. In the national news coverage that followed, Henry's name was in the *New York Times* and his photo ran in *Life* magazine. (He continued to be a leader of the Tennessee Democratic Party. He assailed the 1970 elections of Dunn and Brock as "a plague of Republican locusts," and in 1974 he was elected to the Tennessee Supreme Court on the Democratic ticket.) Dunn did not tolerate Henry's partisan style for long; the new governor dismissed him in November 1971. This triggered two letters to Dunn both defiant and full of righteous indignation.

> Dear Governor Dunn,
>   . . . in 1949, when I was a lowly Captain, and simultaneously served in the Legislature, I vigorously fought Governor Gordon Browning, but Governor Browning, whom I have long since come to admire and respect and whose friendship I enjoy and appreciate, was perceptive of the reciprocities of the rough and tumble of politics, and took no action against me.
>   . . . If you want to throw me out of the Tennessee National Guard because of politics, and in so doing, say to the 13,000 Guardsmen in Tennessee that they forfeit their right to free speech, and are relegated to a role of second class citizenship, then you may instruct your Adjutant General to publish the orders. I cannot and will not live under political dictation. I do not choose to being gagged. I am a stalwart Democrat, a troubled Tennessean and now, an ex-communicated member of the Tennessee National Guard.
>
> With best wishes, I am
> Very sincerely yours,
> Joe W. Henry

MCWHERTER HIMSELF HAD BEEN in the state's Army Guard, joining in 1948 when he was only seventeen years old, and he served until he went to the legislature two decades later. So had Governor Clement in his day, and also his son Bob, the congressman from Nashville. McWherter's cousin Cayce Pentecost, an elected member of the Tennessee Public Service Commission, was a longtime Guard officer. Cavit Cheshier, the long-serving executive of the Tennessee Education Association, remembers meeting McWherter as a fellow second lieutenant in the Army Guard when they were college students at the University of Tennessee at Martin.

Congressman John Tanner, a Democrat and a Navy veteran from West

Tennessee, served in the Army Guard through most of his years in the state legislature. This was true of Andy Daniels and other key legislative staff members during the period. Paul G. Summers, a lawyer from Wilder's hometown of Somerville (who became the state's attorney general in 1999 and an appeals court judge after that), followed the Tennessee Guard service of his own father, Judge Paul S. Summers, who was colonel of the Judge Advocate General Corps. State Representative Walter Bussart and McWherter's chief legal counsel David H. Welles (also later a state appeals court judge) were both JAG officers in the Tennessee Army Guard, as were Nashville businessman Frank Woods and the Sumner County attorney Charles W. Bone, both of whom were allied politically with the Knoxville banker Jake Butcher through the 1970s and early 1980s.

These were notable Democrats all. But as the blue state continued its transition to red, politically connected Republicans likewise moved in greater numbers into the officer ranks of Tennessee's Guard. Charles Anderson, the U.S. attorney for Middle Tennessee appointed by President Nixon, was a Tennessee Army Guard officer. Memphis native Robert L. Echols, a longtime friend of Alexander's from their time as teenagers at Boys State in the summer of 1957, served in the JAG corps and rose to the rank of brigadier general. He served until 1992 when President George H. W. Bush nominated him to the U.S. District Court for Middle Tennessee.

When Echols's presidential nomination to the court came, he hoped his own swearing-in might occur in the State Capitol, but by this time the Democrat McWherter had succeeded Alexander in the governor's office. Echols remembers phoning Harlan Mathews, then McWherter's top deputy, and asking him about the availability of the historic Supreme Court chambers. (Tennessee's Supreme Court relocated to its own building in 1937, and this prominent space on the north end of the capitol's first floor became part of the governor's office. It was later reconfigured as a large formal room, suitable for ceremonies and news conferences.) Mathews returned his call right away, saying McWherter had quickly agreed. For his family's convenience on the swearing-in day, Mathews invited Echols to use one of the governor's private parking spaces on Capitol Hill.

When Echols visited the capitol for a walk-through days before his ceremony, McWherter met him and personally showed him the room. As a final courtesy, the governor then reached into his pocket and handed him two keys to the building. "Those are mine," he told the Echols. "Don't lose 'em."

❖

ONE OF HENRY'S SUCCESSORS as adjutant general was Carl Wallace, a Democrat appointed to the top post in 1975 by Governor Blanton. (Four years later, as the coup to oust Blanton was rushing to its conclusion, Alexander retained Wallace as his own AG in order to thwart Blanton should he learn of the secret plan and preemptively order guardsmen to defend the capitol.) In civilian life, prior to his Guard service, Wallace had been a newspaper editor and publisher in Lebanon, Tennessee, where he and his wife Yvonne operated the daily *Lebanon Democrat.*

Before he became a general, the affable Wallace was for several years the officer in charge of the Tennessee Army Guard's 118th Public Affairs Detachment, which met for monthly "drill" weekends at the Guard's headquarters in Nashville. Into this unit came other Middle Tennessee journalists, many of them staff reporters or editors with the *Nashville Tennessean* and *Nashville Banner* newspapers, local television newsrooms, and a number of advertising and public relations professionals working chiefly in the Nashville area. These included Jimmy Carnahan, Larry Daughtrey, Charles Fancher, Tom Ferrell, Jim Gilchrist, Sam Hatcher, Ryland Hoskins, Hooper Penuel, Bill Preston Jr., Keith Preston, Jim Squires, Al Voecks, and Joe Worley. This was essentially a public-relations office for Guard commanders. Its members often referred to their unit as "the Fightin', Writin' 118th." Many of these, in their civilian jobs as journalists, would report on the actions of the same politicos with whom they served as guardsmen on weekends.

A corresponding public affairs unit in the Tennessee Air National Guard's 118th Military Airlift Wing had as its commander Major Clarence Reynolds, a prominent Nashville banker and member of the Davidson County Election Commission in Nashville. (Serving on Reynolds's public affairs staff on Guard weekends were two *Tennessean* reporters, Tom Gillem and the author.) The former governor Clement, a U.S. Army veteran, was a member of the Tennessee Air Guard after he left office in 1967, serving as a legal staff officer in Nashville. Before Clement's death in an auto accident in Nashville in 1969, he would often visit Reynolds's unit on drill weekends. His son, Frank G. Clement Jr., a lawyer like his father, served in an Air Guard unit based in Memphis; the son became a judge on the state Court of Appeals in 2003.

Between their infrequent active-duty deployments, the routine for state guardsmen was the monthly "drill" weekend, held on Saturdays and Sundays usually at local armories near their homes, plus a fortnight of "annual training" camp each summer. For Tennessee army guardsmen, summer encampments were either at Camp Shelby, in Mississippi, or at Fort Stewart in Georgia. In most cases, participation in summer camp required the cooperation of civilian employers, granting time off without penalty. Once there, military exercises were common during the day, but members were largely free in the evenings.

In the summer of 1981, Wallace arranged a concert for the troops at Camp

Shelby, featuring the Nashville recording artist Tom T. Hall. This became an annual USO-type entertainment tradition for Tennessee guardsmen. Subsequent concerts featured the country music artists Little Jimmy Dickens, Jean Shepard, and Jim Ed Brown. Wallace arranged travel for them from Nashville to the Mississippi post aboard the Guard's C-130 military aircraft.

In my interviews, Guard veterans would recall how friendships made "across the aisle" endured well into their later years, many crediting their Guard service as having been the starting point for what became lifelong relationships with leaders of the other political party. The Republican congressman Jimmy Duncan, of Knoxville, told me it was through his Guard service that he first met Tanner and Bob Clement, both Democrats who hailed from different regions of the long state. (Duncan told me he liked Clement so much he once sent him a $200 campaign contribution.)

"All these guys were my buddies," Paul G. Summers said of his own friendships that came through Guard service. "I got to know hundreds of people from Memphis to Mountain City. We had political discussions and arguments, yes, but nobody ever took those arguments home with them on Sunday afternoon."

Bussart's career as a state judge and legislator spanned the in-between time. In 2017, now an attorney in private practice in Lewisburg and Nashville, he told me his Guard service produced many friendships that bonded him with Republicans as well as Democrats.

"The Guard, particularly in Nashville, was like a big fraternity," he told me. "As Democrats, we didn't see the 'red wave' coming because the people we served with were such nice people. Ned McWherter was such a strong leader, the Republicans were never pushed aside. Ned was inclusive. The Guard made lasting friendships—friends for life. It was a gathering point for politics and personalities."

RELATIONSHIPS GREW ACROSS PARTY lines during this in-between era of politically divided government. This was necessary if anything legislative was to get done. One example was the relationship between the Republican Alexander and the Democrats of the Clement family. They became closer after Butcher defeated Bob Clement for the Democratic nomination for governor in August, 1978.

In the final weeks of the Democratic primary that summer, Butcher seemed to go out of his way to berate and belittle Bob Clement, his closest challenger, and many of Clement's supporters in anger either sat out the general election period or actively supported Alexander, the Republican nominee. Thousands of Clement primary voters switched sides to help elect Alexander in the November general election.

In his first term, Alexander and his advisers looked for opportunities to build on the friendships that had been forged with the Clement family during that 1978 general election period. An early illustration involved a small museum project that was important to the Clement family, in the town of Dickson, their ancestral home.

The Clement Railroad Hotel Museum is housed in the former Halbrook Hotel that sits adjacent to Dickson's old railroad depot. The Halbrook had figured in the family's history; Governor Clement's parents, Robert and Maybelle, had operated the hotel in their early years and lived with their children in the manager's private quarters. Today the museum, which opened in 2009 and is on the state's list of historic sites, commemorates the history and commerce of Dickson County, and it features, on the second floor, a replica of the governor's office at the State Capitol in Clement's time.

Prominent in this display is the governor's desk. Visitors today will see a replica, but the real desk that Clement used while he was in office (his first term began in 1953) was there from 1979 to 2003. How it came to be in this spot, forty-two miles west of the capitol building, is a story of cooperation across party lines.

The late governor's sister, Anna Belle, had been a member of her brother's staff in the early days, chiefly handling patronage matters from her office on the ground floor of the capitol. "Miss Anna Belle" was a charismatic character in her own right—a winning personality, firm handshake, plus the Clement love of people and the ability to draw fresh energy from crowds. In 1974, five years after her brother's death, she was elected to the state House. Two years after that, she won a seat in the state Senate.

In 1979, Anna Belle and her parents (her father was now a state court judge) were gathering artifacts for a future memorial to Governor Clement's legacy at the old railroad hotel, believing it could become an important tourist attraction in Dickson. Hoping to include the governor's desk, Anna Belle phoned Tom Ingram, who was now Alexander's chief of staff, and invited him to visit the Halbrook. He went.

"I had gotten close to Miss Anna Belle during the campaign," Ingram told me, "and she introduced me to her parents, Judge Robert and Maybelle. I went down to Dickson and spent some time with them at the railroad station hotel where they were trying to recreate Frank's gubernatorial office in the front room in that old hotel. They had everything but his desk."

Back in Nashville, Ingram phoned Lois Riggins-Ezzell, the staff director of the Tennessee State Museum, which had custody of many historical artifacts, and he told her, "We're looking for Governor Clement's desk, so we can loan it to the Clements for their museum." A few days later, she reported to Ingram on her search.

"I've got good news and bad news," the museum boss told him. "The good news is, I found the desk. The bad news is, Governor Dunn took it with him to HCA."

When Dunn left office in January 1975, he became an executive of Hospital Corp. of America. In other words, the desk from his capitol office was now in the private sector, sitting in Dunn's executive suite office on the fourth floor of HCA's corporate headquarters in Nashville.

"I asked Lamar if he would call Winfield and ask him if he would loan the desk to the Clements as long as Judge Robert and Ms. Maybelle were alive," Ingram remembers. "But he told Lamar, 'No, it's my desk.' So I said to Lamar, 'Well, can I call him?' He said, 'You can call him, but it's not going to do any good.'"

The call did not go well. "Winfield refused to let us have it, so I put the biggest guilt trip on him I could," Ingram told me. "I said to him, 'This poor couple down there in Dickson, they're old, they're dying, and they've got one last wish—to have their son's office replicated.' He finally said, 'All right. Have someone out here on Saturday morning at 10:00 o'clock and have me another desk in its place.' So I did. We've made up over it, but for a long time it was not pleasant."

I asked Dunn, in 2017, about his memory of this episode.

"That's still a sore spot with me," the former governor replied. "I was very resentful, because somebody in authority had told me to take the desk. Years passed, then the director of the museum, Lois Riggins, told me *she* had the desk and *she* was using it. I don't know how it got to Lois or how long it was kept at the Clement museum. According to Governor Haslam, the desk has been *his* desk since he became governor (in 2011). It never came back to me. It was an historic desk—at least two of the governors before me had used it, Governor Ellington as well as Governor Clement."

Records at the Tennessee State Museum indicate the Clement desk was delivered to Dickson in 1979 on an "indefinite loan" but was returned to the museum in 2003 during the Bredesen administration. (Andy Daniels, a Clement museum board member, told me the late governor's original desk proved to be too large for its allotted space at the Halbrook.) The same logs show the Clement desk was used by Riggins-Ezzell in her museum office until 2011 when it was placed in Governor Haslam's office at the capitol. It was there only about a year, until 2012, when Haslam purchased a new desk, and the old desk went back to storage. On its odyssey over fifty-nine years—over administrations of both parties—the Clement desk had "crossed the aisle" four times.

❖

IN THE SPRING OF 1981, Senator O'Brien invited Alexander to visit her parents, Judge Robert S. and Maybelle Clement, at the Dickson museum. During this visit, with his wife accompanying at an upright piano, Judge Clement sang the hymn "Beyond the Sunset."

> Should you go first and I remain to walk the road alone
> I'll live in memory's garden dear with happy days we've known.
> In spring I'll wait for roses red, when fades the lilac's bloom
> And in early fall when brown leaves fall, I'll catch a glimpse of you . . .

Alexander told me it was the elder Clements' musical performance on that day that helped him understand how they must have inspired the theatrical personalities of their children, Frank and Anna Belle, who had walked onto the public stage just as television was beginning to influence politics. But the cool medium of TV worked against the son. The heat of Governor Clement's famous oratory was at its highest pitch during his keynote address at the 1956 Democratic National Convention, when he delivered a twenty-one-point "indictment of the Republican Party." Clement shouted, "How long, America, Oh how long will he (Eisenhower) stare down the green fairways of indifference?" A correspondent for the *Chicago Tribune* wrote of Clement's speech: "It was only thirty-five minutes but it seemed like an hour and one half." The *Tennessean* reporter David Halberstam said Clement's "thundering, overheated, overlong, overkill" sermon ended his career as a national politician.

After their visit in Dickson, Alexander invited Judge Clement to lunch at the governor's residence to discuss capital punishment. At this time, Alexander was confronted with his first decision on whether to commute a death sentence, and even though he had supported capital punishment while campaigning he was finding the decision difficult. He wanted to hear from the judge how his own son had dealt with the reality of capital punishment. As a Vanderbilt University student, Alexander had admired Governor Clement; he had even voted for him in the 1962 Democratic primary when there were no serious Republican candidates for the office. He knew that Clement, after touring the state prison with evangelist Billy Graham, had eventually pardoned everyone on death row. Over a lunch of sandwiches, soup, and iced tea, Judge Clement shared with Alexander and Ingram that he thought having to deal with so many death sentences was what drove Governor Clement to drink and the reason he had died so early, at the age of forty-nine. The younger Clement, no longer in office, died in a car crash in 1969.

Judge Clement had brought a gift with him to this private lunch meeting. Before he departed for Dickson, he presented Alexander with a vintage walking stick from Franklin D. Roosevelt's 1936 inauguration. Alexander proudly displayed this souvenir of the New Deal in his capitol office, especially for Democratic legislators to see.

The words that Judge Clement had sung in 1981, to his wife's accompaniment, turned out not to be prophecy. He died before her, in October, just a few months after his visit with Alexander. The young governor attended the judge's funeral, at First Methodist Church in Dickson, and was seated in a front pew. When the Clement family entered the sanctuary, Alexander approached the widow to pay his respects.

"You know," Miss Maybelle said, in a whisper loud enough for the entire congregation to hear, "he really liked you, even if you are a Republican."

Laughter then broke the respectful silence among the hundreds of mourners, mostly Democrats of course, who were sitting shoulder-to-shoulder behind them.

IN THE IN-BETWEEN TIME, senior politicos would frequently cross the lines to socialize with their peers in the opposite party. These occasions often involved good food, fine wine, and open bars.

Amon's Duck Blind: In the early years, *Tennessean* publisher Amon Evans convened politicians and advertisers at his well-appointed hunting camp at Springville Bottoms, in West Tennessee. At first, his political guests were mostly Democrats, but both Baker and Alexander were among the earliest of the Republicans there, joining McWherter, Sasser, and others for the weekend of good food and fine wine.

Nashville Chef's Club: This monthly dinner group, which rotated between members' homes, was founded in 1947 when there were few Republicans anywhere in Middle Tennessee. Dunn, McWherter, and Sundquist all became regulars in the in-between time. Governor Bill Haslam is a current member at these club dinners, which continue on the second Tuesday of the month (no guests, membership limited to thirty-six).

August in Naples: Another bipartisan ritual has been an annual golfing trip held each August in Naples, Florida. It was first organized by Republicans: Tom Beasley, Robert Echols, John Stamps, Gary Sisco, and Charles Overby, with both Sundquist and Corker attending, along with Gordon Inman, Denny Bottorff, and Lew Conner. But over the years prominent Democrats joined in, including businessman Clayton McWhorter, the *Tennessean* editor John L. Seigenthaler, and the Washington lobbyist Jim Free.

Gentlemen's Christmas Breakfast: On the second Saturday of each December, Inman hosts an invitation-only VIP event at his Williamson

County home. This occurs on the day of the Symphony Ball in Nashville, theoretically while the women are making final preparations for the big event that evening. It began modestly, in 1999, with a quail breakfast at Clayton McWhorter's farm. Year by year, the crowd would grow—to 220 at the 2017 edition—and included notables from politics, business, and entertainment.

One December during the Democratic administration of Governor Phil Bredesen (2003–2011) the guest list included the incumbent and also the four living ex-governors of Tennessee: Dunn, Alexander, McWherter, and Sundquist. During the pre-brunch reception that morning, Alexander sat down at Inman's grand piano and played a Christmas carol. Inman then gathered the four ex-governors around him for a photograph. As they re-assembled for this second photo, Alexander said, "We ought to let the *real* governor sit in front!" He rose and stepped to the rear of the group, and Bredesen sat on the bench.

EVANS, THE NASHVILLE PUBLISHER, served for many years on the Board of Trustees of the University of Tennessee. This was a coveted appointment over the years for many friends of Tennessee governors, some would say the most sought-after appointment of all. At any given time, the twenty-one trustees considered together would constitute a complex political statement of allegiances, loyalties, and clout. The nine-year terms for trustees meant they would outlast most governors' four-year terms. In special cases a new governor of one party might reappoint a trustee who had been put on the board by a predecessor of the other party, but mostly these were prizes reserved for a governor's most ardent political friends whenever vacancies occurred.

Midway through McWherter's time as governor, a complaint was lodged with his office by his Knoxville nemesis, the Republican senator Victor Ashe. (McWherter once remarked of Ashe: "Victor is like a mosquito flying around your head—he won't hurt you, but he sure is worrisome.") Ashe's complaint was that McWherter had failed to name any Republicans to the UT board, and he stated that this was in violation of state law requiring at least some appointments to be made from "the party opposite the governor." McWherter and his staff studied this. The practical difficulty was that no sitting trustee would likely give up his or her seat in order to create a new vacancy. (The fiduciary responsibilities of university governance aside, there were the complimentary tickets to Tennessee's SEC football games to consider, after all.) Their solution was simple: ask one of the current Democratic members to switch parties.

There was not a more enthusiastic booster of the university than Bill Johnson, a banker in Sparta, Tennessee. Before graduating in 1958, Johnson had been co-captain and an All-America guard on Tennessee's 1957 football team. He and his wife Rena were also important donors to the school over many years. A moderate Democrat, Johnson was first appointed to the UT board, in 1975, by Governor Blanton. Nonetheless, McWherter's staff phoned Johnson, described the problem, and asked him if he would kindly write a letter at his earliest convenience.

Johnson obliged. In his letter, he stated that he had recently become a Republican. Problem solved.

ON RARE OCCASIONS OVER the years a senior leader of one political party would privately approach a significant politician of the other and try to persuade him to change his stripes. This type of recruitment was always a careful maneuver, and it usually failed.

One notable target—on two different occasions, actually—was State Senator Douglas Henry Jr., a fiscally conservative Democrat from Nashville. For many years Henry had held the influential post of chairman of the Senate's Finance, Ways and Means Committee, presiding over the budget decisions each spring. He was a close ally of Lieutenant Governor Wilder, to whom he owed his chairmanship (which was part of Wilder's hold on his own speakership), and no two senators had a closer bond than this pair of courtly Democrats of the Old South tradition.

Nonetheless, two Republican governors—first Dunn in the early 1970s and later Alexander in the middle 1980s—both invited Henry to join the Republican Party. If successful, this of course would help enhance their margins for success in the Democrat-controlled state Senate. Henry, ever the gentleman but of fixed politics, politely declined each time.

Chip Saltsman, who was chairman of the Tennessee Republican Party from 1999 to 2001, recalled meeting McWherter one day in the 1980s. Saltsman was working in his father's road construction business. (The father, Bruce Saltsman, was later Sundquist's commissioner of transportation. In 2018, the son managed the gubernatorial campaign of Republican Randy Boyd.) "I always told Ned I wanted to switch him—that he governed like a Republican." McWherter, of course, remained a faithful Democrat to the end of his life.

In 1991, when the Nashville surgeon Bill Frist was weighing whether to get into politics himself, he visited Senator Al Gore and asked his advice about public service. He remembers Gore suggesting he hoped Frist would consider running as a Democrat.

"Gore pointed out that there was a real opportunity in those days for thoughtful, intelligent, substantive people within the Democratic Party," Frist recalled in his 2009 memoir. "It was advantageous, he (Gore) felt, to be a Democrat in Tennessee, as demonstrated by the long, rich history of Democrats who had dominated Tennessee politics for generations." Four years later Frist ran for U.S. Senate as a Republican and defeated the incumbent Democrat, Sasser. Eight years later, in his second term, Frist became the Senate's Republican majority leader, the lofty partisan post that Baker had held in the earlier time.

In 1997, the chairman of the state Democratic Party, J. Houston Gordon of Covington, had a switch in mind when he approached Bob Corker at a charity golf tournament in West Tennessee. For several years through the 1990s, House Speaker Jimmy Naifeh and fellow Democrats Representative Randy ("Bear") Rinks and the state party treasurer Clark Jones staged an annual golf tournament benefitting St. Jude Children's Research Hospital in Memphis. (Naifeh, also of Covington, was a member of the St. Jude board of directors.) It was held at Pickwick Landing State Park, near Savannah.

The tournament was billed as the "Rural West Tennessee Democratic Caucus Shoot-Out" but leaders of both parties would join in for the good cause. Over the years the event raised more than $1.2 million for the St. Jude programs. Others regulars included House speaker *Pro Tem* Lois DeBerry; majority leader Bill Purcell, and fellow Democrats Craig Fitzhugh, Jerry Hargrove, Tommy Head, Paul Phelan, Don Ridgeway, and John White, and Republicans Ralph Cole, Joe Kent, Steve McDaniel, Charles Sargent, Keith Westmoreland, and Zane Whitson. Other state officials attended, including the state comptroller John Morgan, Secretary of State Riley Darnell, State Treasurer Steve Adams, his successor Dale Sims, the state labor commissioner Jim Neeley, his deputy Dart Gore, and others. Nashvillian Mike Kelly, owner of the popular Jimmy Kelly's restaurant, would donate his staff's time to cook and serve hamburgers for lunch.

The 1997 Shoot-Out occurred soon after Corker had left Sundquist's cabinet, where he was the governor's top finance officer. By this time, Corker had a reputation for working well with legislators of both parties and was seldom viewed as a partisan Republican. He joined in the tournament, adding to the bipartisan support for St. Jude. This was also the year after the Democrat Gordon had lost his U.S. Senate race to Republican Fred Thompson. Gordon, not a golfer, also went to Pickwick that year because he had an audacious proposition for Corker: consider switching parties, run for governor as a Democrat in the 1998 election, and oppose Sundquist's re-election to a second term.

Corker would have none of it.

"I knew it was an outrageous idea," Gordon told me. "But I respected

Corker. I don't even play golf—the only reason I stayed at the golf tournament was to talk with him. Of course, he turned me down."

It was not the first time a ranking Democrat had attempted this with Corker. Naifeh told me that he and other Democratic legislators had similar conversations with Corker in Nashville during this same period, usually over end-of-day "refreshments" in the speaker's office. Both Democrats and Republicans would gather there after the close of legislative business in the afternoons, with Corker often joining in.

"We thought the world of Bob—we all did, Democrats and Republicans," Naifeh remembers. "The House Democratic Caucus tried to get him to run for governor as a Democrat. We talked about it quite often—John Bragg and myself, Randy Rinks, Matt Kisber, Kim McMillan. We were hopeful he would run in the next election. It never happened, obviously."

At this point Naifeh and partisans on his side of the aisle were already desperate to identify their own standard-bearer in the next governor's race against the GOP incumbent. Corker, a faithful Republican, declined them each time, probably more amused than intrigued by political overtures from Democrats. Instead, Corker resumed his business career in Chattanooga, so in 1998 Sundquist won his second term.

Three years later Corker became mayor of Chattanooga, his hometown. Five years after that, running as the Republican Party's nominee, he won his first term in the U.S. Senate.

❖

CHAPTER 8

Jobs for Memphis

"In 1979, the Memphis Jobs Conference was the moon mission of
its day."
    —Ted Evanoff, *Commercial Appeal*, 2013

ALEXANDER'S FIRST EXECUTIVE ORDER was aimed at Memphis. It was
Tennessee's westernmost city and a place of deep contrasts.

In 1979, the Mississippi River town founded in 1819 by the land specula-
tors Andrew Jackson, John Overton, and James Winchester had become the
most populous city in Tennessee. It was also its most racially divided urban
center. Both the poverty level and the racial division were persistent through
the post-bellum decades and had many origins—the legacy of servitude
across the South, where cotton was forever king; migration from plantation
to city jobs; a non-diversified regional economy; the ravages of yellow fever
in the river city in 1873 and again five years later, with even more migration
away to escape the disease; failed schools, machine politics, and scant visions
of hope for successive generations of a threadbare underclass.

This was the socio-economic predicament of Memphis when, in early
1979, the unprecedented coup in Nashville abruptly changed the state government administration. The so-called Bluff City beside the broad Mississippi was also still reeling from the unrest that followed the 1968 murder of
Dr. Martin Luther King Jr., the calamity that brought a woeful new focus on
Memphis from news media around the world.

Like most municipalities in Tennessee, Memphis had both a city government and a county government. The chief executive of both governments
was called *mayor*—meaning that in Shelby County there were (and still are)
two mayors with duties and authorities that were technically separate but
sometimes politically indistinct and often competitive. It was the size of this
city-county locale—a county population of 777,113, according to the 1980
census—that made the job of governing and the solving of complex urban
challenges special in this blended jurisdiction.

The politics of Memphis, especially in the decades of the 1920s and 1940s, was dominated by Edward Hull Crump, once the city's mayor, whom the newspapers called "Boss." Crump was also called the "Red Snapper," a reference to the red hair of his youth and to his speaking style. In a 2010 article, the *Commercial Appeal* described his influence this way: "Crump served only one term as mayor, from 1910–1915, but the charismatic and powerful businessman/deal-maker/politico continued to run the city through the 1950s from his sixth-floor office in the Crump Insurance Building."

Crump also operated from the parlor of the Tennessee Club at 130 North Court Avenue. The building is now home to the law offices of Burch, Porter and Johnson. One of its current partners is Mike Cody, the former state attorney general. In a 2017 visit, Cody showed me the spacious first-floor room where Crump would meet with his state government operatives. The Boss would sit there and review the bills that were being considered in Nashville, brought to him by his agents monitoring the legislature, always with an eye to what was in the best interests of Memphis and Crump's own political agenda. Then he would dispatch them back to the State Capitol with detailed instructions: which bills should be stopped, what amendments should be attached to others, and what else ought to be accomplished inside the legislative meeting rooms two hundred miles to the east.

In Memphis, the races did not mix and power was seldom shared. In Crump's heyday (he died in 1954, at age eighty) significant decisions were made by white men in private rooms, away from public view. This endured over many decades, but by the late 1960s the currents of change were working to displace that mode of municipal decision making. All was trending now toward greater citizen participation and public involvement, especially in regard to city government decisions. This dynamic manifested itself in the rise of black politicians in the 1950s and 1960s, serving alongside their more traditional white counterparts. In 1979, after Alexander signed his first executive order, establishing a "Governor's Economic and Jobs Conference," the gathering notion of public participation in local planning and goal-setting took on a new dimension.

SOME SAY MEMPHIS NEVER recovered from the King assassination. It was here, in February 1968, that the deaths of two city sanitation workers became the flashpoint of a public employee strike over unsafe working conditions and unequal pay. Dr. King visited the strikers on March 18 and returned to the city on April 3 and made his "I Have Been to the Mountaintop" speech. Twenty-four hours later he was dead—shot by a sniper as he stood on a second-floor balcony of the Lorraine Motel.

Among those who demonstrated on behalf of the strikers—wearing T-shirts with the words *I Am A Man* printed boldly—was twenty-seven-year-old Willie W. Herenton. Eleven years later Herenton would become the city's first black school superintendent, and in 1991 the first African American mayor of Memphis.

One of the city's most eminent black leaders at this time was the lawyer and preacher Benjamin L. Hooks. He pastored churches in both Memphis and Chicago and, together with his wife Frances, had been at the forefront of the civil rights movement as it unfolded in Memphis. Hooks was also Tennessee's first black criminal court judge and, in 1977, became the national chairman of the NAACP.

Alexander met this charismatic couple during Baker's successful 1966 Senate race, and they supported Baker again in his 1972 re-election campaign. Two years later, when Alexander first ran for governor in 1974, he became friends with a number of the young black leaders of Memphis, including the Reverend and Mrs. Hooks, Herenton, and the lawyer George H. Brown Jr. Several of these had already become disappointed with Blanton for an ill-advised comment he made about black preachers while campaigning in Memphis that year. Significantly, Mrs. Hooks publicly endorsed Alexander over Blanton. Though Blanton won the general election that November, Alexander carried Shelby County.

When the young Republican ran again and won in 1978, he tried to recruit Judge Hooks to join his new cabinet. He remembers the judge's reply:

ALEXANDER: "I hope you will consider serving on the governor's cabinet."
HOOKS: "Thank you very much, but I don't want to be in the governor's cabinet. I want to be the Governor."

It is plausible that Hooks might have won a race for governor, running as a Republican during this politically turbulent period in Tennessee. A year later, in 1979, George Brown, by this time a Memphis judge, was the GOP's nominee for a vacant seat on the Tennessee Supreme Court; Brown carried both East Tennessee and West Tennessee with a strong turnout in Memphis, but he lost badly in the still-Democratic middle region, losing the statewide race to Judge Frank F. Drowota III. In 2006, Congressman Harold Ford Jr. of Memphis ran a strong race against Corker for U.S. Senate. Hooks died in 2010.

TEN YEARS AFTER THE King assassination, the need for recovery in Memphis and the dreams of civic revival were still much on the minds of the two sitting mayors then in office—the city mayor Wyeth Chandler, and the county mayor William N. (Bill) Morris—and of the city's top-most corporate leaders. At this point, the most prominent leaders of the Memphis business community were the heads of four marquis Memphis-based corporations. These were the particular executives whom the city's newspapers liked to call "the Big Four."

- Frederick W. Smith, the founder and chairman of Federal Express.
- Michael D. Rose, chairman of Holiday Inns Inc. and successor to its founder Kemmons Wilson.
- J. R. (Pitt) Hyde III, founder and chairman of AutoZone.
- Ron Terry, chairman and CEO of First Tennessee Bank, the oldest and largest bank headquartered in the state.

Later on, the cotton merchant Billy Dunavant was also regarded as a member of this elite group of power brokers and philanthropists who made things happen. Sam Cooper, another prominent businessman, who was Alexander's finance chairman in Shelby County, was the first to recommend very early in 1979 that the new governor establish a jobs focus in Memphis. (In 1974, it was S. L. Kopald Jr., the chairman of the Shelby County Republican organization at the time, who introduced Alexander to Cooper, who was an important donor and fundraiser for St. Jude Children's Hospital. Alexander remembers Cooper would often ask him, "Lamar, what are you going to do for Memphis?")

In the early planning for the jobs initiative, it was also Cooper who suggested its name, saying it should be called "the Jobs Conference," according to Bill Gibbons, who became Alexander's lead staffer for the project. Cooper soon became a member of the local steering committee that was co-chaired by attorney George H. Brown Jr., and Tiff Bingham, who was the staff director of the Memphis Chamber of Commerce.

By December 1979, the "Governor's Economic and Jobs Conference" had identified two economic development strategies worthy of a new focus: distribution services and tourism promotion. The central location of Memphis relative to the continental United States was unparalleled, given its connecting web of interstate highways, river transportation, and airport service, and the famous success of Federal Express only underscored this fact. Tourism was also regarded as promising, especially considering the city's music history—the blues, Beale Street, and the legacy of Elvis Presley and his home base at Graceland. Another conference recommendation was a program called "Jobs for High School Graduates," modeled on a Delaware initiative of Governor Pete DuPont.

This might have been the end of the story. At the end of 1979, there was no certainty that the Jobs Conference idea would—or even should—continue beyond that point. Then, in December, came an unplanned conversation at a Memphis restaurant.

RON TERRY WAS A larger-than-life figure not only within his banking organization but also across the upper echelons of the broader Memphis business community. From the windows of his office suite on the 23rd floor of the First Tennessee building, he could scan most of the downtown skyline, a good portion of the broad Mississippi River, and the smooth curves of the Hernando DeSoto Bridge just a few city blocks to the north. Beyond that, the flat expanse of eastern Arkansas spread westward.

From his desk phone, Terry would also maintain his network of local civic connections of the highest order, notably his alliances as one of the Big Four, the most durable Memphis business power base over time, and with the mayors of the city and of the county who would come and go in their turn.

Terry was also close to Donelson, whose law firm Baker and Donelson represented First Tennessee Bank, and he was well known to Gibbons, who had lived in Memphis since he was fifteen. Gibbons, while an undergraduate at Vanderbilt in Nashville, had been research director for Alexander's 1974 run for governor and was a key Memphis organizer in the 1978 campaign. He was now a young policy assistant in the new governor's office. His wife, the attorney Julia Gibbons, had likewise worked in both of Alexander's campaigns and was also now on the governor's policy staff. (She later became the first woman and youngest person to be a judge of a Tennessee trial court of record, by Alexander's appointment. President Reagan nominated her to the federal bench in 1983, and President George W. Bush named her to the federal appeals court for the Sixth Circuit in 2002.)

Both Donelson and Gibbons knew well the leadership matrix in their complicated city—and who fit into it and how. In separate interviews, both Terry and Gibbons recalled for me a chance meeting with Alexander one evening at Justine's in December 1979, after the main body of work for the initial Jobs Conference had concluded. The governor was in town, in part, to help light the city's Christmas tree in Court Square downtown. For Alexander, Justine's was a favorite stop for dinner whenever he was in the city and had the time. The restaurant had a dedicated clientele, especially among the city's business elite, offering New Orleans–style French cuisine in well-appointed dining rooms, all in a pink Italianate stucco house built in 1843.

"That night," Terry told me, "Lewie and I and our wives were having dinner at Justine's, and we didn't expect him but Lamar came walking in with an associate to have dinner before he headed back to Nashville. Lewie and I had been talking about the governor's Jobs Conference and how he thought that it could be the beginning of something. But right now it looked like it was the end of the Jobs Conference. Lewie and I decided to go over and sit down and talk and visit for a while, and it was during that dinner meeting that I told him that if he would continue his support of a future Jobs Conference that we may call the 'Memphis Jobs Conference,' I would agree to organize it and try to make it a success. He did commit to that. He assigned Bill Gibbons to be his contact with us for the remaining two years of the Jobs Conference."

This would establish both a beginning base of influential local leadership, with the possibility of new private financial support, and also a level credibility to advance the initiative into a second year and beyond.

WITHIN DAYS OF THAT evening at Justine's, Terry asked Carol Coletta, who directed First Tennessee Bank's communications and marketing staff, to be his own point person for the accelerated jobs program. ("There wouldn't have been a Memphis Jobs Conference if it hadn't been for Carol," he told me. "She likes to organize and make things work.") Coletta suggested involving the Aspen Institute to support planning and the design of public participation, and the process soon reached out to many other city leaders, including clergy, to broaden the participation in the wider community.

"We worked on the two strategies—tourism and distribution—and so we had task forces working on those two things, and ultimately we also had the money. There were some major projects as part of the economic development strategy that were funded out of the Job Conference. We said, 'Let's broaden the process.' It was a very open, transparent process where people presented their ideas over a period of time. We ended up actually with public voting taking place through the Jobs Conference, to decide on what projects should be funded. I think in a lot of ways, it set the economic strategy, for better or for worse, for some period of time in Memphis because it rallied so much energy and money around those things.

"I thought we should take it as an opportunity to bring people into the conversation who had, so to speak, not been there before," she explained. This was a significant move in a city that continued to be racially divided, with few instances of substantive interactions across that division unless a local election was at hand.

"We were able to get Ron and Fred (Smith) and Pitt (Hyde) and Billy Dunavant and Mike Rose to each sponsor a public session where we brought in outside speakers. I think what was really critical about that was the fact that we went to existing groups all over town and invited people to appoint a li-aison or representative from their group to come to these sessions. It became not just people in the room but the communication links that they all repre-sented to a much broader constituency. Today, you do that with social me-dia, but back in the day we didn't have that option. It really made it, I think, much more powerful to spread ideas in that way.

"The Aspen Institute, to some people, sounded like sort of a liberal plot to influence the outcomes in Memphis, but Lewie Donelson always had this great line—he said, 'There's no Republican or Democrat who was ready to pick up the garbage.' His point was that when you get to a city level, a lot of politics falls away."

Gibbons remembers the Jobs Conference leadership taking deliberate steps to ensure the community meetings would be inclusive of the city's complicated racial composition. Racial divisions have been persistent in Memphis, but the organizers were determined to reach across racial lines in their invitations to both religious and community groups to participate. George Brown, the African American attorney and school board member, and Larry Shaw of the African American consulting firm The Shaw Group were retained to support outreach and messaging, respectively. Brown was designated as a co-coordinator with Gibbons for the conference planning work, and Shaw's office prepared most of the printed materials. Other Af-rican American business, political, educational, and faith leaders were also actively involved in the various committees.

Terry recalls that public participation was key to conveying community consensus for what became the city's principal requests of state government. The conference process marked an important shift from the city's uneven tra-dition of civic discussions that seldom crossed racial boundaries.

"We identified every civic, political, racial organization that had an orga-nization, and we specifically went to their leaders and asked them to come and be part of the Jobs Conference. The meetings were held in the largest conference room at the Peabody Hotel and I imagine at least two-thirds of the people who were seated in that room was a result of the invitations be-cause they were the leadership of some kind of group."

He also credits support of the city's morning newspaper and its editor-in-chief Lionel Linder for committing to give the project regular coverage and editorial support. "I visited with Lionel and told him what we were planning to do over the two years with the Memphis Jobs Conference," he recalled. "He not only gave it a superb editorial support, but he assigned a reporter, Deborah Clubb, who reported on everything the Jobs Conference did. I would say that 95 percent of what she wrote was positive—the other 5 percent were times when she felt she couldn't be quite as positive—but her support was tremendous."

One day, during the planning period, Coletta told her boss that the deacons of Bellevue Baptist Church, a white congregation, had discussed her invitation to participate but replied that they thought it was not an appropriate involvement for them. Terry had been a member of that church.

"I called out there because I had grown up in Bellevue Baptist Church downtown and asked if I could have breakfast or lunch with a half dozen of those deacons," he said. "I explained to them what we were trying to do and told them at the first meeting of the Jobs Conference, I was going to make sure there was at least a half-dozen seats on the front row for them to come and participate. Sure enough, first meeting, I looked down and there were the deacons from Bellevue Baptist, and they became much more friendly to the Jobs Conference after that."

The early steering from Terry's office was an important ingredient in moving the Jobs Conference initiative from its first year to what came next in this broader, participatory concept.

"Frankly, because Ron was willing to put the resources of First Tennessee behind the kind of staff work we needed (at one point, there were five staff members from her public affairs office involved), and we always operated it internally from First Tennessee with a lot of identification of volunteer chairs of committees, and so forth, and kept them running together."

Donelson presided at the final public meeting where the final set of four major city goals were established. These ranged from a new "agri-center" to public funding for a new convention hotel. The latter was a notion that the conservative Donelson personally opposed, on principle, as an inappropriate investment. He did not object publicly, however, and in fact back in Nashville he facilitated its inclusion in the state's funding package for Memphis from his position as the powerful commissioner of the state Department of Finance and Administration.

Terry remembers the county mayor, Bill Morris, "got very excited about it and saw it as an opportunity to learn a lot about what he should do. He not only participated, but he used the goals that were set by the Jobs Conference, basically, as his goals for the county government." The city mayor, Chandler, was less visible in the public process, but Terry recalled that several city hall officials in Chandler's administration "became very active in follow-up to the Jobs Conference."

THE STRUGGLE FOR ECONOMIC renewal has continued in Memphis, especially in the downtown area. Mayor Wharton told me in October 2014: "All the commerce fled downtown. We have one of the largest downtown populations in America, and we don't have a grocery store. It's hard to bring commerce back. I am working every day to get more folks to move downtown. But to shop, it is quicker to go to Arkansas."

But there had also been significant accomplishments by this time, much of it owing to the civic organization engendered by the Jobs Conference. By the end of Alexander's time as governor, he and the city leaders of Memphis, as well as the state legislature, could point to success with the goals first recommended by the Memphis Jobs Conference. The restorations of Beale Street and the Orpheum Theatre were underway. Funding for the new Agriculture Center was secured. The new convention center hotel had opened in 1985, and even Elvis's Graceland was opened to tourists in 1982. By 1986 the northern loop of Interstate 40 was opened, with the long-running Overton Park expressway issue finally resolved.

When the Jobs Conference was unfolding, R. Brad Martin was the youngest Republican in the Shelby County legislative delegation. An Ohio native, he moved with his family to Memphis and enrolled at Whitehaven High School in the tenth grade. At the University of Memphis, he became president of the student government association when he was a junior, and gravitated to Republican politics, admiring Senator Baker and Governor Dunn ("That's when I decided who I wanted to be like," Martin told me) as well as Donelson and the city council member Gwen Awsumb.

Martin credits Ron Terry with "organizing the business leadership to connect with the Alexander administration." He remembers the Jobs Conference, with its focus on civic revival and citizen participation, as a seminal exercise for Memphis. The new capital projects were important, he told me, "but the real significance was it brought together a broad base of county leadership. It got us back on track. It was very important for Memphis—there was no question. In terms of other things that were happening—FedEx was beginning, a very new enterprise at that time in Memphis. It was expanding, and needing to expand. I worked with the administration and we helped relocate some of the National Guard facilities to permit FedEx to expand its facilities early on. So, if you think about business things that had some impact during that era that were lasting, obviously the encouraging and nurturing of FedEx was important."

The Washington columnist Neal Peirce, in his long-running series on innovations in U.S. cities, wrote in 1987, "Memphis has staged a stunning comeback in the '80s."

"Memphis hit the comeback trail when—and only when—it moved to heal its racial divisions, when business moved to strategic economic planning with strong citizen participation, and when a strong business-government partnership was formed. The critical event here was the Memphis Jobs Conference, conceived and initiated in 1979 by Republican governor Lamar Alexander. Attending one of the conference's concluding sessions in 1981, I was astounded to see one of the most 'salt and pepper'—totally integrated—meetings I've witnessed anywhere in America."

In 2013, Ted Evanoff, a veteran reporter for the *Commercial Appeal*, looked back on the conference of three decades earlier as a seminal event that lead to important goals for Memphis and a generational cadre of civic leaders. "In 1979, the Memphis Jobs Conference was the moon mission of its day. Out of the conference came the idea of promoting Memphis as a logistics center. Back then no one realized a fledgling FedEx would eventually employ more than 240,000 people worldwide."

SMITH, THE LEGENDARY FEDEX chairman, credited Alexander with facilitating his company's acquisition of a Tennessee National Guard property that made possible an important expansion of his strategic Memphis hub. Smith also remembers the Jobs Conference as "a formal process with a lot of participation."

"Essentially, it was an attempt—really dreamed up by Lamar, as I recall—to recognize that Memphis was the first of the big cities in the state and what could we do to maximize our advantages and continue to reduce poverty and increase employment," Smith told me. "The governor's personal presence was just hugely important in galvanizing everybody, and at the end of the day we came out with an effort that was quite successful for the area as a whole .... It was an attempt on his part, you know, to focus his efforts on the city that needed it the most—and which politically was least supportive of him—which I think is the measure of the man."

CHAPTER 9

The Phone Call That Changed Everything

"I will never see my grandchildren."
       —Lillian Knight

HOW THE AUTOMAKER NISSAN came to be in Middle Tennessee—and how the state went from having almost no auto jobs to being the top state in automotive manufacturing—is a tale with two beginning points.

One, of course, was in Nissan's own decision-making suites in Tokyo. The other, three years before that, was in a less likely place—a modest home on a Tennessee cattle farm, on Highway 96 near the university town of Murfreesboro.

ON SOME DAYS IT could be a lonely trek, as the candidate walked across the long state from winter to mid-summer in 1978. This particular Thursday in late May had been such a day. Lamar Alexander was still only two-thirds of the way through his journey, walking 1,022 miles on the shoulders of the roads between the mountains and the Mississippi, when he approached the farmhouse in tiny Milton, Tennessee.

It had now been four months since that frozen January morning, in faraway Maryville in the east, when he had stood on the front porch of his own boyhood home at 121 Ruth Street and declared he was running for governor. He then stepped off his parents' porch, launching his unusual campaign: a super-marathon "walk across Tennessee," concluding in Memphis in steamy July.

On May 25, when he arrived walking in late afternoon at the Middle Tennessee home of Billy and Lillian Knight, Alexander was roughly on schedule and the Knights were expecting him. At each of his seventy-three overnight stops, he stayed with a different Tennessee family. The hosts were preselected through communications between the Alexander headquarters staff and local political friends in the given county. The Knights were the candidate's overnight stop Number 54.

The Knights had three sons. The two younger boys—the twins Randy and Ricky—were students at Oakland High School. There was a big game at school that night, and by the time they returned home, Alexander had turned in. They would not meet him until the next morning, over breakfast.

"My mother loved to cook, so they'd had a big country-style supper," Randy told me, years later. "Ricky and I got up the next morning and ate breakfast with Mr. Alexander. We probably had a thirty-minute conversation with him that was mostly about baseball, and we went on our way."

Later that day, Lillian told the boys about the conversation that she and her husband had had with Alexander, sitting in their living room, on the night before. It had been a casual conversation but, according to Randy, this is what she told her sons:

"I asked Mr. Alexander that, if he were elected governor, I wished he would do everything he could do to bring jobs to the state, and in particular to Middle Tennessee, because I really do want you boys to stay at home."

The older son Ronnie was already in the workplace by this time. He held a management position at a Murfreesboro savings and loan. But Ricky and Randy were still in high school, with plans to enroll at Middle Tennessee State University.

"My mother's plea to him was to do everything that he could to bring jobs to the state, and in particular to Middle Tennessee, because she wanted us to stay at home," Randy told me. "She said she wanted to see how we turned out. She wanted to see our families grow. And she wanted to keep her boys close to her. Back then, in the late '70s, before Nissan came along, jobs were not plentiful at all. Jobs were very, very difficult to come by in Rutherford County. And so the possibility to have to move away from home, away from Milton or Murfreesboro, was a very real possibility because there just weren't any jobs. And even if you fast forward, as I was becoming a senior at MTSU and starting to mail out resumes and applications and all of that, I wasn't getting very much response.

"I was going to have to move," he said, "so my mother's fear was looking like it would come true—until Nissan called."

Alexander remembers the conversation that evening the same way. "Lillian Knight told me, 'I'm sad. My boys are talented. They'll never find a good job around here. I'm sad because I will never see my grandchildren.'"

RAY TARKINGTON DID NOT understand why he was sitting in Eddie Jones' office at the Nashville Area Chamber of Commerce.

At his own desk that morning, across the street, Tarkington had picked up a phone message left by Fred Harris, the chamber's vice president for economic development. When he returned the call, Harris was out but his assistant had instructions to transfer Tarkington directly to Jones, the chamber's top staff executive and Harris's boss. This was early March, 1980.

Tarkington was a longtime member of the chamber but had not been especially active in its programs. He had served on the economic development committee, knew Jones in passing, and had met Harris after he moved to the chamber staff from the Tennessee Department of Economic and Community Development. He could not guess why they were calling; this phone call he was returning from Harris was unusual. He held on the line until Jones answered.

"Now, Ray, Fred and I are working on something, and we'd like to talk to you about it a little bit," said Jones, a newspaper reporter in his early career who by this time had been staff director of Nashville's chamber for a dozen years. "So if you get the time I'd like for you to come across the street and talk."

It was a short walk over, just across Fourth Avenue. When he arrived, the chamber boss quickly greeted him and closed the door of his private office. Harris was sitting there.

"We're working on a little project, trying to get a business factory to come to Middle Tennessee," Jones said. "We've got a possibility on a piece of property there, but we need some information about another piece of property right in the front of it, and your name came up as somebody that might check that out for us. What we're doing is Top Secret and we don't want anybody to know about it."

Far from being unusual, this type of secrecy was a standard element in Tarkington's toolkit. Manufacturers and other relocating businesses customarily kept their projects under wraps for multiple reasons, so Tarkington found nothing unusual about this request.

"You don't want to go around and start creating a lot of conversation, and then people wonder what's going on there and either blocking it or getting in there and somehow stopping it. Anytime you're talking about something commercial, we know sometimes people get riled up and file suit against you and stop it. And the price might go up, too."

The Smyrna "site" was in multiple parcels, with different owners, which would have to be assembled. In addition to this obstacle, Tarkington himself was busy—and he also worried about the effects of introducing a new manufacturing facility to this rural location.

"I wasn't sure this was something I wanted to get involved with," Tarkington told me. "I had just become president of the Nashville Board of Realtors. We were in the worst economic period of time that we've been in, in so many years; the interest rate is at 12 percent now, and rising. I'm committed with that. My secretary has just left and I had to hire a new one. The only man that was working with me left, and I'm by myself, and I don't know that I can do it. And I was trying to be president of the Nashville Board of Realtors, three thousand members at that time, trying to head that up—I was constantly getting calls from newspaper, television, everybody about how bad the economy was, and how people were sinking—and trying to do my own business."

Tarkington had been familiar with Smyrna since childhood. He now thought of his own friends and neighbors in Rutherford County and wondered what their reaction might be. In 1946, soon after World War II ended, his uncle Pat Patterson and aunt Lola Patterson bought a small grocery in Smyrna near Sewart Air Force Base. (The base was closed in 1970.) After the war, many military families planning retirement decided to remain in Smyrna. The Pattersons' store thrived, and they later opened a gas station.

"I knew what factories were doing up north," Tarkington said. "Eventually Fred told me it might be a car company, but you don't build trucks and cars down in the South. You raise cotton down here . . . . At that time, you looked at all the factories, and all the strikes and things like that, and I didn't see anything positive. I saw the negative of the factory."

He prayed for guidance. Then he went back to see Fred Harris. One practical problem was the number of individual owners in the targeted tract. Another was that he had no money to compensate property owners who might agree to give options on their property.

"Fred, you want me to take an option on a piece of property. You don't have any option money. There are four or five pieces of property here. In addition to the racetrack, they have flea markets on it. In addition to that, there was a hotel, and a restaurant, and right behind that is a campground and we're going into summer. How in the world can you do this? It's impossible to do."

"Well, let's give it a try," Harris replied, still not naming the ultimate client for this secretive research. "It's the best shot we've got."

THE WORD *NISSAN* HAD not yet been spoken in this initial real estate discussion. It was not until their second meeting, in early April, that either Jones or Harris mentioned to Tarkington who the client was. About ten days after the first visit, Tarkington was invited back to discuss his findings. Once again, Jones closed his office door and spoke in a hushed tone.

"We're working with this company Datsun," Jones said. That was the business name Nissan used at the time for its U.S. sales operation. "They want to put a factory in here and change the name of it. They are looking at us—we are one of the sites they're considering. We don't have it tied up or anything, but we got a promise verbally."

Tarkington unfolded site maps of the proposed rural Smyrna location. Leafing through this paperwork, Jones now provided more detail on the company's specifications. They were tightly drawn and included strict requirements for both highway and rail access.

"If we do something there, and it doesn't face Highway 41, it won't work," Jones cautioned. "There are all these strange pieces of property on Highway 41. If they're going to be interested at all, they've got to have that frontage—they can't be over behind something. They want some identification there, and so what we're gonna need is to see if we could work those out. We would need to see about tying that up. We would like for you to help us on that."

Datsun was the name of Nissan's modest-selling compact sedan. The automaker had introduced it to the U.S. market in California. In our interview years after his early discussions with Jones and Harris, Tarkington told me he knew the company made small pickup trucks but didn't know they made cars.

It also later became clear to Tarkington why he had been invited into the project. It was his previous experience with the Louisville and Nashville (L&N) Railway company, which operated an important Nashville-to-Chattanooga rail line through Smyrna.

"One of the things that I think attracted Nissan to this project was the fact that it was located close to Nashville," Tarkington said. "It was close to the interstates. And it had a railroad track close by. Once the deal was done, the L&N Railroad made an agreement with Nissan, and they said, 'We will put a spur line coming off the main line.'"

Unless L&N cooperated, Nissan would not be able to have access to the rail link essential to receiving many materials and for shipping new vehicles to market from the end of the production line.

"They knew a lot of things," he added, referring to his Chamber of Commerce contacts and the officials they in turn were answering to at the state's Economic Development Department. "I didn't know anything. I knew nothing about what was really going on. I'm walking on stage, but the play is going on behind me."

BY THIS TIME JAPAN had become an economic development prospect of great interest to Tennessee economic development leaders, as well as to almost every other state in the Midwest and Southeast. Governor Ray Blanton and his economic and community development commissioner, Tom Benson, had made recruiting trips to Tokyo encouraging Japanese government and business leaders to consider Tennessee for agricultural imports and business investments.

The Southeast U.S./Japan Association had been established in 1976 with members from both public and private sectors across an eight-state region—Alabama, Florida, Georgia, Mississippi, North and South Carolina, Tennessee, and Virginia—and the governors would rotate the host duties. Japanese government and business leaders had a counterpart organization on their shore. The new president, Jimmy Carter, who had been governor of Georgia, had spoken at a meeting of southern governors and urged them to "look to Japan" for business opportunities for their states.

As late as 1975, Sumitomo Chemical in Mt. Pleasant, south of Nashville, had been the only Japanese plant in Tennessee, and fewer than 1,500 Japanese lived among the state's population of four million. The heightened focus on Japan began to produce results for Tennessee during Blanton's term. Sumitomo Chemical and Monsanto established a joint venture in Mt. Pleasant. Toshiba placed a manufacturing operation in Lebanon in Wilson County. Nissan chose Memphis for a plant producing forklifts.

In November 1978, only days after Alexander's election, he attended a ceremony in Memphis announcing Sharp Corporation's decision to locate its largest U.S. plant there. Alexander remembers that Japan was not prominently on his mind until after that Memphis event.

"I can guarantee you," he said later, "that not one Tennessean said to me while I was walking for six months across the state, 'When you get elected, I sure hope you'll go to Japan and attract some jobs.'"

Then, only three weeks after being sworn in, Alexander and his wife, Honey, attended the annual White House state dinner that the president hosts for the nation's fifty governors and their spouses. This was in early February 1979.

Alexander recalled later, "President Carter said to us, 'Governors, go to Japan. Persuade them to make in the United States what they sell in the United States.' I took what he said to heart. First, he was our president and I felt I should pay attention to what he said. Second, I had just said in my inaugural address that raising family incomes would be my first goal. Tennessee was then among the bottom five states in average incomes, at 81 percent of the national average income. And, at that time, I believed the best way to raise incomes was to recruit good jobs from other places. Plus the American economy was terrible. American companies weren't expanding. Third, while I had never thought about it before, Japan looked promising. It was the world's second-biggest economy, selling everything from TV sets to cars in the U.S., almost all of which they made in Japan. The U.S. government was putting great pressure on Japan to start making in the U.S. what they sold here. So I thought that we might attract some of the first Japanese manufacturing plants. I knew each major manufacturer would only build one or maybe two in the U.S. Finally, after a while I realized I am only one governor and the world is big, so I am likely to get a better result if I focus most of my attention on a single objective—and that objective became Japan."

WHEN HE RETURNED TO Tennessee, Alexander phoned Dean Rusk, President Kennedy's secretary of state who had retired to Georgia. In March, Rusk was his guest for lunch at the governor's residence in Nashville. Rusk shared valuable insights into the business behavior and protocols of Japanese industrial leaders.

"I knew nothing about Japan and had no idea how to go about this," Alexander told me, "so I thought I would ask an expert." He was amused that Rusk spent a good part of the lunch instructing Alexander on official protocol, including how a governor in his home state outranks anyone else except for the president of the United States, and that outside of his home state he outranks almost no one."

One exception to that rule, Alexander discovered, is Japan—where an American governor does command an unusual amount of respect. "Japan is very hierarchical with respect to age and status. I learned quickly that the top man in Japan—and it was always a man—wanted to deal with the top man, and the Japanese assumed that a governor was literally in charge of his state."

A few months later, in November 1979, during Alexander's first visit to Tokyo, the governor had a dinner with two top executives of Nissan: the chairman, Katsuji Kawamata, and the global president, Takashi Ishihara. They discussed how Nissan was looking to locate a manufacturing facility in the United States but had not decided on the location. Joining them at the table was Jim Cotham, the chief of Tennessee's Department of Economic and Community Development, and Mitsuya Goto, a U.S.-educated Nissan executive who served as point man for the company's contacts with American states.

Kawamata, then seventy-five years old, was curious about the young governor's age. With Goto translating, this conversation ensued:

CHAIRMAN KAWAMATA: (*to Alexander*) "May I ask, how old are you?"
ALEXANDER: "I am thirty-nine years old."
KAWAMATA: (*begins laughing*)

ALEXANDER: "Why are you laughing?"

KAWAMATA: "Because I am twice as old as you are, and I am thinking about locating the largest Japanese capital investment ever made outside our country in your state."

FOR THE NEXT SIX months the Nissan project became the most sought-after industrial recruitment prize in the United States.

A regime of secrecy pervaded all aspects of Nissan's internal decisions, as well as its site selection process in the field. Company executives were dealing confidentially with a very select group of officials in at least three southern states. In Tennessee, the company's planning for this major manufacturing plant went by a code name: Project C-30. Tennessee ECD Department officials were monitoring this closely, and Alexander made clear to Commissioner Cotham, who headed the ECD Department, that the governor personally and his staff were available at any time to assist and support the recruitment effort to make Tennessee the winner.

The quiet work to assemble the site went slowly, maybe too slowly.

With Tarkington's help, Harris had identified a number of parcels and their owners quickly enough. But Nissan officials were conducting their own meticulous search. Ishihara himself, the company president, once drove to Dickson County west of Nashville to determine the depth of the subsurface rock. He was a gregarious and bluff man, taller and huskier than most Japanese. It was Ishihara, a Nissan company man since 1937, who had eased Nissan through some of its most important breaks with tradition. He had been in charge of Nissan's exports to the United States since the 1960s, and no one in his company knew the challenges and opportunities better. He was thorough and unusually hands-on for the president of such a large company. When he received the geologist's answer, he immediately rejected the Dickson site, saying it would not withstand the tremendous pounding forces of his heavy stamping machines.

Nissan officials had also determined that they would need at least 400 acres for their new plant. Then, seeming to believe that the state government could produce whatever land it wanted, insisted that the site be a 437-acre tract in Rutherford County, southeast of Nashville, owned by Maymee Cantrell, who lived in Waverly, in West Tennessee. The problem was, she did not want to sell.

Alexander knew this could be the deal breaker. So, on a February morning in 1980, the governor flew by helicopter to Cantrell's home in Waverly. At her kitchen table, she served sweet iced tea with her specialty key lime pie, and they talked about Nissan. Alexander remembers their conversation went like this:

> ALEXANDER: "I hope you will let Nissan buy your land. It will tell the whole world that Tennessee is the best place to do business and bring jobs to people who need them."
>
> CANTRELL: "I don't want to sell. But I believe in what you're trying to do. The problem is our caretaker, Mr. Ward. I promised him he could live on the farm. I'm a woman of my word, and I won't break my promise."

The governor proposed a solution. When he returned to Nashville, he contacted Boyce Magli, a Williamson County real estate broker, and asked him to find Mrs. Cantrell a farm as much as possible like the one in Rutherford County. Magli found such a property only a few miles away from the Cantrell farm. Mrs. Cantrell bought it and then gave Nissan an option to buy the 437 acres that the company wanted.

But then Nissan decided the Cantrell acreage was not enough land. The company now wanted a total of 800 acres, specifically the 260-acre farm owned by the McClary family. So the governor made a second visit. He later wrote, "Mr. and Mrs. McClary were in their seventies, and the farm had been in Mrs. McClary's family for one hundred years. We talked it over on a hot June night, rocking on their screened porch. They finally agreed to sell."

Three years later, when the first Nissan pickup truck rolled off the assembly line at the new Smyrna production facility, Alexander spotted Mrs. McClary and spoke to her after the jubilant ceremony ended.

> ALEXANDER: "How do you feel?"
>
> McCLARY: "We did the right thing for the people of the area. I know that. But if you really want to know the truth, I can't say it makes me happy to lose our farm."

NUMEROUS NISSAN EXECS WERE now traveling into the state on a regular—though guardedly quiet—basis. They were doing C-30 research, including their efforts to understand what it was like to live in an American city like Nashville. Masahiko Zaitsu, the top Nissan executive in Los Angeles, was in Nashville eleven times through 1979 and 1980. Each time he was Alexander's guest at the executive residence on Curtiswood Lane. "I think our children thought he was a Japanese uncle, he was at the governor's mansion so often."

Harris said Zaitsu would typically control discussions on Nissan's side of the table, recognizing which of his executives would make remarks or ask questions. "Mr. Zaitsu was the leader of the whole process for them. He would decide which of their execs would talk, and who would say what. I remember he would say 'I will sit here and be quiet, because I don't understand English so well.' Of course he was the leader and understood English perfectly, but that was their normal routine. They mainly didn't want to go out to dinner, but they loved to come to my house. They would ask us questions like, 'What kind of furniture would I need.' They asked, 'Will the furniture come with house I buy?' Of course, the answer was no."

Harris remembers one evening when he and his wife Laura hosted Zaitsu and another Nissan executive to dinner at their home in the suburban Hillwood section of Nashville. After the meal, the men walked out onto Harris's patio, with its peaceful view of the rolling hills of the Hillwood Country Club golf course. Suddenly, the visitors' attention was captivated by a multitude of fireflies that were flashing across the lawn. They walked into the yard to get a closer view.

"They were just fascinated with the fireflies," Harris remembers. "Most of these guys lived in the cities. We were outside on our patio, looking out over the golf course. I'd never seen that many there."

COMMISSIONER COTHAM'S WIFE RACHEL remembers being asked to accompany Mrs. Ishihara on a day when their husbands were in business meetings in Nashville. When the day came, there seemed to be one minor crisis after another with her Japanese visitor's itinerary.

"I knew they were coming from Georgia, so we knew we were in a competition," Rachel Cotham told me. "It was decided that I would spend the day with her, and we had a driver who was one of the employees at the department. We also had an interpreter for Mrs. Ishihara and me. I had never worked with an interpreter before, so that was kind of daunting, but I decided that I needed to be very careful and remember that I was speaking to her and not to the interpreter. I had prompted my babysitter to be ready just in case Mrs. Ishihara wanted to see a private home. I thought my home was the only one I could think of where I can just walk in with a strange woman. But when we quizzed her on what she wanted to do, she said she wanted to shop for shoes and she needed to go by the beauty salon.

"She was a petite woman—she wore a size four and a half shoe. I don't think there was a four-and-a-half size shoe anywhere, so we had no luck shopping. We got back in the car, which was one of the state automobiles. It was a hot day, and the driver went to turn on the air conditioning but it wouldn't turn on. I thought to myself, 'Oh, gosh, there goes the automobile plant!' But then, I guess by magic, it did come on."

"Mrs. Ishihara was gracious, a 'stylish grandmother' type. She was very easy to deal with, but maybe a little shy. But overall the day was fraught with one crisis after another. And I couldn't help thinking, 'Oh I hope this isn't giving her a bad impression.' I wanted so badly to make a good impression on her, and I just wasn't certain I did. However, on the day Nissan announced it was coming to Tennessee, there was a big party at one of the hotels downtown, and I met Jim down there. And someone said, "Oh, Mrs. Cotham, we are so glad you are here. Mrs. Ishihara has been asking for you.""

ISHIHARA'S ROLE WAS SO decisive that Alexander did his best to stay close to him. During the Republican National Convention in Detroit in July 1980, when Alexander learned Ishihara was in Tennessee conducting his own site selection visits, the governor skipped a meeting with the Republican nominee Ronald Reagan to fly home to see Ishihara.

Alexander told friends later, "I figured that, at that point, Ishihara could do more for Tennessee than Reagan could."

THE PHONE CALL THAT changed everything came late on a Thursday morning—October 30, 1980—a half-hour before noon.

Jim Cotham received word that Nissan had now made its decision and that Governor Alexander should expect a call from Marvin Runyon before noon. Cotham soon joined the governor in his office at the capitol. Yet there was no certainty, even at this point, what the final decision was and whether Runyon's message would signal success or failure. He could be calling, out of courtesy, to say another state had been selected.

Either way, this call would mark the end of the long process. Things had progressed well by this day, and there had been no significant disconnects as the sides continued to negotiate. At this point, Alexander estimates that he had spent two of his first twenty-three months as governor working on the Nissan project, three weeks in Japan and the rest of the time hosting visitors and overseeing his department's careful replies to countless requests for information. Since mid-October the Tennessee officials had believed that Nissan's choice had probably narrowed to two states—their own and Georgia, with Georgia possibly having a slight edge.

Early in the month, Alexander, Cotham, and his senior staffer Joe Davis had attended the fifth annual meeting of the Southeast U.S.-Japan Association at the Pinehurst resort in North Carolina. Alexander had given welcoming remarks to his regional counterparts—including Governor George Busbee of Georgia—and to the delegation of visiting Japanese executives. During one of the breaks, Alexander remembers briefly overhearing Busbee as he spoke on a pay phone near the hotel lobby.

"I can remember seeing Busbee on the phone, and hearing him say, 'We can do better than that!' He was talking in an excited way that made it sound like he might be losing and we might be winning," Alexander told me. "He didn't see me. I was just walking by. I assumed it was his economic development commissioner that he was talking to."

This was also an active period politically. Alexander's daily schedules show days full of official duties on a range of state government issues but also frequent trips in the evenings to campaign fundraisers and other events for Republican legislative candidates. But the priorities shifted immediately when word came from Cotham that Runyon had requested time for a phone call on October 30.

On this morning, hoping for the best, three men gathered with Alexander in the governor's private office: Cotham, the press secretary John M. Parish, and Lewis Lavine, the former deputy campaign manager who was now one of Alexander's top policy advisers. Parish brought his camera. When the intercom buzzed, the governor's executive assistant Virginia Parker told her boss that Runyon was on the line holding for him.

Lavine remembers: "We honestly had no idea what the answer was going to be. As late as the night before, we thought they might be going to Georgia. There had not been a problem that we knew of, and Lamar felt his working relationship with Marvin had progressed to a good point. But still we didn't know."

Alexander wrote of this moment years later: "The first time I had met Marvin—two months earlier for lunch at the governor's residence—I was sure all was lost. Marvin was in a foul mood. A Nashville hotel had lost his suitcase—for the third time—and he let me know right away that he was a *close* friend of Governor George Busbee of Georgia, our closest competitor for the plant. Then he began to discuss concessions that we could not make, ones which I thought we had settled already with the Japanese . . . . When he left after lunch that day, I was ready to call Busbee and congratulate him."

Governor Alexander was seated at his desk when he picked up the receiver. The call lasted only a few minutes, as the no-nonsense Runyon quickly came to his point.

"Lamar," said the ex-Ford executive, "we're coming to Tennessee." The photographer's image captured the moment—a beaming Alexander, holding the phone to his ear with his right hand and flashing a thumbs-up with his left. The many months of outreach, cultivation, travel, and negotiations had paid off.

"My smile was a foot wide," Alexander remembers. "It was the biggest news in our state in a long time."

What Runyon was setting in motion would be a half-billion-dollar construction project—the largest single one-time investment in Tennessee by any business up to that time and, as Chairman Kawamata had said, the largest overseas investment ever by a Japanese company.

A FORMER NISSAN EXECUTIVE, Yoshikazu Hanawa, told *Automotive News* in a 2008 interview that Ishihara had chosen Tennessee because of its distance from Detroit and from what he regarded as the UAW's corrupting influence. Alexander agrees with this estimate of the main reason Nissan chose Tennessee. "It was right-to-work, much more than anything else," the governor said later. "On my first trip to Japan in 1979 I took a print of a photograph of the United States taken at night from satellite. It showed our country with all the lights on and most of the lights were east of the Mississippi River. The west was mostly dark until you got to the West Coast."

"The Japanese knew very little about Tennessee, except for Jack Daniels whiskey, the Tennessee Waltz, and Elvis. They would ask, 'Where is Tennessee?' 'Right in the middle of the lights,' I would answer." Two-thirds of Americans live within five hundred miles of our borders. If you are manufacturing heavy cars and trucks it saves a lot of money in transportation costs to be in the population center, which has moved from the Midwest toward the South since Henry Ford's day. And then I would say, 'Kentucky and Tennessee are now the center of the market, and every state north of Tennessee, including Kentucky, does *not* have a right-to-work law."

Also, not yet trusting of American workmanship quality, Ishihara placed a heavy emphasis on automation in the new facility and restricted the manufacturing program to small pickup trucks. Instead of hiring experienced union autoworkers from the Midwest, he sent three hundred Middle Tennesseans—almost all of whom had never worked in auto plants—to Japan for three months in the fall of 1981 to learn how to build pickup trucks "the Nissan way." Honey Alexander served Thanksgiving dinner to these Tennesseans during one of the governor's trips to Japan.

In the end, Ishihara trusted Runyon, the Texas native and a former auto assembly line worker himself who had long experience leading Ford's auto manufacturing. Ishihara gave Runyon only two specific mandates—quality here must match the standard of Nissan products coming from Japan, and costs must be firmly controlled—then he delegated everything else to his new U.S. president. "The rest," Ishihara told Runyon, "is up to you." Runyon responded by recruiting a team of Ford executives from Detroit who, like him, knew what to do but like him felt restricted by the Detroit environment.

They were eager to start from scratch to build a better truck and car.

❖

Fig. 1. Democrats and Republicans in the Tennessee House of Representatives gather around Speaker Ned McWherter in this 1973 photo in the House chamber. Courtesy of Jim Free

Fig. 2. Nashvillians Ted Welch, left, and Pat Wilson, right, both served as chairman of the Republican National Finance Committee. President Reagan hosted them at the Western White House. Courtesy of Colleen Conway Welch

Fig. 3. NAACP Executive Director Dr. Benjamin Hooks answers a reporter's questions before speaking at Tennessee State University on March 31, 1983. Ricky Rogers/*The Tennessean*

Fig. 4. Governor Lamar Alexander, left, and Finance Commissioner Lewis R. Donelson III confer during the Memphis Jobs Conference on Nov. 3, 1981. Behind them are the Memphis business leaders Ron Terry and Mike Rose. Dave Darnell/ *The Commercial Appeal*

Fig. 5. President Ronald Reagan and First Lady Nancy Reagan join Republican friends and other guests at the home of Senator and Mrs. Howard Baker in Huntsville, Tennessee, following the grand opening of the 1982 World's Fair in Knoxville. Dinah Shore and Chet Atkins are standing to the right of Mrs. Reagan. Honey and Lamar Alexander kneel in front. Courtesy of Senator Lamar Alexander

Fig. 6. Bill Gibbons and Memphis Mayor A C Wharton spoke with the author about their city's struggles through racial and economic turmoil following the 1968 assassination of Dr. Martin Luther King Jr. Author's photo

Fig. 7. Circuit Court Judge George H. Brown became Tennessee's first black Supreme Court judge in 1980. He is greeted by attorney Sabrina Ball at the Shelby County courthouse in this 2005 photo. Matthew Craig/*The Commercial Appeal*

Fig. 8. Federal Express founder Frederick W. Smith waves as he boards the company's first Falcon fanjet in this 1983 photo. He flew the plane from Memphis to present it in Washington to the Smithsonian Institution's National Air and Space Museum. James R. Reid/*The Commercial Appeal*

Fig. 9. Dr. Willie W. Herenton stood on the steps of his childhood home in Memphis soon after he was named superintendent of the Memphis city school system. Dave Darnell/ *The Commercial Appeal*

Fig. 10. Real estate broker Ray Tarkington indicates on a property map the Rutherford County land that Nissan officials wanted for their U.S. assembly plant. Author's photo

Fig. 11. Nissan's global president, Takashi Ishihara, greets Alexander in 1980 on his visit to company headquarters in Tokyo. At center is Shozo Shimizu, a high-ranking member of Nissan's ultra-secret "C-30" team. Courtesy of Judge Andy Bennett

Fig. 12. Alexander receives the call from Runyon—who says "Lamar, we're coming to Tennessee"—and gives the "thumbs up" to ECD Commissioner Jim Cotham after a long recruiting effort. John M. Parish

Fig. 13. Nissan USA president and CEO Marvin Runyon, seated right, was one of four executives receiving the 1985 Advantage Business Awards in Nashville. Seated left is E. Bronson Ingram, chairman of Ingram Industries Inc. Standing are Tom Beasley, president of Corrections Corporation of America, and Wayne Chastain, president of Med Inc. *The Tennessean*

Fig. 14. Runyon and John L. Parish shake hands over the hood of a new Nissan sedan as it rolls off the production line at Smyrna, Tennessee. Personal Collection of John L. Parish

Fig. 15. ECD Commissioner John L. Parish was seated next to Bridgestone president Kanichero Ishibashi at a working lunch in Tokyo. Personal Collection of John L. Parish

Fig. 16. Alexander repeatedly used this NASA satellite image of the continental U.S. at night to show General Motors officials how Tennessee is centrally located to the most of the nation's population. NASA

Fig. 17. The 1984 meeting of the National Governors Association was hosted by Alexander in Nashville. At this casual reception at the Tennessee Executive Residence, Alexander greets Arkansas Governor Bill Clinton. Between them are country music artists Brenda Lee and Ray Stevens. TSLA

Fig. 18. This photo of spider webs on a rural fence became an iconic image of Saturn's pledge to respect the environment in its move to Spring Hill, Tennessee. TSLA

Fig. 19. The 'Tennessee Homecoming '86 Special" ran for one week, making stops at rail depots across the state. At this whistle stop, author Alex Haley waves alongside the governor's mother, Flo Alexander, son Will, and country music artist Ed Bruce. TSLA

Fig. 20. Staff members of the state Tourist Development agency surround Commissioner Etherage Parker in this publicity photo promoting Tennessee Homecoming '86. Courtesy of Charlotte Davidson

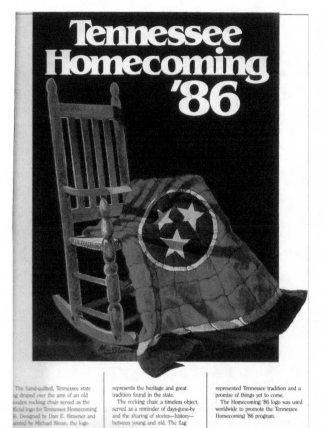

The hand-quilted, Tennessee state ng draped over the arm of an old oden rocking chair served as the ficial logo for Tennessee Homecoming 6. Designed by Dan E. Brawner and ainted by Michael Sloan, the logo

represents the heritage and great tradition found in the state.
The rocking chair, a timeless object, served as a reminder of days-gone-by and the sharing of stories—history—between young and old. The flag

represented Tennessee tradition and a promise of things yet to come.
The Homecoming '86 logo was used worldwide to promote the Tennessee Homecoming '86 program.

Fig. 21. The official Homecoming logo, designed by Dan Brawner, was not licensed but made freely available to any individuals or organizations with a good idea. Tennessee ECD

Fig. 22. Alexander signs the Better Schools Program in a ceremony at Julia Green School in Nashville. He is surrounded by students, Education Commissioner Bob McElrath, and the bipartisan sponsors of the landmark legislation. TSLA

Fig. 23. (*Top*) The Tennessee Main Prison, west of Nashville, was the scene of disturbances on July 2, 1985. The unrest quickly spread to other correctional facilities. Kathleen Smith/*The Tennessean*

Fig. 24. (*Right*) Representative Lois DeBerry, Democrat of Memphis, toured the main prison on August 28, 1985, with other members of the Select Committee on Corrections. Inmates shouted from a window about a shortage of hot water. Kathleen Smith/ *The Tennessean*

CHAPTER 10

Nissan Arrives

"We'll be ready when you're ready."
— Commissioner William Sansom to Marvin Runyon

THERE WAS STILL MUCH to do before a public announcement could be made, before any earth could be moved.

Among many other details of the giant project, highway access had to be arranged and built, government paperwork minimized, and training programs sized and staffed. At this point, Alexander assigned Bill Sansom, then his cabinet-level commissioner over the state Department of Transportation, to be the chief liaison in the remaining negotiations. On Nissan's side of the table would be Runyon, who involved himself personally in this foundational work with the Tennessee government officials.

Two years earlier, Sansom had been running American Limestone Inc., a Knoxville supplier of crushed-stone for highway construction, when Alexander approached him about heading up the highway agency. He was a prominent businessman in the city and also chairman of the Knoxville Chamber of Commerce. Alexander, during his campaign for governor, had asked Sansom what his number one goal for Knoxville was. "Fixing Malfunction Junction before the World's Fair opens," Sansom replied, referring to the 1982 World's Fair planned for Knoxville. "Malfunction Junction" was the derisive local nickname for the long-running, headache-inducing, rush-hour traffic snarl where Interstate 40 and I-75 merge in East Tennessee. Sansom now stressed how essential it was to bring a more permanent solution to this complicated problem of engineering and design.

ALEXANDER: "How would you do that if you were governor?"
SANSOM: "I would hire the very best person I could find, give him a mission, and meet with him once a month to make sure the project was on time and on budget."

After Alexander's election, early in the transition period when he was recruiting his first cabinet members, he had invited Sansom to the Alexander family cabin in Blount County. He recalled their earlier conversation about "Malfunction Junction," told Sansom he was the very best person to fix it before 1982, and therefore he should be the state's new transportation commissioner. Sansom accepted—both the appointment and the challenge with its daunting timetable—and he proceeded to get the job got done, on time and on budget.

So, well before Nissan was even known to be an industrial prospect, the first priority for TDOT in East Tennessee on Alexander's watch would be to fix "Malfunction Junction" before the world came to visit. With Nissan, the recruitment of the businessman Sansom paid a second dividend when Alexander sent him to the negotiating table opposite Runyon.

BOTH TOUGH AND AFFABLE, Sansom was well prepared for this new assignment. He had good relations with both government and corporate leaders in the region. He had enlisted in the Marine Corps after high school. After discharge he enrolled at the Citadel in South Carolina where he was the top graduate in 1964. (His twin brother Bob likewise finished first in his class at the U.S. Air Force Academy). Bill retained a military bearing through his business and civic careers in Knoxville, a city where much of the employment resides in the public sector—at the Tennessee Valley Authority and the University of Tennessee, as well as the big Oak Ridge National Laboratory nearby—and he became a leading business figure, prominent among his fellow private-sector CEOs.

Though Nissan had now settled on Smyrna, there was still much negotiating ahead in order to firmly secure the deal. If these talks did not go well, it was still possible the automaker might push away from the table and choose another state. Cotham had shouldered the lead responsibility for marketing Middle Tennessee to the Japanese, but for the private negotiations over highway improvements and other items of immediate interest to Nissan, Alexander felt he needed a hard-nosed negotiator to deal effectively with Runyon. He phoned Sansom at his home in Knoxville early on a Sunday afternoon, described Runyon, and made clear his sense of the task ahead.

"I just had lunch with a guy, named Marvin Runyon, that Nissan has hired to run Nissan U.S.," Sansom remembers Alexander saying that day. "He's a typical industry S.O.B. and I need for you to handle our negotiations. Jim Cotham isn't tough enough for that. Can you meet with Runyon tonight?"

Sansom drove to Nashville that afternoon. What followed over the next weeks was a series of bilateral meetings, mostly held in a conference room at Cotham's ECD Department headquarters in Nashville, with staff members and technical consultants seated on both sides of the table. The discussions quickly focused on the project timetable for the critical highway upgrades and how to fast track various permitting approvals relating to construction of the massive manufacturing complex.

Though from vastly different backgrounds, Runyon and Sansom soon came to appreciate each other's no-nonsense style and decisiveness. At one point in these discussions, Sansom sensed that a Public Health Department official was wading too tediously into the legislative history of Tennessee's water and air quality control statutes that would apply to Nissan's painting processes. Sansom cut him off—too much background, no time for trivia—and he pointed to Runyon sitting at the table.

"He doesn't care about that," the commissioner declared. "Just tell him where you want him to put the paint."

In other negotiating sessions, highway upgrades were high on the agenda. The rail access was important for raw materials coming to the plant, but it would also be critical for trucks hauling new vehicles from the assembly line to market to have speedy access to I-24, I-40, and I-65, the three expressways that converge in Middle Tennessee. Runyon pressed Sansom on when the highway access improvements would be completed. One particularly tense exchange sent the state officials scrambling to their maps and calendars in search of a firm timetable.

> RUNYON: "You're going to build this connector and you're going to do all of this work, but when are you going to have the work finished? When are you going to be done?"
> SANSOM: "I don't know. When are you going to be done?"
> RUNYON: (*Pause*) "I don't know either."
> SANSOM: "I'll tell you what: We'll be ready when you're ready."

GROUNDBREAKING FOR THE Smyrna plant came on February 3, 1981. Nissan executives were there from Tokyo for the ceremony, together with local and state officials, and news media from all over. This should have been a happy, festive morning, a celebration of new jobs and new hope, the grand climax of months of careful planning.

This was how Alexander described what became a dark and ugly day: "A cold morning rain had made mud out of the pasture that Maymee Cantrell used to own, and the dignitaries' car wheels were plowing mud into furrows. Nissan officials had put up a large tent in the center of the pasture to shelter the groundbreaking and to ward off rain and chill. And I had ordered fifty state troopers to be on hand to ward off the trouble."

The flashpoint for local leaders of the United Automobile Workers was Nissan's hiring of Daniels Inc. of South Carolina, a contractor who used both union and non-union labor. Hearing that announcement, the top labor leader in Tennessee, Jim Neeley, president of the AFL-CIO State Labor Council, met with a company official in hopes of securing some of the new employment on the Smyrna project for UAW and other union workers.

"They had a person in Nashville and I had been meeting with him about using labor on the construction jobs," Neeley told me. "But on the day before the Nissan announcement, he told me they weren't going to use *any* labor union workers. I felt it was a deathblow."

On the day of the groundbreaking, labor struck back.

Runyon's staff had arranged for a novel groundbreaking: a Nissan pickup truck was outfitted with a small earthmover blade for the ceremonial turning of the dirt. This might have been, as intended, a festive scrapbook moment with beaming dignitaries all around. That was not to be.

Suddenly there were shouts and jeers, interrupting the dignitaries on the dais. Remarks by Runyon, Alexander, and Nissan's executive vice president from Tokyo were interrupted multiple times by booing from the jostling crowd. Before the ceremonial action could shift to the small truck outfitted to break ground, a throng of protesters suddenly stepped into its path, blocking its forward movement. Nails were tossed onto the ground where the truck was to be driven, and someone slashed its tires.

The Tennessee Highway Patrol had advised state officials to avoid the event altogether. Alexander had ignored this warning. Some members of the legislature attended but the two top leaders, McWherter and Wilder, did not.

Pat Nolan had been a television reporter for the CBS affiliate in Nashville since 1975. He had traveled to Detroit the previous October for Nissan's announcement of the Tennessee decision, and he met Runyon there. Within a few days, he received a call at the station from Don Corn, a local UAW officer who had worked with Nolan's father at the Ford Glass Plant in west Nashville. Corn was upset that Nissan was not going to employ UAW workers on the big Smyrna project. Nolan mentioned this to his news director, Chris Clark, and they agreed to keep an eye on the labor situation.

On this February morning, Nolan and the cameraman Bob Bosworth flew to Smyrna by helicopter to cover the groundbreaking. This was an unusual mode of transportation for them at the time—years before local TV stations routinely used helicopters to report on traffic—because they anticipated that auto traffic around Smyrna would likely be a nightmare. When the chopper landed in an adjacent field, clouds had formed overhead, the air was cold, and the ground soggy.

"I remember watching Governor Alexander and the Nissan guys sitting on the stage when the rocks were hitting the stage," Nolan recalled. "I didn't see anyone get hit but you could hear the rocks ping off of the platform. They (protesters) were not too far away and in earshot, yelling 'Go Home Jap' and stuff about Pearl Harbor. These folks started the demonstration before they (the officials) got a chance to start the ceremony. They tried to start the ceremony anyway and the protest got louder."

On the dais, Cotham was sitting near Alexander. At home that evening, he told his wife Rachel that a member of the governor's security detail had given him unusual instructions: "I was sitting right there behind the governor," Mrs. Cotham remembers him saying, "and his security detail said to me, 'If anything happens, you fall on the governor. Throw yourself on the governor.' I had no security training. How do you fall *onto* somebody?"

Runyon and Alexander persevered with the official program, speaking over the shouts. Alexander later wrote of this moment,

"When my turn came, the demonstrators were in full voice. I could either denounce them or let their obnoxious conduct speak for itself. I knew something they did not: the microphone in front of me fed sound to all twelve television cameras. The rude shouts could drown out my voice in Smyrna, but the world would still hear on the evening news what I had to say. I welcomed Nissan with these words:

> It would be hard to overestimate the importance of this new facility to the State of Tennessee. Nissan is one of the three or four leaders in what is becoming a global industry. Having their United States headquarters here will not only be of tremendous direct value to us but will be a magnet for other high technology industries from around the nation and around the world.
>
> Twenty years ago, Mel Tillis sang a great country song 'Detroit City' about the thousands of southerners who had to leave home to find jobs in the assembly plants and factories in the North. Now, thanks to Nissan, many members of the present generation can stay here and get those high-paying jobs, and some of the ones who had to go away before can come back home. That's not a cause of protest. That's a cause for celebration."

As for the protests, Alexander remembers he was "more angry than embarrassed" and, most of all, concerned with what the scene at Smyrna might communicate to the outside world about racial intolerance in Tennessee.

"I was angry at these people about to deprive our state of what could be the greatest economic bonanza we were ever likely to have," he told me. "And if they destroyed it, or if they had caused Nissan to change its mind, then other Japanese companies would change their minds. Other auto companies wouldn't come to Tennessee and we would be stuck where we were—so that's what made me angry. It wasn't that they're treating me rudely, or treating the Japanese person rudely, which they did, it was that they were about to ruin a once-in-a-lifetime opportunity for the state. I was afraid that might happen so I tried to challenge that as best I could with what I said, and I know I could be heard because I had the microphone and they didn't. But I was . . . 'seething' is a good word. I mean, I was absolutely—well, there was no hesitation in my going or in what I had to say there, in spite the ugliness of the whole affair."

Neeley was in the crowd that day but told me later he had not been standing close to the trouble. He said he did not personally witness any rock throwing or tire-slashing.

"I was there, but I couldn't get close because there was so many people," Neeley remembered. "It seemed like the entire labor movement was there, and they got all the seats. I was probably two hundred to three hundred feet behind them." Nonetheless, the next day Neeley learned he had been sued in federal court at Nashville for destruction of property. U.S. District Court Judge Tom Wiseman eventually dismissed the complaint.

That very afternoon, the governor's office prepared a sternly worded resolution extolling the future economic benefits of Nissan's arrival, in hopes the General Assembly would swiftly adopt it. The statement condemned the violence of that morning and declared the Japanese were most welcome in Tennessee. (I wrote the first draft for this statement; after a quick review by Alexander, Tom Ingram, and Commissioner Cotham, it was taken to McWherter and Wilder who had it prepared as a joint resolution.) This became "House Joint Resolution 58" and was overwhelmingly adopted the next morning by a vote of 87–4 in the House and 32–0 in the Senate.

The resolution took note of the 2,200 "high-paying jobs" and $40 million annual payroll that Nissan would bring, and how "virtually every state east of the Mississippi River was working for and hoping to obtain the Nissan project." Also noting that fourteen Japanese companies were already doing business in Tennessee, from Knoxville to Memphis, the resolution continued:

> The great majority of Tennesseans wholeheartedly welcome Nissan and recognize the long-term positive effects that this project will have on improved standards of living and the economic well-being of countless Tennesseans . . . it is regrettable and unfortunate that a small group of agitators, many of them from outside Tennessee and others of them from outside Rutherford County and adjoining counties, conducted themselves in a manner unbecoming and uncharacteristic of Tennesseans at Nissan's formal groundbreaking ceremonies on February 3.

❖

ALSO ON THAT NEXT day, Neeley was summoned to Alexander's office. Both the new lawsuit and legislative resolution were mentioned. "Lamar called me and wanted to meet. I met with him and Tommy Ingram at the governor's residence." The labor leader remembers the conversation went like this:

> Neeley: "Governor, I've always respected the governor's office."
> ALEXANDER: "Jim, I had a chance to kick your ass and I did it."
> NEELEY: "Governor, given the opportunity I'm gonna kick your ass up between the shoulder blades."
> ALEXANDER: "I understand."
> NEELEY: "So now that we've got the preliminaries out of the way, what's the purpose of this meeting?"
> Alexander: "Well, we've got to figure out a way to work together."

And they did. Within a few days, Bruce Thrasher, a regional UAW official from Atlanta, arrived in Nashville to coordinate with Neeley. Tempers cooled, and construction of the new plant moved forward.

APART FROM ORGANIZED LABOR, Tarkington remembers hard feelings on the part of older residents of the project area.

"There was a lot of animosity from them. In the war, some of them had flown out of Sewart Air Force Base, and some of those guys got captured over there. So a lot of local people didn't have a lot of love for the Japanese at that time. There were a lot of military people out there that were about as angry as the union was. That generation was still alive and active. A lot of people always retire around the old base. Nashville has a lot of military people around there, and it just was not a good atmosphere."

Yet in the brief but intense period of assembling the Smyrna site, Tarkington told me, he heard no discussion about worries that Middle Tennesseans might not accept a Japanese employer. "I really didn't think about that until after the fact. And some of the people I heard making comments in the newspaper. You know, bringing in a Japanese factory. And here they were twenty years ago, thirty years ago killing us. That was just one of the things that was a little bit negative, along with the union."

Today he calls it "a Tennessee miracle."

EVENTUALLY MOST EMPLOYEES AT the new Nissan plant were Tennesseans who had never worked in an auto plant before, but the first employees were experienced managers Runyon recruited from the Midwest.

The Nissan move to Tennessee thus became a story of assimilation for these Michigan and Ohio natives who relocated south to staff the new plant for the start of production. Many of these early transplants left behind family and generational friends who had worked alongside them on the assembly lines of Ford and General Motors. The word spread rapidly through neighborhood and shop floor that relatives and longtime associates might defect to a Japanese automaker, and the news engendered resentment for some of those who would be left behind.

Mickey Rose had been a supervisor of Ford's computer systems department in Detroit, supporting data processing at twenty-one assembly plants, when he received a phone call from Rick Brown, a colleague at Ford's plant in Louisville, Kentucky. Brown confided that he had taken a job with Nissan in Tennessee.

"I didn't even know what a Datsun was," Mickey told me. "I had to drive all over Detroit looking for a Datsun dealer. I found one in the Yellow Pages and I went and took a look at their products; when I saw the 380Z or 280Z I said—you know, being young and everything—I says, 'Hey, that's a company I'd like to look at.' My grandfather, on my mother's side, was a friend of Henry Ford and they use to come over and play cards at the dining room table and us kids were little kids and we'd run around and they'd kick us out of the dining room. My dad worked for Ford Motor Company. He was a new car distributor."

Mickey took the job and became one of the first hundred Nissan employees at Smyrna. He showed me his employee badge—No. 74—from the first wave of hiring at a plant that has since employed many thousands. He was on the first technical team that went to Japan for training at Nissan headquarters. He said he learned there that the Smyrna facility was to be identical to Nissan's Kyushu assembly plant.

His wife Carol was likewise a descendant of Ford workers, engineers, and managers. Once in Tennessee, they began to put down new roots. Carol and Mickey took up "two-step" dancing with other Ford transplants joining them at a local dance club. Carol especially credits the parishioners they met at St. Stephens Catholic Church for making them welcome in their new Old Hickory community.

Their younger son Mike, who was born in Detroit, was part of the family's journey to Middle Tennessee. Mike eventually trained as a video journalist. He became the chief videographer at the same CBS affiliate in Nashville that had covered the angry groundbreaking in 1981.

❖

THERE WERE SEVERAL EARLY assimilation moves to help ease the transition for the families of Japanese executives moving into the Rutherford

County community, and also to raise an appreciation of Japanese culture among the Tennesseans they would meet.

The Murfreesboro school system began a program of "Saturday Schools" for the small number of Japanese families who moved to Tennessee. These schools taught Japanese language and mathematics to Japanese children. In 1982 the Japan Center of Tennessee was established on the university campus at Murfreesboro, under the direction of MTSU political science professor Esther Seeman, with a $30,000 appropriation from the legislature and funding from Nissan. Its first event was to host a lecture, by Nissan vice president Shuichi Yoshida, on "Japanese Management Innovations." An informal group of business leaders called the Tennessee-Japan Society also formed at Alexander's request, with the Nashville banker Ed Nelson as an important leader. In 2000, the Japan-America Society of Tennessee was established, with Maury Bush of Sharp Corp. as the first director. Leigh Wieland, who had been a staff member in Alexander's ECD Department and later was a policy adviser to Governor Sundquist, became the JAST staff director in 2003. Good sushi became available in Nashville restaurants.

Alexander also raised funds to hire the Pulitzer Prize–winning photographer Robin Hood who spent six months in Japan photographing the surprising similarities of two different cultures: Boy Scouts, maple trees turning red, irises blooming, sticky summers, sumo wrestlers in Japan and World Wide Wrestling in the United States. These and many more images were published in a 1986 book Alexander titled *Friends. Japanese and Tennesseans. A Model of U.S.-Japan Cooperation*. Later, when the governor visited the Tokyo home of Kanichero Ishibashi, president of Bridgestone Tire Company (which later placed its North American headquarters in Nashville) and son of the company's founder, a copy of *Friends* was the only book on his living room table.

The intense publicity surrounding Nissan's location decision, and the multiple efforts to introduce Tennessee to the Asian country on the other side of the world, quickly produced other results. Yoshio Okawara, Japan's ambassador to the United States, said that by the middle 1980s fully 10 percent of all of Japan's U.S. investment was in Tennessee.

JEFF WILSON WAS A journalist in Jackson and Nashville during the in-between time. In 1984, he became a correspondent for the Associated Press, based in the state capital. Years later he described the significance of Nissan's arrival in the state.

"What was happening during the 1980s, and this was especially strong in Middle Tennessee between Nissan and Saturn and the new Nashville airport, was that the sensation of 'BOOM' was dramatic here. I'm sure there were other factors, but those three would just be the major legs on the tripod. And so you had this influx of people, you had this total change in the mind-set, the business mindset. And this really started with Nissan.

"I think Nissan opened our vistas. It's like, 'Wow! If we could do this, then what else can we do?' Saturn was announced in '85, the American Air-lines hub was announced in '85, the new airport opened in '86. It was a total shift in the mindset in Middle Tennessee, in my opinion." Looking much further ahead, some people would say that it was Nissan coming in the first place that, in due course, led to GM picking Spring Hill for Saturn, and ulti-mately Volkswagen in Chattanooga. Nissan changed the game. Nissan was the breakthrough event."

CHAPTER 11

Megatrends Tennessee

"In an information society, education is no mere amenity; it is the prime tool for growing people and profits."
—John Naisbitt, *Megatrends*

SOON AFTER JOHN NAISBITT'S bestseller *Megatrends: Ten New Directions Transforming Our Lives* was published in 1982, his book became a must-read sensation among futurists and also for business strategists eager for a crystal-ball glimpse of the world to come.

In Nashville, Alexander ordered four dozen copies. He gave a book to each member of his cabinet and the cadre of political appointees who headed up the twenty-two departments of state government, as well as copies to his senior staff in the governor's office. Adding his own signature inside the cover of each book, Alexander made it clear that *Megatrends* was required reading for the final year of his first term and looking ahead to the second should he be re-elected.

Finally, the governor invited Naisbitt himself to Nashville to meet with his leadership team. The author accepted the invitation. On the day of his visit, in a conference room at the James K. Polk State Office Building near the capitol, Naisbitt spoke and answered questions for ninety minutes.

OVER THE DECADES, GOVERNORS in Tennessee have utilized the "cabinet" concept in different ways. As a group, the cabinet per se has no conferred authority. The term does not appear in the state's constitution, nor for that matter are any specific departments set forth there for the executive branch. In the beginning, the term was most likely borrowed from the federal government's vocabulary to denote the chief executive's senior council.

In the early 1970s, Governor Dunn did not often refer to his cabinet as such. In the administration that followed Dunn's, Blanton's commissioners rarely met as a group over his four years in office. Alexander, on the other hand, hosted regular dinner gatherings for his cabinet-level officers as well as daytime meetings. The purpose was as much for team building as for planning, but the sessions included planning retreats and sometimes guest speakers. (Naisbitt was one of these dinner guests. Others included the author Alex Haley and Vanderbilt University Chancellor Joe B. Wyatt when the administration was beginning its push for a new "Technology Corridor" near Oak Ridge and Knoxville.)

McWherter conducted a statewide "listening tour" in 1987, very early in his first year in office, and required all his department heads to participate but otherwise did not convene his cabinet routinely. Sundquist convened his cabinet infrequently, two of its members told me. For Bredesen, full cabinet meetings were also rare, but four of his cabinet members recalled "brown bag lunches" with different sub-sets of commissioners grouped by areas of focus, usually organized by the governor himself.

IN 1982, WHEN ALEXANDER'S cabinet gathered for Naisbitt's visit, it was chiefly an exercise in thinking about the future. The author stressed how "trends are not predictions" but are ways for understanding the social currents that might shape how the future unfolds. Alexander, in any case, regarded Naisbitt's book and the author's approach to his subject as a way of thinking for his own policymakers in preparation for a second term.

The upcoming period, 1982–1986, would in fact be a time for pushing new policies before the legislature, notably reforms in elementary and secondary education and new structures and funding for higher education.

During his visit with the Alexander team, Naisbitt described his research, his conception of what constituted a megatrend, and how the notion might apply to public policy. The ten megatrends that he cited were large ideas that, he observed, were sweeping U.S. society at the time.

1. The shift from an industrial society to an information-based economy.
2. The tandem phenomena of "high tech" and "high touch."
3. The expansion of economic borders—formerly national, now increasingly global—and the new reality of international competitiveness among cities and states.
4. The shift in planning focus from short term to longer term.
5. The rise of innovation among cities and states, with governors in particular bringing about solutions to social challenges like crime and education reform.
6. The emergence of self-reliance over institutional problem solving.

7. More participatory democracy.
8. The shift from hierarchies to networks, from vertically organized work teams to more horizontal structures.
9. The movement of populations from north to south, from Rust Belt of the northern tier of states to Sunbelt.
10. More choices, shifting from "either/or" to "either/and" in selection of services and opportunities.

From the perspective of a quarter-century later, not all but arguably most of Naisbitt's shrewd observations proved to be on the mark. And this orientation, their discussion with the author in 1982, helped to focus Alexander's team on the most important work they would undertake in a new term over the coming four years.

MARTHA BROWN LARKIN (then Martha Olsen) was commissioner of the state's Department of Revenue at the time of the Naisbitt visit. She would later serve as commissioner of personnel in Alexander's second term. She remembers the time with the futurist author as "enriching and educational for the cabinet."

"The experience of doing that—of having an author talking about things that were happening in the business world, and the world in general—was good for us because government becomes so insular, especially during a legislative session. You have to shake yourself sometimes and remember there's a whole world out there, outside the little pocket you work in every day. There are other people out there who we are trying to serve and who have other interests, who don't understand a lot of what government does but who expect things to work better and they look to government to be responsible.

"Lamar made a special effort to do that," she added. "When we did cabinet meetings, we didn't just talk about what was on his list. For instance, when Alex Haley spoke to us once, it was thought provoking, and also helped develop some collegiality with your colleagues. It helped develop a relationship between people who may have had nothing in common—either programmatically or in background—and it helped build up a team."

CHAPTER 12

Ground Zero Knoxville 1982

"The politics was just back and forth, back and forth. The World's Fair was probably one of the best examples of bipartisanship you could imagine."
—Bo Roberts

IT WAS THE YEAR of the World's Fair. The world was coming to Knoxville.

By New Year's Day 1982, the East Tennessee city of Knoxville was poised to be the public stage for a rolling drama of several acts and half a dozen subplots—some political, others economic, and all under the glare of the nation's news cameras. Officials in Tennessee's third-largest city, and certainly also at the State Capitol in Nashville, had long known they must make ready. The world was coming to Knoxville, true enough, but before this new year ended the city would become a broader "ground zero" where old politics collided with the new—and a monstrous banking scandal would deepen.

There were many starting points for this turbulent year.

As early as 1975, local civic and business leaders had discussed taking a shot at hosting a World's Fair. It is a type of grand international exposition that occurred only once every five years, and over time the most successful of them always added a new international luster to even the better-known international cities such as Paris, New York, and Chicago in their day. Tennessee had hosted only one other, in Nashville, in 1897.

Knoxville, in the 1970s, was best known as the headquarters city of the Tennessee Valley Authority, as gateway to the Great Smoky Mountains National Park, and as hometown of the University of Tennessee's flagship campus. The proximity to the federal government's Oak Ridge National Laboratory, in adjacent Anderson County, had also made this zone a magnet for scientists and scholars, with one of the South's highest concentrations of PhDs. And yet Knoxville's boosters still winced when reminded how the author John Gunther, in his 1947 bestseller *Inside USA*, had belittled their town as "the ugliest city I ever saw in America," and how as recently as 1980 a *Wall Street Journal* reporter had called Knoxville "a scruffy little city by the river."

True or not, both were still regarded by locals as embarrassing smears. More constructively, the *Journal* piece now fed a new civic resolve to give the world an updated image of Knoxville.

In order to qualify as a sanctioned World's Fair, technically called an "international exposition," Knoxville officials had to prepare and submit a formal proposal and application to the U.S. Commerce Department. The city would also be required to mount a comprehensive financing plan to pay for the six-month extravaganza costing many millions from both public and private sources. For this purpose, in 1975 Mayor Kyle Testerman appointed a seventeen-member committee to explore the idea of hosting a World's Fair. The mayor also designated as its chairman Jake Butcher, who at that time was Knoxville's highest-profile banker.

The new committee proposed a motto for the 1982 Fair: "Energy Turns the World." The hope was to capitalize on the national reputations of TVA with its regional power grid and all the cutting-edge science at the Oak Ridge laboratory. As part of their research the committee visited Spokane, Washington, which had hosted the 1974 Fair. This lead to creation of a new non-profit entity called the Knoxville International Energy Exposition with a bipartisan board of leading citizens. The KIEE board soon employed Bo Roberts as staff director on a six-month consulting engagement to facilitate organization of the many details.

Roberts was a close friend of Blanton's tourism commissioner, Tom Jackson. Ten years before this, Roberts had been Governor Ellington's executive assistant and, more recently, a high-level administrator at the University of Tennessee. His new job title would be president and CEO of the KIEE entity.

"I committed to six weeks of consulting to get the organization set up," Roberts told me. "That six weeks turned into seven years." In my interview with him, Roberts stressed how complicated the political environment became during the 1975–80 period, when both the White House and the Tennessee governor's office would pass from one party to the other. The entire project, from initial planning to execution of the six-month fair, actually occurred over three presidential administrations and two governors. This time span included the year (1978) when Knoxville banker Jake Butcher ran for governor against Alexander, and the year the Fair officially unfolded when Randy Tyree, the Democratic mayor of the host city, opposed Alexander's re-election.

"It all started when President Ford was in office," Roberts recalled. "Then, in 1976, Carter was elected so we were dealing with the Carter administration's Commerce Department. After the 1980 election, we were working with the Reagan administration. The politics was just back and forth, back and forth. That was how important the bipartisanship or multi-partisanship was. We were bipartisan. We had to be. I loved it, but one time I thought it was like the intensity of a political campaign. Like a campaign, we knew there would be an ending date, for better or worse. This was like a five-year political campaign."

In 1975, the Democrat Ray Blanton was in his first full year as governor of Tennessee. He designated Jackson, his commissioner in charge of the Tennessee Department of Tourist Development, to be his administration's liaison with KIEE's Knoxville leaders, who were mostly Republicans. The city would ultimately need the blessing of the U.S. Commerce Department, so it was also important to have good communications with the sitting administration in Washington, D.C.

Successfully navigating the potentially choppy political waters—federal, state, and local—would be essential to a successful application, as well as for assembling the necessary public and private financing for the Fair. The founding board of KIEE was, in fact, well organized to cover all the necessary political bases.

Butcher, the chief executive of the United American Bank chain that extended across East Tennessee, had Democratic friends in high places. He and his brother C. H. Butcher, who ran the sister organization of C&C Banks, were not Blanton allies but their universe included Bert Lance, the Atlanta banker who was currently President Carter's budget director.

The Butchers were also friends with Tennessee's junior U.S. senator, Jim Sasser; the Memphis congressman Harold Ford Sr., who was a member of the House Ways and Means Committee; and Knoxville's Mayor Tyree, who had succeeded Testerman in 1976. (Testerman would later serve another term, following Tyree.)

The vice chair of the KIEE board was Jim Haslam, the founder and CEO of Pilot Oil Corp., the longtime friend and political ally of both Baker and Alexander, as well as others in the state's Republican hierarchy. Together, Haslam and Butcher were the most prominent pair of business executives in the Knoxville region at this time, and other KIEE board members included important large employers in the region: Dick Ray, who was Alcoa's top executive in Tennessee; Roger Hibbs, president of Union Carbide's Nuclear Division, which operated the Oak Ridge laboratories; University of Tennessee president Ed Boling; Bill Sansom, president of American Limestone Company; and Tom Bell, president of East Tennessee Natural Gas.

The Commerce Department's approval would bring some government financial support, but the financing for the Fair would require a significant level of state governmental commitments as well as private-sector bank loans. The federal government appropriated $20 million for U.S. participation in the Fair, including design and construction of the United States pavilion. State government was asked for $11 million in cash and also to cover extensive highway improvements, which were estimated at a billion 1980 dollars. Butcher and Roberts were careful to cultivate support of the Fair not only with Governor Alexander but also with the Democratic speakers of the Tennessee legislature, House Speaker Ned McWherter and Lieutenant Governor John Wilder in the Senate.

The same Butcher-Haslam leadership group, with their high-level contacts across Knoxville's banking community, also helped facilitate the critical bank financing arrangements, both within the region and outside it. When the Commerce Department's final approval was given, a financing plan was established with Chemical Bank of New York as the lead bank, pledging about $100 million in loans. Local and regional banks participated according to their size. The Butcher banks became the largest of the local tier of lenders; Park National Bank, which Haslam was affiliated with, was the second largest. A regional tier that included First Tennessee, SunTrust, and Wachovia banks committed to a total of about $40 million.

Over the course of these loans, Roberts remembers, rising interest rates became a special complication. "Chemical Bank's worst-case projection had been that the prime rate might go to 13 percent. It was at 9 percent at closing, and it actually went up to 21 percent. But all the loans were paid back."

Meanwhile, there was an early leadership change at KIEE, brought on by Tennessee's evolving politics. Butcher had run for governor in 1974 and had come in second in a crowded Democratic primary field of a dozen candidates, losing to Blanton. Four years later, in early 1978, with Blanton's administration in a growing web of scandals, the governor surprised his closest supporters by announcing he would not seek re-election. Butcher quickly let it be known that he intended to run a second time. (By this time, Alexander was already several weeks into his "walk across the state" campaign, having announced his own candidacy in late January.) Butcher, saying he wanted to shield the Fair from politics, stepped down as chair of KIEE, and Haslam became chairman.

This time, Butcher won the Democratic nomination for governor in August, and Alexander was the Republicans' nominee. In the weeks that followed, Alexander made Butcher's banking practices a central issue of the fall campaign. On November 4, Alexander was the victor.

PROBABLY THE TOUGHEST PHYSICAL challenge leading to a successful World's Fair was the urgency of unsnarling Knoxville's legendary traffic congestion—the locally famous interstate highway slowdown zone known as Malfunction Junction.

If the world was to come here in 1982—and if millions of visitors were to have any hope of arriving and departing by car and bus in their own lifetimes—the state Transportation Department (meaning the Alexander administration) would have to devise a more permanent solution to the motorist's nightmare where Interstate Highways 40 and 75 converged to traverse downtown Knoxville. This perpetual snarl was very near to the designated World's Fair site, an old railroad gulch that historically separated the central city from the UT campus on the west side. It was a dilemma that had long defied the highway engineers' attempts to solve it.

The solution began, in part, with Alexander's recruitment of the businessman Bill Sansom to run the state Highway Department. He was a graduate of the Citadel and a director of First Tennessee Bank. The crushed-stone business he ran supplied many highway construction projects, so many road builders knew him. He was a well-known in Knoxville business and civic circles and had served on the KIEE board in its early years.

Sansom considered himself apolitical. He told me he had met Alexander only twice before the new governor-elect asked him to lead the Department of Transportation, and he did not immediately accept. In fact, he says, Alexander enlisted Senator Baker in his recruitment strategy and also deployed Haslam locally to help persuade Sansom to accept. It was Baker who phoned Ralph Hennebeck in New York, the CEO of ASARCO (which owned American Limestone), and Haslam spoke to Sansom's father, Richard E. Sansom, at a Pilot service station in West Knoxville.

"Lamar's a salesman—don't kid yourself," Sansom told me. "I said 'I'm not interested.' He said, 'If you get interested, come up here and let's talk about it.' Then Ralph Hennebeck calls me, and he says, 'Baker has called and asked us to try to make it work for you to go over there.' And my Dad was getting gas one day at Haslam's office, on Kingston Pike, and Jim walks out and says, 'Boy, Dick, I hope Bill goes and does that job for Lamar.' My dad says, 'I told him *not* to. He shouldn't do it. He would embarrass the family if he did it.'"

The son took the job—and was immediately thrust into the task of managing the complex planning to fix Malfunction Junction in fewer than three years. He recalled hearing from DOT veterans that the job would be impossible on such a tight schedule.

"If you think about spending over a billion dollars to fix Malfunction Junction and I-640 between January 1979 and the World's Fair in 1982, I was told, 'You cannot do that. You physically cannot do that. It can't be done.' It's quite a story. We got it done."

IN THAT CONNECTION, THERE was a character called the "Knox Mess Monster."

In November 1979, thinking ahead to the massive road project that would be necessary in Knoxville with its inevitable construction delays, Alexander's press secretary John M. Parish had an idea. He asked Irving Waugh, Jackson's successor as tourism commissioner, to come up with a cartoon-like character that might provide daily traffic reports, even make appearances along the project route, and generally help lighten the mood of motorists driving in and through Knoxville.

Waugh, before his cabinet appointment, had been a longtime executive in Nashville's music industry and president of the NBC television affiliate in the city. He also had been the creator of the annual Country Music Association Awards broadcast that originated in Nashville. (As the station executive, Waugh had helped Alexander's political career following the 1974 defeat by inviting him and the Democrat Floyd Kephart to appear together on a weekly "point-counterpoint" feature on WSM-TV's *Scene at Six*.) Waugh was an older executive, with an elegant demeanor, who had a habit of calling the young governor "Lad." For the assignment from Parish, he turned to Charlotte Davidson, a creative marketing pro who was serving as assistant commissioner in his Tourist Development Department.

"The commissioner asked me to write up some ideas, so I wrote three," she remembers. "One was the 'Knox Mess Monster,' kind of a cross between Big Bird on Sesame Street and King Kong. The idea was motorists would see him on the side of the interstates, always shaking his head and taking the side of the poor motorists—just a diversion to give the motorists something to laugh at. I sent the proposals to Commissioner Waugh, and it went to the governor and he called me, and we decided on Knox Mess."

Davidson then asked a costume designer to make a costume (plus one backup) for an actor to wear. As it turned out, the Knox Mess Monster never made it to Knoxville. "Just as we were going to put the monster on the road, the economy turned down and jobs were being cut, hard times, so it was decided that it was not a time for fun stuff. I just put the costumes in plastic bags and hung them in my attic with my old prom dresses."

JOHN KING, A KNOXVILLE lawyer, had been Alexander's Knox County campaign chairman in 1978, and was now on the governor's cabinet as commissioner of the Department of Revenue. He recalled a 1980 planning meeting at the State Capitol, where Alexander convened a number of Knoxville's leading citizens to discuss plans for the coming World's Fair. King remembers the governor spoke first and then recognized Waugh, to give a progress report.

"Lamar called on Irving for comments on the plans he had seen. Irving told the group, very matter-of-factly, 'The objective of the Fair is to make a tourist destination out of a railroad gulch.' Of course, it was a lot more than that, as we proceeded to clarify."

As the time of the Fair drew closer, Waugh was succeeded as commissioner by Etherage Parker of Hartsville, Tennessee, a tobacco merchant, oil distributor, and operator of Stuckey's convenience stores across the southeastern U.S. Parker was as homespun and country as Waugh was urbane and telegenic, but like Waugh he was a sharp-thinking results-oriented businessman who proved popular with the state's tourism industry.

"I used to laugh to myself when Irving and Etherage would get together and talk about tourism," Davidson told me. "There was Irving Waugh, a former World War II correspondent, former president of WSM-TV, a Virginian with a nose made for looking down. And there was Etherage from Hartsville, who made his money with Stuckey's stores, Texaco gas and convenience stores, and a tobacco warehouse—a man who made deals across the state on a handshake. On the surface, they were as different as could be but, underneath, two of the smartest and most honorable men I have ever known. And they were alike in believing their job was to fill the attractions, hotels and motels and restaurants in Tennessee with tourists. Etherage was a political genius. He had as many Democrat friends as Republican. He knew how to fight on something, come out laughing, and still be friends."

Parker himself remembers the Fair succeeded largely because of its bipartisan support—Republicans working alongside Democrats—and careful coordination with Butcher and the administration's Republican friends in East Tennessee. He also credited the two legislative leaders, the Democrats McWherter and Wilder, with supporting the state's funding commitments to the Fair.

"McWherter and Wilder were both more conservative than Lamar, and he respected them very much," he told me. "They helped him. McWherter and Wilder treated him like two fathers raising a son. They were both astute politicians and knew the feelings of the people of Tennessee. Lamar was a better student and did better in their 'class' than any other governor. He graduated with honors. Today none of these politicians want to work together on behalf of the state. We're heading down the wrong road."

Parker's time commitment to Alexander was to serve as tourism commissioner only up until the October 31 end date of the Fair. This was so he could return to his tobacco business in the important market months of December and January. He left the Alexander cabinet at the end of November.

THROUGHOUT THE FAIR'S SIX-MONTH run, with millions of visitors streaming into Knoxville to see the exhibits and pavilions of twenty-two nations, Alexander was also tending to his own re-election campaign.

One of his campaign strategies that year was a succession of local civic improvement projects known as the "Community Days." These were carefully planned in close coordination with local officials in each town. For this task, Alexander's campaign manager Tom Ingram enlisted five young staff members to handle local organization and planning: the coordinator Jim Fuller, Lisa Barnes, John Crisp, Steve Gill, and Debi Taylor Tate.

Working by regions, these five would coordinate with mayors or other community leaders, help identify and organize the locally chosen project, and carefully advance the day's schedule as each event day approached. There were more than forty of these events across the state, beginning on May 14 and occurring over a five-month period through October leading to Election Day on November 2.

John Crisp remembers that almost all these events would include a walkathon or parade and usually a potluck dinner, all to raise money for a hands-on volunteer project the community had selected. Both Governor and Mrs. Alexander usually attended these. The kickoff project was in Maryville, Alexander's hometown. It was a walkathon in support of Haven House, a shelter for abused women, one of Honey's projects. In Erwin the next day, in upper East Tennessee's remote Unicoi County, the community day restored a fish hatchery, the train depot museum, and nature trails. A community project in Williamson County on May 21 built the new Fairview Community Park. The following day in Chattanooga, a benefit for Red Bank High School athletics starred the Nashville recording artist Pat Boone in concert with "Alexander's Washboard Band," re-assembled from the governor's 1978 campaign road team. On June 5, a walkathon benefitted Johnson City's Little League baseball teams at Liberty Bell Sports Complex. In Memphis, a concert on June 26, featuring the Reverend Al Green, supported restoration of the Senior Citizens Center.

In the state GOP primary on August 5, Alexander was re-nominated for a second four-year term without opposition. His Democratic opponent in the November 2 general election would be Mayor Tyree of Knoxville.

THE WORLD'S FAIR IN Knoxville ran from the first day of May to the last day of October, and it was a spectacular.

President Reagan was on the dais for the opening-day ceremonies, along with the entertainer Dinah Shore, Majority Leader Baker, Sasser, Alexander, Tyree, as well as Butcher, Haslam, and other city leaders who had made the Fair possible. That evening, Baker hosted Reagan and Alexander and their wives for dinner at his home in Huntsville, Tennessee, north of Knoxville. The guest list included Dinah Shore and Chet Atkins.

In the final tally, eleven million visitors had attended the Fair. Knoxville's old railroad gulch had indeed been transformed into a new park that connected the city's downtown with the university campus to the west. The Fair's landmark golden Sunsphere tower remained prominent on the local skyline, and the massive Malfunction Junction fix was generally regarded as a transportation victory.

The larger economic impact of the Fair was also measurable on Tennessee's tourism statewide, with attendance increasing at venues ranging from the Museum of Appalachia in nearby Norris, Tennessee, to the Opryland USA theme park in Nashville, which that year posted its best annual attendance ever.

"It was successful," Bo Roberts said, looking back. "It was a lot of fun while it was happening, and for years wherever I'd go around the state people would tell me how much they enjoyed it. It was probably one of the best examples of bipartisanship you could imagine, because of the important roles everybody had to play. On the day of the ceremony of the burning of the bank notes, October 31 of 1982, the milestone of paying off the notes, the picture in the *News Sentinel* showed Jake Butcher and Howard Baker holding a 'torch' to symbolically burn the notes."

That ceremony made for a happy day for Knoxville officials and the organizers of the successful Fair. For Mayor Tyree, the merriment would not last long, nor for Butcher, but for very different reasons.

TWO DAYS LATER, on November 2, more than a million Tennesseans went to the polls. Alexander and Sasser were both re-elected to their second terms—each winning with about 60 percent of the vote cast in his respective race. In the governor's contest, Alexander defeated Tyree 737,963 votes to 500,937. (On this same day, in Middle and West Tennessee, two congressional candidates who were *not* expected to win—one Democrat, one Republican—were elected to the U.S. House: Democrat Jim Cooper defeated Baker's daughter Cissy in the Fourth District, and Republican Don Sundquist was the winner in his Seventh District race over the Democrat Bob Clement.) "It was," Mayor Tyree told me, reflecting on the momentous year, "the proverbial best of times and the worst of times, but the best of times won out. We got rid of Malfunction Junction!"

What was looming on the very near horizon for Butcher was much darker.

BILLY ADAMS HAD BEEN president of the Bank of Maryville, near Knoxville, and well knew the Butcher brothers' profile in the region. When Alexander won his re-election, Adams was on his prospect list to be the new banking commissioner in the second-term administration, succeeding Commissioner Tom Mottern. Alexander remembers Adams was reluctant to accept his invitation and recalled this conversation:

ADAMS: "Lamar, I'm not sure I want that much responsibility."
ALEXANDER: "Billy, not much happens in that department. We haven't had a bank failure in Tennessee since the 1930s."

Adams took the job in late November and was sworn into office two months later with the rest of Alexander's second-term cabinet. On Valentine's Day 1983, a Monday, disaster struck Jake Butcher's organization. It would be the complete collapse of his banking empire. It would end his career and, in time, send him to prison.

Alexander remembers staying up most of the Sunday night before, on multiple phone calls between Nashville and Washington, D.C., talking with Federal Reserve chairman Paul Volcker. The Fed chairman updated the governor on the regulators' findings in East Tennessee. Around 4:00 a.m., Volker phoned Alexander again and told him the Federal Reserve Board would have to withdraw its support of the Butcher bank, meaning the state would have to close them down. Alexander then phoned Adams, who ordered the bank not to open that morning.

Federal agents fanned out across East Tennessee and conducted simultaneous raids at Butcher-connected banks. Their objective was to confirm a conspiracy that depositors' funds had been systematically shifted from one institution to another in order to make any one bank appear to auditors to have sufficient funds when it did not. These charges had come up initially in the governor's race, during the fall general election campaign, when Alexander drew attention to an alleged "check-kiting" practice among Butcher banks and to Jake Butcher's own lavish lifestyle.

The February raids shut down Butcher's flagship United American Bank in Knoxville and eventually nine other banks in the region that were owned by either Jake or C. H. Butcher. In the regulatory scramble to protect depositors, the Memphis-based First Tennessee Bank became the new owner of Butcher's Knoxville banking operation, along with its marquis skyscraper on downtown Gay Street.

Two years later, in federal court, Jake Butcher was convicted of conspiracy and bank fraud. He was sentenced to twenty years in prison for bank thefts totaling $17 million. The collapse of the Butcher banks would be called the third-largest U.S. bank failure since the Great Depression.

❖

CHAPTER 13

Mothers and Babies

"The statistic that got us focused was the infant mortality rate. We were definitely dragging the bottom."
—Marguerite S. Kondracke

ONE OF THE LASTING burdens of the modern South was the persistent legacy of poor health—a devil's ugly stew of poverty, malnutrition, and a woeful distribution of doctors and nurses.

Of all the victims of this legacy, the saddest were the children, especially newborns. By the 1970s, the links were clear between inadequate prenatal care, low birth weight, and poor performance in school.

Tennessee's response to this, in the early 1980s, was advanced by Honey Alexander, the first lady. She pushed for a new emphasis on policy issues involving expectant mothers, newborns, and a health care infrastructure that was largely missing, especially in rural and inner-city places. The Alexanders had three young children by this time, with a fourth on the way, and Honey remembers how discussions she had with her own family doctor in Nashville influenced her thinking about public policy for a fragile population.

"I was young and pregnant, so prenatal care was interesting to me," she told me. "Our pediatrician, Dr. David Thombs, had done some work in East Tennessee, and he was struck by the number of mentally disabled people back in the hollers, because they never got out. And it seemed like a very particular problem. We felt like we could do more to help those people make better decisions, get better health care, and it would make a difference. So I kept that in the back of my mind. And then Jim Brown (the commissioner of the state Department of Mental Health and Mental Retardation at the time) came to me. He was interested in studying mental health issues, especially in regard to children's services."

She discussed all this with Governor Alexander, and he mentioned the idea to Dr. Eugene Fowinkle, his commissioner of the Department of Public Health, as an important policy area where Mrs. Alexander might help draw public attention. Fowinkle in turn conferred with his number two, the deputy commissioner Jim Word, and in short order a staff person in the department's Cookeville office, Marguerite Weaver Sallee, was assigned to work with the first lady.

Sallee had grown up in Nashville and was a graduate of Duke University. After college graduation, she lived in Memphis where her husband was in medical school. They moved to Tacoma, Washington, for his residency at Fort Lewis, and she became a founder of the new Planned Parenthood affiliate there. After returning to Tennessee, she lived in Cookeville, in the Upper Cumberland region between Nashville and Knoxville. Here, she worked in the regional office of the state Health Department, managing the state's family planning program. It was a program born as a federal initiative during the Johnson administration, encouraging states to make family planning services more broadly available. Sallee logged many hours in Appalachia, where county health departments were the primary source of health care for people in rural counties.

"It was actually Gene Fowinkle who pulled me from the day-to-day duties and said, 'Go create a child health initiative, if you will, for the first lady.'" Sallee said she did "a lot of national research" as a first step and then had her first meeting with Honey Alexander at the governor's residence in Nashville. From that first visit, she remembers her new boss saying, matter-of-factly, "Let's get started."

Alexander remembers: "Honey and Marguerite came in to see me about what they wanted to do," he said. "I had never met Marguerite. She was an impressive woman. I was impressed with everything about her presentation. She's quite a salesman." (After the meeting, he remembers turning to Ingram, and asking, "Who the hell was that with Honey?")

Sallee, in Alexander's second term, became commissioner of the Department of Human Services. After leaving state government, she became the founding CEO of Corporate Child Care (which involved the Alexanders, R. Brad Martin, and Bob "Captain Kangaroo" Keeshan). It later became Bright Horizons Family Solutions Inc., a public company, and Marguerite Sallee Kondracke continues to serve as a director.

THE HEALTHY CHILDREN INITIATIVE got off to a fast start. Honey Alexander remembers her travels across the state in the early planning stage, asking lots of questions of lots of people, both lay and professional. The conversations she had with Tennessee health care providers seemed like a breakthrough and helped clarify for her and Sallee what young mothers and newborns needed most.

"What disturbed me, among other things, was the lack of communication between the various entities. I've always felt that if maybe you could get people talking to one another that maybe you could accomplish more. So that's why I brought in a diverse group of people. And I started with commissioners so they would start talking to each other. They were all interested, because they were working for Lamar, and they wanted him to succeed."

Kondracke remembers how this early work translated rather quickly into a set of new county-based programs, with improved coordination across agencies—and, in short order, new funding for the overall initiative. "We set a goal of prenatal care in every one of the ninety-five county health departments, and we made good use of nurse-practitioners," she said. "We wanted every child to have a medical home. There was a need for more and better daycare and afterschool programs. These were new concepts. We had some pushback from organized medicine where we were trying to leverage county health departments and utilize nurse practitioners."

This opposition became more determined, particularly among the medical establishment, she told me, and at one point Tennessee's federal funding for health programs was targeted. "Suddenly we had to go to Atlanta to keep the federal funding for Tennessee. I'd show up in the regional office and there'd be people from Tennessee, from the state dental society or the state medical association to oppose our proposals. I was stunned to see these people show up in these meetings. I remember being even teary in a presentation and just so stunned and shocked at the degree of opposition. I do remember feeling pretty naïve."

The big break came when the Tennessee Pediatric Society voiced its support of the initiative. "Dr. Hayes Mitchell of East Tennessee threw his personal weight behind what we were trying to do," she remembers. This was a welcome opening for the initiative, and the new emphasis was soon reflected in the Alexander administration's budget requests to the state legislature, eventually growing to $2.3 million annually.

The project had revealed that many babies were being born across Tennessee without a pediatrician available on the first day. The pediatricians group agreed with the HCI task force that in cases where a child was born with no pediatrician identified, the local hospital together with doctors and HCI staff would designate one.

Data on infant mortality was abundant by this time, and it bolstered the cause. "The statistic that got us focused was the infant mortality rate," Kondracke said. "I think we were forty-eighth in the country (among fifty states) in terms of infant mortality rate. We were near the rock bottom. If it weren't for Alabama and Mississippi, we would have been on the bottom, but we were definitely dragging the bottom in infant mortality and that's what got us focused. Then you think, how do you influence a statistic like that, so we set a goal of prenatal care in every county health department and made good use of nurse practitioners, and we set a goal of a medical home for every child born in Tennessee, and we had a partnership with the Tennessee Pediatrics Society to help make that possible. Mainly, that was driven by being sure every child's immunizations were up to date.

"The 'medical home' could be the county health department, and it could be a partnership with a local pediatrician. We made good use of the health departments in the ninety-five counties. Tennessee has a strong system of county health departments, beautifully staffed, so we made better use of that talent. Nurse practitioners were just coming into vogue, so they were a big part of the solution. From there we began to take a more holistic view of child health and started talking about the need for more and better daycare and the need for more afterschool effort."

THE HCI INITIATIVE WAS originally seen as a four-year project. Building on the first-year progress with establishing the "medical homes" regime—making prenatal care available for every pregnant woman—the following years focused on prevention of teen pregnancies and an infant follow-up program to ensure that all babies received developmental services and better coordination between agencies and the private medical communities.

Tennessee's emphasis on prenatal and neonatal health continued to be a priority within the state's Department of Public Health in the years after Alexander left office. The original program name, Healthy Children Initiative, was eventually dropped, but the programmatic emphasis did not wane as many states continued to struggle with socioeconomic factors that contributed to persistently high rates of infant mortality.

A formal assessment of these programs as early as 1985 concluded that the HCI programs were working as intended: "Children have been assigned 'medical homes,' their immunization rate is better, and the medical communities are pleased." Two decades later, during the administration of Governor Phil Bredesen, state Health Commissioner Kenneth S. Robinson gave this assessment in a 2006 letter to the state comptroller's office:

"Our State government's Healthy Children Initiative, dating back to the 1980s, expanded pregnancy testing and prenatal care throughout many local health departments, and subsequent federal legislation which allowed presumptive eligibility of Medicaid for pregnant women facilitated both the enrollment of women by health department staff into Medicaid, and also those women's entry into early, adequate prenatal care . . . . Tennessee is now even far ahead of the curve in having in the Department one of the most aggressive and comprehensive newborn screening programs of any state."

By 2017, Tennessee's infant mortality rate had progressed among the fifty states from forty-eighth to thirty-eighth.

CHAPTER 14

Chattanooga

From Dirtiest to All-American City

"You should be designing the city, not just letting it happen."
—J. Stroud Watson

ON AN OCTOBER EVENING in 1969, the CBS anchor Walter Cronkite declared, on national network television, that Chattanooga was now the "dirtiest city in America."

For civic leaders in Tennessee's fourth-largest city, where both the population and the manufacturing employment base were well into historic declines, this was a shocking new label—an epithet that would add fresh insult to old economic injury.

There was no denying that Chattanooga's air was badly polluted, that a walk through town would reward you with a sooty shirt or dress, not to mention insidious health effects. But Cronkite's words (based on a new report from the U.S. Department of Health, Education and Welfare), coming as it did on *CBS Evening News*, now threatened to quash even a civic booster's sunny spirits and pour cold water on the vision of a better future by way of new investor interest from outside the city.

This, without question, was the wrong kind of publicity. This was a civic nightmare.

BY THIS TIME, CHATTANOOGA'S deeper story had already been one of economic rise and fall, cycling over a long century of boom and near bust. The natural terrain of broad river, deep gorges, and towering mountains—all converging at the line that separates Tennessee from Georgia—had provided stunning scenic beauty, a temperate climate, and a most strategic location for both armies and industry over history.

Through the middle years of the twentieth century, with the coming of the Tennessee Valley Authority with its New Deal hydroelectric dams and cheap electricity, Chattanooga had risen as a thriving manufacturing center. Local leaders took pride in the city's growing dominance as the industrial "Dynamo of Dixie," owing to its enviable position at the shipping intersection of the Tennessee River, railroad lines, and national highways. Some of these very same assets—the scenic mountainous terrain, river, and the confluence of rail and highway access—also brought to Chattanooga the darker demons of urban development. The mountains formed a natural bowl that trapped the pollutants that rose from the smokestacks of steel foundries and textile mills. The environment rivaled even that of Pittsburgh.

On the worst days the sky was dark at noon. Photographs from the 1960s show the city's air sullen and sooty with smoke and smog. The rate of tuberculosis in Chattanooga was now three times the national average. One writer said corrosive emissions from industry along the river were so bad that ladies' nylon stockings would disintegrate. On some days Chattanoogans and their visitors walking the city streets could not even see the crest of Lookout Mountain for which the city was known.

Underneath all that came the waves of deindustrialization, racial turmoil, flight to the suburbs, and recession. Jobs vanished as manufacturing departed the city. Population growth slowed and then stopped; young adults finishing high school yearned to move away, and many did. In a 2008 Brookings Institution report on how Chattanooga eventually overcame these ills in its extraordinary rebound of the 1990s, the researchers David Eichenthal and Tracy Windeknecht summed up the dark downtime that preceded the city's re-birth to come: "By the 1980s Chattanooga was in both economic and population free-fall."

"Like many cities," they wrote, "Chattanooga was hit hard by deindustrialization. After reaching its peak in 1979, the country's manufacturing employment declined by more than 7 percent during the decade. The loss of manufacturing had an even greater effect on Chattanooga. Between 1980 and 1990, the number of Chattanoogans employed in manufacturing declined 28 percent, to 12,231, or about one in five workers. Fifty years earlier, more than one in three Chattanoogans worked in manufacturing . . . . As the number of manufacturing jobs declined, so did the number of city residents. After losing almost 10 percent of its population in the 1960s, Chattanooga lost another 10 percent during the 1980s, and for the first time in a century, Hamilton County's population declined as well. Downtown had—like many other U.S. downtowns—became a ghost town. Few families believed their college-bound children would ever return—there were no jobs and there seemed to be little future."

Chattanooga meanwhile became a divided city. Many of its wealthiest citizens retreated to their homes in the clouds—on Signal Mountain to the west of the town center, and on Lookout Mountain to the south side—and the blue-collar workers toiled in a disappearing manufacturing base in a polluted city below.

For some of Chattanooga's municipal, business, and philanthropic leaders, Cronkite's report about that pollution became a galvanizing wake-up call. They began to collaborate on a broad call to action that, in time, turned their southern city around.

ON THE DAY THAT John T. (Jack) Lupton met J. Stroud Watson, in 1981, they must have seemed an unlikely pair of future collaborators.

Lupton was the richest man in Chattanooga, heir to the vast Coca-Cola Bottling fortune. He was a philanthropist, board chairman of the family's Lyndhurst Foundation, clean-cut and handsome, patrician in his bearing, and a man of strong opinions. Lupton's father, Thomas Cartter Lupton, had endowed the foundation (later renamed "Lyndhurst" after the name of the family home in Chattanooga).

Watson, on the other hand, was a bearded professor of architecture, born in New York City. He was an early visionary in urban design, with his own strong opinions on how modern cities should work. In the 1970s he had helped to design the planned city of Milton-Keynes, near London. He was now lecturing across the U.S. and had recently been invited to join the School of Architecture faculty at the University of Tennessee, in Knoxville.

"The new dean, Roy Knight, said I should go down to Chattanooga and talk to Rick Montague," Watson recalls. "He was Jack Lupton's son-in-law and in his third year as head of the Lyndhurst Foundation. They were very much into what their foundation could do for Chattanooga."

By this time, Montague had served as chairman of the Moccasin Bend Task Force, a group of business, planning, and conservation leaders established by the Chattanooga and Hamilton County governments. Their task was to find the best use of six-hundred-plus acres on Moccasin Bend, a peninsula at the curve of the Tennessee River west of downtown. The group had quickly determined that the original scope was too small and should be expanded to include the entire twenty-two-mile river corridor surrounding the city. Under Montague's leadership, the task force concluded that their priority actually should be the opposite side of the river, where downtown Chattanooga lay. Also, in a move that set an important precedent and tone for Chattanooga's planning through the eighties and early nineties, they wanted to invite input from the public, and thousands of Chattanoogans responded. In 1985 when the Tennessee Riverpark Master Plan was unveiled, some 1,600 citizens came to see it.

WATSON RECALLED HIS INITIAL conversation with Montague, the foundation executive. Montague, he told me, expressed strong interest in seeing the city develop in such a way that young adults would want to return to Chattanooga after college. He asked Watson how that might happen.

"You should be designing the city, not just letting it happen," Watson replied. Soon after this, Montague arranged an introductory meeting with Lupton.

On his first visit to Lupton's office, Watson brought along with him his wife Cynthia and their daughter Bryony, then five years old. As they were taking their seats, Lupton's assistant came into the room and offered the child a cold drink.

ASSISTANT: "Dear, would you like a Coke?"
BRYONY: "Oh, no, thank you. I don't drink Coke. My father said it's bad for me."

Given the setting, this might have been a meeting stopper, but Watson remembers Lupton "just howled" laughing out loud at the girl's candid reply.

During this visit, Lupton asked questions of the architect and quickly warmed to Watson's ideas for more orderly and principled development in U.S. cities. In short order, Montague arranged a consulting contract, giving Watson a formal basis from which to engage other city leaders and design professionals in a new conversation about Chattanooga's future.

THE COLLABORATION THAT ENSUED between Watson, Lupton, and Montague would endure over the next decade. Even so, Watson encountered some local resistance among the city's architectural firms.

Early on, he advocated—successfully—for establishment in Chattanooga of a new entity called the Urban Design Studio. The purpose, he said, was to bring together professionals from different design disciplines to engage in the kind of collaboration and visioning that could yield bold new thinking for the city's benefit. The UDS that Watson advocated became a joint venture of the University of Tennessee and the Lyndhurst Foundation and would be the convener and facilitator for new discussions.

Chattanooga's architectural community did not see it the same way and protested creation of the new agency. At one point, several disgruntled architects wrote a letter to the University of Tennessee system president in Knoxville, Dr. Edward J. Boling, the top administrator over all five campuses across the state. In their letter, the opponents contended that Watson's stirring around their city was an inappropriate use of university resources. Boling turned the letter over to his executive vice president, Dr. Joe Johnson, and asked him to look into the grievance. Lupton, of course, was well known to Johnson as an important donor, especially for his gifts in support of UT-Chattanooga's main library. These local architects who complained were therefore up against a powerful patron.

"The university had supported the establishment of the Urban Design Studio," Johnson told me, "and, yes, some architects who worked in Chattanooga did complain about Stroud's activities there. I talked to them. We felt the design center, and Stroud in particular, were doing very important work that would lead to plenty of work for local architects. We continued to support Stroud's work in Chattanooga."

IN 1983, CITY LEADERS established Chattanooga Venture, a public-private entity that directed the planning for a series of six public meetings, in 1984, designed to engage citizens at large in a visioning process about the future. This culminated in *Vision 2000*, a report that articulated a sweeping set of forty goals for the city's future. Some of the goal statements were specific, some aspirational—all directed toward improving Chattanoogans' quality of life.

The Venture group then organized an implementation strategy of co-ordinated follow-up on the recommendations, aiming to facilitate progress toward the new civic goals. Individual leaders accepted assignments for particular initiatives. The action steps varied by subject, ranging from action on a proposed downtown aquarium, conversion of the Walnut Street Bridge into a pedestrian walkway, more affordable housing, and so forth. (Eight years later, Chattanooga's visioning process helped to inspire a similar city-wide initiative in Nashville called Nashville's Agenda. *See Chapter 21.*)

Alexander remembers a pivotal meeting in the governor's office in 1981, when two prominent Chattanoogans came to call. One of the visitors was Lupton. The other was Pat Brock, whose family had founded another of Chattanooga's best-known businesses, the Brock Candy Company. Both men had been important to Alexander's election in 1978 as influential leaders of the campaign finance effort. This visit occurred not long after the news had broken of the state's $20 million assistance package arising from the Memphis Jobs Conference.

"Jack and Pat came to me," Alexander recalled. "One was my biggest political supporter in Chattanooga, the other was my biggest financial supporter. I had no two bigger supporters in Chattanooga than Jack Lupton and

Pat Brock. When I ran for governor the second time, in 1978, I had to figure out how to raise the money. That was before the modern contribution limits. I determined I would ask ten people to give me $12,000 each. Jack Lupton was the first guy I asked, and he did it. Pat became important in my campaign. They were two guys to whom I politically owed a lot. And they said, 'Memphis got twenty million dollars. We want Chattanooga's money.'"

Alexander asked his visitors what Chattanooga would do with the money. The answer: "We think maybe an aquarium. It would cost $3 million to $5 million."

The governor then told them the Memphis story—how that city had taken a year and a half on a consensus-building effort, how it involved many citizens, and how they had identified important civic goals that both the city's leadership and the grassroots had embraced.

"I asked them, 'Why would you waste our money on just any old aquarium? Why don't you build the best aquarium that everybody on the East Coast would want to see, the biggest one between Miami and Baltimore?' I challenged them to go back and think about a bigger aquarium. They were very unhappy with the meeting, but they came back to me within a year and they'd identified three or four strategic goals for the Chattanooga area. They incorporated their ideas into Chattanooga Venture, the community-wide planning process, and came back soon with a proposal for several projects, including a much more ambitious $35 million aquarium, with Lupton and his foundation paying for most of it. This was an important part of Chattanooga re-launching itself based upon its natural assets such as the Tennessee River and scenic areas and becoming one of the country's most admired midsized cities. The goals supported by the Venture project had to do with preserving the Tennessee River gorge, another with the city's riverfront, one with the Hunter Museum, and the other was the aquarium. Lupton, very bluntly, told me that the aquarium they wanted would be a $35 million project now, and he would pay for most of it. The legislature approved my recommendation for state funding. So the state did the same thing in Chattanooga that it did in Memphis. Chattanooga just ran off with it. They had terrific leadership and broad support."

As it turned out, none of the state's appropriation to Chattanooga was used to pay for the new Tennessee Aquarium. Its project site was privately owned, meaning state funds could not be invested there. Instead, the state government's allocation to Chattanooga went to other new projects in the downtown area adjacent to the aquarium.

In December 1986, Lupton announced that he and the Lyndhurst Foundation would invest at least $20 million as seed money for development of the Tennessee Riverpark. This dollar amount would grow eventually to $45 million.

❖

TEN MONTHS EARLIER, ON the first February afternoon of 1986, a young developer named Jon Kinsey was sitting in the den of his Chattanooga home reading through a week's worth of newspapers. He had not seen the Monday newspaper until Friday because at this point in his career Kinsey was commuting weekly to his office in Hilton Head, South Carolina. The dailies were always waiting for him, in a stack in the den, when he returned home for the weekend.

On this Friday, when he turned to page eight of the *Chattanooga Times* of the previous Monday, his eyes stopped on a headline that contained a familiar name: "Jack Lupton Talks about a City and Its Destiny."

What followed on the page was a long transcription from a rare interview that the normally reclusive Lupton had given to *Times* reporter Bill Dedman. In this interview, the first Lupton had granted in twenty-one years, the philanthropist spoke with great candor about how Chattanooga had become a segregated city—culturally, as well as racially—and how that fact was helping nobody. He praised the Venture initiative, which his foundation had supported, as a breakthrough process that involved many local citizens, on a par with other forward-looking cities he had visited, including Charlotte, North Carolina, and St. Paul, Minnesota.

"The biggest problem that Chattanooga has ever had," he told the reporter, "they've all buttoned it up at night and went home to their little bitty enclaves and nobody communicated with anybody—including him (he points at his father's photograph) and his cohorts. They wanted to keep this place a secret. They didn't want anybody knowing about what a nice little deal they had here. Well, they were full of s—, as far as I'm concerned. And I told him so, in just those words, a good while ago. And that, I think, is what Venture has begun to overcome. St. Paul did it another way. Charlotte did it another way. Strictly business. They got all the business guys together and they went out and did it. 'Like it or not, fellow.' 'Sorry about you down there.' It hasn't been done with this much representation in any city . . . . I think you don't have to have much more than that good-sized nucleus of two or three thousand people that showed up at Venture that really have Chattanooga on their heart to really make a community hum and move forward."

Lupton said his foundation, which was worth around $100 million at the time, would be active in the coming process. The need, however, was for more forward-looking leadership, as well as investments by multiple partners.

DEDMAN: "You said you wanted to raise twenty million dollars, then thirty, then fifty million. How much will Lyndhurst's commitment be?"

LUPTON: "I'm a little hesitant to say to you today, because of ignorance, exactly what we're going to need over the next five years. Ten million may leverage itself enough for us . . . with the financial community coming up with reduced interest loans. This is what happened in St. Paul. The McKnight Foundation gave ten million dollars, and they have leveraged that way up through the skies. So I don't think it's a matter of how much money we get. It's a matter of doing a good job with the first amount."

DEDMAN: "Has the Lyndhurst board met to decide how much it will give?"

LUPTON: "I would be speaking out of school if I said now exactly what Lyndhurst is going to do in the way of dollars. We should have an announcement before too long."

It was that remark that caught Kinsey's eye. In short order he and his partner Jeff Leonard moved their office to Chattanooga.

KINSEY WAS A LIFELONG Democrat. He had grown up in Chattanooga, and at sixteen he found a job in the 1972 Ed Muskie presidential campaign.

"I didn't even know him," Kinsey said of Lupton. "I wouldn't meet him for another four years. But when Jack Lupton said 'I'm going to start doing this' it really changed what people felt could happen in our city. I'd never met him, but because of who he was and him making that statement, we built a $15 million apartment complex a year later, and we ended up moving our company to Chattanooga.

"He is, far and away, the most important person who made a difference in our city. I would not have run for mayor without him. We are who we are because of him. He spent ten years, every day, trying to make Chattanooga a better place. Certainly his money was important, but his leadership and his commitment just inspired so many. He loved this city and was willing to put it all in to make a difference."

Kinsey was mayor from 1997 to 2001. Even then, the *Vision 2000* project was an important catalyst for action. "It's still relevant today. It's called 'the Chattanooga way.' What that instilled in our community was that we need to talk together about what our future can be and decide what we want to do. It's all process. The idea is that you're getting people involved in what our future is going to be. You don't have people at the top deciding—you've got a lot of people voicing their opinions and able to talk about it."

On Kinsey's watch, the city tripled the size of its trade center, built a conference center, and acquired property where the Enterprise South industrial campus was developed (now the location of Volkswagen and Amazon.com operations), plus it put a focus on neighborhoods.

In a nod that crossed the aisle, this Democrat praised two Republican leaders in particular: Claude Ramsey, who was mayor of Hamilton County through this period, and Bob Corker, who followed Kinsey as the city mayor.

"Claude and I served together. We were the best example of a Republican and Democrat working together. We never let either one of us be surprised. I supported him when he ran for tax assessor and for county mayor, over Democrats. We bought the property where Enterprise South was developed. That's where Volkswagen is and Amazon is now. The city had been trying to buy that property for thirty years. We've now got 20,000 jobs out there. There were a lot of local companies that wanted to take fifty acres or thirty acres, smaller parcels that meant we wouldn't have the large parcel to take to prospects. Claude was adamant about keeping it intact and not selling it off, that there would be somebody we could get, and of course we did get Volkswagen."

BOB CORKER WAS TWENTY-SIX years old when he established his own construction business, in 1978, with $8,000 in personal savings. He had accumulated this sum working as a construction superintendent for a company that built shopping centers. In his new venture, the work mainly involved small projects until he was selected by Krystal Co. to build the company's first drive-through customer service windows. As his business grew, he met civic leaders around the city, including Rick Montague, who encouraged Corker to meet Jim Rouse, the Maryland developer who was becoming famous for innovations in retail and "lifestyle" developments. This led to work with Rouse's nonprofit, The Enterprise Foundation, which was involved with low-income housing projects around the U.S.

"I ended up being involved in one of the sixteen goals that Venture had, which was to provide the opportunity for all Chattanoogans have decent housing," he said. "We ended up creating a nonprofit called Chattanooga Neighborhood Enterprises, which, over time, ended up affecting 10,000 families." Corker became the founding chairman of CNE. "That's actually how I got to know Jack Lupton, because the Lyndhurst Foundation was a major donor."

In 1994, Corker ran for the U.S. Senate, losing in the Republican primary to Bill Frist, a Nashville heart-and-lung transplant surgeon. It was the first political campaign for them both. One observer said Frist seemed to learn the ropes more quickly, spending more of his money in the primary than Corker spent of his.

The following year Corker joined the Sundquist administration as the new governor's commissioner over the Tennessee Department of Finance and Administration. This placed him in the prominent role of top budget chief for state government, reporting to the new governor. During his tenure in that post, among other assignments he helped broker the 1995 deal to secure the NFL's Houston Oilers' relocation to Nashville and the completion of the Bicentennial Capitol Mall in time for the 1996 celebration of statehood.

That much is known. What is less well known is that Corker, who by this time had many Republican friends, actually credits Sundquist's predecessor, the West Tennessee Democrat McWherter, with getting him first interested in public service.

"My evolution into the public arena was really a result of Governor McWherter," Corker told me. "When he was running for governor to succeed Lamar (in 1986) he came to Chattanooga and saw what I was working on relative to housing, setting up Chattanooga Neighborhood Enterprise. I wasn't thinking about the public arena. I was a business guy who loved business, but I wanted to make a difference in the world and was spending a huge amount of time as the founding chairman of CNE. McWherter came to town and was running for governor and he saw what I was doing, so after being elected he asked me to serve on a task force on the state level to deal with low-income housing." Soon after this, McWherter appointed Corker to the board of the Tennessee Housing Development Agency.

"That was my first experience, if you will, in public policy—a Democratic governor who had seen what I was doing in Chattanooga. That was my introduction to the fact that in the public arena you can create policies that in some ways surpass, if done right, your ability to deal with things in the private sector. So, we were friends when I was commissioner of finance when he was leaving office and Sundquist was coming in. Whenever I was in West Tennessee in Dresden, I would often stop in and say hello to him. We [the Sundquist administration] were having to do some pretty controversial things because of a budget gap, and on Saturday mornings I would call McWherter and say, 'Hey, Governor, this is what I'm thinking about doing with the prison system, or this is what I'm thinking about doing with this or that.' I knew that a lot of important people in the General Assembly—remember, it was dominantly Democrat—would go by and visit McWherter on Saturdays at his farm or lake house, and he would say to them, 'You know, I talked to old Bob Corker this week and he's thinking about doing this. I think it's a pretty good idea.' He was such a beloved figure by them for his counsel, and it was the West Tennessee Democrats who still ran the state. You can't imagine how helpful that was with Speaker Naifeh and Lieutenant Governor Wilder and others."

IN 2001, CORKER WAS elected mayor of Chattanooga, succeeding Kinsey. On Corker's watch, Chattanooga continued the local collaborations for civic progress, including the introduction of high-speed internet service provided by the local Electric Power Board (EPB). The EPB initiative placed Corker at odds with the state's telecommunications giant BellSouth, which opposed it, but Corker prevailed. (Chattanooga, now called Gig City, and Singapore are the two cities in the world that have done the best job implementing ultra-high-speed internet service.) By this time, many of the *Vision*-inspired developments were well underway, including the Tennessee Aquarium and other new riverfront amenities. Corker worked with his former Sundquist cabinet colleague, the state transportation commissioner Bruce Saltsman, on rerouting a state highway that made possible the "21st Century Waterfront." Today, this stretch of the river features a hundred-mile bikeway, a new bridge, public art, rowing competitions, and an important Ironman event.

"Chattanooga is, by every standard, one of the best outdoor communities," Corker told me. "It transformed our community, focusing on the outdoors in that way. What it has done is it has caused people to want to live there and to visit there and be there. What we saw in the 2003 timeframe was how we were having such difficulties retaining young people in our community. We paid to have them educated, and they would leave our community and head for Nashville or some other place. What we've found is that migration has reversed itself, and our young people want to stay and live there. It's become a hip place to be."

"What we did, in football analogy, was we woke up every day and threw deep on every play. We thought, look, we got four years here to make as much difference as we possibly can in our community and every day it was drop back and throw deep."

IN A 2015 ASSESSMENT for the Brookings Institution, Bruce Katz pointed to the EPB project as "the catalyst of the city's economic revival"—drawing investors and tech entrepreneurs—through the use of local debt financing and application of federal dollars. He also highlighted the collaborative spirit of diverse players and institutions as other keys to the city's modern progress.

"By smartly deploying $228 million in local revenue bonds and $111.6 million in funding from the Department of Energy's Smart Grid Investment, EPB has built one of the world's most extensive municipal high-speed internet networks, installing more than 9,000 miles of fiber throughout 600 square miles across two states. . . .

"Chattanooga's innovation district is the product of genuine, enthusiastic collaboration—not often seen in bigger cities—between public, private, and civic institutions and leaders," Katz wrote. "These players include the city and county governments, EPB, the Lyndhurst and Benwood Foundations, the University of Tennessee at Chattanooga, the Enterprise Center and an entrepreneurial mix of investors like The Lamp Post Group, start-ups like Bellhops, incubators like CO.LAB, and real estate developers like River City Company, DEW Properties, and Fidelity Trust Company. I was continuously struck by the extent to which this diverse set of players—with very different experiences and world views—are truly 'collaborating to compete' and grow something truly unique to their city."

CHAPTER 15

The Fight for Better Schools

"I've run for governor three times, and the school reform fight was
harder than all of them put together."
— Governor Lamar Alexander, Republican

"Lamar was the finest politician I ever met. He was smart enough to
know it's OK to lose every now and then."
— Representative Steve Cobb, Democrat

IN APRIL 1983, a blue-ribbon commission appointed by President Reagan's
secretary of education rocked the U.S. education establishment with a report
entitled *A Nation at Risk.*

"If an unfriendly foreign power had attempted to impose on America the
mediocre educational performance that exists today," the report declared,
"we might well have viewed it as an act of war. As it stands, we have allowed
this to happen to ourselves."

This trouble in the nation's schools had been brewing for some time. By
the middle 1970s, the nation's elementary and secondary schools were facing
a collision of demographic trends and substandard performance. Together,
they portended a dark future. Student outcomes were lagging, especially
when compared to other countries with which the United States fancied itself a global competitor. In cities across America, taxpayers were uniformly
defeating local referenda for improved public funding for their schools.

The demographics of the teaching profession were also deteriorating in
alarming ways. The nation's public school faculty was aging. Many of the
most experienced teachers were leaving the classroom, either through retirement or to take better-paying jobs outside their profession. Retiring teachers were not being replaced by a younger generation of new educators from
the colleges of education, as had been the norm over the preceding century.
Young women finishing college now had more abundant career opportunities than their predecessors. Too few college graduates were choosing careers
in the classroom.

By 1980, the median age of all U.S. primary and secondary school teachers was thirty-six years old. By 2000, that number would climb to forty-three. Over the same time period, faculty members aged forty and older increased from 40 percent of all teachers in 1980 to 60 percent twenty years later. The need to draw more new teachers into the profession was also being driven by growth in the number of primary and secondary students.

All of this contributed to policy concerns that a true shortage of qualified teachers was coming soon. There was also no consensus on what to do about it.

Government budgets were tight, and tradition bound. Teacher associations had traditionally pressed for smaller class sizes and higher salaries, both to reward current faculty for long service and to better incentivize the young college graduate to consider teaching as his or her life's work. Historically, teacher compensation was never based on measurable student progress or observable good teaching. Instead, local legislative bodies provided lump sums to school administrators who paid teachers using rigid tables that measured only numbers of degrees and years of service, a form of compensation that held firm as the status quo through the twentieth century. More radical policymakers were now concluding that educators, parents, children—and ultimately the republic—were reaping a whirlwind of mediocrity.

IN THE SUMMER OF 1969, when Lamar Alexander was twenty-nine years old and a young staffer in the Nixon White House, he met Chester E. "Checker" Finn Jr., then twenty-four. They were two among twenty or so bright twenty-somethings whom older hands in the West Wing called the president's "Kiddie Corps."

They had the credentials to be in this elite group, and they worked for luminaries of the new administration's top echelon. Finn, from central Ohio, a recent Harvard doctoral student in educational policy, had arrived at the White House with Harvard professor Daniel Patrick Moynihan, the president's counselor for urban affairs. Alexander, a lawyer from East Tennessee, was a protégé of Tennessee Senator Howard H. Baker Jr. He had left Baker's staff in the spring of 1968 to become national director of planning for Citizens for Nixon-Agnew. Working in the campaign at the Willard Hotel, two blocks from the White House, Alexander met Bud Wilkinson, the famed Oklahoma football coach. After Nixon won, Wilkinson recommended Alexander to another Oklahoman, Bryce Harlow, who was Nixon's first staff appointee. Alexander became deputy to Harlow, who now headed the new president's congressional relations team. The young Tennessean worked at a desk in Harlow's office on the first floor of the White House West Wing. Alexander would later say of this early on-the-job training: "It was there,

watching how Mr. Harlow did things—and with Senator Baker before that—
that I earned my 'Ph.D.' in politics and government."

On Moynihan's team, Finn specialized in desegregation issues. His infrequent encounters with Alexander during this period chiefly related to coordination on the hot-button issue of forced school busing, which had roiled
school districts in the South and East—Finn advising Moynihan, Alexander
working with Republicans in Congress. At this point the two young staffers
had few opportunities to interact. Alexander left Harlow's team in the summer of 1970, returning to Tennessee to manage Winfield Dunn's campaign
for governor. Finn stayed until 1973; when Nixon nominated Moynihan to
be U.S. ambassador to India, Finn became Moynihan's counselor on the embassy staff in New Delhi.

A dozen years later, in Nashville, Alexander and Finn would meet again.
But first, Alexander would run for governor two times, losing in 1974, then
winning his second race in 1978.

IN NOVEMBER 1978, FOUR progressive young governors were elected across
the South: Democrats Bill Clinton of Arkansas, Richard Riley of South Carolina, and Bob Graham of Florida, as well as Alexander in Tennessee. These
four, together with two other southern governors already in office—Jim
Hunt in North Carolina and William Winter in Mississippi—began discussing how low educational achievement and teacher shortages were depressing
economic growth in their states.

These conversations initially occurred in committee sessions of the
National Governors Association and the Southern Governors Association
and also at meetings of the Southern Regional Education Board. Alexander
had quickly become active in each of these organizations (and eventually
would serve as chairman of all three). Following Reagan's election in November 1980, the NGA chairman at that time, Governor George Busbee of
Georgia, a Democrat, also asked Alexander to serve as the governors' chief
liaison with the new Reagan administration.

These six governors—Alexander, Clinton, Hunt, Riley, Winter, and
Graham—came from different personal histories and political circumstances.
Yet they were now pondering similar realities about schools and schooling in
their respective states, and all that they saw suggested grave implications for
economic growth. While the teacher shortage was unquestionably a national
issue in its scope and depth, the implications were especially acute across the
South. For a host of historical reasons, several states in this defeated region
still languished chronically at the bottom of important national rankings for
family incomes, graduation rates, state government spending, and teacher pay.

The first comprehensive wake-up call to state-level policymakers actually came in the summer of 1981, two years before the *Nation at Risk* report, in a document from the SREB entitled *The Need for Quality: A Report to the Southern Regional Education Board by its Task Force on Higher Education and the Schools.* SREB, based in Atlanta, had been established in 1948 as a nonpartisan nonprofit compact of seventeen member states. Its 1981 report was informally called the "MacKay Report," for the task force chairman, State Senator Kenneth H. MacKay Jr., a lawyer from Ocala, Florida.

MacKay's seventeen-member task force declared that any educational progress that the South had achieved over the preceding generation was good but not good enough—and "should not mask the serious questions about quality that confront us today."

"We reject the notion that the myriad ills of society—such as changes in family life and the distracting effects of television—make it impossible to put education's house in order," the report stated in its preamble. "Difficult and elusive questions of educational quality can and must be addressed in earnest by a strong partnership of higher education and the schools."

The task force went on to enumerate important policy areas that required immediate attention, including issues of teacher training and retention. This was significant at the time because it was a new, assertive manifesto from political as well as educational leaders, notably including governors across the region. Governor Graham was chairman of the SREB at the time.

EDUCATION OUTLAYS AT THIS time in Tennessee constituted roughly half of all state government spending. With no state income tax, outlays for schools came from state sales taxes as well as local sales and property taxes. So much dependence on local taxes created disparities in local support for K–12 education from one county to the next. All this combined to keep state support for education prominent in any discussions of school policy and government finance.

In 1980, the second year of his new administration, Alexander had mounted an education initiative that emphasized basic educational skills and computer literacy for all eighth graders. To this new campaign, which was formulated by the state Department of Education, Alexander gave the slogan "Basic Skills First, Computer Skills Next." He flew to Palo Alto, California, that summer to see what he could learn about computers from Steve Jobs, the co-founder of Apple Computer. These were the very early days in the development of personal computing, even before the Apple Macintosh machine was invented. Out of this meeting came an agreement that the state of Tennessee would buy enough new Apple computers for every middle-school student to have access to one.

The following February, at Alexander's invitation, Steve Jobs spoke to an

NGA committee meeting in Washington, D.C., about the coming relevance of computer technology to the nation's schools. The young inventor was obviously brilliant and certainly accomplished as a renegade innovator in the new field of microcomputers. But in this particular committee setting in the nation's capital, amid governors and their senior staffs, he also came across as politically naïve. At one point following his prepared remarks, Congressman Tim Wirth of Colorado, a faithful Democrat, asked Jobs a series of questions. Around the conference table, placed in front of each participant, were the customary name cards showing title and name. As Jobs listened to Wirth's questions, he misinterpreted the "Rep. Tim Wirth" printed on the congressman's card. Respectfully, Jobs addressed his answers to "Republican Wirth . . . " at least two times, until the Democratic congressman could not contain his laughter any longer. He gave Jobs a good-natured correction.

This early focus on computer proficiency for every middle-school student put Tennessee out in front among most states. But Alexander later said, "I made one big mistake. I forgot about teacher training. The students became comfortable pretty quickly with computers but the teachers weren't, and we didn't take enough time or spend enough money to make teachers comfortable and proficient with these new devices."

IN 1981, WITH REAGAN in his first year as president, the new U.S. Department of Education was under fire from Republicans in Congress, who were calling for its abolition. The department had been created two years earlier during the Carter administration. To head this controversial department, Reagan appointed Terrel H. Bell, who had served as the nation's commissioner of education during the Nixon and Ford administrations.

Originally, Bell had proposed that Reagan name a new presidential commission to recommend reform of the nation's schools. Reagan did not approve a commission, but authorized Bell to establish his own department-level study group, which he called the National Commission on Excellence in Education. It was an eighteen-member group empanelled by Bell in 1981, during his first year as secretary. Its work would consume nearly two years, and this was the origin of what became the *Nation at Risk* manifesto.

When Bell's commission published *A Nation at Risk*, in April 1983, it was strongly worded and added new fuel to the work of the education reform governors, especially in the South, who now had the president for a partner. The language was insistent and painted the nation's educational dilemma as an alarming issue threatening America's position in the world.

"Our Nation is at risk," it began. "Our once unchallenged preeminence in commerce, industry, science, and technological innovation is being overtaken by competitors throughout the world. This report is concerned with only one of the many causes and dimensions of the problem, but it is the one that undergirds American prosperity, security, and civility . . . We report to the American people that while we can take justifiable pride in what our schools and colleges have historically accomplished and contributed to the United States and the well-being of its people, the educational foundations of our society are presently being eroded by a rising tide of mediocrity that threatens our very future as a Nation and a people. What was unimaginable a generation ago has begun to occur—others are matching and surpassing our educational attainments."

The report laid out five specific policy recommendations: "new basics" (including four years of English, three years of math, science, and social studies, and a half-year of computer science in high school); measurable progress standards; a longer school year; better preparation of teachers; and more accountability.

Despite initially resisting Bell's call for a presidential commission, Reagan now took the new message on the road for eleven weeks.

IN THE FALL OF 1981, well in advance of his 1982 re-election campaign, Alexander was planning a second term and building a policy program that would make the most of another four years in the governor's office. In his inaugural address in 1979 he had set as his top goal raising family incomes, and he sought to do this by recruiting new jobs, notably the Nissan manufacturing plant. However, he soon reached these three conclusions:

1. "Most new jobs are grown at home, not recruited."
2. "Growing and holding jobs today requires higher skills than many Tennesseans have."
3. "Better schools mean better jobs."

Education was heavily on his mind, therefore, and the central strategy question was how to fashion a policy package emphasizing progress and performance that the legislature could embrace. He remembers McWherter and Wilder suggesting, during one of their Wednesday morning Leadership Meetings, that the time seemed right to mount a broader initiative for K–12 school improvement.

"They might have figured I was going to be re-elected," Alexander told me, "but education was important to both of them. They said, 'We haven't had a big education push in a long time.' I said, 'Then why don't we have one.' So, we agreed to jointly appoint members of a commission to make recommendations to us by November of 1982, after the election."

BY THIS TIME, IN what both Alexander and Checker Finn insist was a pure coincidence, Finn moved to Nashville to join the faculty at Vanderbilt University's Peabody College, a leading U.S. school of education. His appointment as a professor afforded him time to continue his research and writing. Alexander soon invited Finn to his office. The two renewed their friendship that had begun years earlier in the White House, and the new Peabody professor became an unofficial advisor to Tennessee's governor. Through memoranda and meeting discussions, Finn raised policy ideas that were unconventional at the time, including school choice for parents and performance pay for educators.

Over the following year, while the joint study committee was doing its work downstairs at the Legislative Plaza, Finn suggested to Alexander what became the most controversial component of all: a proposal for performance-based pay to help the state and local school districts attract and retain the best teachers. At this time, as Alexander was fond of repeating, "Not one state pays one teacher one penny more for teaching well."

OVER THE NEXT TWELVE months, planning for education reform and talk of new funding accelerated at Tennessee's State Capitol.

Alexander's daily schedules from this period show at least one meeting or phone call each day on some aspect of educational improvement: meetings with the head of the Department of Education, Commissioner Robert McElrath, and his staff; phone calls with Finn; updates on education statistics from the Tennessee State Planning Office and the state's Higher Education Commission; additional phone calls with other reform governors and NGA staff in Washington, D.C.

Alexander also recalls meeting with the deans of all the Tennessee teacher colleges. Many of these deans, he remembers, were negative toward the idea of providing differential pay to teachers, believing the payment of financial bonuses to teachers based on performance evaluations would be damaging to professional relationships in a school setting, susceptible to favoritism, and probably a nightmare to administer in a data-based way. Alexander became exasperated by the deans' refusal to support or even help devise a plan to pay teachers more for outstanding performance.

"This is really ridiculous," he would say. "IBM pays teachers more for teaching well. University professors are paid more for teaching well. But they (the deans) say they can't figure out how to do the same for high school teachers. If they won't do it, how do they expect those of us who are not professional educators to figure it out?"

So, in the fall of 1981, Alexander, McWherter, and Wilder jointly established a working group to undertake a "Comprehensive Education Study," and this new CES panel met through the summer and into the fall of 1982. The group brought together advocates for many education constituencies, ranging from leaders of the legislature's education committees to the Tennessee Education Association, the state affiliate of the National Education Association, the nation's largest teacher union.

The chairman of the task force was State Senator Anna Belle Clement O'Brien, the Democrat who chaired the state Senate Education Committee. She was the sister of former Democratic governor Frank Clement and the aunt of Bob Clement, who had been a candidate in the Democratic primary for governor in 1978, the year Alexander was elected. O'Brien's committee worked through the fall of 1982. On November 3, Alexander was re-elected to a second term, defeating Knoxville Mayor Randy Tyree.

Four weeks later, the CES task force delivered its final recommendations. It was a ten-point package including these elements:

- Performance-based pay for teachers, which the document called the Master Teacher Program. The joint committee recommended that the state find a way to reward outstanding teaching.
- A comparable bonus system for principals.
- A new program of endowed faculty Chairs of Excellence that was favored by Representative John Bragg, the Murfreesboro Democrat who chaired the House Finance, Ways and Means Committee.
- Full funding for the state's higher education funding formula.
- An array of new "Governor's Schools" for outstanding high school students, modeled on a similar program in North Carolina.
- Reorganization of the State Board of Education, a reform promoted by Wilder.

"I wanted everybody to have a stake in the total package," Alexander told me. "It wasn't *my* ten-point plan. It was from the task force. The Master Teacher Program had come from Checker Finn, but it was now recommended by the Comprehensive Education Study, which included Cavit Cheshier (the TEA staff director). What I tried to do was get most of the task force members' ideas in there so everybody had a share of it."

Alexander's plan, following his re-election, was to work through November and December fine-tuning the education reform package—the O'Brien committee report would be the foundation of the new education policy and funding package—and then to propose it formally to the new 93rd General Assembly when the legislature convened for business in mid-January.

Tennessee's legislature had strong Democrat majorities in both the Senate and House, and the TEA was the most powerful lobbying group working there. Alexander recalls a private meeting of southern governors, in the fall of 1982, when Texas governor Bill Clement, a Republican, asked:

"When do you suppose one of us is going to be brave enough to really take on the teachers union?" Alexander soon answered that question.

While he had taken care to include the TEA in the CES process, the spirit of collaboration and consensus that permeated that process in 1982 soon evaporated after the report was made public. While most elements of the ten-point Better Schools Program were relatively noncontroversial, the Master Teacher proposition drew swift reaction from leaders of the TEA and the NEA as well.

"When I actually recommended it in January," Alexander remembers, "all hell broke loose."

THE "MASTER TEACHER" COMPONENT was touted as an enhancement to the traditional framework of across-the-board raises for all Tennessee teachers, and it would also be voluntary. To begin, the state would pay every one of its forty-three thousand teachers $1,000 more each year so long as the teacher passed the National Teacher Exam. (Almost all did.)

Then, any tenured teacher could volunteer to become a Master Teacher earning as much as $7,000 more per year (including the $1,000 for passing the national exam). This could mean as much as a 70 percent increase in the state share of an individual teacher's pay. Master Teacher credentials could be renewed every five years.

The proposal did not affect teacher tenure. Local governments did not have to contribute, thereby reducing the local disparities in teacher pay. And, as teachers eventually discovered, the higher pay levels would have a dramatic effect on a Master Teacher's retirement pay.

To evaluate teachers under this new regime, Alexander proposed that a new council of teachers devise a process based upon a number of factors including classroom observation, student opinion, principal's opinion, a teacher's own portfolio, and student achievement. And to ensure fairness, teachers would be evaluated not by one peer teacher or principal, but by a panel of three teachers selected from outside the teacher's own school district.

This pay plan was, of course, a radical departure from the traditional pay structure for public school teachers, and immediately it became controversial within the state's education establishment. For many decades, the standard compensation system had calculated teacher pay based on objective qualifications (degrees attained) plus experience (years of service) without any reference to student achievement or progress year over year. Adding a new element of "teacher effectiveness" was therefore seen by some teachers (and especially their TEA officers) as highly disruptive.

ALEXANDER LAID OUT THE full ten-point Better Schools Program in his televised State of the State Address on January 29, 1983. It was a thirty-minute, televised speech, but a dozen words of it became a rallying message for the fight to come.

"Not one state," he repeated, "pays one teacher one penny more for teaching well." The governor wanted Tennessee to become the first, but he told the legislature that his colleague, Florida governor Bob Graham, a Democrat, was proposing a similar program to reward outstanding teaching in his state.

Anchoring his presentation, Alexander stressed his recommendation that base pay for all teachers would be raised. That and the other program improvements would require new revenue, for which he proposed an increase in the state's sales tax rate. But immediately the Master Teacher component became the flashpoint.

Leaders of the TEA seized on it. Cheshier criticized the lack of detail, particularly in the standards and evaluation processes that were to be used. Such details had not been developed, in fact, but were to be established as soon as possible after the broader program was authorized by the legislature. Gene Bryant, a TEA staff member and the editor of *Tennessee Teacher*, the association's member newsletter, told me his leaders had also been unaware of Finn's role in formulating the BSP and were troubled by it. "We were familiar with him as someone who wrote about education policy. We didn't realize that he was then in Nashville, working at Peabody. We knew him as a character who had no teaching experience whatever."

On close examination of the proposed legislation, TEA's staff attorneys reported to the association's board of directors, "This thing is full of poison pills." The TEA board and staff, led by Cheshier and chief lobbyist Betty Anderson, were determined that the Master Teacher component would not become law. But it was clear that any hope for increased salaries for teachers was also weighing in the balance.

"It was extremely complicated, and the weight of the complications caused serious problems," Cheshier told me in our 2016 interview. "We were not opposed to evaluations. We didn't want to stop the momentum. We were too desperate for increased salaries for teachers. Jim Henry (the House Republican leader) told me, 'Cavit, we can't pass the sales tax increase without the TEA's help.' We knew that sales tax was critical."

As the TEA pushback intensified, Alexander pledged publicly a "battle royal" with the union, in the cause of better schools. (This comment, in the retelling by union leaders and their legislative friends, grew harsher as the session moved forward. It became a promise of "bloody battle with the TEA," one TEA staffer said. The House majority leader, Representative Tommy Burnett, a TEA ally, went so far in one public statement as to characterize Alexander's comment as threatening a "blood bath.")

Faced with opposition from taxpayers to high taxes and opposition from the teachers union to the Master Teacher concept, Alexander said, "I'm spending all my time trying to take money from people who don't want to give it to people who don't want to take it."

Bryant remembers: "Some of the (legislative) members we'd supported had trouble dealing with the stress of the situation," Bryant told me. "McWherter was more capable of dealing with it than others were. He was wanting to work toward a compromise. He knew how to take political pressure, and seek relief when he needed to, but he knew how to stand firm. He was just a more skillful politician than others. Very skilled."

IN MARCH 1983, AFTER many long months of negotiation, the legislature's standing committees decided not to approve the reform package in the current session. It was clear the TEA leaders had been active with their grassroots opposition, asking teachers who lived and voted in key legislative districts statewide to put pressure on their local representatives. The Senate Education Committee, chaired by Senator O'Brien, voted 5–4 to postpone any action on Alexander's proposals until the General Assembly's 1984 session.

At that point—in order to keep the reform package alive—together with the hope it offered for new revenue for any across-the-board raise for teachers—McWherter and Wilder agreed to name a new special joint committee to consider the governor's proposals more deeply over the summer and fall.

Normally, such a summer study committee was the death sentence for a controversial bill; typically an out-of-favor proposal would be sent to such a fate, never to be heard about again. But in this case, the new committee that the speakers appointed, in close coordination with the administration, actually gave new hope to the Better Schools Program. Many of its members were already sponsors of the program in their respective chambers, and the new chairman appointed by the speakers was Senator O'Brien.

But the defeat stung Alexander deeply, and he quickly decided on two courses of action. The first would have been a dramatic step, without precedent in Tennessee: he actually considered resigning his office, and running for re-election—exclusively on a "Better Schools" platform. This would be the equivalent of a British-style vote of confidence in the governor, now serving his second term. But the state's attorney general Bill Leech quickly nixed this idea, telling Alexander the state's constitution allowed only two consecutive terms.

"I really wished I could have done that," he said. "My idea was that Lieutenant Governor John Wilder would serve as interim governor, and I would run in a special election in November 1984 and put the issues straight to the people. I wanted to take the battle away from the legislative chambers where the lobbyists for the teachers union were fighting my reforms tooth and nail. I called Attorney General Bill Leech in, and told him I wanted to resign and take it across the state and put the issue to the people and get support that way. I think he saw I was serious, so he was serious."

> LEECH: "No, Governor, you can't do that. You've already been elected twice, and that would be a third term."
> ALEXANDER: "Are you sure about it?"
> LEECH: "I am."

IMMEDIATELY ALEXANDER BEGAN TO assemble a statewide program of public awareness. It would draw on his experiences of the Community Days of his re-election campaign of the year before and would take the Better Schools campaign more broadly public, involving a statewide array of business and community leaders.

For this initiative, Alexander recruited a phalanx of volunteers from Tennessee's business leadership who became advocates for education reform. This new group was called "Tennesseans for Better Schools," and a surprising pair of co-chairs were announced: the governor's mother, Flo Alexander, who had been a kindergarten teacher in Maryville, Tennessee, together with the Nashville attorney Frank G. Clement Jr., son of the former governor and nephew of Senator O'Brien.

Fred Dettwiller, owner of DET Distributing Company in Nashville, one of Tennessee's biggest beer distributors, agreed to lead the fundraising. Other prominent leaders ranged from Jim Haslam in Knoxville to Charles Smith, chancellor of the University of Tennessee at Martin, the college Mc-Wherter had once attended. (Four years later, in 1987, Smith would become Governor McWherter's commissioner of education.) Staffing this effort were Debi Taylor Tate and Bob Weaver.

To finance this broad effort outside the government, Alexander tapped into private sources of money statewide. These included members of the Watauga group, a powerful behind-the-scenes committee of business leaders in Nashville who supported initiatives they believed would help the city. Among them were business leaders Nelson Andrews, Bronson Ingram, Bill Weaver, and Pat Wilson. In Chattanooga, a similar group was assembled with Jack Lupton, Pat Brock, Burton Frierson, Scott Probasco, and representatives of Lupton's Lyndhurst Foundation. Waymon Hickman, the Columbia banker, was another prominent participant in the finance effort.

Their contributions made possible, among other things, new public opinion surveys by the nationally respected pollsters Peter Hart, who normally polled for Democratic campaigns, and the Republican pollster Bob Teeter. This bipartisan duo proceeded to ask Tennesseans their views on the idea of rewarding outstanding teaching with merit-based pay, and the responses showed strong support for the concept and became persuasive with legislators. Another component was a grassroots petition effort. Alexander himself presented the polling results to Senator Carl Moore of Bristol, a Democrat and swing vote on the Education Committee, together with a petition signed by fifteen thousand citizens in Moore's district in support of the Better Schools plan.

ON PRESIDENT REAGAN'S eleven-week tour that year, calling attention to the *Nation at Risk* recommendations, one of his stops was at Farragut High School in west Knoxville. The president made a point to say that Alexander's proposal to create a Master Teacher Program was a substantive state response to his national call to action.

Speaker McWherter, the influential Democratic leader, was one of the Tennessee legislators who attended Reagan's visit that day. The speaker pronounced the idea of paying more for better performance "the American way" and his statement offered hope for Alexander's program in the next legislative session.

Through the summer of 1983, Alexander took his own "Better Schools mean Better Jobs" show on the road outside Tennessee, hoping to spread and dilute the NEA's resources among multiple state-based fights over teacher pay across the U.S. This effort took him literally from coast to coast, north to south. He spoke to audiences of policymakers from Virginia and the Carolinas to California, and from Michigan to Arizona. Following a ten-day family trip through the Grand Canyon, he met the leaders of the Utah legislature at a breakfast at the Utah executive residence, hosted by Governor Scott M. Matheson, a Democrat.

While the summer study committee was beginning its work, back in Nashville, Checker Finn arranged an introduction for Alexander to Albert Shanker, the head of the American Federation of Teachers, the rival national union to the NEA. The three met in the corridor outside an AFT meeting in Washington, D.C. The AFT had almost no members in Tennessee, and Shanker, who was an independent thinker on education policy, sensed an opportunity for his union. He invited the governor to address the AFT annual convention in Los Angeles, and Alexander quickly accepted. (When Alexander later told his mother, the kindergarten teacher, about his proposed trip to Los Angeles to address the union, Mrs. Alexander him: "Son, be careful.")

In Los Angeles, Shanker introduced the Republican governor to several thousand skeptical union activists, telling them that he was always willing to listen to governors who were willing to support more money for teachers' salaries. And, he said, "If you can have master plumbers, why not have master teachers?"

Following Alexander's address, the union members gave the Tennessee governor a standing ovation.

CONTINUING HIS PURSUIT OF McWherter's support, Alexander invited the speaker to travel with him to North Carolina to visit that state's residential math and science Governor's School. The cost of the program in North Carolina was $5 million. After this visit, the two decided that cost was too much for Tennessee to swallow, and they agreed instead to amend the Better Schools Program to authorize several summer Governor's Schools for students and one for teachers of writing. "We could reach more people at a lower cost," Alexander explained.

During the fall of 1983, Alexander continued his efforts to build public support for the school reform program, especially the Master Teacher component. He hosted a forum at Vanderbilt University that included Shanker and retired Admiral Hyman Rickover as speakers. Through that fall, a time of intensive negotiations between the administration and the legislative study committee members, the principal disagreements were over how to ensure fairness in the peer evaluations of classroom teachers. The TEA leaders stressed the virtual impossibility of removing all bias if educators, both principals and teachers, were required to judge one another's performance. That's when the Alexander team offered that the evaluation teams would come from outside the teacher's (or principal's) own school district.

This period was therefore characterized by daily communications between elected officials and senior staff in both branches. Representative Steve

Bivens, Democrat from Cleveland, Tennessee, was the chair of the House Education Committee and intimately involved in the final negotiations. Other House leaders on the pro-reform side were Representatives Steve Cobb, Democrat, a Nashville lawyer; Jim Henry of Kingston, the House Republican leader; and the Democrats John Bragg of Murfreesboro; Dana Moore of Johnson City; and Jimmy Naifeh of Covington. In the Senate, closely involved with all discussions of policy and legislative process, were the GOP leader Tom Garland of Greeneville, and the Democrats Anna Belle Clement O'Brien of Crossville, John Rucker of Murfreesboro, and Douglas Henry Jr. of Nashville, the long-serving chairman of the Senate Finance Committee.

At the staff level, in addition to Commissioner McElrath, Alexander's team included both policy analysts and lobbyists. Legal counsel Bill Koch was the governor's lead for developing or approving specific language amending the master legislation. (The author was the point person for day-to-day liaison with the TEA leaders, chiefly Betty Anderson.) The administration lobbyists Granville Hinton and Jeff Combos were principal liaisons with members of the General Assembly. On the legislative side, Billy Stair was McWherter's senior policy adviser, taking the lead on coordination decisions on amendments and committee processes.

Bivens, years later, recalled this period of back-and-forth negotiations as a demanding time for the part-time legislators. At one point, administration and TEA staffers planned to fly together to Bivens's hometown for what they believed could be a final discussion on a set of key amendments. But on the scheduled morning, Cleveland's small general aviation airport was fogged in. Bivens offered to drive to Chattanooga and meet the plane there instead.

In the homestretch, negotiating sessions were usually held in committee rooms at the Legislative Plaza in Nashville, including McWherter's own conference room, with both legislative and administration leaders at the table. These sessions were intense, with advocates on either side pressing for concessions from the other.

"Speaker McWherter, at the end, told us he wanted us all to stay in his conference room and not to leave the room until we had it worked out," Bivens told me. "And that's what we did. I remember one afternoon we'd gotten it down to a final disagreement over one word—I forget what the issue was—and somebody suggested we should substitute the word 'shall' with the word 'may' and, at the same time, create an oversight committee to monitor the progress.

"We all looked at each other, and it looked like we had agreement among the legislative members. Then we looked at you [the author] and you said, 'Well, I need to go upstairs and check with somebody about that.' You came back a few minutes later and said y'all were in agreement with the change. And we had it."

The performance pay component was not the only negotiating point. Bragg's support, as chairman of the House Finance Committee, was crucial. His judgment and experience on budget matters were highly respected in both chambers. His House district included his alma mater, Middle Tennessee State University, at Murfreesboro, and Bragg became an advocate for a college-level innovation he called the "Chairs of Excellence." These would be distinguished professorships at state universities, with the cost shared 50/50 between state government and private sector contributions. They were not part of Alexander's original plan but, Bragg thought, would complement the new Centers of Excellence, helping the universities focus their resources on specialized programs they do well.

Alexander invited Bragg to the governor's office.

BRAGG: "I prefer the Chairs of Excellence."
ALEXANDER: "Those are a good idea, but Centers of Excellence are more likely to create programs on our campuses that are really distinguished."
BRAGG: "I'm not sure I can support the program without Chairs of Excellence."
ALEXANDER: "Then why don't we just do both?"

The result of the meeting was an agreement for the state to fund half the cost of one hundred $1 million Chairs of Excellence, and a recurring appropriation of $25 million allocated to Centers of Excellence on the university campuses. This agreement helped to secure Bragg's eventual support for the Better Schools Program.

Representative Steve Cobb, a Democrat and House co-sponsor of the Better Schools plan, recalled the detailed preparations for the 1984 session—and the escalating tensions between legislative leaders and the TEA operatives. He also remembers the other key senators and representatives in the bipartisan coalition who helped to engineer passage in the 1984 session.

"I remember one afternoon," he told me. "There was a key vote coming up in the (House) Education Committee, and we needed every vote. Representative Dana Moore was not in the room. She told me later somebody from the administration followed her into the ladies' room and told her she was needed back in the committee meeting. She came back and voted with us."

Cobb said the credit for the hard-won success went to the personal leadership of Alexander and McWherter, and their capacity to cooperate both on the policy framework of reform and also the details of nose counts and persuasion.

"Of all the people involved," Cobb told me, "the number one and number two were Governor Alexander and Speaker McWherter. Without both of them, it would not have passed. Both were essential and did what needed to be done. "Lamar was the finest politician I ever met. He was smart enough to know it's OK to lose every now and then. It was hard not to like him and respect him."

THIS PROCESS, WITH REGULAR communications between the administration and the legislative leaders, culminated in two separate bills. One was the improved Better Schools Program, now called the Comprehensive Education Reform Act of 1984, or CERA, in which the term *Master Teacher* had now disappeared. (It was replaced with *Career Ladder*, which the TEA leaders preferred for the new differential pay regime. Pay supplements were the same but were now labeled as Career Level I, II, and III.) The other bill provided for the governance reorganization of the State Board of Education, which Wilder had championed throughout the process. Alexander supported all these changes, calling them "improvements" to his early proposal.

Therefore, when the new year arrived there were wide expectations that the CERA package would be the marquis newsmaker topic for the 1984 session. But on January 4, after consulting with McWherter and Wilder, Alexander issued a call for the legislature to convene in a special session six days later, in advance of the regular session. This strategy meant that nothing except the Better Schools Program and the money to pay for it could be considered. Alexander believed this maneuver would weaken the hand of teacher union lobbyists and strengthen his hand by putting a public spotlight on the legislature's deliberations.

It was during this extraordinary session that the reforms were adopted, together with the sales tax increase to pay for them. Crucial to the success of the bill was the package of adjustments, which was called the Weakley County Amendment, invoking the name of McWherter's home county in West Tennessee. McWherter sponsored the amendment, and this brought enough Democrats on board to pass the final bill.

ALSO CONTRIBUTING TO SUCCESS, on the Senate side, was a quiet visit to Nashville by Governor Graham, the Florida Democrat, who came at Alexander's invitation. Graham had been one of those early reform-minded southern governors who had collaborated across party lines. The purpose of his Tennessee trip on this day was to meet with Senator O'Brien, a meeting that Alexander arranged knowing that Graham was proposing his own new program to reward outstanding teaching in Florida.

With great respect and deference, Graham said to O'Brien he hoped she would support the new Tennessee bill in spite of the union's opposition. There was no way, he argued, to continue to attract outstanding teachers to the classroom unless the very best teachers could earn higher salaries and know their excellence was appreciated. He also put the matter on a more personal basis, speaking eloquently to Senator O'Brien as a fellow elected official.

"I try to remember," Graham said, "that none of us are in these elected positions really for very long. The question, for me, is how to make the most of the time we've been given." Senator O'Brien later cast the deciding vote that moved the Better Schools Program out of committee, onto the Senate floor, and into law.

"I have always admired Bob Graham for that," Alexander told me later. "He didn't have to come to Tennessee to meet a legislator he didn't know. He was actually hoping Florida, not Tennessee, would be the first state to pay teachers more for teaching well. And he did it at considerable political risk; he was often mentioned as a Democrat candidate for president, and 20 percent of the delegates to the Democrat National Convention at that time were members of the National Education Association, who hated pay for performance."

IN THE MIDST OF all this, there was new trouble in Memphis.

St. Jude's Hospital, the world-famous children's hospital founded and placed there by Danny Thomas himself, was threatening to move to St. Louis. Hospital leaders were citing Washington University, in St. Louis, as having superior research facilities to the University of Tennessee's Health Sciences Center in Memphis. Hearing this on a weekend, Alexander phoned UT president Ed Boling and, within a few days, also met with members of the Shelby County delegation to the legislature.

The main result of these rapid discussions was an agreement to allocate twenty-five of the proposed one hundred new Chairs of Excellence to UT's medical center in Memphis, with the university committing to raise the required matching funds from private sources. This opened the prospect of an influx of additional research talent into Memphis and helped persuade the St. Jude's board to remain in the city. It also helped to persuade Memphis lawmakers to support the Better Schools Program, which would create the new faculty chairs.

St. Jude's leaders also wanted two seats on the University of Tennessee governing board. Sam Cooper, the Memphis businessman and major St. Jude's supporter, was already on the UT board. St. Jude's suggested adding Ron Terry, the chairman of First Tennessee Bank. After conferring with Boling, Alexander phoned Terry, who accepted.

"I couldn't say anything but okay," Terry told me later. "I did tell them (his new fellow UT trustees) that when the University of Tennessee played Memphis State University, I was going to sit on the Memphis side."

ON MARCH 6, 1984, Alexander sat at a teacher's desk on the "cafetorium" stage at Julia Green School in southwest Nashville. A student sat beside him, and the legislators who had co-sponsored the reforms—Democrats and Republicans together—stood behind them. There the governor signed the two new laws making Tennessee the first state to pay teachers more for teaching well.

Eventually, ten thousand Tennessee teachers climbed the career ladder voluntarily. The law created the hundred new Chairs of Excellence at Tennessee universities. By 2017 these chairs had a total endowment value of a quarter-billion dollars. The Centers of Excellence established by the new law still operate—for example, in the UT-Knoxville Science Alliance, the East Tennessee State University's Center for Appalachian Studies, and the University of Memphis. In the summer of 2017 there were eleven Governor's Schools on university campuses for rising eleventh- and twelfth-grade students. (The Governor's School for the Arts and Sciences at MTSU, in the late John Bragg's district, was by then in its twenty-ninth year, having attracted more than seven thousand students to its month-long summer program.)

These new programs were paid for by the largest increase in state education funding—and the largest single tax increase earmarked for schools—by any General Assembly in Tennessee history. The state's higher education funding formula was fully funded for the first time in many years. An unprecedented three-year budget plan, designed by Alexander and approved by the legislature, made sure the new funds would be spent as intended.

FOR THE REVAMPED STATE Board of Education, Alexander recruited Nelson Andrews, the Nashville businessman, to be its first chairman. Andrews was well known to both McWherter and Wilder. He was also one of the business leaders who had helped raise money for the Tennesseans for Better Schools campaign of the previous year.

In the early 1970s, Andrews had been involved in a wide-ranging study of the state's higher education system, during the Dunn administration. It was a tangled web of issues, ranging from governance to funding. In the process, Andrews began to understand that what happens in postsecondary schools affects the K–12 system in myriad ways, from the preparation of elementary and secondary teachers to college admission standards.

"We thought at the time, 'What should we do about K–12?'" Andrews recalled in a 2006 interview. "You looked at the system and you kept going back to how we're not succeeding when our kids get to higher education in Tennessee. And the figures were pretty startling. Kids out of high school who went into higher education had a success rate—if you say graduating from a two-year institution in three years, or a four-year institution in six years—had a success rate of about 30 percent, which is terrible. That meant over two-thirds of your kids were failing.

"So I said, 'The problem we've got is down on the K–12 end of it.' And I kept hollering about that. Should have kept my mouth shut, I guess. And then here along came Governor Alexander, and he asked me to serve on a new state board." Andrews would continue as the chairman for the next nine years.

CHAPTER 16

Landing Saturn

"I think we're doing our best work when we work together. When you
don't worry about titles and you work together for the common good,
we accomplish a lot. The same goes for our government."
— Mike Herron, United Auto Workers chairman at Spring Hill

BY THE LATE 1970S, Detroit's bedrock industry—the U.S. automotive industrial machine—was facing a new type of competition from automakers
on the far side of the Pacific Rim.

In its postwar recovery, Japan had become an innovative new titan of
productivity, technological skill, and economic strategy, and its automotive
industry in particular was poised for a dramatic rise. By the early 1980s, Detroit and all the industrial Midwest were reeling from a stagnant economy
and new consumer choices: the 1973 energy crisis, rising gasoline prices, and
popularity of smaller, energy-efficient cars, dramatically lowered domestic
auto sales and depressed employment across the auto industry. Meanwhile,
the Japanese were making better cars.

In his 1977 bestseller *The Reckoning*, former *Tennessean* reporter David
Halberstam said the Big Three domestic automakers and the United Auto
Workers had together formed an oligopoly. And it behaved as if they could
forever get away with selling big vehicles at big profits that got only thirteen
miles on a gallon of gasoline. And when they did try to make small cars,
they were such clunkers that American consumers were persuaded to keep
on buying Japanese products.

To the south of this economic devil's brew, Nissan had planted an important flag in 1980 by placing its first U.S. production facility in Middle
Tennessee, initially making light trucks. The Nissan manufacturing model
of advanced automation and nonunion hiring had been a disruptive new element among domestic U.S. automakers. General Motors, in its boardroom
and C-suite, was now considering how best to respond. The path forward
was not at all clear.

The engineers and managers of General Motors, like their counterparts at Ford and Chrysler, knew well how to design new-year models; to establish production lines and staff to assemble them; to array the parts suppliers to feed into the assembly plants; and to distribute the new models to thousands of retail dealers across the hemisphere and beyond. Those components were relatively easy. The harder new question now for executives on the upper floors of GM's futuristic Renaissance Center headquarters was how to accomplish all of those moving parts with a different workforce model than in the past. The traditional management-labor mode had become saturated by decades of complex labor agreements with the United Auto Workers, and the challenge specifically was how to make this hidebound relationship less sluggish, more dynamic and participatory, and more productive.

This is how the Saturn program was born inside General Motors.

In 1983, GM CEO Chairman Roger B. Smith announced a new corporate resolve by his company to win back sales that had been lost to Toyota, Honda, and other Japanese car companies. Success in this mission, he said, would come from American ingenuity and an innovative management structure that would be new to his industry.

Initially, a planning team was assembled at GM's technical center at Warren, Michigan. On July 5, 1984, President Reagan visited the Warren offices and congratulated GM for working to keep the U.S. auto industry competitive.

Six months later, GM announced it was establishing a new operating subsidiary called Saturn Corp. This was not to be just one more new model line but "a new kind of car company"—a separate operating unit within the GM corporate structure, with its own brand-new production location somewhere within the United States. It would be a partnership of GM and the UAW, with different work rules and practices designed to build a small car that would complete with those made in Japan and Germany.

SMITH'S INITIAL ANNOUNCEMENT, in 1983, had fueled immediate speculation around the country about where this new production site would be placed. By the time GM formally announced its new Saturn division in January 1985, other details made the interest of business recruiters even more intense: the new facility would be a $5 billion plant—said to be the largest one-time investment ever by a U.S. company—and would employ as many as six thousand workers, producing a half-million vehicles annually. In short order, there was an accelerated scramble among governors hoping to win the coveted new plant for their states.

Over the next twelve months, this scramble would play out in state capitols, boardrooms, hotel rooms, and even on national television. Hundreds of communities across the nation pushed their locations as being prime for the new Saturn plant. But the biggest spectacle in the Saturn recruitment race came at the end of February 1985, when seven governors appeared together on *The Phil Donahue Show*. Seated together on the set in Donahue's Manhattan studio, pitching their respective states, were the governors Richard Celeste, Ohio; Jim Thompson, Illinois; Dick Thornburgh, Pennsylvania; Terry Branstad, Iowa; Rudy Perpich, Minnesota; John Ashcroft, Missouri; and Mark White, Texas.

Two other governors—Alexander of Tennessee, and Governor Jim Blanchard of Michigan—declined. Alexander, in fact, had been excused.

"I saw Roger Smith at the Gridiron Dinner in Washington, and I mentioned the Donahue thing," Alexander recalled in an interview later. "I said, 'Do I need to do that?' He said, 'Of course not. That's not the way we locate plants.' But he said what we did need to do was pass the seat belt law, which we did."

Congress had first considered mandatory installation of seat belts in automobiles in 1966, but the idea was highly controversial at the time. Automakers complained it would lead to higher productions costs. In 1984, the National Highway Transportation Safety Administration proposed new regulations to require restraint systems in all new vehicles unless mandatory seat belt laws were in place to cover at least two-thirds of the U.S. population by September 1989. At that point, auto manufacturers joined with safety advocates to encourage states to adopt such laws. New York had been the first state to pass a seat belt law, in December 1984. Tennessee's law would be enacted the following April 21, less than a month after Alexander's conversation with Smith at the Washington Gridiron Dinner.

"It was hard to pass," Alexander remembers. "I had all of these legislators who said requiring Tennessee drivers to use seat belts in their own vehicles was against their principles. They didn't have any principles against recruiting six thousand new jobs."

DURING THE TIME THAT GM executives were in their site-selection phase, Smith and Alexander would meet face-to-face at least two more times. The next was in a more private setting than the swank Gridiron Dinner, and it was not on network television. Nor was it in Washington, D.C., but in Memphis.

This was a high-level presentation to a VIP audience of one—and involved an easel whose metal legs had been hacked off for the occasion just that morning. Howard H. Baker Jr., the Tennessean who was majority leader of the U.S. Senate, was the intermediary who arranged this private encounter for Alexander and his team. It was in the late spring of 1985, in a private suite at the Peabody Hotel, where Smith was to speak to a regional meeting of the United Way of America.

"Senator Baker was going to be there, and they were friends," Alexander told me. "I asked Baker to arrange an appointment with Roger Smith so that he and I could talk to him."

This would be the most important chance Alexander would have to present Tennessee's case for winning the largest industrial investment in the state's history. The preparation for the meeting, therefore, was painstaking. It was also different from how the state officials had dealt with Nissan's leaders in that earlier recruitment campaign. There had been, for one thing, more frequent encounters and communications with Nissan representatives. GM's mode was more secretive, even with the Tennessee officials who understood the need for discretion.

"We knew for several months that Nissan was interested in Tennessee and we were working with many Nissan executives, regularly, every day," Alexander told me. "That went on for months. But Saturn was very secretive. General Motors didn't tell anybody anything. In fact, the economic development people in Maury County didn't even know they were coming. They had all of this huge publicity. Governors were making fools of themselves by going on *The Phil Donahue Show.*"

On January 14, 1985, the governor sent the GM chairman a letter. He wrote out the draft on a legal pad, with his black felt-tip pen, and he pulled no stops to use the extraordinary economic case study that had undergirded Nissan's success in Tennessee to this point:

Dear Mr. Smith—

I am following up on Howard Baker's telephone conversation with you on Friday.

Howard and I look forward to a visit to let you know why Tennessee is the only logical location for GM's new Saturn plant!

As you suggested to Howard, we will wait until you let us know when such a visit is convenient for you.

Tennesseans proudly use lots of GM products. We make a good many parts for GM cars and trucks.

But I'm sorry to say we have never had a GM assembly plant in our state. In fact, our only automobile and truck assembly plant is the new Nissan plant.

Nissan is in Tennessee because it studied every state in the Eastern U.S. for seven years and figured Tennessee was the best place to make quality trucks and cars and a profit.

To get Nissan we did not promise the moon as some states did.

We offered a good business environment, a trained workforce (we do help pay for training), and a location that is at the population center of the U.S. Because of Tennessee's location, Nissan saves a few dollars every time it ships a truck.

The Nissan plant has hired 3,500 terrific Tennessee employees, has been ahead of schedule in everything it has tried to do, and was named one of the 10 best managed companies in the U.S. by Fortune. In May Nissan will start making cars in Tennessee.

Most dealers say their customers think Nissan trucks made in Tennessee are better than those made in Japan.

The reason I am writing all this about Nissan to the GM Chairman is that GM might find that Saturns made in Tennessee would be better than Saturns made anywhere else in the U.S., and because of our location, a little cheaper to deliver.

I look forward to our visit.
Lamar

cc: Hon. Howard H. Baker Jr.

THE MEETING WAS AGREED TO, and this established a hard deadline for making ready a critical presentation. All the materials were prepared and assembled under the supervision of EDC Commissioner Bill Long and his deputy commissioner Ted vonCannon, a veteran development professional and career state employee. But Alexander was never far from the process, giving his comments and edits to presentation documents either directly to Long or via Tom Ingram to the PR consultant Hank Dye, president of the Dye, Van Mol and Lawrence firm. Dye's shop was generating the final charts and graphics to those strict specifications. The production process ran smoothly, but the sensitive inter-office communications were constrained by mid-1980s technology: no one was using email this point, and facsimile transmittal was limited and fitful. This meant the team had to rely on personal delivery of documents, including the back-and-forth drafts, markups, and final clean copies. The early technology also made for slow deliveries from Nashville to GM's headquarters in Detroit, requiring numerous personal deliveries by hand to the Motor City.

"There was a lot of pressure on this," Dye explained. "It was very, very secret. Bill Long, as commissioner, was former military and was a stickler for code names. Everything we did had a code name on it. The code name for this project was 'HFS'—which was 'Home for Saturn'—and everything we did, every invoice I sent, every file we made, was filed under the 'HFS' code."

ON THE MORNING OF the meeting with Smith, Alexander met his small entourage at the state hangar on the east side of the Nashville airport for their flight to Memphis. VonCannon had been in charge of preparing the presentation boards and other materials Alexander would use for this critical encounter with GM's top executive.

With only a few minutes before flight time, Alexander asked for a final run-through before he boarded the King Air. VonCannon quickly found a private conference room inside the hangar building. He propped the boards up on the tray of the metal easel and quickly flipped through them while Alexander watched.

"Governor, what do you think?" vonCannon asked. "Are we ready?"

"Okay, that looks pretty good," Alexander replied, "but I want to tell you something. That easel—that's too high. We're going to have Roger Smith sitting in a chair. He's not going to be standing up, so we need to have that easel lower. We need to get it lower."

VonCannon looked at his three-legged easel again and realized he had an engineering problem: its height was not adjustable, and the metal construction meant its legs were fixed and could not easily be shortened. He asked the governor for a quick break, picked up the easel, and exited the room with it. Down the hall, he found the door leading into the flight hangar, his eyes rapidly scanning the space. He spotted an aircraft mechanic standing in a far corner.

"You got a hack saw?" vonCannon shouted to the man.

"I do," the mechanic said. "Right over here."

The technician quickly grabbed the tool and with a few quick motions lowered the height of the easel to vonCannon's hasty specifications, making it nearly three feet shorter. Moments later, the Tennessee officials were in the air—their very short easel stowed in the rear of the plane—flying west to Tennessee's largest city.

Their mission: to persuade the largest industrial prospect in the state's history.

"BAKER AND I MET with Mr. Smith in the hotel room before he made his speech," Alexander remembers.

"I had figured that Nissan's presence in Tennessee was either the hook or the kiss of death and I was trying to figure out how to counter it. So I worked on these boards to make a presentation to him. My daughter Kathryn saw me practicing these at the governor's mansion, and she said, 'Dad, this is the silliest thing I've ever seen. You're going to talk to the president of General Motors with boards like that?'"

"My argument to him was, 'You're trying to build a car that people will compare to the Japanese cars, so why don't you put your plant right next to your Japanese competitor? Tell your union and tell your management if Nissan can do it in Tennessee, you can do it. Don't just compete at the dealership. Compete at the plant site. Let the competition make your car better.' So that was my pitch to him."

When the meeting ended, Smith, Baker, and Alexander departed for the United Way luncheon in the ballroom downstairs. In a follow-up letter from his desk in Detroit, Smith wrote to Alexander, "I was indeed impressed with the opportunities available in the State of Tennessee and the progressive attitude that prevails." He signed the letter, "Sincerely, Roger."

LATER IN THE PROCESS, but before GM signaled its final decision, there was one particularly frantic scramble to meet a GM deadline. The materials were assembled without a hitch, but then the agency discovered that all the flights from Nashville to Detroit were fully booked. The package had to be in GM headquarters by 8:00 a.m. the next morning, meaning that not even FedEx could get it to downtown Detroit on time.

"It was supplemental to the main proposal," Dye told me. "We had been working on it into the wee hours. All of the commercial flights were overbooked, and back in those days you didn't have all of the options of communication that you have today. FedEx wasn't going to be quick enough. Somebody had a brother-in-law or cousin or friend or something in the Air Guard. He went home and got his Air National Guard uniform on and we took him out to the airport. We tucked it under his arm and sent him up there. He played the 'uniform card' and got on standby and got on a flight and delivered our proposal package up to Detroit."

GM's DECISION WAS NOT long in coming at this point, but the company kept its project tightly under wraps. Both GM's real estate officials and the executive of the new Saturn division, while cordial to Tennessee officials, gave little indication of which way they were leaning relative to the final plant location.

They were working, meanwhile, to secure options to a massive tract of agricultural land in the rural southern region of Middle Tennessee, near Columbia, south of Nashville. For this secretive work, Ed Dillworth, a GM legal counsel who had now become the general counsel for Saturn and right arm to Saturn president Bill Hoglund, reached out to Maclin Davis at the prominent Nashville law firm of Waller, Landsden, Dortch and Davis. Inside the Waller firm, two attorneys, Lew Conner and Wes Shofner, were assigned to the Saturn case. Conner coordinated the business aspects of Saturn's work with state government and Maury County officials. Shofner, a real estate lawyer, took the lead on the options work, a painstaking process that involved identifying target parcels, running title searches, and making initial contacts with property owners, usually through local real estate agents.

Conner was particularly close to Alexander—best friends since their Vanderbilt days, former law partners, political allies, fellow coaches on their sons' baseball teams—but both insist they did not communicate about Saturn during this fast-moving period of the automaker's decision making.

Not that Alexander didn't try. "As a matter of fact," Conner told me, "Lamar got wind—not from me—that General Motors was seriously looking, and that the law firm was helping General Motors. He would call twice a week toward the end, four to six weeks out, and Ashley (Conner's wife, the phone was on her side of the bed) would answer, sometimes between 6:00 and 6:15 in the morning."

> LAMAR: "Good morning, Ashley, it's Lamar. Could you tell me if Lew has anything to tell me today?"
> ASHLEY (*HOLDING THE PHONE*): "Lew, it's Lamar. Have you got anything you need to tell him today?"
> LEW: "Tell him no, and to have a good day."

Conner remembers he was, meanwhile, urging both Dillworth and Bill Hoglund to communicate with Alexander as quickly as possible. "I'm begging them, 'You've got to trust the governor of Tennessee. Let me show you how receptive the governor for the State of Tennessee, and the rest of the state of Tennessee, will be if you will just come down here and talk to them. I promise you. I give you my word that they will not let it out. I said the only person to trust is the person I know I can trust beyond anything and that is Lamar Alexander.' Hoglund didn't know Lamar; Dillworth didn't know Lamar. Didn't know if they could trust him."

At last Dillworth phoned Conner, asking him to set up a private after-hours meeting with the governor. "Bill Hoglund wanted to look at Lamar Alexander and know that he would be able to trust him to keep his mouth shut." Around 6:00 p.m. Conner and Hoglund met in the lobby of the Loew's Vanderbilt Plaza Hotel in midtown, across West End Avenue from the Vanderbilt campus. The two of them loaded into Conner's Cadillac and drove seven miles south to the governor's residence on Curtiswood Lane.

Until this night, Saturn's president had not met Tennessee's governor.

With no staff present, Hoglund, Alexander, and Conner sat in the governor's study, a small wood-paneled library, and Hoglund went through the checklist of components they would need in order for Saturn to land in Tennessee.

They talked for three hours.

THERE WOULD BE ONE more face-to-face encounter between Smith and Alexander. It occurred in Washington, in late June, in a conference room inside Butler Aviation, a general aviation service at National Airport. It was a day trip for Alexander, who flew on state aircraft for the private meeting. Another state employee made the trip, though she did not attend the discussion with the GM chairman.

Jennifer Barker Schettler, who worked in the governor's press office, was eight months pregnant on this day. She had asked for permission to fly to Washington, if a seat might be available on the state airplane. Her purpose was to retrieve a special family heirloom, an antique cradle then at her cousin's home, and bring it back to Tennessee.

When Alexander's private meeting with Smith concluded, Schettler was waiting in the Butler Aviation lobby—with a problem. The unwieldy cradle would not fit onto the King Air. Observing this, Smith offered to help. Before boarding his own corporate jet, the top executive of the world's largest industrial corporation sized up the situation. He suggested they remove the rockers from the cradle, and it fit snugly then into the baggage hold.

IT WAS NOW EARLY July. Saturn's public announcement would not come for another four weeks. As the date approached, Alexander insisted that the announcement be given sufficient context. They would, after all, be disclosing an immense economic development both for the U.S. auto industry and for regular Tennesseans. A multi-part communication plan was assembled, involving members of the governor's staff, officials at the ECD Department, its Nashville ad agency Ericson, and the PR firm Dye, Van Mol and Lawrence.

One element of this plan was to prepare a full-page advertisement to run in selected newspapers, most significantly in the *Wall Street Journal*. Alexander wrote the copy himself, and the Ericson agency executed and placed the final layout design. The ad was to run for ten days in most national newspapers.

The governor later wrote, "For $450,000 the state bought a ride on the largest advertising blitz in automotive history. General Motors had not spent a penny on advertising Saturn, but the intense competition for the plant made front pages for months in 1985. As a result, twice as many people can identify a Saturn as can identify a Pontiac, even though Pontiac has been building cars since 1926 and Saturns won't be produced until 1990."

A news release was also prepared, though carefully couched in anticipatory, subjunctive-case verbiage:

> "Saturn—if it comes to Spring Hill—will become the model for Tennessee's crusade to keep yesterday's values while we're getting tomorrow's jobs . . . "

> "The Saturn decision will be a national verdict that declares the best home for tomorrow's jobs. No one can remember a bigger commotion about where to put a plant . . . "

> "Tennessee has emphasized three points in presenting our case to General Motors: a central location that lowers transportation costs, a work environment that encourages efficient work practices and high quality, and our massive push for better schools."

> "Tennessee is in the center of things. Three-fourths of the U.S. population lives within 500 miles of Tennessee. If you move far away from the center of the national market, transportation costs begin to overwhelm every other cost. That's why Bridgestone, Northern Telecom and Nissan are headquartered in Nashville. That's why Federal Express brings all its packages to Memphis every night."

That final point was intended to lay some foundation for subsequent work to recruit not only with other types of manufacturers but also, in particular, some of the hundreds of auto parts suppliers that would feed the Saturn assembly line.

A **HIGH LEVEL OF** secrecy was still the order of the day.

Neither GM's executives, nor their lawyers at the Waller firm, nor any of the state officials, were to tell anyone what was now being negotiated. Alexander began to worry about the scope of the surprise that would befall Maury County—like a bomb about to be dropped on an unsuspecting city—since there was no way to pre-brief any local officials, even at this late date.

"I was immediately thinking of all of the problems," Alexander recalled. "In the Nissan case, we had had Mayor Sam Ridley (of Smyrna) and the whole community involved and active, helping to make the pitch. But with Saturn, this now meant that General Motors might be coming into Maury County with five-billion dollars—the largest investment ever by an American corporation in a plant—and Maury County wouldn't even know about it until the decision was made. So I persuaded Bill Hoglund that he needed to allow me to pick one person who could help guide them in how to deal with the local people, and I picked Waymon Hickman. He turned out to be a good choice."

Hickman had lived in Columbia all his life, and was its most prominent and respected business leader. His prestige and public profile as a banker and business leader were unmatched—so was his discretion. He was chairman of the Farmers and Merchants Bank and well known to state, county, and municipal officials. He had been a contributor to Alexander's political campaigns and also to the Tennesseans for Better Schools program of 1983.

The prospect of a new manufacturing plant was welcome news to Hickman. Unemployment had been high in Maury County ever since the large employers Monsanto and Stauffer Chemical had departed. Their phosphate mining operations had ceased when detergent manufacturers stopped using the chemical.

Very quickly, Hickman found himself in secret meetings with Conner and top GM officials, including Dillworth, Guy Briggs, Jim Lewandowski, and Tom Manoff, as well as Hoglund. "We were all sworn to secrecy," he remembers. "Their business cards had nothing about General Motors on them. They even drove Toyotas. I mean, they were here in this community without anyone really knowing."

BY THE THIRD WEEK of July, the nation's automotive press was at full stride, with multiple reporters scrambling to learn details and break the news of the coming announcement by GM. Speculation was high but unconfirmed that Tennessee might be the winner of the Saturn prize.

Toward the end of this final week of careful preparations in Nashville, probably on Wednesday, a young press aide in Washington had a brainstorm—mixed with a dollop of good-natured political mischief.

Suddenly, on Thursday, there was a news release from Tennessee's U.S. senators. The announcement from the offices of Senators Sasser and Gore provided no substantive detail, and the names General Motors and Saturn were not even mentioned—only that "an important announcement" was expected in Tennessee in the coming days.

The source of the information remained murky, but Sasser, as Tennessee's senior Democratic senator, had communication channels with leaders on both sides of GM's labor relations. A center-left labor Democrat from Nashville, where Ford's glass plant had been an important employer for decades, Sasser was well known to the United Auto Workers, and his seat on the Senate Appropriations Committee likewise kept him on GM's Washington radar. (In May 1988, GM invited Sasser to Talladega, Alabama, to be grand marshal for the kick-off race of the Winston 500 series. He was given the honor of a ceremonial lap in the official pace car, a Pontiac, with the head of GM's Pontiac division riding with him.) Gore had been Tennessee's junior senator only six months by July 1985, but he also had labor connections owing to his previous four terms in the House. In any case, it was possible that someone in GM's executive suite or the UAW might have tipped off someone in either senator's office.

Gore's press secretary at the time, Mike Kopp, told me later how the attempted preemption actually happened from that point forward. First came a phone call from an automotive reporter in Detroit.

"I remember having one phone conversation with a reporter from a Detroit newspaper. It made me nervous because I thought, this guy knows more than I do. He's in Detroit and I had no contacts and had no idea what was going on. I'm twenty-something years old, but I remember the guy saying, 'What can you tell me?' I kept telling him we can't really talk about that. I remember thinking, the best way I can get through this interview is to make him think I know something by saying, 'I'm sorry, I can't comment on that'—as opposed to just being honest with him and saying I don't know. I didn't have a clue what was going to go down."

Kopp ended the call. Then he picked up the phone on his desk again and dialed the governor's office in Nashville. At this time, the Tennessee governor's press office issued a weekly listing of upcoming public events, gleaned from the official schedule but without reference to internal meetings. Kopp remembers his call was transferred, probably to the press office, where a female staff member answered.

"Can you tell me if Governor Alexander has a news conference coming up in the next few days?" Kopp asked her.

"Yes, he does," she replied. "On Monday."

With this new nugget of information, Kopp quickly conferred with two of his senior colleagues in Gore's Washington office—Peter Knight, the chief of staff, and Roy Neel, another top adviser—and also with at least one staffer in Sasser's press office.

"It seemed to me nobody would be announcing there was going to be a news conference unless it was good news," Kopp reasoned. "In politics, you don't announce bad news. Based on that, both offices—our staff, Sasser's staff—came up with this strategy to put out a statement that there was going to be a major announcement in Tennessee. We weren't going to lie and say we knew what the announcement was—we just said it was good news and 'We're very happy for Tennessee.' We would not have taken that step if we weren't deluged with the media inquiries. I can't recall a single other time when I was with Gore, for almost nine years, that we got so many media calls about any one thing. It was a feeding frenzy. People were looking for just any nugget."

Neel, who was later Vice President Gore's chief of staff in the Clinton White House, recalls this episode with a mischievous smile. "I remember Gore and Sasser made some announcement, and there was blowback. It was, for them, a no-lose announcement. All we announced was there was going to be 'an announcement' the next day."

Nonetheless the ploy sent a shockwave through the governor's office in Nashville, especially among the team preparing the big announcement event. The effect was to give Alexander's team a momentary case of the bends, now worrying that their best-laid plans for a spectacular news day—months in the making—might suddenly be falling apart.

ON THE SUNDAY AFTERNOON before the official announcement, eight men gathered for a final private meeting at Conner's home in the fashionable Sugartree development on Nashville's Woodmont Boulevard. Alexander had signaled, through Conner, that this button-up planning meeting should not be held at the official executive residence and also that he himself would not attend out of caution, lest they draw unwanted attention from news media.

Conner and his wife Ashley lived at 163 Charleston Park. The men gathered in a bonus room above the garage. In attendance were GM's Dillworth and Hoglund; Commissioner Long and two members of his ECD Department staff; and two men from Maury County, the banker Hickman and the county executive Taylor Rayburn.

"We were going through the final plans for tomorrow's press conference and literally walking through everything that was going to be done," Conner remembers. "The negotiations were done. We've now dotted the I's, we've crossed the T's. All that's left is for Saturn to land."

In all the hubbub, Conner had forgotten about his next-door neighbor—another man who, had he been aware of it, would have been keenly interested in what they were discussing inside No. 163.

"As God is my judge, I look out the window, across the service driveway, and through the neighbor's window I see Marvin Runyon inside, riding his exercise bike." Runyon, the top executive of Nissan, owned the home that fronted on Prospect Hill, sharing the service driveway with Conner's residence. Conner also noticed Runyon's "President's Car," a special Nissan model the company provided to its elite global executives, parked in the driveway below. Conner could not contain himself.

"I called the others over to the window and said, 'Guys, you see him? What do you think the Chairman and CEO of Nissan is going to think in the morning when he hears our news?"

IN ONE OF HIS final preparations, Alexander dictated a personal Telex message to his old friend Takashi Ishihara, the Japanese executive who fifteen years before had approved the coming of Nissan to Tennessee, and the man who had hired Marvin Runyon from Ford to come from Detroit to run the new operations at Smyrna. Ishihara was now the chairman of Nissan Motor Company, Ltd.

With this note, which Commissioner Bill Long was instructed to transmit on Sunday afternoon before the momentous news of Saturn would break on Monday, Alexander had a single purpose: to thank Nissan "for being the first."

> Dear Mr. Ishihara,
>
> General Motors will announce on Monday afternoon (July 29) that Saturn will locate in Spring Hill, Tennessee. I wanted you to know that, in part, Tennesseans have Nissan to thank for the Saturn decision. If Nissan had not come to Tennessee and created such a fine environment for building high quality cars, I do not believe Saturn would have come to Tennessee. While we are glad to have Saturn, we continue to be grateful to Nissan for being the first major automobile company to show confidence in Tennessee. Please extend my best wishes to our other friends at Nissan.
>
> Lamar Alexander

SATURN OFFICIALLY "LANDED" the next day, with formal public statements by the company, both in Detroit and Nashville.

In spite of all the speculation that had gathered in the automotive trade media over many weeks—and even the moments of political mischief in the Senate office building in Washington—the announcement that Saturn was heading to Tennessee was momentous.

The Nashville event was at the Maxwell House Hotel, where a celebration banner and other materials proclaimed: "Saturn Has Landed." There was joy among the economic-development professionals, much celebration among the political leaders, but also a measure of anxiety among people whose families had resided in Maury County's tranquil countryside over their lifetimes. Their peaceful way of life was sure to change by the mega-development at Spring Hill, soon to become a major U.S. industrial center.

SATURN WAS TO BE "a new kind of car company," prominently including a new formal operating relationship between management and labor. The internal Saturn arrangement was meant to improve on many decades of experience with the United Auto Workers. In GM's traditional manufacturing hubs in the North, labor-management relations had become layered and bureaucratic over the years. Either side had complaints about the other, including blame for GM's slowness to innovate. Now, with the Saturn model, GM executives sought a do-over with the new company, beginning with a fresh approach to collaboration from the shop floor to planning systems.

Mike Herron was born in Flint, Michigan, and joined the Saturn project in 1990 as the first vehicle was shipped. Four decades earlier, his grandparents had migrated north from Tennessee and Arkansas, looking for work in the auto industry. By 2017 Herron has been elected to six three-year terms as UAW chairman at Spring Hill. (The chairman is responsible for the union's side of collective bargaining in the plant, while the local president runs the union's internal business affairs.)

"I've had numerous opportunities to leave here and always opted to stay in Tennessee," Herron told me. "We love Tennessee. I've had the opportunity to see and work with Lamar and McWherter and Bredesen on up through Governor Haslam and I've had a wonderful working relationship with all of them. It's critical," he added. "If you don't have the ability to grow the state, grow the jobs, and do what's best for the state, you don't have a right to be in office. They have always put the people first and created a positive business environment in the state of Tennessee and they have always worked well with each other. They would get things done. That's why this state is a shining example. A lot of the partisanship you see today in Washington, and in some of the other states, you just don't see here."

"I think we're doing our best work when we work together," he said, referring to Saturn's internal culture; but then he made a connection to the broader culture and the capacity for making progress when even politicians make their party labels secondary.

"When you don't worry about titles, and you work together for the common good, we accomplish a lot. The same goes for our government."

THE BANKER HICKMAN TOLD me that his own early encounters with the UAW representatives were pleasant.

"This one guy with the union (Jack O'Toole, a UAW business unit planner) wore a white hat all the time," Hickman remembers, "so I went up to him one day and asked him about it."

> HICKMAN: "What's with the white hat?"
> O'TOOLE: "We want the people down here to know that the union wears white hats and not black hats."

Long-time residents of Maury County began to see changes very quickly, first with the rising level of employment at the construction site. The owner of the local radio station, Bob McKay, described how his family had lived in Spring Hill for years and how the community had fundamentally changed by Saturn's arrival. Sam Kennedy, publisher of the Columbia *Daily Herald*, told me how the automaker quickly began to inject newcomers into the county and the towns of Spring Hill and Columbia, the county seat. Looking back, he now judged the coming of Saturn, overall, as a positive.

In the first weeks after the announcement, state officials invited the county government leaders to the governor's mansion in Nashville, hoping to help them anticipate the growth issues about to descend on their communities. Alexander remembers a particular exchange at that meeting: "Maury County is the home of the Tennessee Farm Bureau, where zoning is a bad word. I remember hearing two county commissioners saying to each other when they left, 'If we don't get busy writing some zoning rules, we'll never see another cow graze or a stalk of corn grow in Maury County.'"

Peter Jenkins, the Connecticut native and author of the bestseller *Walking Across America*, had recently moved with his family to quiet Spring Hill after seeing most of the country on his famous cross-country trek. He told me that when he heard the Saturn news, he phoned Alexander in Nashville.

"Holy smokes, Lamar, I walk across the United States. I find one peaceful, pleasant little place, prettiest little place in the whole United States, where I want to live. I buy a house, put down my roots, and here comes Saturn right on top of me."

THIS LATTER CONCERN—the fear of upheaval, disruption, possibly of a way of life—was much on the minds of Alexander's team in the closing weeks and months. It also permeated their final round of talks with GM's senior management.

Over the coming months of site planning and construction, Dillworth, working directly with Hoglund, was particularly determined that the official assurances to the local population—that the Saturn development would not destroy their small-town atmosphere—would be honored. Hoglund voiced GM's assurance that construction plans would keep Maury County's tranquility in mind.

"Spring Hill is a lovely part of the world," the president of Saturn declared on the day that Saturn landed, "and we're not going to rape the land with smoke-stack factories."

Concerns over the impact of such a huge industrial development on Maury County's way of life took many forms, and two different experts were made available to city and county leaders. Alexander reached out to his South Carolina friend Charles Fraser, who had been the visionary developer of Hilton Head, and Conner introduced the Vanderbilt Law School Dean John J. Costonis, an expert in land-use planning. Alexander owned a home in the Sea Pines community at Hilton Head and met Fraser there. Costonis had been involved in planning Brazil's new capital of Brasília, as well as in other nations of South America, prior to his deanship at Vanderbilt where he met Conner. Both Fraser and Costonis were subsequently hired by Saturn as consultants on the Spring Hill project.

Three decades later George Jones, who had been mayor of Spring Hill at the time, remembers Fraser brought in a new level of planning expertise that proved helpful to local officials. He remembers, with some bitterness, his own dealings with the state officials, but now assesses as a positive the zoning protections that the Saturn project introduced in the county.

"That is one thing that Lamar did do—furnish the money that helped get the community stabilized in terms of zoning and planning," the former mayor told me. "The state did pay the ticket to get Charles Fraser, who designed Hilton Head, to come work with us. That has been a plus for the Spring Hill area. It was a big plus for us to be planning for the stabilization of the community. We all, with General Motors, worked together on the zoning. They didn't want the beer joints and barbecue places popping up on the highways, and neither did we. It still happens, some people abuse the system."

Jones also commented on the growth that occurred in Saturn's wake—and why the planning and zoning protections proved so important. When he moved from Erwin, Tennessee, after high school graduation, he remembers the residents of Spring Hill numbered only about 350. By 2018 the population had risen to 39,602.

❖

As a more artful way to benchmark the commitment to planned growth, Alexander arranged for two staff photographers from state government—Jed DeKalb and Earl Warren—to shoot pictures in Spring Hill and Maury County, cataloging pre-construction images for the historical record. In this way, he thought, people could later remember what the town of 1,100 was like before the arrival of the largest industrial investment ever. One of the photos that Warren captured was a pastoral scene of a split-rail fence line, with a large spider web clinging to it in the morning dew.

On the day Saturn landed in rural Maury County, Alexander gave a print of that photograph, with this challenge: "If the spider web is still here when the first Saturn rolls off the line, you will have done your job."

Top Saturn executives kept the spider web photo in their offices as a reminder of their commitment to preserve the environment while bringing in so many new jobs. For the next dozen years, they would also present a commemorative copy of that photo to company people who had been key to setting up the company—both labor and management.

They called it "The Spider Plaque."

CHAPTER 17

The Roads to Better Jobs

"Mr. Jim said, If you take care of the schools and the roads, the politics will take care of itself."
— Representative John Bragg quoting the late House speaker Jim Cummings

GARY GARFIELD SHOWED ME through his suburban skyscraper office, with its view of downtown Nashville on the western horizon. Arrayed on his credenza and walls were the memorabilia of a proud company, Bridgestone Americas, Inc., employer of fifty-five thousand across fifty facilities.

Garfield's desk had been Harvey Firestone's own. On the credenza were trophies and photos of winners of the Bridgestone golf tournaments. And on the south wall were a pair of enlarged photo portraits—one of Firestone in his prime, and the other of Shojiro Ishibashi in his own. These were the honored founders who had matured and risen to corporate power in different, distant lands.

The parity in size and placement of these two images was intentional, symbolically important to Bridgestone's internal culture. Since 1988, when Bridgestone acquired Firestone (with both sides calling it a "merger") the combined company had sought to honor both of its legendary founders.

In 2016, at the time of my visit to Garfield in his offices near the Nashville airport, his executive team was making preparations to relocate their U.S. headquarters once again—this time into the city's central business district. The new office tower was rising on Demonbreun Street east of Fourth Avenue, at the busy downtown epicenter of Music City's tourism and cultural life. On opposite corners of that intersection—unofficially called Nashville's "Crossroads of Music"—are the Country Music Hall of Fame and Museum on one side, and the Schermerhorn Symphony Center across the street.

It was not always so. Just three decades earlier, neither Japanese businesses nor the automotive industry were generally recognized as significant employers in Middle Tennessee. The advent of Nissan and later of Saturn, and the explosive expansion of their supplier networks, would change all of that. Bridgestone was not the first automotive supplier to follow Nissan's and Saturn's leads in coming to Middle Tennessee, and by no means would it be the last.

But in the middle 1980s none of this was guaranteed. First, Tennessee would have to figure out how to draw automotive suppliers here at all, and that would require a very different system of roads.

In September of 1985, two months after General Motors announced it would place its $5 billion Saturn plant in Spring Hill, Tennessee, Alexander met with GM executives again and asked them a question:

"How will you locate Saturn's suppliers?"

"We use computers," one of the executives replied.

"And what do your computers look for?"

"They look for intersections of the best four-lane highways," the man answered. "We want our supplies to arrive at our assembly plants reliably and on time. We call this 'just-in-time' delivery."

Alexander and his team were familiar with the "just-in-time" concept from their earliest discussions with Marvin Runyon and other top Nissan executives. It was a manufacturing supply concept first developed in Japan (Toyota has been credited with leading the way on the JIT concept among automakers), and it had become how modern car and truck factories were moderating their costs by minimizing the need to stockpile large inventories of parts essential to the manufacturing process. Suppliers either had to locate close to the assembly line, or in any case be capable of filling orders quickly.

Now, four years later in this new conversation with Saturn's top brass about their own supply chain, Alexander could see both a challenge and the glimmer of a rare opportunity.

The problem was that Tennessee's four-lane highways were in an acknowledged state of mediocre condition. Many of these roads were in poor repair, but more fundamentally even county seats in many parts of the state were not directly linked to the interstate highways that connected Tennessee's major cities and supply-chain routes. But here was the opportunity: at Spring Hill, Saturn would need to count on as many as 650 first- and second-tier suppliers on a tight "just-in-time" relationship that would keep the assembly line moving without delays. This is why Nissan had chosen as it did, placing its first U.S. manufacturing facility so close to dedicated rail access and to Interstate 24.

Accessibility for these suppliers became a new driving vision associated with the auto industry's success in Tennessee—and vice versa. During the next year or two, decisions about where to locate Saturn's supplier plants would be made. As the governor later told the state's lawmakers, "Almost all of Tennessee is within 250 miles of Spring Hill—as well as the Nissan plant a few miles away in Smyrna. So is almost all of Kentucky and so are parts of eleven other states. You can bet your bottom dollar that recruiters from all those states are going over those lists of suppliers.

"So how," he asked, "are we going to get them to Tennessee?"

His answer was a massive "Better Roads Program" costing an estimated $3.3 billion and designed to "give Tennessee one of the best networks of interstate and primary highways in America." On February 17, 1986, he proposed to the state legislature an initiative that would accelerate 312 projects along 7,100 miles of interstate and primary highways. The intersections of these four-lane highways, he predicted, would become prime locations for 95 percent of the new automotive supply plants. Because of the new funding, this plan would cut the time for building the priority road projects from twenty-eight to thirteen years.

For the first time, Tennessee would build 110 miles of interstate-quality highways with 100 percent state tax dollars, instead of the usual 90–10 federal-state split. These priority projects would include the long-planned Interstate 840 (later called "840 Parkway" in the plan) that would loop some thirty miles to the south of Nashville. The plan would attract to Tennessee auto jobs headed to the American southeast and spread them across the state. "We do not think all the new jobs in Tennessee ought to be in Spring Hill and we do not think people in Spring Hill want them there," the governor said.

The breadth of Alexander's proposal became clear in a lengthy letter dated April 1, 1986, from Dale Kelley, the commissioner of the Department of Transportation, to the chairmen of the finance and transportation committees of the state Senate and House. It was a twenty-five-page document listing projects across the state, and also identifying the number of miles and specific cost of each.

This ambitious plan was not well received by a weary legislature. After all, weren't governors in their final year supposed to fade away quietly? Alexander, with McWherter's support, had wrangled the legislature into raising the gas tax twice before. And with the significant assumption that the new plan should avoid new highway debt, there was no easy out this time, either: this new plan would require a four-cent increase on a gallon of gasoline and a three-cent increase in the diesel tax. When the governor invited the House Transportation Committee to the executive residence to preview the plan, its chairman Representative Robb Robinson spoke plainly.

CHAIRMAN ROBINSON: "Governor, I have just one question."
ALEXANDER: "Yes, sir?"
ROBINSON: "When are you going to go away and leave us alone?"

There could not have been a less convenient time especially for Mc-Wherter, who was preparing to run for governor himself that same year. He did not relish campaigning as the sponsor of a big tax increase. Plus, he had planned for an accelerated road initiative to be the signature program of a new McWherter administration. Privately, he told Alexander in one of their early Wednesday morning meetings, "You're not going to leave me anything to do."

Also throughout this period, the veteran Democratic State Representative John Bragg of Murfreesboro, chairman of the House Committee on Finance, Ways and Means, would mention the advice he had received as a young legislator from his mentor, the late Representative Jim Cummings of Woodbury, once the speaker of the House:

"Mr. Jim said, 'If you take care of the schools and the roads, the politics will take care of itself.'"

SPEAKER MCWHERTER'S TOP policy aide, Billy Stair, told me later, "We fundamentally misjudged Lamar's intentions for his last year in office. We did *not* anticipate he would come back with something that would require a tax increase, like on gas and diesel fuels.

"That last year, when we were slogging through the counties, he [Mc-Wherter] talked about the road program at every stop—that was going to be a central plank of his gubernatorial campaign, the need for a large-scale upgrade of Tennessee's road system. It was legitimate, we really did need to do it. It had broad appeal; everybody had a road that needed improvement of some type. It sort of gave you a built-in way to localize your message. So we were just shell-shocked when Lamar came out with that program. We all tipped our hats to him. That we needed to have it was something Ned absolutely needed no convincing about, but it really threw a curveball into his preparations for running for governor—it really caught us flat-footed—but how could you oppose it? You couldn't do that."

DALE KELLEY WAS ALEXANDER'S third commissioner to run the Department of Transportation. He had served two terms in the House but was best known around the state as a veteran basketball official in the Southeastern Conference. After one heated committee hearing on the road program, fielding many questions from legislators he had previously served with, Kelley brushed off any suggestions that their needling had gotten under his skin.

"The abuse doesn't mean a thing to me," the longtime SEC referee replied. "I've been booed by twenty-four thousand people at once." Kelley would later serve seven terms as mayor of his hometown of Huntingdon, in West Tennessee.

If Alexander, McWherter, and Wilder had not once again combined their considerable political skills in their final year of working together in state government, the Better Roads Program would have been dead in the water. As it was, the governor's bill soon became stuck in the Senate Transportation Committee, but Wilder resurrected it by amending another bill that had already passed the Senate.

THERE WERE TWO IMPORTANT road programs during Alexander's years in the governor's office. The first had come in 1983, in the year following Alexander's re-election. Passing this early road program required a high level of coordination with the legislative leaders—together with a high level of retail politicking by the chief executive himself.

One uncommitted Democrat, whom McWherter specifically mentioned to Alexander as a problem, was Representative Lincoln Davis of Pall Mall, in rural Jackson County on the Upper Cumberland plateau, an area of many small, hilly farms and few if any Republicans at that time. Granville Hinton, the administration's chief lobbyist, soon invited Davis to a private meeting in the governor's office.

"Governor," Davis protested to Alexander, "I can't vote for this tax. They'll defeat me back home if I do."

Alexander suggested that Davis invite him to a public meeting in his rural legislative district, where the governor could make the case to his constituents. Davis obliged, and on an early evening in March 1983 Alexander appeared in a packed Overton County courthouse.

"This will spread the jobs across the state, including Overton County," Alexander said. "For less than the cost of one tank of gasoline, or $15 a month, you can cut in half the time it takes to build the roads we most urgently need. You will pay a third, the truckers will pay a third, and the tourists will pay a third. And some of the new tax money will come to Overton County, which means you won't have to raise your local property taxes to build county roads."

As the evening concluded, both Davis and Alexander remember one county commissioner who was seated in the rear of the courthouse meeting room, stood and said, "Lincoln, if you DON'T vote it, we'll beat you."

Davis voted in favor of the bill.

❖

THREE YEARS LATER, IN presenting his 1986 program, Alexander refused at first to discuss financial details with legislators until there was a consensus on the 311 projects to be built. This was achieved through an arduous survey that involved Kelley and his department team working with members of the legislature identifying the highest priority projects in each district. The highway construction map that Alexander presented to the legislature thus had something in it for every county.

Soon the retail selling of the program began in earnest. The governor barnstormed the state with that map, visiting civic groups and local news media. He buttressed his appeal by arguing that all the cost would be paid for only by those who used the roads and that state taxpayers would be left with zero road debt. Therefore, instead of paying back interest and debt, all the new money could be used for road maintenance and new construction.

Once, when McWherter himself seemed reluctant, Alexander telephoned Frank Robinson, the publisher of the *Elizabethton Star* in northeast Tennessee. The governor told Robinson, a Democrat, that the highway bill—especially important to the publisher's mountain region—would never pass without McWherter's help. And if it did not pass, he added, that would be the end, in particular, of the proposed four-lane "bicentennial highway" from Johnson City to North Carolina. Robinson called McWherter, and the speaker soon stepped up his efforts. In 1987, two years after McWherter became governor, he persuaded the legislature to add two more cents to the gas tax to speed up construction.

Representative Jim Henry, the Republican leader in the House at the time, remembers the importance of emphasizing how new tax revenues were a responsible way to present the highway program of the future. Both the 1983 Alexander education program and this 1986 road program had had that aspect in common.

"The way we liked to look at it," Henry recalled, "was 'How much more conservative can you be than to propose a program and propose a way to pay for it?' When the governor proposed road programs he said, 'This is what it's going to cost and I'm going to be up front about coming to you. We're not going to borrow the money or kick the can down the road—we're going to pay for it.' To me that was the most conservative way to do it and everybody knew the system—what the program was that you were going to do. They knew it was going to cost money and, really, by the time it got to the General Assembly, Lamar had done such a good job of convincing the business community, the educators, and the general public that it wasn't difficult to vote for any kind of tax. It always had been, but this time it wasn't—the homework had been done and that's the way he handled so many things.

You know, when you've got the general public on your side and the legislature is at all reflective of it, you've saved a lot of wear and tear."

In the state Senate, it was immediately clear the program did not have enough votes for passage. It was stalled in the Senate Transportation Committee where its chairman, Senator Riley Darnell of Clarksville, was opposed at this point. Lieutenant Governor Wilder, the Senate speaker, coordinated a maneuver that gave the plan new life, working closely with two other Democrats: the veteran senators John Ford of Memphis and Douglas Henry Jr. of Nashville. Ford had already won adoption of a new program called the Transportation Equity Fund that would establish a revenue source in support of rail, aeronautics, and river commerce. They engineered an amendment to the TEF bill, adding the Alexander roads program, and the enhanced package was now adopted on the Senate floor 26 to 6—bypassing the Transportation Committee.

As the final vote approached in the House, Alexander the Republican and McWherter the Democrat were in close collaboration to gather the necessary votes for passage. "That was one thing about Lamar and Ned," Henry remembers. "They always ended up together on almost everything. Sometimes Ned couldn't support publicly what Lamar was doing, but he supplied enough votes to where it supported him."

Alexander confirmed this. "Ned told me one day, 'Governor, you get all of the thirty-eight Republican members to vote with us. And I'll tell you the twelve Democrats we need . . . and one of them might *not* be me.'" They agreed on this, relied on this mutual calculation, and Jim Henry went to work on his side of the aisle. On a daily basis, he would coordinate closely both with the speaker's office and with Alexander's legislative staff.

As the time for counting noses drew down, the administration became more confident of the outcome. This was the result of the combination of targeting road improvements to key districts and the steady, quiet pressure from McWherter and his floor leaders. House members, working with their district Senate counterparts, also knew this closing period was a time of opportunity, and several submitted new amendments that would benefit their areas. Alexander held daily update meetings with his lobbying team and Kelley, together with Lewis Lavine, the governor's chief of staff, to keep track of all the legislative traffic.

There were squeeze points, to be sure, when even the House speaker would question the legislative dynamic, always with one eye on the election in the fall. Failure in this session, with the massive road program in the balance, was not an option.

"On the last day before the vote," Lavine remembers, "everybody was sure it was going to pass, but McWherter got spooked somehow. The House was in session and there was some new amendment that appeared that was a surprise to him. He left the speaker's podium and came off the House floor and waved me over. He put one of his big arms on each of my shoulders and he said, 'Lewis, what in the hell does this bill do?' We went into his office with Dale Kelley and some others and talked about it, and everything settled down." The final vote in the House was 54–37 with one abstention.

Counting the projects added by the legislature in the final weeks of wrangling, including establishment of a twelve-year cycle for resurfacing the new highways, the final cost of the total highway package had grown from $2.8 billion to $3.3 billion. Alexander signed the measure into law on May 1, 1986.

❖

SIX MONTHS LATER, McWHERTER was elected governor. He won the office running on a simple campaign formulation of "Schools plus Roads equals Jobs." Over the next three years, his administration followed through with the subsequent tax increases on gasoline and diesel fuel that had been agreed to in the original program.

In this work, McWherter was firm in his personal advocacy with reluctant legislators who preferred to avoid voting for a new fuel tax increase. Representative Jimmy Naifeh, the McWherter ally from West Tennessee who was now the Democratic leader in the House, sponsored the bill raising taxes, but he understood both the political and practical reasons other members wanted to avoid a tax increase. "We all were worried the trucks wouldn't stop in Tennessee if we went up on diesel, if our tax was going to be so high. We were afraid they'd fill up in West Memphis, Arkansas, and not stop in Tennessee. So McWherter had us phase it in, a little bit each year over three years, and this gave other states a chance to raise their taxes also."

Nonetheless, the selling job in the legislature was not easy, and one of McWherter's tactics became legendary. This involved a toy that he kept in the lower-right drawer of his executive desk: a miniature model of a yellow road-grader, the type of heavy construction equipment that road builders used. His staff would bring resistant legislators in, one at a time, and the member would state his reasons for opposing another fuel tax increase. Naifeh sat in on many of these encounters and remembers the routine that unfolded in the governor's office many times that session.

"Ned would bring the members in—it wasn't just the Democrats. If a member was hesitant or just said they couldn't vote for the bill, Ned would pull out the toy road-grader, about twelve inches long." The governor would listen, then place the miniature road-grader on the top of his desk. Then he would look the recalcitrant legislator in the eye.

McWHERTER: "You know what that is?"
LEGISLATOR: "Yes, sir, it's a road-grader."

McWHERTER: "Yes, it is, and if you don't vote for this bill, it'll be the last goddamn road-grader you'll ever see in your district."

One senior McWherter staff member, who sat in on several of these learning moments, told me: "After he did that, he didn't have to do it too many times—the story spread like wildfire."

On other occasions, the governor's language could be even tougher in these moments. Another of his staffers remembers McWherter lecturing one male House member who persisted in wanting to avoid a tax vote: "Look," the governor, out of patience, said sternly, "you've got two balls—use one of them."

OVER THE NEXT DECADE, trade publications serving America's trucking industry began to rate Tennessee's road system among the nation's best. In 2001, *Overdrive* magazine reported that Tennessee now ranked first, having moved from second—surpassing Florida—in the publication's annual survey of truckers. Arkansas was rated the state with the worst roads; the article quoted John Hoard, a professional driver, observing that driving from West Tennessee into Arkansas was now "like going from heaven to hell."

Three decades since passage, it would appear that Alexander was right to claim, "This one tank of gasoline per year is the best investment in new jobs Tennesseans can make." Over that time $5.7 billion had been spent implementing the 312 individual projects including the 100-percent state-funded 840 interstate-quality loop south of Nashville, the Knoxville airport–to–Oak Ridge parkway, and the Johnson City–to–North Carolina parkway. By 2016, Tennessee was one of the few states in the nation with zero state highway debt.

The result, though hard won, was achieved because Democrats and Republicans in the middle 1980s were willing to look at each other across the aisle, acknowledge the same set of facts, and agree on what the future required of them. Horse trading for public improvements in individual legislative districts also played an important part; this is another remnant of the in-between time that had largely expired by the time the twentieth century drew to a close, in many state capitols as well as in Washington. In Congress, the practice of legislative "earmarks"—allocating funding for local projects that critics called "pork barrel" was disdained. By then, in a new environment of more extreme partisanship, the rising conservative majority had taken a dim view of such deal making.

"It was a different mindset," Lavine reflected in our interview years later. "It was possible to engineer a swap—this project for that vote, in support of the larger package. Some people today might find that distasteful, but it was acceptable and practical—and successful."

AS MEASURED BY THE automotive supplier jobs that eventually came to Tennessee, the bipartisan road program of 1986 was a remarkable long-term success.

In 2016, more than 832,000 cars, trucks, and SUVs were produced at manufacturing plants in Tennessee. This scale of production requires a multitude of suppliers—the makers of engine components, windshield wiper blades, tires, and sophisticated electronics—all reliably operating on tight delivery schedules. By December of 2017, according to the state's Department of Economic and Community Development, the roster of the Tennessee-based suppliers now stood at a total of 919 companies employing over 130,000 workers.

Even a notable failure along the way turned into success. When Tennessee pursued—and lost—Toyota's new manufacturing plant toward the end of the Alexander administration, the company told the governor it would, as a concession, place a small supply subsidiary called Nippondenso in Blount County. They expected this firm might employ a hundred workers.

Today, operating under its new name, Denso Manufacturing Tennessee, Inc., which opened in 1988, it employs more than four thousand people at Maryville, making electronics for Toyota, Honda, GM, Chrysler, Ford, Hyundai, and Subaru.

CHAPTER 18

The Homecoming

"Rising, Shining Tennessee"
—Headline in *National Geographic*, May 1986

ON THE WEDNESDAY BEFORE Saturn's new home was announced on a Monday, a group of auto executives from Detroit and their spouses were seated at round dinner tables inside the governor's official residence. Honey and Lamar Alexander had thought carefully about what to serve their Michigan guests and also whom they might ask to provide entertainment.

It was a warm summer night in Nashville—July 23, 1985—so that dinner was being served in the cool indoors, rather than on the back terrace where guests could look across the broad manicured lawn that sloped gently down toward Curtiswood Lane.

Interspersed among the executives seated in the dining room were leading citizens of Nashville, all eager to help present Middle Tennessee in its best possible light for the out-of-town guests. Competition had been so fierce that according to a recent poll the name Saturn was already better known than Pontiac, the established brand line that GM had been selling for sixty years. What none of the locals knew as yet was that their visitors had made up their minds about where to put the largest capital investment ever made in the United States.

For the dinner entrée and the music, Honey and Lamar had settled on country ham and Charlie McCoy. The ham would taste of Tennessee, and so in his way would McCoy, the harmonica virtuoso and recording artist (who, thirty years later, would be inducted into the Country Music Hall of Fame). Both the cuisine and the musician would be unfamiliar to the visiting executives, most of whom lived in the fashionable Grosse Pointe suburbs outside Detroit.

There were two reactions to these choices.

Bill Hoglund, the designated Saturn president who was the Alexanders' houseguest for the night, told them the next morning he awoke very early "dying of thirst"—having eaten so much of the salty ham. But even as the guests were departing, on the evening before, one Nashville matron had approached the governor.

"Why," she asked him, "would you serve these elegant people from Detroit country ham and then have that harmonica player? Why didn't you offer them Chopin? What will they think of us?"

"Ma'am," the governor replied, "why should we offer them average Chopin when we have the best harmonica player in the world?"

ALEXANDER, A SEVENTH-GENERATION Tennessean, knew his native state had something of a problem with self-confidence. *We aren't as good as they are,* too many people thought.

Maybe this was a symptom of mountain culture, where outsiders looked down on those living in Appalachia as unfortunate and downtrodden, and Tennesseans resented this. (Once, when producers of the television show *College Bowl* asked the University of Tennessee's team to participate wearing overalls, the Knoxville students in defiance showed up in the studio wearing tuxedos.) Or maybe the poor self-image dated all the way back to the end of the Civil War and the legacy of defeat among Middle and West Tennesseans.

The young governor tried whenever possible to follow his grandfather's advice: "Aim for the top. There's more room there."

This is one reason, he would say, why it was important to be the first state to pay teachers more for teaching well. Not just because the state needed better teachers—which was true—but because Tennesseans needed to be first in something. This is why Nissan's decision in 1980 to choose Tennessee was doubly important. Every state wanted Nissan, so when Tennessee won that competition, outsiders thought better of Tennessee and, more importantly, Tennesseans thought better of themselves. To win the Saturn competition as well when so many states were scrambling for it (New York had offered a billion dollars in incentives) would finally make it clear that Tennesseans were capable of playing well in any competition.

This also is why a program called "Tennessee Homecoming '86" became such a big deal. It started simply enough—in a conversation on a bus, somewhere between Nashville and Memphis—and then it got way out of control.

"CHARLOTTE," THE DETROIT TRAVEL writer asked the state tourism official, "just what does Tennessee have that would make somebody want to spend their vacation here?"

Charlotte Davidson was the assistant commissioner of the state's Department of Tourist Development at the time, and she remembers this exchange quite clearly, thirty-five years later. Partly because it led to Homecoming and all that trouble.

"Without thinking, I blurted out, 'Because we have big mountains, big fish, cold beer, country music, blues, and barbecue—all you could want, whenever you want. It's a hell of a deal. Hell of a deal."

Two weeks later, the Detroit reporter sent Davidson a tear sheet with the article she had written. "And there, on the travel page across the top, was my quote—attributed to me. Yuck. But under that was this great story about how the whole state of Tennessee was a tourist attraction." At about this time, her department was surveying motorists who stopped in at the state's welcome centers, hoping to capture fresh data to help shape a new out-of-state advertising program. Davidson added a new question: What is the first thing you think of when you hear the word Tennessee?

"When I studied these surveys, I was shocked," she remembers. "We got some of the expected answers—Jack Daniels, Elvis, Grand Ole Opry—but to my surprise a huge percentage of them said, 'It's like going home.' In fact, a lot of them had said, 'I always think everything will be all right when you get to Tennessee.'"

Davidson discussed this new data with her boss, state Tourism Commissioner Irving Waugh.

"These people are not from Tennessee so they aren't talking about going to a house when they say 'going home'—they're talking about a *feeling*. They think of Tennessee as a return to Mayberry. They think the whole state is one Jack Daniels Lynchburg ad. Coming here is like returning to a time of good friends, good food, front porches, and good times. How can we have an event or something they can come home to. Irving said, 'What about having The Year of the Tennessean?' Then we discussed how everybody who lives in Tennessee could throw a big party for everybody who ever lived in Tennessee, and everybody who wants to live in Tennessee—a big Tennessee homecoming. I don't remember who said the word *homecoming* first, but it was Homecoming from then on."

IT WAS, IN ANY case, an audacious idea—asking Tennesseans in cities and towns, hamlets and hollows across the long state to invite their families back home to celebrate local history and whatever made their living places different and special.

This would become Tennessee Homecoming '86 and it was announced by Alexander in his second inaugural address, in January of 1983. The target year of 1986 would be his last full year in office and also ten years prior to the state's bicentennial observance. Whatever might happen in 1996 would be in another decade and on another governor's watch.

This helped to shape Alexander's second inaugural message. He asked Tennesseans "in each of the three thousand places with names that we call home" to do three things:

1. *Find something special in your community.*
2. *Plan a celebration of that special something during 1986.*
3. *Invite everyone who ever lived there to come back and join your community's celebration.*

To anyone who might think that another state had more to be proud of, Alexander insisted, Tennessee had much to celebrate.

THE PLANNING FOR ALL this had, in fact, begun in 1981 when Alexander and his political team were deep into organizing for his re-election campaign of the next year. Central to the early vision for Tennessee Homecoming '86 was Doug Bailey, the Washington political consultant.

Bailey had helped design Alexander's 1978 campaign and his unorthodox "walk across the state." Three months after Alexander won the election that November, the governor-elect reached out to Bailey again, on the day of the coup that ousted Blanton three days early. Bailey helped Alexander shape his message to the public when he took the oath of office that evening, explaining what had happened and why. Over the following eight years, Bailey would visit with Alexander in Nashville on an almost weekly basis, assisting with messaging and other political planning.

The statewide celebration that became known as Tennessee Homecoming '86 did not, in fact, begin as part of a long-term master plan for community engagement by the Alexander team, but it might as well have been. By the time the Homecoming year concluded, in the fall of 1986, Alexander could look back over at least three large-scale engagements with the public in his eight years in office (not counting the 1978 campaign walk) that had dramatically raised his profile as a candidate with news media and the public.

His 1982 re-election campaign had featured that series of statewide "Community Days" centering on local civic improvement projects. This program, like the five-month walking campaign of 1978, was well organized and meticulously planned, with Bailey advising closely. In a 2016 interview, John Crisp recalled: "From a political standpoint, the Community Days allowed us to build coalitions with local folks, including Democrats, Republicans, and independents. We were running a general election campaign from the get-go."

Even Alexander's Democratic opponent in 1982, Knoxville mayor Randy Tyree, later told me, "Lamar put it out of the park with those Community Days." Following the 1982 primaries the Alexander campaign team invited Tyree to participate in the local events whenever his campaign schedule permitted. This might have created some political difficulty for Tyree, but he joined in at least one of the local events, in Dickson County. (Tyree was a native Middle Tennessean and remembers first encountering Alexander in 1957 when they were both chosen from their high schools—Tyree from Gordonsville in Smith County, Alexander from Maryville—to attend Boys State at Castle Heights Military Academy in Lebanon.) At the Dickson event, Alexander introduced Tyree to the crowd, and the Democrat pitched in on the carpentry work alongside local volunteers.

"I remember I wanted to show Lamar up," Tyree told me later. "Even though he had been kind to me, I wanted to show I could paint or drive nails better than he could." A TV news crew asked the two nominees to demonstrate for the camera. "We wound up nailing something together. Lamar was on my left, and I was on his right. We were driving nails like mad, but both of us bent our nails, we were so interested in showing off for the cameras. I think people could appreciate the good sportsmanship. They may not end up voting for you, but the situation could unify people together. Politics is the best place in the world not to take yourself too seriously."

Organizationally, the Community Days experience established a model and a staffing framework that, in turn, lead to the city-by-city advocacy operation called Tennesseans for Better Schools in 1983 to build support for the Better Schools Program legislation and its final adoption in the legislature the following year. Two years later, Homecoming '86 was the beneficiary of that tactical innovation with comparable large-scale engagements across the state—always featuring regular Tennesseans, their local government leaders, and their communities' causes, sharing the civic spotlight with the young governor.

"**HOMECOMING WAS CRAZY,**" Diane Hayes remembers. "It was probably the best job I ever had."

She had worked in public relations in Nashville and came to state government, in the Tennessee Department of Economic and Community Development, to assist with organization of the National Governors Association conference that would be held in Nashville in 1984. There she met Lee Munz, a political appointee from Oak Ridge who was running the state's Energy Office. Munz became coordinator of Homecoming '86 and offered Hayes the job of director of special projects.

By this time, planning for Homecoming was well underway. Alexander had described it in his second inaugural address, in January 1983, with the goal of every one of Tennessee's ninety-five counties to have at least one official Homecoming Community. By summer, two famous Tennesseans—the author Alex Haley and country comedienne Minnie Pearl—were announced as the honorary co-chairs of the celebration. They were both natives of the state, and in announcing the pair the governor declared they were "perfect examples of what Tennessee has to celebrate."

Davidson convened town meetings across the state to help communities determine what their local celebrations might be.

"I would ask, 'What are you famous for?' And usually they would say 'Nothing,' but once you got them going, I remember in one town someone said, 'We made bullets for World War II.' Great—so you could get out all of the pictures from that era and on Saturday night have a big Bullet Ball. Every town had something they could build a theme on. Some already had a recognized festival like Mule Day, a Strawberry Festival, or the Catfish Fry—and they could build their Homecoming festival around that.

Thirty-nine pilot Homecoming Communities were announced in early 1984, with work underway on their selected projects. These included Minnie Pearl's Hickman County, west of Nashville, and Alex Haley's hometown of Henning in West Tennessee.

The first corporate sponsor of the celebration was Memphis-based First Tennessee Bank. One popular exhibit called "Tennessee Celebrates" toured most of the state's museums with colorful displays on traditional local observances. Karin Bacon, a New York event planner (and sister of the actor Kevin Bacon) designed the exhibit.

TO BE A HOMECOMING COMMUNITY, there were four requirements of each local committee: they had to research their past to identify what was special for preservation, create a visionary plan of where the community was heading and what should be done to reach those goals, complete a community-wide project, and, in Hayes' words, "invite everyone who had ever lived in the community to come home in 1986 and join in a celebration of the whole thing."

"At first the communities were so wary of it," she remembers. "They weren't going to get any state money. They had to come up with their own money if they were going to do it. When the community committed to do these four steps, they had to finance it themselves. Homecoming didn't give any money to it."

Nonetheless, there were eventually eight hundred official Homecoming Communities by early 1986—all with new roadside signs bearing the *H* logo. An impressive list of local projects emerged. Daycare centers were developed. Many towns published written histories. East Tennessee State University, in Johnson City, produced a video history of the university. Etowah restored its old railroad depot into a museum and office for the historical commission. Tullahoma erected a twelve-foot granite obelisk at the former site of Camp Forrest, which had served as a U.S. Army training center and prisoner-of-war camp during World War II. (Tullahoma's homecoming reunion welcomed hundreds of veterans from all over the U.S., and former POWs from Germany also attended the monument dedication.) Manchester, home of a pajama manufacturer, had a big pajama party on the town square. A time capsule was buried in the Memphis Court Square—to be opened in 2036. (There were so many local projects that Alexander quit trying attend them all. "They didn't need me," he said.)

Eighteen projects with a statewide focus did receive some state funding. These included a "journalists reunion" held at Vanderbilt University in Nashville, an event honoring "outstanding scientists" in Oak Ridge, and a new annual Storytelling Festival in Jonesborough. These were partially funded by the legislature, which agreed to allocate $250,000.

A SPECIAL HOMECOMING TRAIN was a popular feature for communities along a rail line between Bristol, Tennessee, and Memphis over five days, from May 19 to May 23.

The planning for this was complicated. Tom Beasley, the former state GOP chairman, introduced Munz to executives with Seaboard System Railroad and Norfolk Southern. One of the state officials involved was Andy Bennett in the Tennessee attorney general's office. Bennett was an assistant attorney general who had worked previously on the statute establishing the Tennessee Claims Commission, the new agency created in 1985 to resolve citizen claims against the state government. The Homecoming Train would obviously be an unusual activity for state government, and Bennett's assignment in early 1986 was to anticipate the types of problems that might occur as the train moved along its excursion route.

That route was a simple one, but people who experienced it recall some memorable moments along the way. Members of the legislature were hosted at a special stop in Spring Hill in southern Middle Tennessee to tour the forthcoming site of GM's new Saturn manufacturing facility.

❖

THE NASHVILLE ARTIST Dan Brawner designed the official Homecoming logo, featuring a Tennessee state flag draped over a rocking chair. The design eventually inspired an assortment of other adaptations. Soon there was also a new popularity for the iconic wooden rocking chair.

"The logo really came alive," Hayes remembered. "They made a decision that people could use the logo any way they wanted to. No one had to get permission to use the logo on anything, anywhere. So people started to use it. There was Homecoming stuff everywhere with the logo on it, all across the state. For a while there was a collection at the Tennessee State Museum of all the ways people had used the logo.

"The communities could do anything they wanted. In the beginning, because Lamar was involved in it, people thought it was political. But what happened, when the first thirty-nine communities came together, was people didn't think Republican or Democratic. It became their personal project. When they saw they could do anything they wanted, as long as they did the four-step process, it was their decision and it took off like wildfire. People forgot about it being anything political. That's when it mushroomed, and it did kinda get out of control.

"It seemed like a good idea to not try and control it. If state government in Nashville had told everybody what to do, it would've been a government project. In fact, it became a personal project in each place, and that was a fun thing to watch."

ANOTHER OF THE EIGHTEEN special projects was a musical based on the history of Tennessee, which was produced for the Homecoming central office by Gary Musick of Bookends Productions. The production was called *Comin' Home, Tennessee* and was produced for $50,000, with Kroger as the lead corporate sponsor contributing $25,000, and the balance coming from the fund established by the legislature. Communities could rent the production. "It was booked hundreds of times during the year by Tennessee communities. The show premiered in a performance for members of the legislature in January at the Opryland Hotel ballroom. Months later, the finale was the half-time program at the Liberty Bowl in Memphis.

"IT WAS A BIG LEAP of faith," Hayes told me, reflecting on the year-long event. "It was an exciting time.

"In the beginning people couldn't figure out what Homecoming was. Lamar kinda threw the idea out there and said 'I want y'all to figure it out.'

That took until the end of '85, really. By that time the communities had begun to figure it out. That night when they saw the musical, it was like light bulbs went off in their heads. It tied together the state's history and music."

Another component was founding the first Southern Festival of Books, which became a long-running annual event. It was fashioned along the lines of the popular Miami Book Festival, which Hayes visited together with the Nashville author John Egerton and Robert Cheatham, staff director of the Tennessee Humanities Council. In Miami, they met with Stephen Mason, an executive of Ingram Book Company, the large book wholesaler based in Middle Tennessee, and this lead to Ingram becoming the first of the major corporate sponsors for the new Southern Festival, which debuted, in downtown Nashville, in 1989. Now a popular annual event, the autumn festival on the War Memorial Plaza and the nearby Nashville Public Library remains a popular meeting place for readers and authors with new titles.

THE HOMECOMING PROJECT SPUN out of control, intentionally, into hundreds of community celebrations statewide, with only a minimum of central coordination. "Nobody in the State Capitol gave anyone in the counties permission to do any of this," Alexander said later. "The government spent very little tax money on it. And there was almost no 'news' of it—because Homecoming was a celebration of lives coming *into* order, not tumbling out of order. But by 1986, Homecoming had spread like a prairie fire."

In May of 1986, *National Geographic* magazine published a blockbuster thirty-six-page essay with photography, describing the transformation of Tennessee. The title on the cover read, "Rising, Shining Tennessee." This was a new level of national attention to Tennessee, its diverse people, old traditions, and new progress. Priit J. Vesilind, the senior writer, said he had never set foot in Tennessee before, and his essay—together with photography by Karen Kasmauski—gave the *Geographic*'s global readers a stunning interpretation as seen through fresh eyes. The pages told the stories of Tennesseans from east to west—from the zinc mines, roaring waters, and Smoky Mountains in the highlands of the east, to Nashville and now Nissan and Saturn in the middle, to Graceland and the Mississippi in the west.

"Today, like the country boy made good," Vesilind wrote, "Tennessee greets the dawn with a sophisticated eye. Business is booming. Yet in many ways its soul remains unchanged from earlier times. And in a world increasingly hungry for yesterday's values—hard work, loyalty, love of place—Tennessee's frontier virtues may well be the secret of its newfound success."

CONNIE VINITA DOWELL WAS one who had moved away early. Years later she came back to Tennessee, with a special take on what Homecoming '86 had meant to her home state.

She told me of her childhood in Cumberland County, Tennessee, outside Crossville up on the Cumberland Plateau, where she had been the youngest of five children of hard-working parents. They grew tobacco, strawberries, and corn. They raised hogs and milked the cows. Connie taught herself to type, and at thirteen she worked behind the counter at Mitchell's Drug Store in the town. In high school, her English teacher let her borrow books to read. She remembers, too, when television came into their rural home, and how the images it brought of the wider world were a treat but could also be an embarrassment for her.

"TV came in our house when I was five years old," she remembers, "and early TV had a huge influence. The south, including Tennessee, was presented for laughs, held up for ridicule. I was embarrassed by the culture here. I had felt we were the 'Beverly Hillbillies' to a lot of the country, which is part of the reason why we felt the way we did about our heritage."

As a teenager, she watched many of her contemporaries move away. By the time young adults finished high school, especially in the Tennessee mountains, they imagined more promising futures somewhere else. Connie herself began a journey that took her to Knoxville, then to Murfreesboro for college, then across the United States and back. Always, she told me, there was a mixed feeling about home: "I would cringe when someone would ask me, 'Where are you from?'"

In 2009 she settled in Nashville to be Vanderbilt's first dean of libraries. It was, by this time, a changed city—with a growing population, new symphony hall and art center, professional hockey and football, and a deepening diversity of new restaurants and nightlife. Now, more young people including the college graduates of Nashville universities were staying, not leaving.

Soon after this, Alexander gave his gubernatorial papers to Vanderbilt. As Dean Dowell's librarians began to curate them, she came to appreciate the larger effect that she believed the 1986 Homecoming experience had imparted—chiefly a new level of Tennessee pride of place.

"Talking with Senator Alexander, hearing his stories, reflecting now about his days as governor and how important that walk across the state was to him, he had stayed with families like mine," she told me. "He was hearing them say, 'Our children are leaving. We've got to have jobs and reasons to keep them here.' He listened to those people and I see it in Homecoming. I wouldn't have imagined it."

❖

CHAPTER 19

The Prison Problem

"The legislature then wasn't nearly as polarized as it is today."
—Former Correction Commissioner Steve Norris

THE TROUBLE BEGAN AROUND dinnertime on a steamy Monday night in deepest summer. It was the first day of July 1985.

The initial bulletin came into Correction Department headquarters in Nashville from the warden at the Turney Correctional Center at Only, Tennessee, about a hundred miles southwest of the State Capitol: inmates have set fire to three buildings, he reported, and they have taken twenty other prisoners hostage. Later updates would report that six hundred men had become involved, that one inmate was stabbed and another had suffered a heart attack. A prison guard was held but then released.

The central issue, a prisoner spokesmen said, was the new requirement that they wear striped uniforms. Other complaints were quickly piled on, including rancid food in the cafeteria, but the trigger was that this was the first night of the first day that the new prison uniforms became the enforced dress code behind the walls. The new striped clothing was a requirement imposed by an act of the legislature (to take effect on the first day of the new fiscal year) in response to a number of escapes across the Tennessee system. Prisoners didn't like the look of this standardized attire, and the first night of July revealed how much.

By the next morning, three other prisons across Tennessee were involved, including the main penitentiary in west Nashville, where news photos showed smoke billowing into the sky. Trouble also erupted at two of the state's regional facilities in rural Bledsoe and Morgan counties.

There had been escapes and riots before this angry week, and Tennessee was not the only state to feel the pressure of courts and reform advocates, but this particular week of rage behind the walls became a wake-up call for both governor and legislature. They commenced an intensive period of investigation and understanding. Within five months, Alexander and legislative leaders had agreed to a new program that would involve prison construction and a wave of operational reforms.

❖

Depending on whom you asked, Tennessee's prisons were either barely acceptable or a bare-faced outrage that no one in authority seemed willing to address. In truth, the issue was national in scope; multiple lawsuits had been filed across the U.S. by prisoner advocates naming governors, department heads, and other officials for neglecting the health and welfare of inmates in their custody.

The driving case in Tennessee was *Trigg v. Blanton* in state Chancery Court, naming Alexander's predecessor in the governor's office as the lead defendant. A decision in *Trigg* came in September 1978, in the final few months of Blanton's term, declaring the entire state prison system unconstitutional. The order cited a host of specific ills—ranging from overcrowded, "archaic" housing units and unsanitary food service to substandard ventilation, inadequate mental health and medical services, and the "violence and the constant fear of assault."

A subsequent federal court case styled *Grubbs v. Alexander* also declared Tennessee's prison system unconstitutional. The courts placed Tennessee's correction system under the jurisdiction of an appointed master who would approve action plans, including new construction. The eventual solution would require the attention of at least five successive state administrations— three Democratic, two Republican—before that federal court order was finally lifted.

Steve Norris had been a career state employee and executive director of the state planning office when he was appointed deputy commissioner of the Department of Employment Security early in Alexander's new administration. Commissioners were the political appointees who headed the twenty-two departments. By long tradition their deputies were usually non-political professionals who had seasoned longevity in a given department and saw to its day-to-day administration.

By April 1985, with concerns about prisons escalating, Alexander and his senior staff decided that Norris's organizational and management skills would be needed most on that troubled front. Legislative leaders knew Norris and trusted him.

"I was summoned to the governor's office for a 5:00 p.m. meeting by Virginia Parker (Alexander's executive assistant). She said 'come and see me,' and I went up and she put me in that small conference room. The governor came in and said he wanted me to be commissioner of corrections. Of all the things I thought we might be talking about, this wasn't on the list. But I thought about it for a few minutes and said if this is something he wanted to do, I'd do it." When he was sworn in, Norris became Alexander's fourth commissioner to manage the Department of Correction.

The Norris appointment was the start of an intensive period of policy planning by Alexander and his senior team, coordinating closely with the Democratic legislative leaders. The internal discussions focused on how best to relieve prison overcrowding—the hardest challenge was the court's order to stop the practice of housing two inmates in one cell, which had immediately raised the prospect of expensive new construction to create greater capacity.

"When I first got there," Norris remembers, "we weren't credible with anybody—the legislature, the press, or the general public. What we had to do was fix that one issue. Then, in the disturbances in July, there were three million to four million dollars in damages, but it turned out to be a pivotal event that let us establish some better controls. Correctional officers at the main prison told the warden and me that we needed to have more controls. We were under a tremendous amount of scrutiny at that time. I think the governor just made up his mind that we had a problem that needed to be dealt with, and this was the way to do it."

The administration's response was a comprehensive reform package that included creation of a new sentencing commission to rewrite the state's sentencing laws and two new maximum-security prisons to replace the obsolete main prison at Nashville and also the old Fort Pillow Prison in West Tennessee, as recommended by the special master. To enact these improvements, Alexander, in concert with the two speakers, McWherter and Wilder, called an extraordinary session of the General Assembly to consider both the policy and financial remedies.

"Several in the legislative leadership were surprised when Governor Alexander called a special session," Norris told me. 'They had had a special corrections oversight committee. But the special session was a pivotal event that caused the department to work its way out of the court order."

The session proceeded at a fast pace and lasted only about a month. Norris remembers five members who were particularly active in the negotiations: Senators Bob Rochelle and Milton Hamilton, and Representatives Tommy Burnett, David Copeland, and Bill Richardson. All were Democrats but Copeland, who was a Republican House member from Chattanooga.

IN HIS DAY, BURNETT was the most colorful and charismatic member of the Tennessee General Assembly. His gifts of personal charm and soaring oratory lifted him through the leadership ranks as a top McWherter lieutenant, and he became the majority leader of the House Democrats. When McWherter would gather his committee chairmen around his desk in the speaker's suite, Burnett was prominently seated near him and was never shy in voicing his own opinions.

Burnett's boyhood home was Goodlettsville, near Nashville, but after law school at the University of Tennessee in Knoxville he settled about halfway in between—in tiny Jamestown, Tennessee, on the Cumberland Plateau. There he established his law practice and launched his political career. He was elected to the legislature ten times, representing a district that covered three rural counties on the scenic plateau.

Two years before this, Burnett had had his own prison experience. He was convicted in 1983 on a federal charge of willfully failing to file an income tax return and he served ten months in detention at Maxwell Air Force Base. While he was there, voters in his district re-elected him to the legislature in a 1984 race against two other candidates. (In 1991, Burnett was convicted following an FBI probe, called "Operation Rocky Top," into the state's regulation of charitable bingo games. He lost his law license and was barred from public office, ending his twenty-year career in the legislature.)

Part of the federal court order was to cap or halt further admissions to Tennessee's prisons, including incarcerations of prisoners referred by local courts. This put great pressure on local authorities, especially in the larger cities, and as the special session began on November 4, Commissioner Norris quickly found himself in a legal jam.

"A Knoxville judge called me into court to explain why I couldn't take one inmate back to Nashville," Norris recalled. "I was convicted of criminal contempt and sentenced to five hours in the Knox County jail, while the special session was going on."

Alexander sent his staff legal counsel, former Judge William Inman, to Knoxville to appear before the local judge. "Judge Inman got me out, and we got on the plane and came back to Nashville and we went to the governor's office. Then I went upstairs (the Senate and House chambers are on the second floor of the capitol building) and was given a standing ovation. Next day, I'm in the Legislative Plaza, and Tommy Burnett comes up to me. He puts a note in my hand, and it said: "Steve, As one inmate to another, welcome home. —Burnett"

The legislature wasn't nearly as polarized then as it is today," Norris told me in our 2017 interview. "There was a greater spirit of cooperation then. A lot of the people I worked most closely with in the legislature were Democrats. I used to go over to testify in front of those guys. Rochelle would just tear the hide off of me in the committee hearings, but every day they'd meet he and I would have breakfast together at the Cracker Barrel on Stewarts Ferry Pike. We'd explain our relative positions, and then we'd move on. I'd know what I was going to get, and what I wasn't going to get. At the end of the day, there were no hard feelings. It worked fairly well. After the special session, we began to make some really meaningful progress toward reform.

We gained better control from a purely management perspective. We'd also been very honest with our publics—the legislature, the courts, and the press. We had a policy that we're gonna tell you the truth, and we began to get a better hold on our own credibility."

Stair, McWherter's top policy assistant, described the mood in the legislature at this point.

"The riot at Turney prison was the spark that ignited it," he told me, "but there was resistance to the feds telling us what to do about our prisons. We didn't have the competence or the experience to offer any alternative. Shame on us, but we didn't. What the state ultimately agreed to in the federal court order was far beyond the required minimums. For example, there was no standard against double celling but we agreed to that . . . . We were really behind the curve on prison overcrowding. On the floor of the House, there was a frustration on the part of McWherter and his leadership; they grated at the idea of being forced by the feds to do this. They went along and supported it."

THE PROGRAM WAS ADOPTED. This set in motion the construction of the new prison facilities—which would extend into the next administration—and administrative improvements in the housing and treatment of prisoners, including a sweeping update of sentencing standards.

Eleven months after the special session, McWherter himself was elected governor. One of his first acts was to tell Norris that he would like him to stay on as commissioner of the Correction Department. This signal came from Harlan Mathews, McWherter's top deputy (and later U.S. senator).

"I was in a meeting in Murfreesboro, and Harlan called me. He asked me if I would stay, and I told him yes, I would stay. Later I talked with the governor, and we agreed on a two-year timeframe. We'd reassess where we were at the end of the two years."

Norris's service as commissioner thus spanned the two administrations of Republican Alexander and Democrat McWherter, from 1985 to 1989. He had the point position for overseeing the administrative reforms and also the massive building program, working closely with the State Building Commission, the legislature's Corrections Oversight Committee, and Attorney General Mike Cody.

THE SPECIAL SESSION ON corrections appropriated $200 million for corrections. McWherter became governor in January 1987. Jerry Preston, who facilitated the prison construction program, remembers McWherter at that point was concerned that little had been accomplished by the time he took office.

"It really irritated McWherter that nothing had been done with that money, and he wanted to do something," Preston told me. "He gathered a group of people—Harlan Mathews was one of them—and brainstormed about what to do." Later that year, a Special Projects Office was established, and Preston was appointed to run the facilities side of the shop. Jeff Reynolds, who later succeeded Norris as commissioner of correction, was appointed to be the policy advisor on the prison program.

They built six prisons and renovated twenty of the existing facilities with major improvements. Overall, about $400 million had been spent by the time it was finished, with the legislature authorizing the additional outlays as recommended by the administration.

"McWherter was really focused on getting that done," Preston added. "He wanted us to build prisons in counties and areas that had really high unemployment to produce employment opportunities. He wanted to build one in Sneedville, in Hancock County, and I went up there, but it's really hard to put prison property together."

Stair observed, "Building a prison is not a simple thing, particularly then because Tennessee hadn't built one in a long time."

TEN YEARS AFTER THE special session, when Alexander was running for president, John L. Seigenthaler was candid in his assessment of the former governor's record on prison reform. For a *New York Times* profile of the former governor, the retired editor and publisher of the *Tennessean* newspaper told the reporter, "Overall he was a damn good governor . . . but he was insensitive to the fact that [prison] reform could make a difference."

Alexander himself told the same reporter, "I believe a chief executive, a governor or a president, should have priorities. My priorities were better schools and jobs."

CHAPTER 20

The Game Changer

"Sometimes I ask myself, 'Could I play for me?' The answer's not always yes."
    —Coach Pat Summitt

IN THE IN-BETWEEN TIME there was one topic that Tennessee's General Assembly always agreed on—to the last man and woman, year in and year out, no matter which party held the legislative majority or the governor's office. That topic was Coach Pat Head Summitt of the University of Tennessee.

Summitt's storied career in sports made her a hero to young girls, a leader of athletes, and an icon among collegiate coaches. When her teams began to win national championships, the legislature would regularly invite her to Nashville to be honored by them. It was always a celebrity moment.

They knew she had persevered on the hardwood, reaching the pinnacle of the sport. But some of them knew she had also persisted in a courtroom, years earlier, in a case that changed the game of women's basketball.

IN THE FATEFUL SUMMER of 1974—the summer that Nixon resigned in Washington, Patty Hearst was kidnapped in Berkeley, and sixteen men ran for governor in Tennessee—an irresistible new force in sports met an immovable object.

The stubborn object was "Title IX of the Education Amendments of 1972" updating the Civil Rights Act of 1964. The new force was a rising young Tennessean named Patricia Head.

Like the birth of a new star in a galaxy light-years away, whose significance isn't discernible on our planet until much later, even the brightest sportswriters could not know the true import of Title IX without the perspective of time. Yet in the fullness of time this new statute and the young prodigy from Henrietta, Tennessee, together would accelerate opportunities for girls.

When Coach Pat Head Summitt died at sixty-four in July 2016, she was hailed as the "winningest coach in college sports"—of either gender, in any sport. Writers cited her win-loss records, that perfect 39–0 season in 1998, and her legendary eight national championships at the University of Tennessee in Knoxville. All true, and the praise richly deserved, but few remembered a very early leadership role she played, four decades earlier, that arguably had made the most difference of all: the conversion of girls high school basketball from the six-player/divided-court mode to the modern five-player/full-court system.

In 1971, eighty years after Dr. James Naismith had invented the five-player game for men, the NCAA made the full-court game and thirty-second shot clock official for women's basketball at the college level—but not for high schools in Pat Head's home state. That would be up to the Tennessee State Secondary Schools Athletic Association (TSSAA), which governed high school sports.

In 1972, while Pat Head was a sophomore and a standout player for the University of Tennessee-Martin in West Tennessee, Congress passed the new federal Education Amendments. Title IX of the new legislation declared that no college receiving government assistance could exclude anyone from participation in any sport on the basis of gender. This provided the legal foundation for non-discrimination in college sports—and opened a new future of opportunities for women in sports.

Two years later, President Gerald Ford signed the new legislation into law at about the time that Pat Head, now a graduating senior, was offered the head coaching job for women's basketball at UT's flagship campus in Knoxville. At twenty-two years old, she took the job and the graduate assistant position that came with it.

She quickly identified the TSSAA half-court rule as a disconnect. When it came to recruiting new players, it was difficult for college-level coaches to recruit Tennessee prep stars because of what she regarded as the state's demeaning rules for girls basketball. She knew this system well from her own high school playing days at Cheatham County High School. She herself had played under the old six-player/divided court rules and knew its limitations. She remembered how girls in the traditional system had either trained as guards on defense or as forwards on offense—but not both—and how this limited their possibilities when college-level coaches made their scholarship decisions.

By 1976, Tennessee was only one of six states in the country that still followed the six-on-six rule. Then the family of young Victoria Cape, a high school player in Oak Ridge, sued the state's rule-making body for high school sports, the TSSAA, claiming discrimination. The six-player system was beginning to change in other states around the U.S., but in Tennessee the system was a drag on the progression of talented athletes from high school to college with scholarship support. In the trial, a TSSAA official even testified that the half-court mode was more suitable for girls, who, he contended, did not typically have the stamina for full-court competition. He said it was appropriate, especially, for "the clumsy girl" athlete who was unable to run and play with skill on the full basketball court.

"And what about the clumsy boy?" Victoria Cape's lawyer asked the man. "Do you offer the half-court rules to boys also?" Of course they did not.

Pat Head testified in that Knoxville trial of *Cape v. TSSAA*. She insisted that as coach of the UT women's team she could not recruit in her own home state because individual girls started out at a disadvantage. Tennessee girls, playing the high school game under the current rules, were not prepared to compete successfully on both ends of the court. They were limited in their experience and training, and some athletes found this both frustrating and demeaning.

Judge Robert L. Taylor ruled in the Cape family's favor. The TSSAA appealed, but in the end changed to the five-player/full-court rule.

I ASKED FORMER COLLEAGUES of Coach Summitt's about the importance of that change four decades ago.

"Women's basketball has always been very popular in Tennessee, but when the nation started changing to the five-men game, it was obvious that we needed to change," said Joan Cronan, former women's athletic director at UT. Teresa Rotier Koeberlein, who later became chief of staff to U.S. Representative Diane Black, was the head manager of the Lady Vols (1988–92) and reported directly to Coach Summitt in Knoxville. "Everybody talks about how many wins and her graduation rate, which are great, but when you look at significant change in the history of the state, this was a pretty significant change," she said. "In order to build a powerhouse Pat Summitt had to be able to recruit in state, and to do that she had to restructure what was being done in Tennessee."

In Middle Tennessee, Betty Wiseman was Belmont University's coach for sixteen seasons and compiled a 248–152 record. She is considered the founder of Belmont's women's athletics program. She grew up in Portland, Tennessee, and like Summitt was raised on a family farm.

"The early '70s was a critical time for women's sports at the collegiate level," Wiseman told me. "Title IX required the state institutions to look at their population and make some changes. Pat became the agent of change for five-on-five. When she came into the picture, she became the spokesperson.

She had the vision. She was really the one who initiated conversations. We all just jumped on the bandwagon, but Pat was our leader—the one who was most vocal about it. I do remember her going to court. That's just who Pat was. She didn't mind speaking how she felt. She challenged them."

Today we take all this for granted. At many colleges, women's basketball outdraws the men's on game day. In the much earlier day, when Pat Head played at Cheatham County High School, young guards in the backcourt may have yearned to take a shot at the bucket, but the rules held them back to the midcourt line. For many, the dream of a college scholarship was likewise out of reach.

Now girls everywhere, whether on the court or off, know they are eligible to take their best shot.

IN THE EARLY YEARS of Summitt's program at Knoxville, she and her small staff had to rely literally on bake sales and other fundraisers to make ends meet, especially to maintain their travel schedule. Through the early 1980s, Summitt would use her own van to drive team members to away games. From the same van, they would sell doughnuts to raise what travel money they could.

There was no travel budget for the women's program, Cronan told me, so the players and coaches would have to make do by sleeping in the gymnasium of an opposing team on the night before a game.

By the early 1990s, Summitt was probably the best-known Tennessean in America. As her Lady Vols continued to amass winning records and championship laurels, she became a familiar face on national television at NCAA tournament times. Her popularity within the state was unmatched.

And so it came to pass, as it sometimes will, that someone thought Coach Summitt could also be a winner in politics. Susan Richardson-Williams was one. She had been chair of the Tennessee Republican Party from 1982 to 1985. A UT alumna, she joined the UT Women's Athletic Department staff in 1988 as associate athletic director for development, reporting to Cronan. She remembers, in 1991 or 1992, putting the political question to Summitt.

At this point, McWherter was in his second term. Because of the state's term limits for governor, he would not be able to seek a third term. It was too soon for much serious speculation about others, from either party, who might run for the open seat in 1994.

"Pat was just a force of nature, and not just around athletes but anybody who came around her—little girls, big girls, women, anybody," she told me. "She was a true leader—decisive—and she would've been in it for the right reasons. She was as good a decision maker as any leader I'd ever seen. She had no hesitation to 'pull the trigger' and never looked back. She had power, naturally. Every man and every woman I knew would have voted for her. So, yes, I asked her about running for governor."

Summitt laughed it off. In the conversation, Richardson-Williams remembers the coach made a reference to her brother, State Representative Tommy Head of Clarksville. Tommy was a prominent Democratic leader in the state House.

"You'll probably make me run as a Republican," Summitt told Richardson-Williams. "What do you think Tommy will say?"

Brother Tommy didn't have to worry or even weigh in on the matter. His sister had her own plans, bigger than politics.

ON MARCH 2, 1998, Summitt was on the cover of *Sports Illustrated*, under the headline "The Wizard of Knoxville." In 2009, she became the first Division 1 coach to reach a thousand wins. That same year, the *New York Times* noted another part of the legacy she was establishing in Tennessee, and called her Knoxville program "a cradle of coaches" for the astonishing number of former players and assistants who had advanced to coaching and top administrative positions at other colleges and universities across the country. CBS Sports and the Associated Press reported there were seventy-eight women in such positions who had been mentored by Summitt in Knoxville.

Dr. Joe Johnson, president emeritus of the University of Tennessee, recalled how the state legislature would regularly honor Summitt and her national championship teams with unanimous resolutions and standing ovations when they came to the State Capitol. "Many of the state's political leaders, both Democrat and Republican, came together often to celebrate Coach Summitt's success," Johnson said.

Late in her career, after her teams had earned eight national championships and collected a stunning record of 1,098 career victories, Summitt told a colleague that it was "not the numbers I remember, but the faces."

It was her memories of young women who had played the game for her on innumerable courts across America. Her most profound statistic may have been that all her former players graduated with college degrees. Many became superstars of the game, in college and later in the Women's National Basketball Association. Some went on to careers as television sportscasters—as did Candace Parker and Kara Lawson—and an astounding number became winning coaches themselves.

But dig beneath the headlines and the pages of the record books, and look to the careers of many other women who were also connected to her program and were shaped by it. You will find a further world of women who also learned life lessons when they were under Summitt's influence. While some became superstars in the sport, even more took the lessons with them into dozens of different careers.

In August 2011, Summitt herself announced she had been diagnosed with early-onset Alzheimer's. She also declared in an interview, "There's not going to be any pity party. I'll make sure of that." (She finished the 2011–12 season and stepped down in April.) Soon after the diagnosis, hundreds of former players and staff wrote letters to Coach Summitt. One of them was Teresa Koeberlein, Summitt's team manager in the early years, who by this time had much on her heart.

October 19, 2011

Dear Pat,

I have started this letter many times, and always find it difficult to find the right words. As you know, I was blessed with two great parents that taught me the value of hard work, compassion for others, and dedication. I learned from you how to put this into practice. I experienced on a daily basis that a person can be a true success in their professional field, while maintaining the values that I was taught at home.

You taught me to believe in myself. My parents always told me that I could do or be anything I wanted, but, in my mind, my parents had to tell me that. A young college kid being trusted by you, the greatest coach of all time, made me believe that what they said was true. The lessons I learned from you, I practice daily in my professional life. The ones that stick out the most are:

Every role is important to the team, be the best you can be in your role. It takes everyone to be successful.

You must be willing to do what needs to be done. None of us are above any job that makes the team move forward.

Teach your team to solve their problems. If you bring me a problem, bring me a solution.

Use every opportunity to teach people about life, utilizing the tools and experiences you have.

Most times, you learn more from the losses than the wins.

The final thought that comes to mind is the importance of loyalty. The voice of my conscience is a basketball coach with steel blue eyes. If I ever question what I should do, I go back to that place of loyalty. If you are loyal to yourself, your values and the people you surround yourself with, you can't go wrong. Of course with that, comes the responsibility to be careful and discerning with your loyalty. It must be an amazing feeling to know how many people like me, have an unwavering loyalty to you.

This five foot tall kid with the bad knee, that came to you wanting to be around a game that I love, was blessed with the experience of a lifetime. I still find it hard to believe that you had so much faith and trust in me, from taking care of Tyler on the occasions the nanny came a few days late, to managing the payroll for basketball camp, to managing the daily logistics of the team. Your trust in me, has always made me feel special.

I am so happy to write down my thoughts for you, and to join with everyone else. You are so humble that you do not have the ability to actually see and comprehend the vast numbers of people you have influenced and impacted over the years. I hope this gift gives you a small insight into that impact.

I often heard you say that you consider yourself a teacher. You teach young women about life, and you use basketball as your tool for teaching. Thank you for teaching me about life, friendship and loyalty.

Love,
Teresa Rotier Koeberlein
Head Manager 1989–92
Manager 1988–89

ON MARCH 24, 2012, when the Lady Vols won again, their victory pushed Summitt's total to 1,098 career wins, making her the winningest college coach ever, in either gender, across all sports. That record stood for six more years. When the Duke University men defeated Rhode Island in the second round of the NCAA tournament on March 18, 2018, the legendary men's coach Mike Krzyzewski paid Summitt possibly the ultimate compliment across time:

"Pat," he said, "would have won hundreds of more games if health had not taken her from us."

❖

Fig. 25. The reigning leaders of the "West Tennessee Caucus": Lieutenant Governor John S. Wilder, Governor Ned McWherter, and House Speaker Jimmy Naifeh. TSLA

Fig. 26. With Nashville's downtown arena almost complete, Mayor Phil Bredesen gave a private tour for Dr. Thomas Frist Sr. and Tommy Frist Jr., co-founders of HCA. Also pictured are Kenneth L. Roberts, president of the Frist Foundation, and project manager Peter Heidenreich. Author's photo

Fig. 27. (*Top*)
NHL commissioner
Gary Bettman, right,
talks with news
reporters as Nashville
Predators owner Craig
Leipold listens in this
March 20, 1998, news
photo. Randy Piland/
The Tennessean

Fig. 28. (*Right*)
Memphis Mayor
Willie W. Herenton
was all smiles after the
unveiling of his life-
sized statue on Walker
Avenue on April 23,
2003. Dave Darnell/
*The Commercial
Appeal*

Fig. 29. Houston Oilers owner Bud Adams and Nashville mayor Phil Bredesen sign the 1985 development agreement for the team's move to Nashville. Standing behind them, left to right, are Mike McClure, Joe Huddleston, Byron Trauger, Dennis Bottorff, and Steve Underwood. Courtesy of Byron Trauger

Fig. 30. Three co-chairs of Nashville's "NFL Yes!" referendum in 1996—Dick Darr, Robin Fuller, and Rick Regen—celebrate victory with the Oilers' Mike McClure. Courtesy of Mike McClure

Fig. 31. Tennessee politicians often came together over music. Grand Ole Opry legend Roy Acuff, center, greets Democrat McWherter at the home of GOP fundraiser Colleen Conway Welch. Courtesy of Colleen Conway Welch

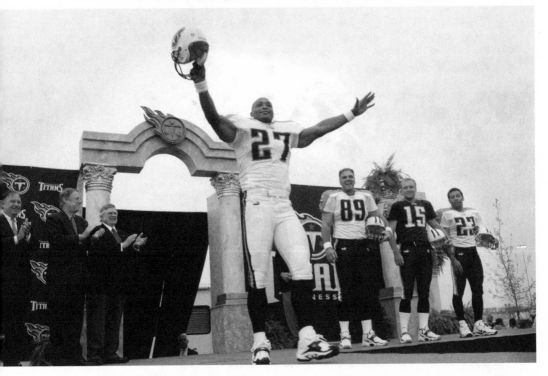

Fig. 32. Star running back Eddie George (27) and teammates show off new uniforms for the Tennessee Titans at an unveiling on April 13, 1999. At left are businessman Denny Bottorff, Mayor Phil Bredesen, and Titans owner Bud Adams. Jared Lazarus/*The Tennessean*

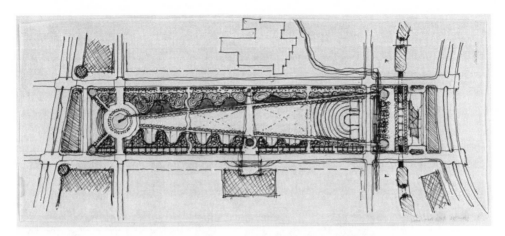

Fig. 33. The original sketch by Architect Kem Hinton for the downtown tract that became Tennessee's Bicentennial Capitol Mall. The new state park opened in 1996. Courtesy of the Architect

Fig. 34. Monumental towers of the ninety-five-bell carillon anchor the north end of the Bicentennial Capitol Mall. Rob Gordon, WPLN

Fig. 35. Coach Pat Summitt leads the cheering in Austin, Texas, after her Lady Vols captured their first Women's NCAA National Championship on March 29, 1987. From left are Melissa McCary, Kathy Spinks, Bridgette Gordon, and Dawn Marsh. Miles Cary/*Knoxville News-Sentinel*

Fig. 36. The iconic glare of Coach Pat Summitt. Here she leads her University of Tennessee Lady Vols to a 64–54 victory over Rutgers in the NCAA semifinals at Philadelphia on March 31, 2000. Delores Delvin/*The Tennessean*

Fig. 37. Pat Summitt and Wilma Rudolph attend a 1993 Nashville reception, hosted by Governor McWherter, to kick off fundraising for the soon-to-be-built Women's Basketball Hall of Fame in Knoxville. Bill Steber/*The Tennessean*

Fig. 38. Senator Bob Corker greets Jimmy Haslam, James A. Haslam II, and Governor Bill Haslam. The two families have been close since Corker and Jimmy Haslam lived together in college. Courtesy of Governor Bill Haslam

Fig. 39. Governor Bredesen and Carlos Ghosn, Nissan's global president and CEO, descend the capitol steps following the announcement that Nissan's headquarters for the U.S., Canada, and Mexico will move to Franklin, Tennessee. Sanford Myers/*The Tennessean*

Fig. 40. Four governors—Sundquist, McWherter, Alexander, Dunn—and former U.S. Senator Jim Sasser, right, attend the 2001 memorial service for Drue Smith, longtime radio reporter and member of Tennessee's Capitol Hill Press Corps. Randy Piland/*The Tennessean*

CHAPTER 21

Nashville and the "Civic Furniture"

"Successful leaders never take credit for what they're doing. The most successful, in fact, are never even known."
—Nelson Andrews

PHILIP NORMAN BREDESEN WAS out of a job when he first drove into Nashville in 1975. In the passenger seat beside him was Andrea Conte, his wife of one year.

In the HR jargon of the day, Phil was the trailing spouse. Drawing the couple to Nashville was Andrea's new employer, the mammoth Hospital Corporation of America, the pioneering for-profit hospital management company that was founded in Tennessee's capital city. HCA had recruited Andrea to be the director of nursing management systems. She had met HCA people while working as a consultant to the King Faisal Hospital in Riyadh, Saudi Arabia.

Phil and Andrea each hailed from well above the Mason-Dixon Line. Andrea was born in Great Barrington, Massachusetts, Phil in Ocean Port, New Jersey. They met in London. Phil had arrived in the UK in 1971 where he became division manager for the pharmaceutical giant G. D. Searle and Company, the parent company of Andrea's consulting firm. They married in Wheatley, Oxfordshire, in 1974.

Other opportunities soon came the couple's way. HCA later offered Andrea the position in Nashville, and meanwhile Searle asked Phil to relocate to the home office in Skokie, Illinois. He declined that job. He had lived in Skokie, the northwest Chicago suburb, for six months previously and had no interest in going back there permanently.

For their first six months in Nashville, Andrea was the breadwinner. They rented a one-bedroom apartment on Welshwood Drive, in the southern part of the city. Their art collection consisted of posters bought at museum stores. Meanwhile, Phil was trying a number of new business ideas.

At one point he made computer lapboards and sold them through classified ads in the local newspaper. He once contacted Gene Wyatt, one of the top editors at the *Tennessean* daily newspaper. Wyatt was in charge of features, society news, and the Sunday book page. Bredesen pitched him on the idea of paying him to write book reviews. He even brought a couple of sample reviews he had written. Wyatt was either unmoved or too busy, or both; he didn't hire Bredesen, but gave him a stack of books from the editor's slush pile.

Bredesen later met Wyatt's boss, John L. Seigenthaler, the influential editor-in-chief at the morning daily. (Years later, after his terms as Nashville mayor and Tennessee governor, Bredesen told me, "I always gave John a hard time—about that one time they had a chance to hire me—but, no, they were too busy.") The early Seigenthaler friendship would prove fortuitous for Bredesen, leading in 1986 to a key introduction that would help Bredesen focus his sights on politics.

"I had pushed HMOs [health maintenance organizations] when I was working in England before I came to Nashville. I used to go down to British United Provident Association, which was a customer of the division I was running for Searle. One day they asked me to drive a gentleman back to the Heathrow airport. He was a doctor and one of the founders of Kaiser Permanente. I had never heard of Kaiser or HMOs at that point and so he was telling me all about them, and I remember thinking 'That's a pretty good idea.'"

Then came Hospital Affiliates International, another early hospital management company and early competitor to HCA. At first Bredesen worked in a cubicle at HAI, then moved up through the ranks and became an assistant to the president, Jack R. Anderson. HAI was later acquired by Insurance Company of North America (now part of CIGNA), but an early assignment for Bredesen took him to Hendersonville, Tennessee, where the company was seeking state regulatory approval for a hospital. Through his HAI duties, Bredesen learned more about HMOs. "I thought they were intriguing and very much a sidebar for the company, so I did a lot of research on HMOs."

BREDESEN TOLD ME IT was the birth of their son, Ben, in the summer of 1980 that "precipitated things."

"Anyone who has had children knows that gives you a sense of your own mortality, and also of how the future is no longer 'the future' but life is here when you start having children," he said. "So I started thinking I ought to start my own company. Andrea said, 'You know, I'm very happy for you to quit your job and go out and start a company. I'm also very happy, you know, if you don't want to do that—it's absolutely fine with me—but you need to be one or the other. You need to go start the stuff you're talking about.' I said, okay."

Bredesen plunged more deeply into his new business idea—providing management for multiple HMOs. He spent time in the business research room at Nashville's downtown public library and soon developed a business plan. He also visited the Nashville investor Richard Eskind, who was a director of HAI, "basically to ask him how you go about raising money to do something like this." Eskind suggested a meeting with three other Nashville investors involved with HAI. Out of this came Bredesen's new company.

"They all invested money in the new venture, which became Health-America. It was $10,000 from each of five people—one of them was me—and a line of credit for $250,000 at a local bank," he told me. "I had to visit several banks to find one that would lend it to me. That was our capital to start the company."

They took it public in 1983 and the business grew rapidly. Bredesen sold his controlling interest three years later, in the fall of 1986, to Maxicare Health Plans, Inc. He remembers the original investments of $10,000 by each founder, including his own, had grown to about $40 million.

The question for Bredesen now became: What next?

"WHAT I DIDN'T WANT to do was what I've seen a lot of people do, which is sit there and you're forty years old and you've probably got the thirty-five most productive years of your life ahead of you. So I wanted to do something different. I was really kind of interested in politics, so I just jumped up and leaped into the dark."

He had tried politics once before. In 1969, before Searle posted him to London, he had run as a Democrat for a seat in the Massachusetts state Senate. He lost to the Republican nominee, Ronald MacKenzie, but the appeal of politics never left him. In the fall of 1986, after making his fortune in the HealthAmerica sale, Bredesen set his sights on public office.

"I didn't know anybody in town on the political side of things," he told me. "The first thing I did was I tracked down a guy named Joe Napolitan. I had read that Joe Napolitan was probably the world's first political consultant. He'd worked for the Kennedys, and I had read, probably sometime in the early '70s, his book called *The Election Game and How to Win It*. I always thought it was a smart book about politics, so I tried to find him. He lived in New York, so I just called him up on the phone one day and he let me come see him." After that first meeting, the consultant phoned Seigenthaler in Nashville to check out Bredesen. The editor told Napolitan, "Yeah, I know him," Seigenthaler said. "He's a good guy—and not a felon. You ought to talk to him."

Napolitan went to work. Bredesen had his eye on the mayor's office, but polling in Nashville confirmed that he had very low name recognition in the city. He also had few connections with the broader business community, outside his own business venture. With Napolitan, he began to address these deficits—meeting new people, speaking to civic groups, convening young leaders in various settings—both to understand the city more deeply and also to discern his own opportunities.

Among their earliest friends in Nashville, Phil and Andrea met J. Richard and Gina Lodge. The Lodges would figure prominently in Bredesen's political future: Dick Lodge was a well-connected lawyer and lobbyist, a principal in the city's largest law firm, and was chairman of the Tennessee Democratic Party at this time. When Bredesen became governor in 2003, Gina, who had a degree in social work, would become his commissioner of the state Department of Human Services.

NASHVILLE'S MAYOR AND COUNTY council members are elected in off-years relative to presidential elections, with municipal elections occurring in the first week of August. In the summer of 1987, with Mayor Richard Fulton's third and final term ending, Bredesen found himself in a large field of candidates, but on election night he finished second behind Bill Boner, placing the two of them in a run-off election in the fall. Boner, the Nashville native and four-term congressman, quickly began to hammer Bredesen as an outsider. Bredesen lost the run-off.

Boner's win meant he would be leaving Congress, and a special election was set for January 1988. Bredesen entered this race and lost it also—to Bob Clement, then president of Cumberland University in Lebanon, Tennessee. Bredesen thus remained in the private sector for another few years but soon began to study a second race against Boner, opposing his re-election to a second term as Nashville's mayor in 1991.

In a backhanded way, Boner himself provided the breakthrough opening for a fresh challenge near the end of his first term as mayor. He appeared on national television with his girlfriend while still married. The event was an embarrassment for the city, making 1991 a very different political environment for Bredesen to make a second bid for the mayor's office. This time he won.

BY THE TIME BREDESEN took office, Nashville was beginning to benefit from a number of civic innovations that would eventually make for improved citizen collaboration across racial, ethnic, and cultural boundaries. For the most part, each of these rode outside the traditional pathways of local politics and formal municipal government.

Metropolitan Government: Voters, in 1962, ratified a new local government charter that consolidated the old city and county governments into one "Metropolitan Government of Nashville and Davidson County." Nashville was only the second municipality, after Indianapolis, to adopt this unified form. It was a breakthrough at the time, and civic leaders still praise the innovation for streamlining and simplifying governmental decision making. Before this, important measures with countywide significance could require the approval of two governments, two chief executives and two legislative bodies, as well as duplicate departments and agencies. Technically, the school systems and public works departments did not overlap, but in daily practice there were conflicts that produced delays. Progress took more time.

Approval of the consolidation did not come easy. In fact, the final approval of the unified charter did not come until the second attempt. One issue had been the composition of the new legislative body. Leaders in the city's African American districts generally opposed the move, fearing it would dilute black voting power relative to their numbers within the old city limits. A final compromise, as drafted by the charter revision commission, set the council membership at forty with thirty-five members elected from districts and the other five serving in at-large or countywide seats. (The vice mayor, who is elected independently of the county mayor, is the council's presiding officer and may vote in case of a tie.) One result of this compromise was that when the newly elected Metropolitan Council finally took office on April 1, 1963, Nashville had the third-largest local legislative body in the United States, behind only New York and Chicago.

Liquor by the Drink: Just four years later, a second game changer for the city came in the form of a successful push by the business community to permit so-called liquor-by-the-drink sales of alcoholic beverages within the county. A countywide referendum was set for September 28, 1967.

"It wasn't a question of whether or not it was right or wrong, at least in my book," recalled real estate developer Nelson Andrews, who would go on to become the most prominent booster of the campaign in the public eye. He spoke about the effort in a 2006 interview for Nashville Public Library's oral history program.

Andrews himself did not drink alcohol, but he was a realist. "Unless you could ban the process of making alcohol, it was going to be made and people were going to drink it," he said. "So the key was moderation." The Nashville Area Chamber of Commerce created a committee to take on the task of bringing liquor by the drink to Nashville. Behind the scenes, the Watauga group—a private circle of top business leaders who quietly pushed economic development initiatives in town—clearly had a hand in the effort as well.

"Watauga was never directly connected with the chamber," Eddie Jones, later the longtime chamber executive, recalls, "but everyone on the committee was also in Watauga." The committee hired Jones, who was leaving his state position as press secretary to Governor Clement, to provide the political coordination the campaign would need. Opposition was centered in many church congregations. Public debates were heated. At one point, Andrews's home mailbox was destroyed with dynamite. The measure passed.

Leadership Nashville: This civic training program, later replicated in many cities across the U.S., was established in Nashville in 1976 to give community leaders a broader, three-dimensional view of their city. One important trigger had been the state government's routing of the new Interstate 40, which divided many sections of Nashville's African American community on the inner-city's north side. The hope was that with a broader gauge for understanding the complexity of the city, new leaders would make smarter decisions.

Serving on the steering committee, in addition to Andrews and Jones, were Honey Alexander and Jean Caplinger Farris, both members of the Junior League of Nashville; Shirley Caldwell-Patterson, member of League of Women Voters; Vice Chancellor John Mallette of the University of Tennessee's Nashville campus; May Shayne, member of the National Council of Jewish Women; Robert Hawkins, president of the Junior Chamber of Commerce; Cathy Anderson, mayor's office representative, and Corinne Franklin, who would become the first executive director of Leadership Nashville.

Nashville's Agenda: Boner's time as mayor, though brief and free of official scandal within government, nonetheless left in its wake a general civic malaise in the city. (By this time, of course, former governor Blanton had served his prison time, and the Butchers were famously gone from the banking industry; with Boner and his personal controversies now departed from city hall, locals would often refer to "the three Bs"—Blanton, Butcher, Boner.)

Soon after this, I proposed a civic exercise modeled on Chattanooga's groundbreaking "Vision 2000" initiative of the previous decade, to re-engage Nashvillians in talking about their city's future. Early supporters of this notion included Kenneth L. Roberts, former chairman of First American National Bank, who was now managing the Frist Foundation, and Nelson Andrews, chairman of the development company Brookside Properties. Both Roberts and Andrews had been leaders of the Chamber of Commerce, as well as trustees of Vanderbilt University. The discussion quickly accelerated among alumni of Leadership Nashville, who then numbered about a thousand.

Very early in Bredesen's first term, and with his blessing, the detailed planning moved forward. In an organizing meeting in early 1993, two Chattanooga leaders shared their experiences with three-hundred-plus participants at Vanderbilt's Stadium Club. The visitors were Mai Belle Hurley, member of the Chattanooga City Council, and Jack Murrah, then president of the Lyndhurst Foundation. Plans quickly came together for Nashville's own visioning project—called Nashville's Agenda—to commence after Labor Day of that year. As in Chattanooga, Nashville's Agenda was open to all citizens and eventually involved twenty-six public meetings across Davidson County. Some two thousand Nashvillians turned out for these facilitated brainstorming sessions, and from this process a steering committee drafted a set of twenty-one goals that ranged from education and the arts to housing and race relations.

Over the years that followed, both public and private interests in the city worked together on a host of civic improvements and institutional amenities that were consistent with the recommendations of Nashville's Agenda. These included the Nashville Housing Fund, the Frist Center for the Visual Arts, and The Davidson Group, which sought to improve race relations by pairing citizens from different racial backgrounds. While the results typically required public funding or private capital, Agenda steering committee members avoided taking credit. Andrews, who was always encouraging civic collaboration and cooperation to make great civic things happen, often said, "Successful leaders never take credit for what they're doing. The most successful, in fact, are never even known."

Some of the projects took years to complete, but by the end of the 1990s, efforts were underway for what became the new downtown public library and the Country Music Hall of Fame and Museum, as well as the Frist Center on Broadway.

KEN ROBERTS, WHO HAD brought the Frist Foundation's support to the Agenda project very early in its planning, had been close to Thomas F. Frist Jr. since their undergraduate days at Vanderbilt. In the intervening years, with the legendary growth of Hospital Corporation of America, the foundation became the largest philanthropic entity in Middle Tennessee.

Among health care entrepreneurs, HCA is considered the touchstone— the original success story of Nashville's burgeoning for-profit health care industry. The Nashville Health Care Council, founded in 1995, publishes an elaborate wall poster called the Health Care Family Tree. It is updated annually and helps newcomers visualize not only the numerical increase among related businesses based in Nashville but also the organic growth as one unique business has given rise to one or more others. In the center of this graphic family tree is HCA.

The 2017 edition of the Health Care Council's poster identifies more than five hundred companies that can trace their lineage in one way or another to the Big Bang that was triggered in 1969 by Jack Massey, Dr. Thomas F. Frist Sr., and Frist Jr. This growth in Nashville has been dramatic over that period, as early HCA executives went on to found complementary new start-ups in the sector, and those begat still others. By 2015, Nashville was home base to sixteen publicly traded health care companies, employing more than a half-million people globally and with revenues of $73 billion.

This explosion of entrepreneurship and enterprise also brought, in time, significant new levels of personal wealth to the Nashville area. Frist Jr. him-self has regularly appeared on the *Forbes* 400 listing of wealthiest Americans. This concentration of wealth in Nashville has also had political significance the U.S. presidential elections. During the election cycles of 1992, 1996, and 2000, three of the five highest contributing zip codes in the country were in Nashville and Brentwood.

Frist and his family became important philanthropists. The Frist Foun-dation has supported a wide range of nonprofit organizations, from the United Way and Vanderbilt University to Nashville's city parks and the es-tablishment in 2001 of the Frist Center (now the Frist Art Museum), an out-growth of the Agenda visioning project. In 1981, he organized twenty-seven other high–net worth Nashvillians to establish the Alexis de Tocqueville Society. (The name evoked the eighteenth-century French historian who traveled and wrote extensively about the young United States.) Each mem-ber committed to give at least $10,000 annually to United Way, giving it a substantial new financial underpinning, with an initial goal of covering all administrative overhead so that other donors' gifts could be applied totally to nonprofit grantee organizations.

The Tocqueville Society was soon replicated in other cities; by 2016, it had become the world's largest giving society of individual leaders, with 430 chapters and nearly 26,000 members worldwide. (The founding group in Nashville was eventually named the Alpha Chapter.) A decade later, Frist Jr. was elected chairman of the board of governors of United Way of America.

THE SEMINAL EVENT THAT determined the new future for Nashville's modern downtown in the twenty-first century—the most influential single action that opened the way to new museums, hotels, restaurants, symphony hall, and office towers—was Bredesen's decision to locate a new entertain-ment arena in the central city, now called Bridgestone Arena and home of the NHL's Nashville Predators. Final authorization would need to come from the Metropolitan County Council, but it was Bredesen who plotted the new arena in the precise spot where it was built—between Broadway and Demonbreun street, on the west side of Fifth Avenue.

An arena had been proposed before, during the Boner administration, but it had not advanced beyond preliminary studies, with only general notions about making such a facility suitable for large concerts and sporting events. There was also no consensus about the optimum location. Suggestions ranged from locations downtown to suburban building sites.

It was not a popular idea at the time. Bredesen told me his initial polling showed only 18 percent support for a publicly funded facility of this type. In our interview, he recalled the many objections: "Nobody comes downtown anymore." "Why build a sports venue with no NBA nor NHL team agreeing to occupy it." "It's crazy for a southern city to imagine attracting an ice-hockey team tenant." "Aren't there higher priorities for tax dollars." But he persisted.

"I felt the city had over-invested in some government programs and under-invested in 'civic furniture.' It was an active decision on my part to get some civic furniture going here," he said.

PETER HEIDENREICH HAD BEEN the city's Director of Public Works for eight years, and he was applying for the CEO job at Nashville Electric Service, the city-owned electric power utility, when Bredesen called him. In a brief meeting in the mayor's office, Bredesen asked him to be the arena project manager. Heidenreich told me their conversation went like this:

> BREDESEN: "We're going to build an arena."
> HEIDENREICH: "Do you have any money?"
> BREDESEN: "No, but we'll get it."
> HEIDENREICH: "Do you have a site?"
> BREDESEN: "No, but we'll figure that out."

"It was his vision," Heidenreich said, years later. "He believed it was the downtown that influenced the image of the entire region. Nobody was living downtown at that time, and the area was in some state of disrepair. In one of his early 'State of Metro' addresses—long before we had an arena—he took his listeners on what he called a 'helicopter ride' describing how the city could be." On that imaginary tour of a future Nashville, Bredesen described a re-born central city, thriving as an entertainment mecca with residential housing and new amenities.

BREDESEN MADE A NUMBER of early hands-on decisions that proved criti-cal to thrusting the project forward. First, he unilaterally declared where the specific building site would be, pre-empting months of competition and po-litical maneuvering.

"I asked other cities who had tried to do this and failed, 'How did you fail?' One of the answers was that everybody got caught up in selecting the site, and it never got done. Once you start arguing about sites, they told me, you just generated unnecessary friction."

The physical placement of the new arena was one of the hottest issues very early in the project. Before Bredesen stepped in there was no consensus at all on the best location. Dozens of ideas were floated for where the new facility ought to go, with suggestions for building sites ranging from the east side of the Cumberland River across from the city's central business district to an agricultural tract on the campus of Tennessee State University on the far northwest side of the city.

Bredesen swept all that aside. On a map of downtown, spread across his conference table, he pointed to a more central spot—a prominent but un-derdeveloped block south of Broadway west of Fifth Avenue and essentially he said, "We'll put it here." This immediately ended the speculation and changed the project dynamic. Very soon, hopeful architects and builders as well as enterprising developers focused all their attention on this large block and not on a dozen other places. In doing this, Bredesen had created a new reality for Nashville's central city, and so far as developers and city council members were concerned, the site selection was settled.

Next, with help from State Architect Mike Fitts, the mayor also took charge of the design phase in 1993. Competing architectural firms developed five final design proposals, and Bredesen then recruited an elite "design jury" to analyze them. This group included two celebrities—country music star Vince Gill and Anthony Mason, the basketball star who went from Ten-nessee State University to thirteen seasons in the NBA. The mayor did not hesitate to make unilateral decisions on design details he thought were im-portant. Heidenreich recalled this example: "The common thinking, among architects, was that the arena should not have a door on Broadway, that they didn't want people exiting the building onto Broadway, didn't want people on Broadway. He ignored all that."

Fitts was well known in Nashville's design community, as well as in other Tennessee cities where state government had building and renovation proj-ects. (When Fitts retired in 2010, after thirty-nine years in state government, Bredesen had become governor.) Fitts added an extra layer of impartiality and agreed to organize the architect selection process, to help assess designs, and to manage the jury.

"That arena," Bredesen told me, "was always designed to be the anchor around which we were going to rebuild the downtown environment. Music and entertainment were going to be the real anchor. You would have a place that would accommodate sports, but if you want to have a big music concert you'd have to go downtown. If you remember Nashville in 1991, you could have gone out in the middle of Second Avenue and set off a bomb and no one would have heard, and Lower Broadway had some of the least desirable elements. The thrust of this was you wanted to have 'anchors'—get a number of anchors going—to bring people downtown. The arena was number one, but one you sort of had to drag into being."

PHIL ASHFORD WAS A top policy adviser to Mayor Bredesen. He remembers how the original broad purpose of the proposed arena was entertainment, not sports.

"We had always said it was not being built necessarily with pro sports in mind, but we should just have a great arena. But of course, always in the background, there was always the possibility of getting a sports team, basketball or hockey. We were saying it should be performance focused and it should be adaptable for hockey or basketball in the event that something like that comes along, but that we're doing it because this is what the city should have. It was part of the mayor's tax increase package that was approved by the council. He rolled up a pay package (for city employees), a pile of money for schools, and bonds for arena construction."

The financing plan also assumed the Minnesota Timberwolves of the NBA could relocate to Nashville. That never happened.

Ashford continued, "I think the Timberwolves were also flirting with New Orleans at the time, but who knows how serious they were and whether they were using us to negotiate with Minneapolis. Who knows, but the deal would have involved them playing for a couple of years at the Municipal Auditorium (a 1960s structure near the State Capitol) and we would have probably had to come up with some sort of subsidy for them. That seated about seven thousand so we probably would have had to support eight thousand non-existent seats for two years. So that was always a long shot, but you know, I think Phil always took the attitude that we'll see where these things can go. Nothing much came of that. So, there was nothing particular cooking for a year or two. I think everyone would have loved to have had a basketball team, just in terms of the community of people. People in Nashville know basketball. Hockey was going to be something new."

RUSS SIMONS ARRIVED IN Nashville in 1994 after his company, Leisure Management International, won the contract to manage Nashville's new arena. Simons had grown up in Connecticut, and after graduating from the University of Connecticut he landed an internship for 1981–82 at the Summit in Houston, home of the NBA's Houston Rockets. He moved to Memphis in 1989 to manage the Pyramid ahead of its opening in 1994. Then to Nashville, three years ahead of the arena's opening.

Mayor Bredesen, Simons remembers, "didn't seem to know a lot about sports. He was more interested in creating a facility that would help transform things downtown, not because he was personally a sports nut. I knew then he was trying to do the right thing.

"When we were planning the arena, the idea was to build it for entertainment and possibly sports. We knew, no matter what, that we would have entertainment but the building should be flexible enough to accommodate the NBA or NHL if they came. The conventional wisdom was that the most likely would be the NBA. But the arena should be flexible and adaptable enough to respond to the opportunity, when it occurred."

FEW NASHVILLIANS IMAGINED AT the time how influential Bredesen's arena decision would prove to be on the future of the central city over the coming decade. There was still no professional sports team in the picture yet, at this early point, but once the arena construction was underway local attention began to focus on this long-languishing zone.

A hundred years earlier, this low-elevation section of Nashville near the Cumberland River was called "Black Bottom" for all the rich topsoil that washed into it over time. On a map of the old city, the zone also included the city's haymarket east of Fourth Avenue, where grain and horses were bought and sold, and the city maintained a fire hall on that same spot for most of the next century.

In 1996, it was clear that Nashville had a hot new development zone emerging downtown on the south side of Broadway. MDHA, the city's development agency, selected the Gateway Partnership to design a comprehensive development plan for seventeen acres south of Broadway almost surrounding the new arena's position. The principal Gateway partners were the Mathews Company, Gaylord Entertainment, and Central Parking Corp., with design support from Earl Swensson Associates and Gresham, Smith and Partners. Their final report noted the reality of this central core of the city's downtown and the promise of its future:

> The perception was that the core was not a safe place and that there
> was little to keep workers downtown. In addition, there was very little

to bring the tourists downtown. Over the past five years, the downtown area has emerged as a growing entertainment area and has been bolstered by Nashville's reputation as a tourist destination. The goal is to develop a strategy for implementing those elements, and establish a detailed development plan for the 17 acres adjacent to the Arena owned by MDHA.

THIS VISION WAS LARGELY implemented. Within two years, in or near this same downtown neighborhood, three other now-iconic Nashville projects were set in motion:

The Country Music Hall of Fame and Museum rose across Demonbreun Street from the new arena.
The Frist Center for the Visual Arts at Tenth Avenue, between Demonbreun and Broadway.
Nashville Public Library in its new central building, between Commerce and Church streets.

All three of these opened to the public within an extraordinary three-month period of celebration in the spring of 2001: the Frist Center in April, the new library in May, and the country music museum in June.

Each of these was also a private-public partnership with the metropolitan government, though at different levels on the city's side. While the library was fully a city project, boosted by private donations, the new Country Music Hall of Fame and Museum involved mostly private-sector philanthropy, with the campaign led by E. W. (Bud) Wendell, the former executive of WSM Radio, National Life, and Gaylord Entertainment. The new Frist Center for the Visual Arts, championed by the Frist family and the Frist Foundation, was established in a major renovation of the 1933-vintage main post office on Broadway; Bredesen proposed, and Metro Council agreed, that Metro Government invest $19.9 million in the art center project, including the $4.4 million needed to buy the old building from the U.S. Postal Service.

This burst of new institutions gave the city's spirits a perceptible lift and soon the synergy lead to other civic architecture in the area south of Broadway (which now was going by the hip nickname "SoBro"). In 2003, on the old haymarket block, across a new public park east of the arena, construction now began for the Schermerhorn Symphony Center. This new home for the Nashville Symphony Orchestra would debut in the fall of 2006. And new hotels, restaurants, and office structures soon followed.

This period of building and downtown revival through the middle 2000s would later be called "the Nashville Spring."

❖

CHAPTER 22

Hockey Skates In

"We would tell people hockey was like NASCAR without the yellow
flags or football without timeouts."
      —Predators president Jack Diller

FINALLY IT WAS TIME for a lunch break, and Craig Leipold decided to take
a walk. After an all-morning business meeting, closed up indoors, he was
ready for some fresh air.

It was a sunny spring day in April 1995, the day of his first visit to Nashville. Strolling along the downtown sidewalks, he found the weather mild
and a pleasant relief from the icy slush and drear cold he had left behind that
morning in Racine, Wisconsin.

What brought him to town on this day was a meeting of the Levy Corporation, in a conference room on Second Avenue. That's where he met Dick
Evans, another newcomer to Music City, now a senior officer of Gaylord Entertainment, owner of the Opryland Hotel complex, as well as the Ryman
Auditorium downtown.

Evans was aware of Leipold's standing in the world of professional
hockey. Leipold was not yet a team owner in the National Hockey League,
but he aspired to be.

"WE WERE HAVING A board meeting in Nashville," Leipold told me, "and
Levy was in the process of developing a partnership with Gaylord for what
later became known as the Wildhorse Saloon. It was a beautiful day in Nash-
ville. I got to Nashville a little early. I had left Racine on a cloudy, messy,
slushy day and I landed in this paradise. At the break I was walking along
Broadway, and there's this big hole in the ground. The sign says 'Future
Home of the Nashville Arena.'" Back at the board meeting, Leipold asked
Evans about it.

LEIPOLD: "What's going on with that site on Broadway?"

EVANS: "Why don't you come back down here in the next two weeks and let's meet the mayor."

BY THIS TIME EVANS was widely known in the industry as a well-connected player on the highest levels of American professional sports, and his stature in that world was chiefly why the Gaylord organization, based in Oklahoma, had brought him into its Nashville operations. He had begun his career with the Walt Disney Company and by this time had been a member of the board of governors of the NBA, NHL, MLB, and NFL.

When Evans arrived in the city, Bredesen had already proposed a new entertainment arena for downtown. Gaylord had important assets in the central city, notably the historic Ryman Auditorium, and was supportive of Bredesen's efforts to revive the area.

"I was recruited to come in as the chief operating officer," he told me. "It was anticipated that Bud Wendell would be retiring in the near future. Two projects that were on the drawing board, that hadn't been started yet, were the Wildhorse Saloon and the renovation of the Ryman, which had been the home of the Grand Ole Opry for many years. The Ryman had sat empty for a number of years, and the building had several limitations—they didn't own any land around it, needed to build dressing rooms, didn't have an adequate air conditioning system. The Wildhorse was a part of rejuvenating downtown. We did not want to be the Lone Ranger on Second Avenue. We brought in the Hard Rock Cafe and, together with the Wildhorse and the Ryman, the arena created a four-legged stool that would energize the area."

The first week Evans was in the city, in April 1993, he visited Bredesen and quickly found a receptive audience in the mayor's office, where the focus was tight on the need to recruit a lead tenant for the forthcoming arena. He recalled this exchange:

BREDESEN: "Can you help us attract a team?"

EVANS: "Indeed I will."

"From that day on," Evans explained, "we worked together very closely on the whole concept of attracting teams. I took him to New York. We met with (NHL Commissioner Gary) Bettman and David Stern (the NBA commissioner). Subsequent to that, we have a couple of clandestine meetings in Nashville with Gary Bettman, at Opryland Hotel." At this early point in Evans's time with Gaylord, his own office on the Opryland campus was in a trailer near the hotel.

Just as quickly, Evans involved himself with the city's business leadership, both for political support when the time came and also because "if we were successful, we would need the business community to buy boxes. I was asked to meet with Tommy Frist and Bronson Ingram, had breakfast with them. We talked about the importance of the chamber in Nashville, how it was participated in by the senior executives, that they never delegated but participated themselves. Denny Bottorff was chairman of the chamber at that time. I was asked to chair the Entertainment and Sports Committee that year. I found there was a great interest in sports, but there was sort of an inferiority complex about sports—about whether we could ever have a major-league professional team."

PART OF WHAT EVANS discovered in Nashville was a core group of private-sector leaders who were sports enthusiasts. These men and women believed in the promise of sports as a visible tool for economic development. They had championed, for example, the recent establishment of the Nashville Sports Council, recruitment of the BellSouth Senior (Golf) Classic, and the collegiate Music City Bowl. Among these influentials were BellSouth's Tennessee president Dewitt Ezell, the lawyers Lew Conner and Chase Cole, the banker Ron Samuels, the Gaylord executives Terry London and Karl Kornmeier, and American General CEO Joe Kelley. Many of these had been athletes in high school or college or both (Kelley, for instance, had been quarterback at the University of Alabama) but they were all sports fans and true believers.

"The leadership of the business community, from the very beginning," Evans continued, "was building the interest but also the ability to execute a two-fold strategy: involve the senior leadership and also prepare them to execute and sell PSLs and seats, and generate the enthusiasm in the community."

BREDESEN TOLD ME THAT he found Evans to be a solid decision maker who could be as bold as he was.

"My nature is to want to stop talking 'bits-and-pieces' and get down on paper what we could show people, but Dick was the one who knew what needed to be on that piece of paper," Bredesen remembers. "Dick wasn't always one-hundred percent on the page with Gaylord. He wanted the team there. He wanted Gaylord to manage the arena. He wanted Gaylord to have an ownership position in a team; I don't know whether they ever did. He was doing it as a good citizen, but he also had a strong business interest in having a sports team here. We had developed a friendship. We talked regularly. He was exactly the resource I needed."

Nashville was already on the radar of team owners and sports entrepreneurs outside Music City. The new facility, though unfinished at this point, would be capable not only of hosting important large amateur competitions but could figure privately into the internal calculations of professional sports organizations, particularly inside the NBA and NHL. In fact, this had already happened by this time in each of those leagues.

In May 1996, Nashville boosters had been teased by speculation that owners of the NHL's New Jersey Devils might be thinking about leaving New Jersey for friendlier confines. Owner John McMullen complained that his organization did not make enough money under terms of their current lease at Byrne Meadowlands Arena. Evans and the Devils owner were friends, and he had privately introduced Bredesen and McMullen by this time. Evans and his Nashville attorney, Tom Sherrard, had met with the Devils owner several times in Manhattan.

Nashville's new $120 million Nashville Arena that was under construction downtown made this a plausible possibility, so Bredesen eagerly jumped on the opportunity posed by the Devils situation. He quickly came up with a $20 million package of inducements, and the forty-member Metro Council as quickly gave its consent. But when the New Jersey Sports and Exposition Authority learned this, they answered the very next day with a sweetened counter-offer to McMullen. His team also won the Stanley Cup at about this time, and McMullen's interest in moving anywhere else suddenly cooled.

During this same period, the NBA's Minnesota Timberwolves had been mentioned in similar trade media speculation about Nashville. The Timberwolves remained in Minneapolis, just as the Devils had remained in Newark, but the new inducement package that Bredesen had devised had now become a new factor—a known prize waiting—in the broader sports environment. The mayor called it a "hunting license."

In Evans's words, "That gave me the ability to go out and talk to people. 'Here's the deal I can deliver; it's a lease that's been approved. If you move here or buy a franchise for Nashville, here's the deal, and it's been approved by the mayor and the city council.'"

LEIPOLD DESCRIBED HIS FIRST meeting with the mayor in Nashville. Evans introduced them over lunch in a quiet booth at Planet Hollywood on Broadway.

"We sat down with Phil Bredesen, and we hit it off very well. I was so encouraged by the vision Phil had, and we partnered at that time. He said, 'Craig, here's your hunting license. It was a deal that already was negotiated with the New Jersey Devils. Sort of an agreement in place and it did include a twenty-million dollar package of incentives to bring a franchise to Nashville.' Phil said 'All right, you're my guy.' We shook hands and we together went out to visit the NBA and NHL. They were interested in Nashville. You had a lot of growth in Nashville, the automotive industry, the health care industry. We kind of locked onto the NHL as the more likely candidate for Nashville as a place for an expansion franchise. He suggested, 'You make an application for an expansion franchise.'

"Phil Bredesen is one of the smartest men I've ever met," he added. "He's no-nonsense, because he says what he means and means what he says. When he tells you in a conversation 'We're going to do this,' that's what we're going to do. I trusted him. He knew nothing about sports, honestly. In the meeting he and I had with the commissioner of the NHL, Phil kept referring to the ice, the playing surface, as a 'court'—he knew *nothing* about hockey. The first time I watched a game with him and Andrea, when the third period ended, I think he was waiting for the fourth quarter! Who became the true hockey fan was Andrea. She was there all the time.

"But this was a mayor who was driven to change the face of Nashville. He was smart enough about what sports can do for a community, in bringing it together, in giving it swagger, in making it more known throughout the country."

IN JANUARY 1997, Leipold made a formal request for an NHL expansion franchise.

He recalls that Nashville "was the first city to make an application to the NHL for an expansion franchise (rather than recruit an existing team to move) and within a month, there were ten other markets who applied for NHL expansion teams, eleven total. The league decided to expand by four not two." Evans told me he committed Gaylord to buying into 19 percent of a new franchise, if granted.

All this set up a spirited effort in Nashville that would involve not only Leipold's organization and Gaylord's but all the boosters of the Sports Council and a surprising number of NHL hockey fans already living in the region. (Many of the latter had moved to the Nashville area ten years before when Nissan and General Motors had established a new footing there for the automotive industry.)

In early April of 1997, Commissioner Bettman and the NHL Governors'

Expansion Committee made a tour of six cities where ownership groups were hoping for a new franchise: St. Paul, Minnesota; Columbus, Ohio; Atlanta, Georgia; Houston, Texas; Oklahoma City; and Nashville. At each stop, their purpose was to test the city's commitment to professional hockey through visits with important employers and other local leaders. The availability of a suitable arena—or a plan to build one—would be a crucial test.

In Nashville, the NHL entourage was on the ground less than five hours, but the reception was extraordinary in three respects. An elite executive reception, hosted by BellSouth's Ezell, introduced the group to some two hundred of the city's business leaders. This was held on the south side of BellSouth Tower's twenty-first floor, which provided a sweeping view of the area south of Broadway. From this vantage point up high, the sweeping contours of the new arena below brought to mind the Starship Enterprise and stirred notions of the future.

Bredesen and Governor Sundquist attended this VIP gathering. When it adjourned, the visitors exited to the street below. They walked one block and into the arena for a private tour inside. This made a strong impression on the group, Leipold wrote later: "I think the arena just blew these guys away. It is so classy, so well done . . . . One owner said to me that this would be the premier building in the league if we got the franchise. I was feeling pretty good."

But the biggest, most emotional moment was yet to come. When the NHL group exited the building, they were greeted by a cheering throng on the plaza outside at the corner of Fifth Avenue and Broadway. Suddenly, on either side of a red carpet running from the arena's front door to a waiting van, the visitors stepped into a jubilant crowd estimated by a *Tennessean* reporter at between 2,500 and 3,000, most of them wearing NHL jerseys, waiving signs, and cheering wildly.

"It was crazy," Rick Regen, a Nashville businessman who was at the forefront of the boosters, remembers. "It was just amazing. The place erupted. When we opened the doors, the roar of the crowd just came in and echoed off the walls. When we opened those doors, we proved to the NHL owners we could be a hockey town."

Even as the NHL dignitaries made their way by van back to the Nashville airport, they got a further taste of what hockey fever could be like in Music City. At several intersections along that route, the visitors saw more fans cheering, most of them wearing hockey team jerseys from other cities. Many of these garments, now faded some, had doubtless made the long journey from Detroit and Cleveland a decade earlier when the car companies came.

Commissioner Bettman now declared that Nashville was "a very strong applicant" among the six cities the committee had visited.

The big announcement came on June 27. In a news conference, Bettman announced, "Nashville will join the league in 1998–99." The difference, to Bredesen's credit, was the new arena. Nashville was the only city of the six contenders with a completed facility that was ready for play.

IT WAS EVANS WHO also introduced Leipold to Jack Diller, who had worked for the San Antonio Spurs and the New York Nets. (Diller, Evans told me, "had expressed to me that one of the things he wanted to do, to cap off his career, was to start a hockey franchise.") Diller became president of Leipold's new Predators organization. David Poile was named general manager, Barry Trotz was appointed Nashville's first head coach.

Diller, in our interview, recalled the challenge of the early marketing of ice hockey in a southern city. He confirmed that many of the early season-ticket holders were those auto industry transplants from the north. For others, hockey was a new thing.

"We would tell people hockey was like NASCAR without the yellow flags, or football without timeouts," he said.

BREDESEN ACKNOWLEDGES THAT he learned important lessons from these early sports experiences. "We had gotten a number of these approaches that didn't turn out to be anything. While I did my best . . . there was the whole idea of the first one or two of these using the city as a foil."

That lesson would guide him later—in fact very soon—when the owner of the Houston Oilers came calling.

CHAPTER 23

How the NFL Came to Tennessee

"The first time they met, Phil told Bud Adams, 'Bud, I've got a confession to make: I've never seen an NFL game.'"
    —Byron Trauger

"So, let me get one thing straight here. We have a pro football team now, but they're in Nashville?"
    —Tom Hanks as Chuck Noland in *Cast Away*, Twentieth Century Fox Film Corp., 2000

JUNE, 1964

Two young men in a snappy blue convertible—top down, radio up loud, heading west across America.

Paul, the tall one, is behind the wheel, Lamar on the passenger side. Both twenty-three, with two years of law school under their belts, summer jobs waiting in Los Angeles two thousand miles ahead.

In the fullness of time, they will have other futures. Paul will become the fifth commissioner of the National Football League—the most elite job in American sports—and Lamar the forty-fifth governor of Tennessee, the fifth U.S. Secretary of Education, then in 2002 a United States senator.

But not yet. None of that glory will come for many years. First, this buoyant trip west to sunshine and summer work in southern California.

LAMAR ALEXANDER AND Paul Tagliabue had met two years before this road trip, back in the fall of 1962, while waiting in the registration line at New York University School of Law. Both were there as Root-Tilden Scholars. Paul, from Jersey City, had been a star basketball player at Georgetown University. He set the school record for rebounds, one that stood unchallenged for many years. Lamar, from Maryville in East Tennessee, had excelled on the Vanderbilt track team but had also made his name as editor of the student newspaper, the *Hustler*, urging desegregation of that conservative Nashville school.

Somewhere in the long registration line, signing up for classes and needing to buy books, Paul reached into his own pockets, searching, and realized he had forgotten his checkbook. He also had no cash. With no time to fetch his checkbook from home across the river, he turned and asked the fellow behind him for help. Lamar wrote Paul a check for $200 on the spot, and the Yankee and the Tennessean became fast friends.

On their cross-country road trip to Los Angeles, two summers later, they discussed the news of the day and politics and school and their families and life. On holidays, they had sometimes traveled to each others' distant homes and enjoyed the hospitality of each others' parents. "That's how the relationship kind of blossomed," Tagliabue told me. "I had met Lamar's parents when we were in Maryville, and he met my parents in Jersey City when we would go there for Thanksgiving."

Alexander remembers it was Frank Wheat, a senior partner at the Los Angeles firm of Gibson, Dunn and Crutcher, who recruited them both for the summer internships. "He sent us two airplane tickets," Alexander recalled. "We cashed them in and rented a convertible. We put the top town and off we went."

They shared the driving. The top was down most of the way, both remember, and the radio blared Top 40 tunes. There were long talks about the war in Vietnam, campus unrest, civil rights, and life in general. At one point midway, they spent the night at Alexander's grandparents' farm in Tassville, Missouri.

"In the car," Tagliabue recalled, "we spent a long time listening to the congressional debates in Washington on the Civil Rights Act, which was passed in early July that summer. President Kennedy had been assassinated the prior November, and then through that spring there was more and more growing debate around the Civil Rights Act. We were driving when that whole contentious debate was moving forward in Congress. There was a lot of talking about experiences we each had had—what was different, what was similar, what were our ambitions or plans for the future. And a lot of conversation about seeing parts of the country that we had never seen before.

"I don't think I had ever been west of Chicago," he continued. "Most of the places we were going, neither of us had ever been through or to, so a lot of it was about what we were seeing in different parts of the country and ethnic groups that made up the population, and industry that was there, and probably a lot of it was about civil rights. That was the topic in front of the nation during that summer, that and the war in Vietnam, which was beginning to heat up. Eventually the Goldwater-Johnson race in November '64. It was assumed that Johnson was going to be the Democratic candidate. At the Republican convention, they selected Goldwater."

Once in Los Angeles, the two young men rented a small apartment downtown and were soon at work at one of the city's largest law offices.

Alexander remembers, "This was one of the blue-chip law firms, maybe fifty lawyers at the time. It was the firm where William French Smith, Reagan's attorney general, had worked. One of the other law firms, Latham and Watkins, took ten of us out to dinner one night. We had drinks, and they kept us out until two o'clock. They wanted to see how serious we were about becoming lawyers. At dinner, I was sitting next to Mrs. Homer Crotty, the wife of a senior partner, seated around a table in beautiful Pasadena. I looked down and I saw this dish with liquid in it and beautiful greenery. I ate the salad in the bowl, and then so did the other nine lawyers. I noticed Mrs. Crotty was looking more and more alarmed. What I'd eaten were the leaves out of the finger bowl—and so had the other lawyers. I was green."

"What I learned that summer in LA," Tagliabue told me, "was that no matter how smart you are, there is going to be a group of people who are smarter. And no matter how hard you work, there is going to be a group of people who will work harder, and no matter how innovative and ingenious you think your organizational unit is, there is going to be a group of people with a better idea about a better organizational unit and you'd better understand that."

At the end of the summer, on the way back east to their final year of law school, they took a more southerly route through Shelbyville, Tennessee, so that Lamar could be best man at the wedding of Barney Haynes, another NYU classmate.

Lamar, Paul, and Barney would remain friends for the rest of their lives. After Paul became the NFL commissioner, in 1989, each winter he would invite Lamar, Barney, and two other law school chums, Bill Plunkett and Ross Sandler, to be his personal guests at the Super Bowl.

JUNE, 1993

For more years than anyone liked to count, the business and civic elite of Memphis had been hungry for the NFL.

These were accomplished men, titans of industry—men like Fred Smith, Pitt Hyde, Mike Rose, Billy Dunavant, Ron Terry. They were the very kind of prospective owners that the ruling lords of the National Football League most liked to cultivate as their colleagues.

Over their careers, these Memphis leaders had also helped the city navigate through many of its trials—using their contacts across the nation to draw new employers to town, through the long civic struggle of recovery after the assassination of Dr. Martin Luther King Jr., and the hard tasks of rebuilding the city's downtown and its spirit.

What people called "the Bluff City" on the Mississippi would seem to have been the ideal selection for a new pro football team. For many years, in fact, sports boosters across Tennessee had believed that if the NFL ever came within their state's borders, it would most likely happen in Memphis, not Nashville. Memphis was the thirty-ninth largest television market in the United States, and was near four other major media markets. Memphis was also within driving distance of many midwestern cities that currently had no NFL team.

There was also some relevant history. In 1984–85, Dunavant, the cotton industrialist and innovator of the cotton futures market, had owned the Memphis Showboats of the short-lived U.S. Football League. Then the USFL, and all its affiliated teams, ceased operations after losing a lawsuit against the NFL. Yet Dunavant's dream of drawing the NFL to Memphis did not die.

Memphis's shot did eventually come, in 1993, when the league announced it would expand by two new teams. And the same prominent business leaders who had helped bring about the Memphis Jobs Conference in 1979–81 resolved to work together again in earnest. They configured a new ownership group. In addition to Smith, Hyde, and Dunavant, the group now included Dunavant's cousin, the Wall Street money manager Paul Tudor Jones II; NFL Hall of Famer and now businessman Willie Davis; Mike Starnes, chairman of the trucking company M. S. Carriers, Inc.; Willard Sparks, the commodities firm founder; together with the considerable estate of the late Elvis Presley. (One of the team names this group initially put forward was the Memphis Hound Dogs, invoking Presley's 1956 hit recording.) Smith was considered the leader of the group.

At this time, Memphis had no other professional sports franchise. Memphis State University (now the University of Memphis) was then a Division 1 powerhouse in college basketball; the Tigers had gone to the men's Final Four in 1985. MSU's football stadium, the 63,000-seat Liberty Bowl, was central to the initial plan that the group presented, but it was in need of a serious upgrade. A $60 million renovation plan would increase seating to 68,000 and add 8,300 club seats and 100 skyboxes. The larger dream was to build a new NFL stadium next door to the Liberty Bowl, then demolish the older structure.

Four other U.S. cities had the same hopes in 1993—Baltimore, Charlotte, Jacksonville, and St. Louis—but among the five only two could succeed in this high-stakes competition. Beneath all the competing market analyses, high-powered presentations, and local boosterism, the final choice would come down to which of these cities were prepared to build a new stadium, and how quickly.

❖

IT WAS ALEXANDER WHO introduced Tagliabue, his law school roommate, to Fred Smith, the chairman of FedEx. First by phone, then later when he invited them to a college football game in Knoxville.

The first introduction came when Robert Irsay, owner of the Baltimore Colts since 1972, had let it be known he would consider a move from Baltimore to another city. He eventually relocated his team to Indianapolis, in 1984, but first he had considered both Jacksonville and Memphis.

Tagliabue remembers, "Irsay went to Memphis and Jacksonville. With a lot of fanfare, he flew in and was greeted by the mayors of those cities and business communities, and there were pep rallies and cheerleaders. I was outside counsel for the league at that time, and Lamar probably would have said to Fred, 'Why don't you call Paul Tagliabue, and he can tell you what's going on and what you have to do to 'get in the water' with Irsay. But then he (Irsay) ended up thumbing his nose at both Memphis and Jacksonville and going to Indianapolis, where they did have a new stadium—the Indianapolis Dome was new, funded by the Eli Lilly Foundation—and neither Memphis nor Jacksonville was in a position to offer a new stadium anything like the Indianapolis Dome."

Smith's next encounter with Tagliabue, in Knoxville, came about after Alexander invited them both to attend a University of Tennessee football game. Alexander was now president of the University of Tennessee, the state's land-grant college system. By this time, Smith and the other Memphis business leaders had designated Pepper Rodgers, the savvy former head coach of the Memphis Showboats in the short-lived USFL, as the coordinator for their new NFL push. Dunavant was now lead investor in this aspiring ownership group, and Smith would participate as one of several minority investors.

"Lamar invited Pepper Rodgers, and we attended the UT–Notre Dame game in Knoxville," Smith remembers. "Paul Tagliabue was in attendance."

Tagliabue also remembers that meeting. "Memphis was one of the cities in the running. Roger Goodell was managing that process—in terms of liaison with eight to ten candidate cities—and we got down to five." (When Tagliabue retired in 2006, Goodell succeeded him as commissioner of the league.) "It was made clear to all of those cities that they had to have a new stadium."

On his determined NFL mission for Memphis, Smith was prepared to use all the elements of his considerable network of business friends and institutional involvements—both local and national—to help his hometown succeed on this complex chessboard.

And it almost worked.

❖

"OVER THE COURSE OF a year or so, Pepper and I probably saw two-thirds of the [NFL] owners, and most of them were appreciative and supportive. Some of them were not," he told me. Early on, Smith and Rodgers had a clarifying—some might say sobering—visit with Goodell at NFL headquarters in Manhattan. "He told me, straight up, 'If you don't build a stadium, you're not going to be considered for this.'"

In Memphis, building a new NFL-caliber stadium to completely replace the old Liberty Bowl would require local bond financing, meaning a significant commitment from city hall. At a minimum, this meant the new Memphis mayor, W. W. (Willie) Herenton, would need to support such an investment, and more likely he would need to provide proactive leadership, explaining the merits of a landmark stadium project to the city council and taxpayers. The mayor's own leadership and personal advocacy, in other words, would be crucial to a municipal decision.

Methodically, the local leadership group began to create the conditions they thought would make a new stadium possible. Smith told me, "We were going to put forward this very aggressive public relations and political push to build a new stadium, which was the key requirement that the NFL had." Smith was also on the board of directors of Scripps-Howard Newspapers Inc. which then owned the Memphis morning daily *Commercial Appeal*, the highest-circulation newspaper in Tennessee's largest city. So the first stop was a visit with its top editor, Lionel Linder.

This meeting went well. Linder pledged his editorial support for the stadium campaign. In due course, the *Commercial Appeal* was not only providing news coverage and its editorial endorsement of the cause, but Linder even arranged for a billboard across the street from his office proclaiming the newspaper's enthusiasm for a new NFL-grade stadium. Ron Terry still praises Linder's strengths as a civic-minded editor willing to champion important civic causes. "He was the best editor I ever knew in my lifetime," Terry told me. "Outstanding man. He broke the mold. When he believed in something, it showed in the newspaper."

In Smith's memory, it was this strong backing from the city's main newspaper that helped encourage Herenton, who had been reluctant at first, to throw the weight of the mayor's office behind the NFL project.

"He had just been elected mayor—and he became a very long-serving, well entrenched, and highly controversial mayor at the end—but in the early days he was quite unsure of himself," Smith told me. "He was very close to Ron Terry and some of the other people who were involved in this. Of paramount importance to the mayor was the support of the newspaper. In other words, he didn't want to get out in front of this issue, supporting the use of public money when we had so many other needs and so forth. You know how controversial these things are everywhere."

So now things were looking up for Memphis and its NFL dream—with the morning newspaper, the corporate titans, and the new mayor all lending their positive blessings.

Then disaster struck.

"Everything was sort of going along for Memphis," Smith continued, "and we had our group, and we had the political support, and we had the newspaper support. Then, tragically, on New Year's Eve, Lionel Linder was going home from the *Commercial Appeal* down Union Avenue . . . and a young man hit him head-on and killed him."

It was the very night of the Liberty Bowl in Memphis. When Smith heard the news by phone, he was attending the FedEx Orange Bowl in Miami.

To REPLACE LINDER, SCRIPPS-HOWARD sent Angus McEachran, a deeply traditional newspaper editor with little patience for boosterism or supporting civic causes. With him now in the editor's chair, the tone of the newspaper's treatment of the stadium project shifted from positive back to neutral.

McEachran had been the metro editor of the *Commercial Appeal* in the mid-1970s and meanwhile had been assigned to two other Scripps-Howard newspapers. When Linder died, the chain assigned him back to Memphis. I asked him about his decision to change the newspaper's stance on the campaign to bring the NFL to the city. The stocky, gruff new editor did not mince his words.

"What I told them was to hit the road," he told me. "I wasn't going to hang a billboard every Sunday while they were debating whether Memphis was going to get an NFL team. Literally, Lionel was on a billboard across the street from the *Commercial Appeal* office. I didn't think that was the proper thing for a newspaper editor to do." There were no more billboards, and editorially the boosterism ceased. (It was this same traditional approach to newspapering that held McEachran in good stead as a journalist over his long career. When he retired, in 2002, newspapers McEachran had edited for Scripps-Howard had earned three Pulitzer Prizes, including one for the *Commercial Appeal* editorial cartoonist Michael Ramirez.)

McEachran continued, "When it was announced that I was retiring, Fred Smith and some of his establishment buddies—Pitt Hyde, others, people like that—they all got on Fred's Challenger jet and flew to Cincinnati and requested a meeting with the Scripps-Howard news executives. They said, 'We wouldn't presume to tell you who Angus McEachran's replacement should be, but we'd hope it would be with someone like Lionel.' Now, I personally like the guy [Smith] but his idea of running a newspaper and mine were not the same. I told him one time, 'I wouldn't presume to tell you how to run FedEx.'"

Smith told me, "Angus was quite a different guy than Lionel, and he was not in favor of the newspaper taking cheerleading positions and I think it was distasteful for him . . . to be involved in a sports team stadium project and so forth, so the support from the newspaper evaporated. They weren't antagonistic. They just weren't cheerleaders. With that, Willy (Herenton) got cold feet. So our bid was a revamped Liberty Bowl, which was much, much less expensive—and then we were up against four other cities who had pledged to build a brand new stadium.

"As it turned out," he added, "we would have actually gotten the franchise had it not been for the evaporation of the support of the Memphis paper and lack of (local political) willingness to build a new stadium. We would have gotten the one that Jacksonville got."

JULY, 1995

As complicated as Nashville's sports picture had become in the early summer of 1995—with the announced coming of NHL hockey—that situation was about to get even more tangled, and fast. "NFL" was about to enter the local vocabulary, and it would soon roil both state and local politics in the process.

Nearly eight hundred miles to the west, Houston Mayor Bob Lanier was done negotiating with Bud Adams, owner of the Houston Oilers and one of the founders of the NFL. Months earlier Adams, the wealthy oilman, had signaled to Lanier that he wanted a new stadium for his team. The mayor, at this point, was no longer interested.

The chill in Houston had blown in from many directions. The Oilers had not excelled on the field in recent seasons. The glory days of the first championships of the American Football League were stories in history now, and the legendary on-field heroics of Elvin Bethea and Earl Campbell and Warren Moon were at this point only Hall of Fame memories. In the 1994 season, the Oilers won only two games, and the 1995 record was seven wins and nine losses. At the end of the 1995 season, Adams pressed for a new stadium. But it had been only eight years earlier that he had requested—and local officials had consented to—significant improvements at the Astrodome.

Houston's storied Astrodome, though one of the earliest and most famous cathedrals of professional football, by 1987 actually had the smallest seating capacity of any NFL stadium, accommodating roughly fifty thousand fans. Adams told Harris County officials that he was prepared to move his team to Jacksonville, Florida, unless the Astrodome was updated for modern competition, fan experience, and team revenue. The county government responded with a $67 million plan to add ten thousand more seats and sixty-five luxury boxes. This plan was adopted and financed with higher taxes on real estate and hotel rooms and municipal bonds.

The memory of this 1987 transaction was still fresh enough on Mayor Lanier's mind when, in early 1995, Adams was again lobbying for a new, grander stadium—this one with club seating and other revenue generators that were now common to more recent NFL stadiums. The reception the team owner received this time was, at best, lukewarm. The city was still reeling from the oil collapse of the 1980s. Houstonians wanted to keep the Oilers but elected officials were now resisting the investment of even more money so soon after the Astrodome improvements of only eight years before. This time, Lanier turned the oilman down.

This was the precise moment when Adams and his inner circle began in earnest to consider other cities. Within days, Adams gave one of his closest advisors, Mike McClure, the green light to develop a new plan. It would be called "OPERATION CHEROKEE."

The first step forward in this secret strategy would be to reach out, through one or more trusted intermediaries, to the mayor of Nashville.

THE INITIAL CALL TO Nashville was an indirect one, and Butch Spyridon remembers it well. When the phone rang in to his desk, in the first week of July, 1995, he heard the voice of an old acquaintance. This was a back-channel type of outreach, an unofficial third-party feeler—the type that would leave no fingerprints if the answer were no.

Spyridon's desk at this time was in an upstairs office of the Nashville Area Chamber of Commerce, where he was the executive vice president in charge of the city's Convention and Visitors Bureau. This was the side of the house that promoted tourism and ran convention bookings for Music City.

"I remember it like it was yesterday," he told me, "because it was so random, so unlikely, and almost bizarre in how it unfolded. It was a business acquaintance of mine in Houston who called me, Carl Martin. Carl was in the hospitality industry, and actually I think he was between jobs. We were friendly. Carl said, 'Would Nashville be interested in talking to an NFL team?'"

By this time, because of the new arena project, Nashville had been mentioned as a possible expansion city but for NHL hockey or possibly NBA basketball, not for the NFL. Spyridon had become a Steelers fan growing up in Pittsburgh, before moving to Nashville for college at Vanderbilt, but even to his ear Martin's words sounded preposterous.

"Carl did not say who, or which team," Spyridon remembers. "In my cynical, doubter manner I just said, 'Yeah, sure, let me know. Be glad to.' Carl was not a person affiliated with sports. But I remember him saying they had reached out to somebody in Nashville previously and they were told that Nashville wouldn't be interested. I thought, well, that's just not accurate. I thought Nashville would be open to the conversation."

There were more calls over the next several days, then Martin phoned again, and there was this exchange:

> MARTIN: "Butch, I'm sure you've figured out who I'm talking about and what I'm talking about, and we'd like to have further conversation."
> SPYRIDON: "Carl, not only have I not figured out who you're talking about, I really haven't given it a second thought."

"It was so ridiculously unlikely," Spyridon told me, "I just didn't believe it." But Martin became more insistent. Then came another phone call that convinced the tourism chief he should proceed very carefully.

> MARTIN: "Confidentially, I need you off the record and you can't talk about it. It's the Oilers. They'd like to meet. They want to meet. But they don't want to meet in Nashville, and they don't want to meet in Houston. They don't want any politicians, and they don't want any press. Can you put a group together?"
> SPYRIDON: "Yeah, I think I know the right people for what you're describing."
> MARTIN: "We want to meet in Chicago. We want to meet at the Admiral's Club at O'Hare, and we want to meet tomorrow."

Spyridon placed the receiver in its cradle and took a deep breath. Then he walked, quickly, to his boss's office. Mike Rollins, the chamber staff president, was in. Spyridon stepped inside and closed the door.

"I THOUGHT PEOPLE WOULD think I was out of my mind," Spyridon told me. "I already had some of that reputation, and I was not going to be the guy to screw this up." Three years earlier, he had written a letter to the owners of the Hard Rock Cafe chain, urging them to consider Nashville for a new venue. He suggested a specific site on the north side of Broadway between First and Second avenues, near the Cumberland River.

"Mike (Rollins) was always a doubter. When I wrote the CEO of Hard Rock a letter in '92 and said, 'You ought to look at Nashville,' our Second Avenue was dead. Mike asked me then, 'Why are you doing that? It's a waste of time.' I said, 'We need something downtown—something non-country.

Back then there were maybe seven Hard Rocks around the world, so it had some cache."

The Hard Rock gambit had worked. (A Hard Rock Cafe is on that spot today.) But an NFL feeler was on another order of magnitude.

ROLLINS'S FIRST CALL WAS to Dennis Bottorff, one of Nashville's top banking executives who was currently serving as chairman of the chamber's board of governors. Both men remember this brief phone conversation, and agreeing that the best route to Mayor Bredesen would be through his closest adviser in the private sector, the Nashville attorney Byron Trauger. Rollins authorized Spyridon to reach out to Trauger, whose law office was just a block away up Fourth Avenue.

"I knew Byron a little bit," Spyridon said. "I knew he did not have an official governmental role, so to me he was the perfect person to represent the mayor and also not be obligated in any public information scenario. I called him and asked if I could come see him. Mobile phones were mostly analog at this point and everybody heard everything, so I drove up the street and pulled up almost in front of Byron's office and sat there curbside. I think this may have been my best sales job ever—I call him, he's in, and I said, 'I need to talk to you. It's legit, but I'm not willing to do it on this phone.' He invited me up."

Spyridon left his car parked across the street from Trauger's Southern Turf Building, with its ornate grillwork balcony overlooking Fourth Avenue. In its heyday a hundred years earlier, this structure had been a saloon and brothel; now it housed the firm of Trauger and Tuke, which occupied four floors above the street level. In Trauger's private office, Spyridon laid out what little information he had.

"I need you to go with me tomorrow to Chicago," he told the lawyer, "and I'll buy your ticket, and I can't tell you why." Trauger questioned Spyridon for several minutes. He registered doubt about the sincerity of any such outreach from Houston, believing some owners would readily play one city off against another. But he agreed to go.

"Next morning," Spyridon remembers, "we got on the plane with Mike. Byron is looking at me like, 'This better be good.'"

IT WAS MIKE MCCLURE who had authorized the reach-out to Spyridon. McClure reported directly to Adams in the Oilers' front office in Houston.

A news reporter in his early career, McClure was now the Oilers senior vice president for marketing and public relations. By this time he had long experience in professional sports and high-stakes negotiations.

McClure had recently finished negotiating a new television contract for the Oilers with a Houston station owned by Gaylord Broadcasting. An early call was to Gaylord's Dick Evans in Nashville, testing his interest in Nashville having an NFL team. "Dick was working on the new arena, which was already under construction, and understandably they were going to bring hockey to Nashville—and the last thing in the world he wanted was somebody coming in there with a football team. But I didn't give up."

McClure explained to me the origin of his secret code name OPERATION CHEROKEE.

Throughout his life, Adams had been deeply proud of his own native-American heritage—his mother was half Cherokee—and McClure felt invoking the Cherokee name would have emotional appeal for the Oilers owner in two ways. Tennessee had been the beginning point for many Cherokees forced onto the Trail of Tears by the Indian Removal Act of 1830. In McClure's words, the code name "sent the message, 'Wouldn't it be great to go back to the state of Tennessee as a conquering hero and bring your football team to Tennessee—and also be the number one sports attraction in the state of Tennessee—and somehow restore some of the Cherokee pride that you have in your great heritage?'" Adams "seemed to embrace the idea," McClure remembers.

Over the years, Adams had also been to Nashville in his connection to an unrelated business. In the 1970s and early '80s Adams had been on the board of directors of Kusan Inc., which had been headquartered there.

"I had been to Nashville," McClure told me. "I saw that from Atlanta to Cincinnati, and from Washington all the way to Texas, at that point you didn't have any NFL football. I knew that Fred Smith had tried unsuccessfully to get the expansion franchise in Memphis."

McClure continued, "I had done some research. We didn't have the benefit of computers and Google and all that stuff back then, so I went to the old library file cards and began looking up things like TV ADI's for Chattanooga, Knoxville, Nashville, and Memphis, and determined that, while there was no single market in Tennessee that could compare with the Houston TV market, if we made the team a *statewide* team, rather than just a municipal team, and combined those four TV markets, you would have more viewers than you would have from a Houston television station.

"And I checked out a few more numbers, the feasibility, comparing the business environment of Memphis to the business environment of Nashville—which was by far number one in the state of Tennessee and one of the best in the Southeast, if you excluded Atlanta and Charlotte. So, armed with that information I put together a memorandum to Mr. Adams."

McClure was keenly aware he would face skepticism on the part of his Nashville counterparts, chiefly because the Jacksonville gambit by Adams had become widely known in the sports world. He felt he was prepared for this.

"I figured that if the people in Nashville had done any due diligence they would have known that Adams had already played Jacksonville for a fool," he said. "So I'm sitting there thinking I'm going to go into a meeting with people from Nashville, Tennessee, and I'm going to have to convince them of the sincerity of Bud Adams, and how this is a different ball game and I'm a different guy . . . and I would not be sitting there talking to them if I didn't believe, one, that he was serious and sincere and, two, that if we could put together a viable deal we would actually be willing to go through with it.

"So I felt a burden of responsibility from the standpoint of having to take someone whose reputation in Houston, and whose team, is no longer good. He's got a bad football team, and he's been trying to build a new stadium and get out of a lease where he spent $85 million of taxpayers' money, which wasn't to his benefit but as far as the public is concerned they never distinguish the difference. I'm certainly not going to go in there and pretend these Nashville guys don't know anything and haven't done any due diligence."

McClure had reserved a private meeting room inside the Admiral's Club at O'Hare.

Here the Nashville team of Rollins, Trauger, and Spyridon now met McClure; Steve Underwood, then the Oilers' general counsel (and later president); Craig Skien, a stadium marketing consultant; and John Elsner, of the Houston Sports Association. (It was Elsner who had specifically recruited Carl Martin to place the initial call to Spyridon.)

"After introductions, Mike [McClure] went right into what it was and what they were looking for," Spyridon remembers, "and they covered a lot of ground. They absolutely assured us they were serious, that this was not a fishing expedition. Houston had just fallen apart for them, so they told us Bud was now willing to leave his hometown. Mike McClure was a pretty serious deliveryman. He was carrying the water for the Oilers, and he was charged with finding a home. And they had done their homework. They knew about the geographic area, they knew about the population, they knew the competitive marketplace. They had done their homework on this market."

The Jacksonville experience came up rather quickly. McClure told me he "vividly" remembers that very soon after introductions he touched on Adams's recent Jacksonville drama: "Yes, he did go to Jacksonville, and yes he did come close to moving his franchise to Jacksonville but ultimately he stayed in Houston where he has been since 1946, almost fifty years, and Houston has been the base of operations."

Inside the Admiral's Club, their discussion went on for several hours. When the meeting ended, Trauger said he would convey the interest to Nashville's mayor. All shook hands, and the Nashville group flew home.

LATER THAT AFTERNOON, Rollins briefed Bottorff. Trauger went to see Bredesen, then phoned Rollins to report on the mayor's reaction. Rollins promptly shared his words with Spyridon.

> ROLLINS: "The mayor just thinks they're playing us, and we're wasting our time. 'Are they just using us to try to get a better deal in Houston?'"
>
> SPYRIDON: "Let's just suppose they are playing us. What do we have to lose? As long as we're not spending any money, we're going to learn a little bit, and we're going to make some friends in the NFL. If we can get a meeting with the owner of the Oilers, why wouldn't we do that?"

Bredesen remembers that he, too, was skeptical at first. Fresh on everyone's mind, locally, was the ordeal of developing the new downtown arena, without a sports tenant in hand, and the very recent public discussions to bring an NHL team into that now-rising venue. There had also been the flirtations from the New Jersey Devils and also the Timberwolves. Both of those, of course, had evaporated.

But after further discussions with Trauger and Bottorff directly, the mayor began to analyze the best way to undertake a delicate first conversation with a representative of the Oilers organization. Within a few days Bredesen, working on his own personal computer at the mayor's desk, personally designed what he called a "term sheet." He believed the right kind of basic initial agreement, if signed by both parties, would undergird any discussion with Adams or his representatives and provide a deadline. This document could therefore drive the secret discussions forward, he figured, while also protecting the city government and its taxpayers.

❖

ALL OF THIS MOUNTING activity, while complicated and full of stress, seems to have come at a good time personally for Bredesen.

Staff members who were close to him during this period say the explosion of sports opportunities in the summer of 1995 was also the "best medicine" for the mayor in his recovery from a bruising political defeat—his loss to Sundquist the previous November. To say that the first half of 1995 had been a downer for the mayor would have been an understatement.

In 1994, hoping to succeed McWherter, he had run for governor and won the Democratic nomination. Then he faced Sundquist, the five-term Republican congressman. (This time neither nominee was a native Tennessean;

Sundquist came from Moline, Illinois, and Bredesen from Shortsville, New York.) The race had turned into an ugly fight, which Bredesen lost by 142,000 votes, almost a 10 percent margin. It was a painful loss, and the months following were a time of reflection and emotional healing.

But now there were two nationally significant opportunities he would need to manage—with the possibility, if smartly navigated, that Nashville could snare two major league sports franchises with the NFL and NHL. People close to Bredesen at the time remember that this sudden collision of opportunities not only did not seem to faze the mayor but rather seemed an emotional charge for him and a new focus. While others in his circle at city hall were feeling the crush and pressure of cascading new challenges, Bredesen himself seemed to find a new energy.

THE NEW TERM SHEET that Bredesen devised would require of the Oilers organization an exclusive bargaining agreement. Adams or his emissaries could not approach or consider any other city for sixty days while the Nashville talks were pending, and for its part the city could not have discussions with any other team. The mayor believed this stipulation would quickly reveal any possibility of an insincere "fishing expedition" on the part of the Oilers owner—that, if this proved unsuccessful, could leave city officials in Nashville out on a limb.

He asked Trauger to share the document with Adams through McClure. The two sides fleshed out the final language over the following weeks—most importantly preserving Bredesen's insistence on the sixty-day exclusive stipulation. Adams and his team quickly agreed to the conditions.

There would, of course, be a multitude of other details—most notably where a new stadium might be built, and how to pay for it. Based on recent stadium construction in other cities, Bredesen's team working with McClure settled on an estimated construction cost of $250 million. This was a huge figure by Nashville standards, and the discussions centered on the necessity of state government participation. This, in turn, made it necessary to broach the subject, and very quickly, with the taciturn Governor Sundquist.

For this careful assignment, the Democrat Bredesen enlisted the help of two people, both with distinctly Republican credentials. One was Bottorff, and the other was Tom Ingram.

BOTTORFF ALREADY KNEW ABOUT the Oilers gambit, from the day of the first contact when Rollins had passed him the word.

Like Evans in his Gaylord element, and Tommy Frist in his own, Bottorff was in this context now the quintessential connected guy for Bredesen's purposes. From his position at the top of Nashville's First American National Bank, his network reached from the Vanderbilt Board of Trust and into the city's business and finance sector where he was widely respected. Politically, he spoke as a friend to both Republicans and Democrats—including, significantly now, both Sundquist and Bredesen. He had even been a leading figure in Sundquist's finance effort for the 1994 race.

Ingram's career had extended from his David Lipscomb College days, when he was a young campus correspondent for the *Tennessean*, to his prominent roles later in all of Alexander's campaigns. He was the deputy governor (essentially chief of staff) when he left Governor Alexander's office following his 1982 re-election. He then established The Ingram Group, a consulting firm offering government relations and strategy counseling to businesses and individuals. An early client was the GOP mandarin Jim Haslam of Knoxville and his growing Pilot Oil Co. In the early nineties Corker also came to Ingram for advice on whether he should get into politics, and so did many others.

Over the following weeks, Bottorff and Ingram proceeded to reach out to others in their respective realms who likewise knew Sundquist. These included Haslam in Knoxville, and Corker, who now as finance commissioner sat atop the governor's new cabinet. The central agenda was to get Sundquist onboard with a stadium deal. This meant the state government's financial participation.

And it worked.

TIME WAS NOW OF the essence for getting the term sheet document signed, and Adams committed—personally and publicly—to dealing with Nashville on a fixed timetable.

The signing of the term sheet occurred in Nashville on August 11, over a private lunch at the Wild Boar, an exclusive restaurant in midtown known for wild game, fine wine, and high prices. Adams had flown into town the day before. Joe Huddleston, the mayor's finance director, and Trauger were there, and so were Underwood and McClure, accompanying Adams. It was in this setting that Bredesen and Adams signed their names to the mayor's term sheet and shook hands.

Phil Ashford and Jenny Hannon remember the moment that same afternoon when they heard the news. Following his lunch with Adams, Bredesen stepped into a hastily called staff meeting at city hall and surprised everyone there but Huddleston with his update about NFL football.

"I remember Phil called all of his staff into the conference room," Ashford told me. "He said, 'We've got an opportunity for an NFL team. The

Houston Oilers are interested in moving to Nashville.' And my immediate reaction is, 'Yeah, right.' You know, this is another case of us being used."

Hannon remembers the news shocked her. She had grown up in Lebanon, Indiana, and was an athlete in college at Indiana University. She was recruited to Nashville in 1993 to be the first staff director of the Nashville Sports Council. That organization was a joint venture of local government and the Chamber of Commerce, designed to recruit important amateur sports tournaments to the city. Her work was showing some early success, especially with the new lure of the coming arena, where site-prep work was already underway on this hot August afternoon.

"I'll never forget it," Hannon told me, "when the arena was literally just a hole in the ground, we were in a meeting in Mayor Bredesen's office, and he said, 'I just signed an exclusive agreement to bring the Oilers to Nashville.' I had just launched the Sports Council, we were building the arena, and I'm thinking, 'I don't want a stadium and a professional sports team. I don't want this to happen. We're working on the arena!'"

By this hour, of course, the Oilers relocation was in motion.

The news would not be publicly announced until the end of this same day. At lunch, Adams had agreed to appear with Bredesen on the stage of Gaylord's big Wildhorse Saloon on Second Avenue near Broadway. The main order of business at this quick staff meeting, as far as Bredesen was concerned, was for his team to scramble and pull that event together—hoping for maximum attendance by Nashville's business leaders and news media.

Reaching out to VIPs would consume the mayor's staff for the rest of the day. Local news media were also summoned for a major announcement downtown, but no details would be provided.

AT THIS MOMENT, COINCIDENTALLY, some of the national sportswriters who covered the NFL were converging on Tennessee, but not Nashville. Their destination was two hundred miles to the east, in Knoxville, where the Oilers would play the Washington Redskins on Saturday in a preseason exhibition game at UT's Neyland Stadium.

Sundquist had not been in Nashville when the big announcement was made the day before at the Wildhorse. But he was quoted in the *Tennessean* the next morning, saying he looked forward to helping make the Oilers move possible. The governor went on to say he was looking forward to meeting Adams in Knoxville.

On Saturday, McClure recalls, Sundquist's state aircraft landed first at the general aviation facility at McGhee-Tyson Airport. He was waiting inside the terminal and greeted Adams there.

The Oilers lost the exhibition game to the Redskins (16–13). But in a private skybox high above the gridiron, in a meeting facilitated by Ingram with help from Haslam, Adams and Sundquist had a brief visit and a good conversation, all agree.

❖

THE TERM SHEET, NOW agreed to, had been complicated enough, but it would lead to many weeks of further negotiations and a much bigger document. The more detailed development deal was hammered out in many secret meetings, some convened in Trauger's law office, others in private rooms at the Loew's Vanderbilt Plaza hotel.

Occasionally the sessions grew heated, according to participants on both sides. Huddleston described how it went: "There were accusations of 'disingenuous representation' but that was more bluster than reality. Some of these sessions would go until two or three in the morning. People would get very tired. The Oilers were very meticulous, and we were trying to be as meticulous as possible. We would go line by line. They of course wanted everything. We wanted to limit what they got, because every time they wanted something it had a cost. If there was yelling across the table, I was probably as guilty of that as anyone. I got tired of hearing their demands, and at one point I got up and walked out of the room. Byron followed me out. Ralph Voltmer, a lawyer with Waller, was kind of the monitor and scribe and would make sure that everything we agreed to was gotten down in writing. Ralph came out of the room with this absolutely white look on his face, like I was about to blow the whole thing up. Byron said 'Joe, can't you chill out.' I started laughing at him; Ralph looked at me, like 'Why are you laughing?' I said it's all part of the process; we'll go back in and get a better deal. They know we'll come back in, but at some point you have make them think you will walk away.' I thought I had scared Ralph to death.

"What the Oilers really wanted," Huddleston continued, "was our commitment that nothing would be put to a public vote. We couldn't agree to that, because we knew that at some point there would be a substantial bonding proposition, and once that issue got into Metro Council, Phil certainly understood there was a strong possibility all this would be kicked over into a referendum. My recollection is we never committed to that, we committed to our best effort. They (the Oilers negotiators) were really afraid of a public referendum; that would come at the end of a process, and at that point they would be so strung out that their options would be extremely limited."

Trauger told me, "This thing could not have happened without Phil framing the deal and responding at each of the critical moments during negotiations. He was able to look at the term sheet that they presented and have enough experience and enough savvy to say, 'Of course, we're not going to agree to all of that, but it is not so outrageous that we can't cut a deal within that framework.'"

ONCE THESE TALKS WERE concluded, there was now clarity on the financing requirement, for which Bredesen and his team would need to muster support in order to provide the $250 million stadium. This shifted the focus to Capitol Hill and working out a deal with the State of Tennessee on its hoped-for share that would need to be in the neighborhood of $55 million.

The participants in these discussions included neither Bredesen nor Sundquist—more than one participant in the discussions used the expression "bad blood." Instead, a high-level negotiating committee of five members was established to find the path forward. On the state's side of the table was the governor's top deputy, Peaches Gunter Blank. For Metro Nashville it was Trauger, Huddleston, and Jim Murphy, the city's legal director. Bottorff served as a "private sector representative." While their meetings were tense at times, this group worked well together. Their work also took the place of any direct discussion between the mayor and the governor; neither man relished the idea of direct communication with the other. Bredesen's chief contact, other than his discussions with Bottorff, was actually Corker. Both men told me later it was in this negotiating process that they first met and developed a mutual respect.

"That's where I actually got to know Bredesen very well," Corker told me. "He was in the mayor's office and we talked nonstop on the phone, at night. I remember going down to his office late in the evening. Bredesen was an interesting guy in that we would, you know, negotiate back and forth. He would send me talking points that he typed up—I didn't even have a computer on my desk as commissioner of finance in 1995 and '96. Literally, I got them to take it out. It wasn't something that was useful to me. Bredesen, on the other hand, was this techy-oriented guy and he literally would fire it off himself and send it up. And we would negotiate six bullet points."

Bredesen remembers that Sundquist "wanted no part of it. He was distant. It had been a tough campaign; he had won, we were not friends. Sundquist delegated Bob to work with me. . . . We're cut from very similar cloth. He was the core that made it work. We became friends in that process and have remained friends. When I go to Washington now, I see him and we have dinner."

Bottorff remembers, "I think Corker and Bredesen really gained a great deal of trust for each other during that time period." Also helpful to this process was a financial analysis that Bottorff had First American Bank's treasurer, Terry Spencer, perform that deemed the bond-financing package he was proposing for the state to consider a solid approach.

"It was very attractive for the State of Tennessee," Bottorff said. "The $60 million in bonds was just a slam dunk deal to do." He remembers discussing the proposition with State Senator Douglas Henry, chair of the Finance Committee in the state Senate.

> HENRY: "You know, Mr. Bottorff, if I'm walking down the sidewalk and I see a dollar bill laying on the street, I'm going to pick it up and put it in my pocket."
> BOTTORFF: "That's right, Mr. Henry. That's how easy this decision is."

APART FROM THE FINANCING particulars, the physical location of the new Nashville stadium presented additional challenges. For Bredesen the prime site would be the east side of the Cumberland River across the water from the city's central business district on the west side.

The east bank had an assortment of owners and uses, mostly industrial, at this location. Most prominent among these were a manufacturer of heavy marine barges that served river-towing companies, and a commercial sand yard where heavy trucks would load construction sand from barges for local truck delivery to thousands of building projects across the mid-state region.

Where some downtown business owners regarded this heavy-industry view across the river as a sign of a vibrant local construction economy, critics would complain it was an eyesore too near Nashville's front door. Some even urged the city's redevelopment agency to declare the zone "blighted" but Gerald F. Nicely, then executive director at the Metro Development and Housing Agency, had resisted such notions. Better, he said, to wait for a tangible business opportunity coming the city's way, and only then consider city intervention. With Adams's OPERATION CHEROKEE setting its sights on Nashville, the moment had now come.

Ingram Materials Inc., a subsidiary of the Nashville-based Ingram Industries Inc., owned the sand yard. This privately held business had acquired the eastside property in 1962 when it bought the old Cumberland Sand and Gravel Co. and created Ingram Materials in its place. Bredesen assigned Nicely to approached Ingram quietly and explore any willingness to give up the land they had owned for three decades.

This was a difficult time for the Ingram family. The founder of Ingram Industries Inc., E. Bronson Ingram, had been diagnosed with cancer the year before this, and he had died in June 1995. In his absence, several Ingram executives objected to letting go of the sand yard site, fearing a disruption to their regional business operations. Also, the initial offer that Nicely proposed—$1 million—was regarded as much too low.

After Bronson's death, his widow, Martha R. Ingram, had become chairman of the parent company's board of directors. She now viewed the city's request as an opportunity for Nashville that transcended normal operations. She had gotten to know Bredesen over the preceding decade, and she trusted him. Before he was elected mayor, Bredesen had served with Mrs. Ingram on the board of directors of the Nashville Symphony Association, when Bredesen had personally led the symphony management's contract negotiations with the local musicians' union in the late 1980s. More recently, he had supported Mrs. Ingram, a prominent donor to the arts, in her goal of increasing the city's public funding for grants to local arts organizations.

"Bronson had thought someday we'd build a five-star hotel on that property—not that we'd build it ourselves, but that the land would become prime for that type of use at some point," she told me. In that event, the value of the old sand yard would likely rise to well over the million-dollar figure that Nicely was now suggesting. "I said to our people, 'Look, here's what we're going to do: We're going to take a box at the fifty-yard line. But more importantly I have known Phil Bredesen for quite awhile and he has been enormously helpful to me, and this stadium is important to the city of Nashville.' I trusted him to do the right thing."

Philip M. Pfeffer, who was Ingram's executive vice president at this time, remembers it took several months to reach agreement with MDHA. The Ingram sand yard operation was then relocated to another industrial zone near Omohundro Drive, farther upstream on the Cumberland. Bredesen could now commit to Adams the possibility for a new NFL stadium site.

BREDESEN ASKED HANNON TO change jobs and become executive director of TENNFL. This new entity would be charged with building awareness of the NFL opportunity, sales of club seats and the personal seat licenses to anchor the stadium funding, and the initial season ticket sales. Hannon worked out of a loaned office at the local NationsBank headquarters downtown, and her team grew quickly.

Part of Bredesen's agreement with Adams involved a set of financial guarantees, provided by some of Nashville's largest employers. The top executives of a dozen local companies—most of them Republican—had embraced the Democrat Bredesen's appeal for what an NFL team could mean for Nashville's national profile. They quickly provided a set of financial guarantees, some as high as $750,000, to backstop the local financial commitment, if needed. These included HCA, Gaylord Entertainment, First American National Bank, and Ingram.

PSL sales were promising early on as a majority of them sold, but the effort stalled after the initial burst of NFL enthusiasm in the city cooled. In a second push, Bredesen made another appeal to the larger guarantors, and a special marketing committee was formed to design a supplemental sales push. A "virtual tour" on video was developed to show prospects how the stadium—designed but unbuilt—would look. This worked, and the guarantors were soon off the hook.

IN THE FINANCING PLAN that Bredesen and Huddleston designed, it would be essential for Tennessee's state government to participate in several ways. One of these was to authorize Nashville's metropolitan county government to retain a share of sales tax revenues to support construction of a new stadium.

Apart from the bonding and revenue sharing decisions, Sundquist's team insisted on two additional things: One was a solid commitment to Tennessee State University, based in Nashville, to use the new stadium as its home field during college football season. Corker lead the way on this, and it was agreed to. The other was the team name. It would need to be more broadly called the Tennessee Oilers, or whatever new name might be selected, not the Nashville Oilers. This also was agreed to, in recognition of the state's substantial financial participation: $55 million of the $292 million project.

"From the very beginning," Trauger said, "we knew this was going to be the Tennessee team although it's going to benefit Nashville a whole lot more than it's going to benefit the rest of the state. You had to get people to vote for it in the legislature for the rest of the state. The whole deal had to be a really good financial deal for the state. So, the way we structured it, basically, they were going to issue bonds—thirty-year bonds—and they would be paid off in twenty or twenty-one years, but they would keep getting the payments after that time, which would be gravy, so it was a really good financial deal for the state. Bob Corker understood that and went through the numbers with Phil."

NASHVILLE'S SHARE EVENTUALLY involved the use of surplus city water utility fees as an additional source of dedicated revenue, as well as the local bond financing. Both became part of the rallying cry for local opponents of the big project. Prominent in the opposition was the Reverend Bill Sherman, pastor of the big Woodmont Baptist Church in suburban Green Hills. Another was the city councilman Eric Crafton, who launched a petition drive to force a countywide referendum vote on the bond issue. His effort was successful, collecting 43,600 signatures.

In response, the pro-stadium side launched the "NFL Yes!" campaign to ensure a win. Bredesen pressed his former chief of staff Dave Cooley into service as chief strategist and fundraiser, and also detailed his press secretary Shannon Hunt to manage the campaign from a small office at Cooley's PR shop. Three campaign co-chairs were announced—Dick Darr, Elaine Goetz, and Rick Regen—and two prominent Nashville restaurateurs, Mike Kelly and Randy Rayburn, held fundraising receptions so the campaign could afford TV commercials. One featured the silver-haired Mrs. Goetz, who appealed to seniors.

The initiative passed, with 58 percent of Davidson County voters approving, and the construction project moved swiftly forward.

THERE WAS A FINAL timing problem for the Oilers organization to navigate, and it was a big one.

Soon after the referendum passed, the new stadium was quickly under construction, but it would not be ready for NFL games for another two years. This created a need for the Oilers to find an interim site for the two upcoming seasons. Two sites were considered—Neyland Stadium in Knoxville and the Memphis Liberty Bowl. McClure's recommendation was for the team to play in Memphis for the first two seasons in Tennessee.

The choice of Memphis would prove to be a disaster, all around. For the Oilers, attendance was embarrassingly low that next season. The team's marketing efforts in Memphis were aggressive, but there was scant interest among Memphians in turning out for this new "Tennessee team." Bottorff personally offered to fly friends over from Nashville, but he had few takers. Adding insult to injury, some sportswriters and other observers blamed the low turnout on the frustration of Memphians having been so recently spurned by the NFL.

Kelly, the Nashville restaurateur, was chairman of the Tennessee Restaurant Association at the time. He remembers traveling to Memphis for the Steelers game. "Steelers Nation" was there in great numbers, making the Liberty Bowl look more like a home game for Pittsburgh.

"I stayed at the Peabody," Kelly told me, "and I remember getting up that Sunday morning and reading the *Commercial Appeal*. The headline in the newspaper, in four-inch-tall letters, said 'Our Dream, Their Team.' That was just a prelude to what happened. Of course the stadium was full of Steelers fans. That was the turning point. That was the one where Bud said, 'That's it. We're going to Nashville. I'm through.' I think he was through with Memphis at that point." Soon the decision was announced that season two in Tennessee would be played not in Memphis but in Nashville, at Vanderbilt's Dudley Field.

McEachran, the newspaper editor, gave me his take on why the Oilers' Memphis season didn't work out.

"If you can't be the bride, you sure as hell don't want to be the bridesmaid," he said. "That's why nobody showed up. People said 'Screw the Oilers!' And Bud Adams—you talk about being the turd in the punchbowl—he had said how blessed Memphis was to have the Oilers for the little time they were going to be there. I didn't have a favorable impression of him, and the city of Memphis didn't either. They told him to go stuff himself—he couldn't have sold tickets to a whorehouse."

BUT FOR NASHVILLE, the Titans capture was like a tonic for a torpid real estate market, like the time a dozen years earlier when Nissan came. One Nashvillian who observed the "NFL effect" up close was Mark Bloom, a prominent real estate investor who also became close to Adams.

"When the commercial real estate market went up 15 percent overnight, the interest level was because we had an NFL team. The commercial real estate market became a much more interesting play, people coming in from out of town willing to take a chance. That was the beginning of it—when he moved that franchise here. This has been the metamorphosis over the past fifteen to twenty years, from $10 per square foot to $300 per square foot. Only five or six cities in our country have escalated like that in the past twenty years.

"All of a sudden people were saying, 'Nashville got an NFL team? How did that happen?'"

CHAPTER 24

History and Handoffs

"These were not slogans. They were not abstractions."
  —Gordon Bonnyman

AT THE END OF any administration, there is usually in the executive branch some unfinished work. From McWherter, Sundquist inherited two especially high-profile priorities—both of them expensive, deeply complicated, and politically fraught.

One was a huge capital improvement project, smack in the geographic center of Nashville, called the Bicentennial Capitol Mall. The other was TennCare, McWherter's hallmark program to reform Medicaid. Then there was a third initiative that arose from this same transition period, and it was Sundquist's own, called Families First. As TennCare would be to Medicaid, the big idea was to take over from the federal government a central program of social welfare.

The Bicentennial Capitol Mall

As Tennessee's two hundredth birthday approached, the McWherter administration started early preparing for the 1996 commemoration of statehood, though the observance would not occur until almost two years after his successor was elected.

After much planning and design work, the central project that emerged was an ambitious reimagining of nearly a hundred acres immediately north of the State Capitol building, beginning with the north slope of Capitol Hill. This would be a monumental undertaking, covering a distance of almost a half-mile from end to end, between James Robertson Parkway on the south and Jefferson Street on the north. There were several facts of geography and history that made this tract appealing for something big and important. One was the history of Jefferson Street, which had played a visible role in Nashville's civil rights history at mid-century, making it an important reference point for the movement. This tract also had been the location of Nashville's

Farmers' Market, operated by a city government agency, but for years it seemed the passing state administrations gave it very little attention, regarding it as Nashville's responsibility.

Also, because of historically swampy conditions in this area of Nashville, this broad tract had never been suitable for the kind of high-rise construction that occurred on the capitol building's other three sides through the twentieth century. But here was a silver lining: This absence of tall construction also had left the north aspect of the capitol—the vista from Jefferson Street—as the last unobstructed view of the iconic building.

The person who seems to have noticed this architectural opportunity first—and, in any case, who proceeded to do something about it—was a Nashville inventor named John A. Bridges. His sister, Nancy Hardaway, lived in the Germantown neighborhood north of the capitol. Bridges remembers standing in an empty classroom inside the old Elliott School building, on the north side of Jefferson Street, when he looked out a south-facing window and observed the unobstructed sightline to the State Capitol building in the distance.

A graduate of the industrial arts program at MTSU, Bridges was working at the time as a product designer for Aladdin Industries Inc., the Nashville-based maker of the iconic Aladdin Lantern and other inventions. (His name is still on the original patents for Aladdin's ubiquitous insulated mug and also the insulated food trays used by many hospitals and airlines.) Bridges imagined this area north of the capitol could become a state park, capable of transforming this acreage and reactivating the north side with a park-like homage to two centuries of proud history. Otherwise, he believed, in time the opportune sightline would be lost forever as Nashville continued to grow and construction technologies advanced.

Bridges drew a sketch of his vision for a redesign of the linear tract, and he wrote a brief narrative describing it. But he needed an advocate for his idea, a champion who might bring his sketch to the attention of the right people in state government. He showed the concept to his boss, company chairman and CEO Victor S. Johnson Jr., a prominent civic leader in Nashville. Johnson had been an important voice in the fight for consolidated metropolitan government in the early 1960s, and later he was the volunteer board president of the Chamber of Commerce. He also knew McWherter.

Johnson liked Bridges's idea, and he took the sketch and narrative with him to a subsequent meeting at the capitol. There, the Aladdin chairman asked the governor to consider it. McWherter promised he would, then handed the package to Jim Hall, one of his top staff advisers, and asked Hall to evaluate it. Hall had already been thinking about options for how the state might observe its bicentennial in 1996, and soon he became a champion of the Johnson/Bridges concept.

Hall grew up in Chattanooga but over the years his family made frequent visits to Nashville when his brother John Hall was a student athlete at Vanderbilt. Jim Hall had also been to the capital many times prior to McWherter's election in 1986. By the time of this meeting with Johnson, Hall had been studying ways the state might observe its bicentennial. He learned how the Tennessee Centennial Exposition, a century earlier, had included a full-size replica of the Parthenon in Athens, Greece, and had led to the founding of Nashville's Centennial Park. (Nashville's original Parthenon was a temporary structure, reconstructed over the 1920s, and today remains the centerpiece of the midtown park.) But the centennial exposition had also been a year late in opening, finally occurring in 1897, and Hall knew any such delay in the forthcoming bicentennial would be unacceptable to his boss.

"Without Ned the Bicentennial Mall would never have happened," Hall told me. "When I first discussed it with him, he was quite *under*whelmed, as he usually was. He would later call it 'Hall's Mall.' Victor Johnson brought a concept of doing something with the capitol and the area north, and Ned gave me permission to move ahead with it. We got Martha Ingram involved. You also had to get the property available; there were some state offices there, and you had to deal with the L&N Railroad, because it was a main line. Also with the farmers' market down there, you had to deal with Mayor Fulton and quite a constituency for the farmers' market. What we wanted was something that would mark our bicentennial as effectively as Centennial Park had done for our first hundred years. That, to me, meant we had to come up with the grand idea. We decided to have a mall, like you have in Washington."

McWherter put his finance commissioner, David Manning, in charge of this complex project, knowing it would require not only substantial funding but also careful coordination—financial, bureaucratic, and political—among many agencies, local and state as well as federal. In addition, negotiating with L&N would be critical since the old train trestle would need to become a suitable southernmost feature of the new mall. Manning in turn relied on two of his assistant commissioners, Jim Graves and Jerry Preston, and also Mike Fitts, the state architect. Graves was assigned the lead on assembling the big project site, acquiring parcels from many separate property owners. Preston, who ten years earlier had managed the complex program of building updated prisons, would now manage coordination among architects and engineers and of getting a final design approved.

"You could stand up at the capitol," Preston remembers, "and look out over the 'North Forty' and it was pretty easy to think about a mall. You'd think about the U.S. Capitol in Washington and its mall. It was an easy concept to visualize, but difficult to implement. There were multiple studies done about how to use that land—how to use the north slope of the capitol. Then in the early '90s the idea of the mall started taking shape. In 1992 (this was about midway through McWherter's second term) we had worked on the master plan for two years, with the goal of getting it right. There were six or more different concepts for what to do on the mall." Meanwhile, Mc-Wherter established the Tennessee Bicentennial Commission on June 1, 1992. It was a bipartisan group, Hall remembers. McWherter asked Martha Ingram to be its chairman and Vice President Al Gore to be the honorary co-chair. Former Governor Dunn, the Republican who lost the 1986 race to McWherter, was also a member.

Preston and Fitts established a project workshop on the seventeenth floor of the James K. Polk State Office Building near the capitol. He described the early design and approval process: "We wanted people from East, West, and Middle Tennessee to be involved," he told me. "We had different schemes laid out around the room and we had a charette up there with architects, landscape architects, urban planners, and civil engineers from Memphis, Knoxville, and Nashville."

Kem Hinton, principal in the Nashville firm Tuck-Hinton Architects, was a participant in that early charette. He became the lead designer for the mall portion of the redevelopment, which would cover nineteen central acres of the total project. The design team also included Ross Fowler Landscape Architects and SSOE Engineers. In the spring of 1993, their concept for the mall, as well as proposed revisions to the rest of the Capitol Hill plan, were shown first to Preston and then to Manning. This material included Hinton's own first sketch showing more detail of how the mall could be configured. Hinton still credits Bridges with the early vision, but he explained how establishing a new park alone would likely fail to sufficiently activate the site for tourists, residents, and the full mission of the bicentennial observance.

"With nothing in the area except the relocated farmers' market, the new park had to be a destination itself," Hinton remembers. "We convinced the state that the mall needed to be much more than the simple lawn as suggested by John Bridges. Our design theme was 'the land, people, and music of Tennessee,' and this guided us on the development of the symbolic physical elements and features. We hoped that one day, cultural facilities would eventually line the sides of the park." (Twenty-five years later, a new Tennessee State Museum was under construction on the west side of the mall, and ground was broken for a new Tennessee State Library and Archives complex on the east side.)

At the end of May 1993, in a private meeting at Hinton's office, details of the master plan and design scheme were presented to the main decision makers: McWherter, Manning, McWherter's chief of staff Jim Kennedy, and

Hall, together with the state's constitutional officers who served on the State Building Commission. After this meeting, Manning gave the green light for a formal presentation to the full Building Commission, which approved the plan. On June 2, the concept was taken public, with an unveiling on the Fisk University campus. In its final layout, the nineteen-acre mall would become a new state park heavy with symbolism: prominent features would include a two-hundred-foot-long map of the state, an amphitheater, a "Rivers of Tennessee Fountain" and a "Pathway of History" leading to a monumental ninety-five-bell carillon, a musical element and tribute to all the state's counties.

The absolute finish date, of course, was Statehood Day on June 1, 1996. Manning and Hall were careful to get all the construction work under signed contracts before McWherter left office, to ensure the project could not be derailed by whomever might be elected next. So the first of the construction agreements was signed on June 23, 1994, and four days later McWherter presided at a groundbreaking ceremony. This was less than five months before Sundquist's election the following November, and seven months before he would take office as the new governor.

Oddly, Gore's ceremonial appointment became a problem for Sundquist. Very soon after his inauguration, in January 1995, the new Republican governor began to express personal disdain for the mall project. He privately complained, in particular, about McWherter's inclusion of Gore, who was the state's highest-ranking Democrat, in the honorary leadership. Coming from a new governor, all this began to affect the internal dynamic among the central players in the extended mall project team. Some of this was moderated by Bob Corker, whom Sundquist had appointed to follow Manning as the finance commissioner. Among his other new duties, Corker now became the prominent intermediary through the final sixteen months of construction. From his office on the northwest corner of the capitol, Corker was careful to keep the lines of communication open between legislators, leaders of the bicentennial commission, the design team and builders, and most of all with his new boss down the hall.

By the time Statehood Day arrived, the new mall with its many design features had risen and Sundquist's political heartburn over Gore's role had seemed to subside. (It was a brokered peace, with the lion's share of credit going to former senator Howard Baker and also the GOP super-fundraiser Ted Welch, both of whom had interceded with Sundquist on the project's behalf.) In the end, Gore was among the featured speakers on the day of the big celebration, along with McWherter and Sundquist.

The architect Hinton, among many other details, had taken care to give the project a visible, bipartisan balance in its final memorializing touches.

Consider the pair of long pathways that run the length of the mall, beginning on the south end closest to the capital. As these vectoring lines arrive at
the mall's northern end, they almost touch—but not quite—at the "Court of
Three Stars" surrounded by the monumental columns of the carillon.

Like a silent and respectful nod between a Democrat and a Republican
across the partisan aisle that divides them, the visitor finds a raised granite
seat. It bears many names, most prominently McWherter's and Sundquist's,
and it has the feel of a complicated history.

TennCare

This became a signature initiative of the McWherter administration—a bold
revision of the federal Medicaid program. It was designed by David Manning and the state's Medicaid director Manny Martins, and was approved by
the Clinton administration very near the end of McWherter's final term as
governor.

Medicaid, the federally mandated health care program for the poor, had
been established in 1965. Three decades later, the rising cost of health care
was consuming an ever-larger share of state government outlays in many
states, including Tennessee. TennCare was designed as a managed-care system that could also enroll uninsured citizens who were not necessarily eligible under the older Medicaid rules.

Manning's plan would require approval, in the form of a waiver, from the
Centers for Medicare and Medicaid Services (CMS) and both Manning and
McWherter himself were diligent about working their proposal through the
federal system, including discussions with members of Tennessee's congressional delegation. The lawyer Nancy-Ann Min, who would become director
of CMS in 1997, was McWherter's first commissioner over the state Department of Human Services. The governor was close, as well, to both President
Clinton and Vice President Gore.

The CMS ultimately approved Tennessee's waiver, and the implementation of TennCare officially began on the first day of 1994. That January was
also a time of fundamental transition in the governor's office. These were the
final days of McWherter's time as governor, and the very first days of Sundquist's. Manny Martins, who with Manning had designed the TennCare
program, was appointed its first executive director.

As long and complicated as the waiver negotiations with Washington
had been, the complexity of putting TennCare into place in Tennessee was
only more so in the early years. Many external pressures shaped its early
administration—the many millions of dollars at stake, the sorting out of
multiple managed-care organizations, demands (and ultimately lawsuits)
from program advocates wanting more, and state legislators ever wanting

answers along the way. This made for a rocky first decade, with the struggle of balancing cost containment with appeals to admit new categories of citizens in need. (TennCare would have ten different agency directors over its first ten years.)

TennCare's later years were also rocky. The cost of care and the pressures to cover more Tennesseans with new categories of need made for crushing financial trend lines. It would become a Gordian knot, not only for Sundquist but also, and even more acutely, for Bredesen, who would follow him. Bredesen and his finance commissioner Dave Goetz would make the hard choices on their watch, "decertifying" hundreds of thousands of recipients, triggering demonstrations at the capitol that were both angry and heartbreaking.

A Nashville lawyer named Gordon Bonnyman, who directed the Tennessee Justice Center, was another prominent player in all this, but from outside the government, as the TennCare program unfolded. Through litigation that his office would file, Bonnyman challenged the fairness of TennCare on behalf of its recipients, and he became a fixture in how the state proceeded with its implementation of the program. In so doing, he became Sundquist's adversary, nemesis, and foe.

On almost all issues, save one.

Families First

Mention the name Don Sundquist to a journalist, a lobbyist, or any regular citizen who followed Tennessee government and politics in the 1990s, and you are likely to hear stories of this Republican's push for a state income tax, its failure, and of the public anger and acrimony that came with it.

Tennesseans of a certain age, looking back on the Sundquist years (1995–2003) that came between two Democratic administrations, are most likely to mention that bruising fight over taxation. The income tax did not pass— didn't come close—and along the way Sundquist's "tax reform" proposal generated unceasing protests, sign-waving pickets at the capitol steps, and motorists circling Memorial Plaza honking their horns in a discordant and disruptive harangue of the legislators considering the proposition inside the building.

On the radio, the policymakers could hear conservative talk-show hosts berate the very notion of income tax as civic blasphemy. These included a couple of Nashville radio personalities—Steve Gill and Phil Valentine—who added heat to the clamor by speaking at the daily rallies downtown. In hindsight, all this presaged the later grassroots activism of the Tea Party movement and, even later, the "populist" energy that animated Donald Trump's base in 2016. But, now, Sundquist's was the name and the face of the issue the demonstrators denounced.

This noisy controversy had erupted over an old policy discussion that had come around again, and logically enough. The state government's budget, for all its proud tradition of conservative fiscal controls, was on a collision course with economic reality. The state's constitution prohibited an income tax. In fact, business recruiters in Tennessee's Economic Development Department—as well as leaders in the urban chambers of commerce—would proudly trumpet this absence of a payroll tax as a competitive advantage over neighboring southern states. But Tennessee's heavy dependence on the sales tax for the bulk of its general revenues also made its state government's budgets ever more susceptible to swings in the national economy. As basic program outlays continued to mount, especially for schools and in the Medicaid program, the very long-term stability of government finance was looking untenable.

In modern times, most governors had come to the same conclusion as Sundquist now had—that the responsible step was to put a new and less regressive revenue stream tax on the table, pairing a new income tax with a rollback of the old sales tax on groceries and medicine. Reformers like Lewis Donelson, even when he was the Republican Alexander's finance commissioner, would invoke the importance of "tax fairness." He and other advocates argued that the consumption-based sales tax was certainly regressive and punished people living on low incomes. As a practical example, they always cited how the sales tax on a loaf of bread was more of a burden for a poor family than for a wealthy person who was better equipped to pay it. But public opinion, as expressed by unwilling elected legislators on their own or by citizens more loudly, would regularly freeze any talk of reform before it could ever be advanced.

Yet Sundquist, in his second and final term, insisted that the government's old system of finance needed fixing. Leaders in the Democratic-controlled legislature largely agreed with him, too—in the beginning—and so the governor proceeded. He proposed amending the state's constitution to authorize a payroll tax, pairing it with a set of tax relief measures including sales tax reduction. To this day, Sundquist insists he had sufficient support in the legislature to pass his package, but that key members who had committed to his reforms ultimately bailed, retreating from the heat of popular pushback. His initiative failed, and as the protests outside the capitol faded back to silence, Tennessee's government finance laws remained essentially unchanged.

But there were many other issues that were successfully transacted by the Republican governor and Democratic legislature during Sundquist's time. When I asked him later what he was proudest of from his tumultuous eight years in office, what achievement he valued most in hindsight, without a moment's hesitation the former governor replied with two words: Families First.

This was an initiative, born in Washington, to reform what had become a bedrock federal program of social welfare, dating to the Great Society of President Johnson. Called Aid to Families with Dependent Children, and usually known by its acronym AFDC, this program of cash assistance to the poor was signed into law by Johnson in 1965. Three decades later, AFDC would not have been an issue that voters in Sundquist's conservative GOP base might have expected from this governor. But an opportunity for reforming it now had a bipartisan impetus in the nation's capital—and its completion at the state level would likewise require a high level of cooperation across the aisle.

President Clinton and the Republican house speaker Newt Gingrich had found some unlikely common ground on the AFDC issue. Clinton, as early as his election campaign in 1992, promised to reform welfare—to "end welfare as we know it," he said. Gingrich, like President Reagan, missed no opportunity to push for deep reform of the federal government's system of social welfare. The Clinton administration cited AFDC as a prime opportunity to adjust welfare rules to make the system more supportive of families, limiting the benefits to five years while imposing work requirements, and turning all of it over, ultimately, to the states willing to take it on.

Enactment was not without controversy, as advocates for the poor worried that multiple state governments could produce uneven administration. In fact, by the time Clinton's new policy approach finally became federal law, in August 1996, the Democrat had vetoed two previous bills sent to him by Congress. Advocates also challenged this third attempt, but Clinton signed it into law in the White House Rose Garden, even as its opponents protested on Pennsylvania Avenue.

"Today," he declared, invoking his own catchphrase from the 1992 campaign, "we are ending welfare as we know it. But I hope this day will be remembered not for what it ended, but for what it began." Barbara Vobejda, the *Washington Post* reporter covering that signing ceremony, wrote that Clinton suggested that his acceptance of the bill should remove welfare from the political arena. "The two parties cannot attack each other over it," said the president. "Politicians cannot attack poor people over it.... And we have to all assume responsibility."

SUNDQUIST, WHO HAD SERVED six terms in Congress, was now at the midpoint of his first term in the governor's office. His election in 1994 had returned the state to a new period of divided government, with a legislature still controlled by the Democrats. This meant the Republican and his staff and cabinet would need to coordinate carefully.

On the governor's senior staff, Leonard K. Bradley became the point man for shaping Tennessee's response to the AFDC changes in Washington. As the policy planning director in the office, he coordinated with departments on their myriad legislative programs, always with a special eye to Sundquist's priorities. Bradley was a thoughtful analyst and planner with deep experience in state government over many administrations, Democratic and Republican, dating back to the Ellington and Dunn years. In fact, as head of Ellington's Office of Urban and Federal Affairs, he supervised the receipt and application of the huge new funding afforded by the Great Society. Dunn later asked Bradley to be his own director of policy planning.

Tall, lean, and laconic, Bradley over the years had thus established a rapport with legislative leaders of both parties and their staffs. Uniformly, they liked him and appreciated his grasp of policy, his style of give-and-take over making and amending laws, his sense of fairness, and his mainly calm demeanor. (When he retired from state government, in 1996, he was invited to teach courses in government and public policy at two schools: Tusculum College in East Tennessee, and Vanderbilt's Peabody College of Education and Human Development in Nashville.)

Bradley and Sundquist, in some respects, were an unlikely pair to collaborate on welfare reform. The issue itself was more in Bradley's wheelhouse as a veteran policy man whose domain reached across many departments and subject areas. Sundquist, on the other hand, was a known fiscal and social conservative from his time in Congress and before that when he was president of the National Young Republicans. So far his time in the governor's office had been more about keeping the ship steady and the budget balanced.

Over many hours Sundquist and Bradley discussed the future of AFDC. Bradley told me the governor had warmed to the subject, seeing it as a reform that could strengthen low-income families by restoring some balance to the relationship between work, personal pride, and responsibility, and the hope of a future off welfare. Bradley conferred with many professionals outside the government, as well as inside the state's Department of Human Services. This work resulted in a new bill, which Sundquist proposed to the General Assembly. On Bradley's recommendation, it was titled Families First.

Just as Washington activists had done in the congressional debate over AFDC reform, advocates for the poor in Tennessee raised issues with Sundquist's proposal, seeming to doubt a Republican's sincerely. They pressed hardest on the aspects of childcare and transportation. Many AFDC recipients were single mothers who did not own automobiles, so they would need help at home in order to go find and hold the required new jobs.

In an editorial on November 12, 1995, the *Tennessean*, normally skeptical of Sundquist's motives, nonetheless praised the administration's willingness to strengthen the Families First proposal. From that editorial:

> Despite the obvious holes that would need to be filled, the program has much to admire. The concept of having an individualized contract between the recipient and the state, if adequately administered, could give welfare recipients the attention they need to make the transition to independence.

Gordon Bonnyman was closely involved in this same process and was keenly tuned in to the fate of a vital welfare program. He was interested, both programmatically and personally, in what might become of AFDC now that it was being turned over to the state—from a Democratic administration in Washington to a Republican one in Nashville—just as he would in the policy battles over TennCare that would come over the next twenty years.

When the new legislation went to the General Assembly, its co-sponsors came from both sides of the political aisle, giving the administration's reform proposal bipartisan leadership in a still-Democratic majority legislature. On the House side, the lead co-sponsors were two Nashvillians: Republican Representative Beth Harwell, who was the administration's floor leader for the bill, and Democratic Majority Leader Bill Purcell.

Neither Harwell nor Purcell was a Tennessean by birth. They were both born in Pennsylvania, in fact—Harwell in Norristown, Purcell in Philadelphia.

Harwell had worked in the legislature since her college days at Nashville's Lipscomb College, starting as an intern, and was elected to the House in her own right in 1988. She was chair of the state's Republican Party from 2001 to 2004, the period when the GOP took control of the Tennessee state Senate for the first time in 105 years. In 2011, Harwell would become the first female speaker of the Tennessee House and was a candidate for governor in 2018.

Purcell also became an effective House leader, on the other side of the aisle. He was elected majority leader five times by his Democratic House caucus. (Purcell left the legislature at the end of 1996. He became director of Vanderbilt's Child and Family Policy Center—where he coordinated the annual Family ReUnion conference, hosted by Vice President Gore—and was elected mayor of Nashville in 1999.)

Purcell and Harwell were thus part of a new generation of bright young lawmakers in Tennessee and made an effective team as co-sponsors for Families First. The measure was adopted in both houses and sent to Sundquist's desk, where it was signed into law.

Bonnyman followed all this closely, and in the end praised it as a step of genuine progress in public policy. He gave much of the credit to Bradley as well as Governor Sundquist. "There was a lot going on in Washington at the time, during the Clinton administration, about 'ending welfare as we know it'—that was Clinton's expression and his brag," he recalled. "But in Tennessee, Families First was much more sophisticated than what happened under Clinton."

"With Leonard, you had a policy person who was humane and skilled and smart. He understood the issue and how real people were affected by the AFDC program. Bill Purcell had actually represented poor people and understood the only thing keeping them from living in squalor was the AFDC program. (Purcell, after law school at Vanderbilt, had worked for Legal Services in Jackson, Tennessee, before moving to Nashville.) AFDC had been around a long time. It had been helpful, at best, and at worst destructive to intact families and demeaning to low-income people in vulnerable circumstances.

"You could say 'AFDC is welfare as we know it' and that was a guaranteed applause line for Clinton and Gingrich. Clinton was trying to move the Democratic Party to the right and capture more of the Reagan voters. Gingrich had come with his 'Contract with America,' which had provisions about welfare and legal services. That was about politics, not making good policy, and I don't think they were very invested. I felt Don Sundquist *was* invested. I think he is a very decent person. I think Leonard was able to take his own notions of what good policy was and find a 'market' in Sundquist—someone who wanted to do the right thing by people who were most vulnerable. For them, these were not slogans. They were not abstractions. So Families First was designed, in Tennessee, by people who *actually* cared about what the national politicians *claimed they* cared about. Sundquist and Bradley wanted to address the real issues affecting families."

At the National Governors Association, Sundquist's file biography still includes these words: "In four years, his Families First welfare reform program reduced the number of families on welfare from 70,000 to 30,000." A 2001 study of four hundred families who had left the program found that 69 percent either found a new job or reported a pay raise, and 67 percent of people who had left Families First for work were now employed full-time.

IN 2014, SUNDQUIST WAS invited to speak at a charity roast for Bonnyman in Nashville.

Considering all the topics on which the two men had clashed over the years, the governor might have declined the invitation. He did not. True to the tradition of celebrity roasts, the governor began with a few good-natured jokes (*"When I was first asked to participate in this roast, I just figured it was another ploy by Gordon to serve me with another lawsuit."*) But he soon turned serious.

"All Republicans can have a heart," Sundquist said, "and we need to have more who can have a heart. It's probably true for some Democrats, as well. Gordon, I hope one of us makes it to the Pearly Gates—I hope *both* of us—but whichever of us makes it first, we need to tell St. Peter, 'We tried to make it work.'"

CHAPTER 25

Fast Forward

"The story goes on and leaves the writer behind, for no story is ever done."
—John Steinbeck

AFTER THE DAY OF the frightful plane ride in 2002 and the private meeting in Washington of governors and senators and mayor with Carlos Ghosn, it would be another full year before Nissan began to make internal plans to move its U.S. headquarters away from Los Angeles. And Ghosn would not publicly unveil the final decision until two full years after that.

"This week," he said on November 10, 2005, on the first floor of Tennessee's State Capitol, "the board of Nissan North America made the decision to relocate our North American headquarters, and we are coming to Tennessee."

When the world heard these words that Thursday, there was jubilation in Nashville, shock in Los Angeles (where the company employed some two thousand), and a resigned disappointment in Sacramento. Governor Arnold Schwarzenegger told the Associated Press he had gotten wind of the possible relocation two or three weeks earlier and that he had immediately reached out to Nissan executives in Southern California. From them, he learned the company had been studying such a move for two years.

"I wanted to find out, 'What is it that you need, to stop you from moving to another state?'" Schwarzenegger said. "And they said, 'Look, the things that we need are so overwhelming that you can never provide them—because you would need to change a tremendous amount of laws, the tax code, and so on.' So it's just, the other place, the other state is just so much more competitive, they [Nissan] already made that determination."

It was too late for California. For Tennessee, it was a joyful confirmation of the state's ascendance in the world of auto manufacturing. To the news reporters in Nashville, Ghosn provided more detail of what drove the relocation choice. He pointed to lower real estate and business taxes as major reasons for the move. Tennessee government officials explained that they offered Nissan a package of incentives, including tax breaks and other credits. Nissan received about $197 million in total state subsidies, including $64 million ($50,000 per relocated employee) from the new credit. The company also received a property tax abatement of 47 percent from Williamson County, estimated to be worth $32.5 million at the time.

For Nissan, Ghosn said, the bottom line was this: "The costs of doing business in Southern California are much higher than the costs of doing business in Tennessee." The difference in Tennessee, he said, was 44 percent less than in California—a critical consideration in view of the transformation that was already coming to the auto industry.

"We're going to be facing—in 2006, 2007—I'd say, at best, stagnation," Ghosn said. "It's an industry where you have to move all the time. You have to question yourself all the time. You have to challenge the way you're doing business all the time."

In doing so, he challenged conventional notions in his industry and startled the Nissan employees still based in Los Angeles. There was fallout among Nissan's workforce there, many of whom ultimately chose not to make the move. But by the time the new corporate office campus opened for business in Middle Tennessee, in 2008, nearly half of Nissan's staff had decided not to remain in California.

Nissan had established a foothold on the West Coast in the 1960s, selling the funny-looking diminutive Datsun sedan at the disappointing rate of about one car a week. Now, probably half the Californians viewed a possible move to Nashville like coming to the original home place of the Beverly Hillbillies, and more than half of them chose to stay put in California. The elation in Tennessee was balanced by deep disappointment in California among Nissan's Los Angeles workforce. *Automotive News* later called Jim Morton "Nissan's point man for the unpopular relocation to Nashville." He retired in 2007.

Nissan opened its new U.S. headquarters in the Cool Springs suburb south of Nashville in 2008. By 2015, the company's Tennessee workforce stood at approximately ten thousand people, counting the assembly lines at Smyrna, the powertrain plant in Decherd, and the headquarters offices at Cool Springs. By this time Nissan was selling enough cars and trucks to spend nearly $19 billion annually with 917 parts suppliers spread across eighty-five of Tennessee's ninety-five counties—not counting wages and salaries for employees at the three locations.

IN 2002, BOB CORKER was on a mission to complete Chattanooga's new vision for Ross's Landing on the riverfront downtown. The former developer and finance commissioner to Governor Sundquist was now the mayor of his hometown, and by this time much was happening in the river city.

Much of it had begun with Jack Lupton's enabling of the urban planner Stroud Watson, the early sketches by the design teams Watson had recruited to the task, and also the Vision 2000 process in the early 1980s. All this had garnered the support of a succession of Chattanooga mayors, as well as the city's leading philanthropists.

Driving the broader evolving game plan for the larger city was also the goal of bringing new life to the old industrial zone now called Enterprise South. In that initiative, in particular, Corker the Republican found an important ally in Bredesen, the Democrat who was now governor.

A FEW MINUTES PAST 6:00 P.M. on September 26, 2007, Corker served a dry Riesling and Atlantic salmon to a group of Volkswagen executives at his home on Lookout Mountain. Together with a bipartisan team, the senator had been courting VW since the time he was mayor of Chattanooga.

Just before this private dinner, Bredesen had signed papers ensuring that the U.S. manufacturing plant for Europe's largest auto company would be built in Tennessee. After toasts, Senator Lamar Alexander sat down at Corker's piano and played "Chattanooga Choo Choo" while the happy guests sang the melody and the words, which were familiar to the Germans as well as the Americans.

To usher in the twenty-first century, Bredesen had helped Tennessee win the national "Race to the Top" competition for educational excellence and began allocating more state dollars to colleges that improved their graduation rates.

In 2009, Republican governor Bill Haslam smoothly took the handoff from Democrat Bredesen. Haslam pushed teacher evaluations, helped the state post the nation's biggest improvement in K–12 academic scores, and announced he was putting Tennessee on course to become the first state in the nation to offer tuition-free community college.

Eastman built a new $100 million headquarters in Kingsport, the Korean tire giant Hankook put its North American plant and headquarters in Clarksville, and FedEx employment reached 325,000 worldwide. For the third consecutive year *Automotive News* named Tennessee the number one state for new auto manufacturing jobs. The Boyd Center at the University of Tennessee reported in June 2016 that Tennessee's job growth was at its fastest pace since the 1990s and its "economic momentum" was sixth in the nation.

By 2016, Tennessee was ranked a leader in the U.S as measured by foreign direct investment. The state clearly was sustaining its long-term growth in jobs, especially owing to the automotive industry and the supply chains the automakers required. *Automotive News* reported that Nissan's Smyrna manufacturing center was now the most productive auto assembly plant in North America, producing more than 633,000 vehicles in 2015.

Randy Boyd, a Knoxville businessman, became Haslam's commissioner of the state ECD Department in January of 2016. "Nissan's arrival here was such a catalyst for so much that has happened in Tennessee thirty years later," he told me. By this time, the auto supplier sector had also grown dramatically, with a total of 917 companies now doing business in the state.

The University of Tennessee report also pointed to an ominous shadow on the horizon: the 2008 Great Recession had driven many out of the workforce, leaving Tennessee the tenth-lowest in labor participation, a standing exacerbated by low education levels and poor health.

THE STATE'S POLITICS NOW had a new complexion: a supermajority of red not blue.

Tennessee had again become a one-party state, but with Republicans now ascendant just as the state had been majority Democratic fifty years earlier.

Some observers of this new scene wondered if the competition in politics—the type that had produced leaders who worked together during the in-between years to create *National Geographic*'s "Rising, Shining Tennessee" summation—might now revert to the one-party doldrums.

Doldrums had dominated the state before—for a long century, in fact, after the Civil War.

BY 2017, NASHVILLE'S Bridgestone Arena—the local project that had little public support and no professional sports tenant when Mayor Bredesen proposed to build it in 1995—had become the fourth-busiest building of its type in the United States. *Pollstar*, a trade magazine covering the touring concert industry, said the Nashville venue had become the twelfth-busiest venue in the world.

The arena had also become home of country music's premier TV event of the year, the CMA Awards Show. In 2016, the Bridgestone hosted the National Hockey League playoffs, with the Nashville Predators taking the Stanley Cup championship finals down to the last game, losing only in the final game to the Pittsburgh Penguins.

IN THE GOVERNOR'S OFFICE, the weekly Leadership Meeting that commenced in 1979 continues at this writing. It is still held at 7:00 o'clock each Wednesday morning whenever the General Assembly is in session in Nashville.

The participants have changed over the decades, as new administrations have taken office and the respective party caucuses have chosen their own new leaders. The number of officials invited to attend has grown, with some insiders noting that this has put a chill on the candor.

In 1985, when Alexander called a special session of the General Assembly to consider a prison reform plan, he invited his Correction Department commissioner Stephen Norris to sit in each Wednesday. The next spring, when the massive 1986 road program was under consideration, Alexander had Transportation Commissioner Dale Kelley attend. In both cases, the speakers and their principal floor leaders in this way had steady access to the administration's top officials, and thus all had ample time to float ideas for amendments and program enhancements that could pull in more yes votes.

In the 1990s, the two speakers also began to invite the chairmen of their respective finance committees, who usually worked in close coordination with the state's commissioner of finance and administration. One of the longest tenured participants was Senator Douglas Henry Jr., a Nashville Democrat, who chaired the Senate Finance Committee throughout this period. It was not until 2007, when Republicans took numerical control of the upper chamber following the 2006 elections, that Henry lost his committee chairmanship and thus his seat at the Wednesday leadership talks.

During Sundquist's administration (1995–2003) certain staff members were included in this exclusive meeting for the first time, and this expanded in later administrations. Governor Bill Haslam (2011–2019) told me he continued the tradition, believing it was a healthy form of communication among top leaders as issues and government itself had grown ever more complex.

Curiously, over more than three decades that followed, news reporters have only rarely attempted to invade the private space where this meeting has continued to occur. It remained private—no news reporters in the room—through Alexander's time as governor. The plainspoken McWherter, who early in his own legislative career had co-sponsored Tennessee's open-meetings "Sunshine Law," as governor seldom closed his office door. On the infrequent occasions that a reporter or two might look in the meeting room, McWherter would say, "OK, you dog-asses, come on in. Sit down over there, and be quiet." It didn't happen often.

Purcell, who was the majority leader in McWherter's House for six years in the 1990s (and later mayor of Nashville), gave me his explanation for why this low level of news media intrusion was so constant over time.

"By 1990 it was very clear the meeting was open, and anybody could come in," he remembers. "If a reporter wanted to come in, they could come in. It was an early meeting. I think reporters knew their presence in the room probably would have an impact on the conversation, but more importantly McWherter, his staff, and the leaders in the room would tell them what happened anyway, so it wasn't any particular advantage to be there when the conversation occurred. I can remember rare occasions when reporters did come in toward the end."

Purcell suggested it was chiefly the early hour that discouraged the comfortable Capitol Hill reporters from attempting to sit in. Seldom would anyone in the capitol press corps even ask.

GENERAL MOTORS, IN 2004, began planning for a conversion of the Saturn plant at Spring Hill. The 2007 model year would be the last for Saturn, but the manufacturing facility was given a new life.

The company invested nearly a billion dollars in the modernized plant and began producing the Chevrolet Traverse. Currently, the products that roll off the assembly line at Spring Hill also include the Cadillac XT5 and the GMC Acadia.

When the production of Saturns ceased, in 2007, the Spider Plaque award was also discontinued.

AS IT TURNED OUT, Lillian Knight did live to see her grandchildren and to know them as cherished family residing with her in Middle Tennessee.

She was eighty-one years old when she died, on July 27, 2013. Her extended family was with her when she passed, including Randy's adult sons Griffin, now twenty-seven, and Spenser, twenty-three. By this time, Griffin was working at Nissan, too. Like their father and uncles, both these young men remained in Rutherford County.

"They were there at the end," Randy told me. "She knew we were all there."

By 2015 Randy Knight had become the Nissan executive in charge of manufacturing at the sprawling Smyrna facility, and Ricky became head of supply-chain management. That year Randy presided over a festive ceremony at the plant heralding the rollout of Nissan's latest Smyrna product, the 2016 Maxima. Alexander was the featured speaker, and the two shared a brief, private conversation.

"I told Senator Alexander that if my mother was still living, there wouldn't be anything I could do to keep her from being here today. She was so prideful about her family, and about the boys, and being able to see us grow up and get good jobs. There probably wouldn't be anything we could do to keep her from being on the stage."

You wouldn't have known it from reading the national news, or watching the shrill political talk shows on cable TV in the first decade of the new century, but in the final two years of the Obama presidency, some of the old Tennessee-style bipartisan cooperation was still at work in Washington, albeit quietly.

But by this time most of the work "across the aisle" was conducted necessarily behind the scenes.

There were two significant examples in the modern era, even in the midst of a widespread belief in the demise of inter-party cooperation. One came in a major update of national education policy, and the other brought new promise for accelerated health care research. Both became possible on a freezing Friday morning in the middle of January 2015, during a presidential visit to East Tennessee.

The White House had planned a late-morning event for the president on January 9 at Pellissippi State Community College, a two-year postsecondary school on the highway between Knoxville's McGhee-Tyson Airport and Oak Ridge in Anderson County. The Pellissippi Parkway was an interstate-quality four lane built as part of the 1986 road program to connect the airport with the nation's largest energy laboratory; Alexander called it the "Oak Ridge Corridor" and hoped it would provide a symbol (like Route 128 in Massachusetts or the Research Triangle in North Carolina) to bring attention to this economic nexus in Tennessee. There were some three thousand PhDs clustered in that zone, but it had been a largely unknown concentration of brainpower. The order of the day was to unveil Obama's "America's College Promise," his proposal to make community college tuition-free for students nationwide. It was similar to Haslam's Tennessee initiative of the previous year, called Tennessee's Promise.

This day had begun early for Alexander. He arrived at Andrews Air Force Base, in suburban Maryland, well ahead of Obama and his entourage. When Corker and Congressman Jimmy Duncan arrived in a waiting room off the tarmac, they were escorted together aboard Air Force One. They walked past the president's on-board quarters to a rear section where other invited dignitaries are seated. Here, they joined three administration officials: the deputy secretary of the U.S. Department of Education, a member of the White House congressional liaison staff, and the president's domestic policy adviser for education. A voice on the intercom announced that President Obama was ten minutes away, then five minutes away. The plane lifted off at 10:45 a.m.

Once airborne, Obama entered the guest cabin having doffed his suit jacket. He sat and talked with the three Tennesseans for about twenty minutes. This conversation touched briefly on Middle East issues (Corker was chairman of the Senate Foreign Relations Committee), then turned to domestic education policy (Alexander chaired the Senate Committee on Health, Education, Labor, and Pensions), particularly the need to reform the controversial No Child Left Behind program of the Bush years and its heavy emphasis on national standards and rigorous student testing tied to performance measures for both teachers and schools. Many educators and parents had complained that the tests were imposing unnecessary and unproductive burdens on the classroom. The national teacher organizations—the National Education Association and American Federation of Teachers—insisted that linking students' test results to their teachers' evaluations was unfair and unproven.

When Air Force One landed in Tennessee, the president's party gathered in preparation to exit the plane. "You've just been re-elected, so you can go first," Alexander remembers Obama telling him, well aware that he was arriving in a congressional district that had not elected a Democrat since Lincoln was president. But when the forward door opened, Obama appeared first, with Alexander just behind the president at the top of the steps. Corker and Duncan came next, then Governor and Mrs. Crissy Haslam. Vice President Biden and his wife, Dr. Jill Biden, were the first to greet the president at the foot of the steps. They moved into waiting cars, and the motorcade proceeded onto Alcoa Highway and then Pellissippi Parkway.

On campus at Pellissippi State, the audience was already assembled and waiting in the Arts and Sciences Building when the presidential entourage arrived. The program was brief, with Haslam speaking first to greet the president. Obama was upbeat and took care to praise Tennessee's leadership in education reform. Alexander was the final speaker.

When the public program ended, the White House staff served lunch in a private room for Obama and Biden with Alexander, Corker, and Haslam, together with the Bidens and the governor's wife. Their discussion over fish and vegetables touched on the work of Alexander's committee to accelerate the work of the Food and Drug Administration and also NCLB.

"I told the president about our FDA priority, and he said it was one of his also," Alexander remembers. "The president had formed a group to take a look at how the FDA deals with precision medicine. 'We should be able to work together on this under the radar and do something really big,' I said. He agreed. I told him Bill Frist (the physician who was the former Senate majority leader) would be helping and he liked that.

"The president said it is disappointing that there is so much 'noise' around Washington that makes it so difficult to reach across party lines and get results," Alexander continued. "He said this has gotten worse, and he said to Governor Haslam that the governor's job must be more enjoyable because there is less of the noise in states. He said that one congressional visitor to the White House, when asked if he would make a concession on an issue, had replied, "I've already made one. I'm here."

In this lunch discussion, Obama must have sensed he could work with these particular Tennesseans in Congress. That evening Alexander wrote this in his journal: "In these settings the president is engaging, relaxed and confident. He is aware that he is in unfriendly territory but understands that Corker, Haslam and I are Republicans with whom he can work."

The Pellissippi State meeting made clear there would be opportunity for agreement and compromise on several initiatives: reform of the Bush-era No Child Left Behind policy, by this time regarded as federal government overreach; the Obama administration's push for "precision medicine," and the Cancer Moonshot initiative that Biden was driving; and also the 21st Century Cures Act—all residing in the committee of which Alexander was now chairman. Over the next two years, this work progressed even as the nation otherwise witnessed a rising level of partisan bitterness between the candidates of both parties hoping to succeed Obama, and through the extraordinary election of Republican Donald J. Trump over Democrat Hillary Clinton in November 2016.

The specific vehicle for reforming No Child Left Behind came as Congress took up the reauthorization of the federal Elementary and Secondary Education Act (ESEA), centering in the Senate's Committee on Health, Education, Labor and Pensions. Alexander had become the committee chairman when Republicans won control of the Senate in the 2014 elections. Senator Patty Murray of Washington State had been the chairman until that point, and she was now the ranking Democrat on the panel.

In contrast to the daily reports of deepening partisan rancor, which was driving the larger Republican-majority Senate and the Obama White House into many stalemates, Alexander and Murray had not worked together until January 2015, when Murray became the ranking member. After a rocky start, the two soon developed a level of trust and mutual respect. Alexander's preference for forging alliances—very much in the old Baker mode, leading to quiet progress and results—helped Murray find an important ally. With very rare exceptions, Alexander eschewed any public attention to the work he did behind the scenes.

The two worked over the next twelve months—usually with no fanfare whatever—and the final vote on the Every Student Succeeds Act was unanimous. The committee members' views ranged from Bernie Sanders to Rand Paul, an extraordinary achievement and emotional moment for several senators. The measure was adopted by the full Senate and then the House, and Obama signed it into law the following December, 2015, calling it "a Christmas miracle." The editorial board of the *Wall Street Journal* called ESSA "the largest transfer of power from Washington, D.C. to states and communities in 25 years."

ESSA ultimately had the support of both the national teacher unions. Weeks later, in a recognition that would have stunned any Tennesseans who remembered the NEA's bitter fight with Governor Alexander over the Better Schools Program of 1983–84, the NEA presented both Alexander and Murray with the NEA's Friend of Education award for 2016.

Then, also in 2016, Alexander's committee proceeded to hammer out the 21st Century Cures Act, which Senator Majority Leader Mitch McConnell described as "the most important legislation this year." The bill would, among other things, support the development of a universal flu vaccine, a vaccine for the Zika virus, non-addictive pain medication, and the ability to identify individuals at high risk of Alzheimer's before symptoms develop—and speed those cures and treatments through the regulatory and investment process and into doctors' offices and the medicine cabinets of consumers.

Largely unknown to Washington news media, Alexander was also quietly continuing to promote this new legislation with the Obama administration, including three visits with the president himself, one of those in the Oval Office, as well as phone conversations with the president and White House Chief of Staff Dennis McDonough, even as the 2016 presidential race was lurching to its surprise conclusion on November 8. The final Senate approval came during the so-called lame duck session the following month, one of only two bills to succeed to passage during that period. In one of Obama's last official acts, the departing president signed the Cures bill into law.

"My goal is not bipartisanship," Alexander told reporters, after the victory was secured, sensitive to how that word and labels like "moderate" and "compromise" had become anathema in the hypercharged environment of Washington. "My goal is results."

The new Cures law thus went into a category of largely quiet results along with the ESSA reform of No Child Left Behind.

DEATH CAME TO MCWHERTER on April 4, 2011. It was not unexpected. His cancer had been diagnosed months earlier. The loss of weight from his famously large frame had made his features gaunt, but he had stubbornly maintained his sense of humor, his many political friendships, that twinkle in his patient blue eyes, and his broad popularity. One of his early campaign slogans was "He's One of Us!" After he had left office in January 1995, when the Republican Sundquist succeeded him, many of McWherter's followers high and low proudly brandished a colorful bumper sticker on their cars, printed with the lament "I Miss Ned."

McWherter's physician, Karl VanDevender, remembers a blunt phone call near the end, so reminiscent of the former governor's cordial but no-nonsense manner. VanDevender had been the personal physician to every Tennessee governor since Winfield Dunn except for Alexander (his physician, Dr. John Sergent, has been a close friend since their Vanderbilt undergrad days). McWherter had recently been in for more tests and now was calling his doctor for an updated prognosis.

> McWherter: "So, Doc, am I on a short fuse, or a long fuse?"
> VanDevender: "Well, Ned . . . I'm afraid it's a short fuse."
> McWherter: "I understand."

❖

ON THE DAY HE DIED, as word of McWherter's passing circulated rapidly, one of his toughest partisans, the attorney J. W. Luna, was sitting in his law office in Nashville.

His law firm is in a mid-rise building in downtown Nashville, at 333 Union Street, on the same site where Andrew Jackson, the founding Democrat, had operated his own law practice in the time before he became president in 1829. Luna had been one of McWherter's most loyal and scrappiest allies over the long years, both as campaign adviser and cabinet member.

Luna now got word that Alexander would shortly be giving a tribute from the Senate chamber in Washington. He quickly rose from his desk and closed his office door for privacy. Then he tuned his television to C-SPAN. In a moment Alexander appeared on the screen, standing in the well of the Senate chamber.

For years, working at the governor's side, Luna had known and well remembered now the tumult of the campaign trail, the cheers and applause of friendly crowds who always pressed in for a glance and hopefully a handshake. Now Luna sat alone, in silence, to hear what a Republican had to say about his old boss.

As Luna watched and listened, on this saddest of days, the tears streamed down this tough man's face.

❖

"THERE ARE A LOT of people in our State who come in and out of politics," Alexander was now saying on the TV screen. "Maybe they are appreciated, maybe they are not. Only a few leave a lasting impression. Ned McWherter will be among the very few who leave the most impression. Part of it was his big, burly, infectious, lovable personality. Part of it was his good sense of politics and openness around the State Capitol. But a lot of it was his willingness to say to people, such as a new young governor of the opposite party: I am going to help you succeed, because if you succeed, our state succeeds.

"Governor McWherter and I talked many times. I talked with him most recently about one week ago. He was going to see his doctor again to find out whether, as he said, he had a short fuse or a long fuse. Apparently, he had a short fuse. He didn't have much life left in him, although he may not have known it. Perhaps he did. He used to joke and say, 'The size of the crowd at your funeral will depend a lot on the weather.' I think all of us in Tennessee would say the size of the crowd at Ned McWherter's funeral will have nothing to do with the weather, because I imagine it will be standing room only, with people pouring out of the back doors. . . .

"I am sad to report he is gone. But it is an important time to celebrate the life of a public servant whose lessons of how to achieve consensus and still be a good politician will be a good lesson for everyone in Washington, DC."

THE MOURNERS TURNED OUT in great numbers—twice.

There were two funerals for McWherter: a large service at the War Memorial Auditorium in downtown Nashville, near the State Capitol and the speaker's old legislative offices, and another gathering of family and closest friends on the following Sunday on the front lawn of his Dresden home in West Tennessee.

Thousands attended the Nashville service. The turnout there was bipartisan, though it certainly leaned Democratic, and nonetheless was a reminder of McWherter's long career in public life, when he worked with Republicans also. Baker and Alexander were there, and Seigenthaler was present also, along with a host of the speaker's colleagues from the General Assemblies of yore. Among the speakers were Clinton and Gore, and also McWherter's son Mike, the late governor's longtime adviser Billy Stair, and the current Republican governor, Bill Haslam.

Standing room only.

YEARS LATER, IN AUGUST 2015, I sat down for lunch in Nashville with Mike McWherter. He was en route from his home in Jackson to a TVA Board meeting in Knoxville. By this time, Mike's daughter Bess, granddaughter of the late governor, was working in government on the staff of Corker's Foreign Relations Committee.

Mike spoke candidly with me of his father's complex relationship with Alexander, their starkly different backgrounds, and their uncommon mode of working together across the aisle, both in public and in private, for the common good. Mike told me, among things, that in hindsight it was the coup, the extraordinary ouster of Blanton in 1979, that seems to have made all the difference.

"That whole process," he said, "when Lamar got sworn in, in such a radical manner—in the coup—I think it forged a respect and a relationship between the two of them that held forth to the day my father died."

Timeline 1978–2002

What Happened in the In-Between Time

1978   Republican Lamar Alexander kicks off his second campaign for governor in Maryville, his hometown. Begins a 1,000-plus-mile walk across Tennessee.

Nashville swimming prodigy Tracy Caulkins, age fifteen, wins five gold medals at the World Championships. She is predicted to win multiple gold at the 1980 Olympic Games in Moscow.

U.S. Senate ratifies Panama Canal Treaty.

Pope Paul II elected.

Anwar Sadat and Menachem Begin sign Middle East accord at Camp David.

Senator Howard Baker re-elected to third term, defeating the Democratic Party's nominee, Jane Eskind.

Alexander elected governor, defeating Democratic nominee Jake Butcher.

FBI agents arrest three aides to Governor Ray Blanton, including his legal counsel, at his State Capitol office, seizing cash and documents relating to suspicious clemency cases. National news media focus on Tennessee's "clemency for cash" scandal.

Top country single is "Mamas, Don't Let Your Babies Grow Up to be Cowboys" by Waylon Jennings and Willie Nelson.

1979   Blanton signs commutations for fifty-two state prisoners, including double-murderer Roger Humphreys, son of a political friend.

FBI agent informs U.S. Attorney Hal Hardin they have new information that another round of commutations are being prepared for Blanton's signature. Hardin phones Governor-elect Alexander, asking him to take the oath of office three days early.

Chief Justice Joe W. Henry administers the oath to Alexander at 5:55 p.m. in the Supreme Court chamber. Democratic leaders present include House Speaker Ned McWherter, Senate Speaker John Wilder, Attorney General Bill Leech, and Secretary of State Gentry Crowell.

Attorney Fred Thompson begins duty as Special Counsel to Governor Alexander, sorting out which of the Blanton-issued clemencies are valid.

Alexander takes his oath of office for second time in public ceremony on War Memorial Plaza.

President Jimmy Carter urges the nation's governors to "Go to Japan" to find new opportunities in economic development.

Iranian militants seize U.S. Embassy in Tehran.

Alexander's Executive Order No. 1 establishes a "Memphis Jobs Conference" to be held November 28–29 at the Cook Convention Center.

Margaret Thatcher elected Prime Minister of the United Kingdom.

The Tennessee Film, Tape and Music Commission established in the governor's office to recruit film and TV production to the state. Actor Jerry Reed and director Delbert Mann appointed co-chairs of the new fifty-member commission.

Knoxville mayor Kyle Testerman appoints businessmen Jake Butcher and Jim Haslam as chair and vice chair of local organizing committee for the 1982 World's Fair.

The Reverend Jerry Falwell, chancellor of Liberty University in Virginia, founds the conservative political organization Moral Majority.

Top country album is Kenny Rogers's *The Gambler*, whose title song was written by Nashvillian Don Schlitz.

Tennessee Secondary Schools Athletic Association adopts five-player, full-court rules for high school girls basketball.

The movie *Coal Miner's Daughter* starring Cissy Spacek is filmed in Nashville.

Gannett Co., the nation's largest newspaper chain, buys the *Tennessean* and sells the afternoon *Nashville Banner* to a local ownership group lead by John Jay Hooker.

Top-grossing movie is *Kramer vs. Kramer*.

Soviet Union invades Afghanistan.

1980   Tennessee Performing Arts Center opens in Nashville.

President Carter announces U.S. will boycott Moscow Olympic Games if Soviet troops are not withdrawn from Afghanistan within one month. Leonid Brezhnev refuses.

Carter tells swimmer Tracy Caulkins, hurdler Willie Gault, sprinter Joan Pennington, and other elite U.S. Olympians they will not go to the Moscow Summer Games.

Nissan announces its first North American manufacturing facility will be built in Smyrna, Tennessee, to produce small pickup trucks.

Jane Eskind elected to Tennessee Public Service Commission, first woman to win statewide election in Tennessee.

Tennessee's Chief Justice Joe Henry dies.

Howard Baker runs for president.

U.S. Women's Open Golf Championship held at Nashville's Richland Country Club. Amy Alcott wins.

Republican National Chairman Bill Brock selects Detroit as site for 1980 GOP convention over Sun Belt cities other party leaders preferred, wanting the party to be seen as issue-centered problem solvers.

Alexander appoints Memphis attorney George H. Brown Jr., to the Tennessee Supreme Court succeeding Justice Henry. Brown becomes first African American to serve on the state's highest court.

State Democratic Executive Committee nominates former chancellor and appeals court judge Frank F. Drowota III of Nashville to run against Justice George Brown. Drowota elected on August 7, succeeding Brown, who had served six weeks.

Nashville businessman Phil Bredesen founds HealthAmerica, a health care management company.

Paramount Pictures releases the movie *Urban Cowboy* starring John Travolta and Debra Winger, creating a surge of new interest in country music.

Top rock album is *The Wall* by Pink Floyd.

Remodeling begins on Beale Street and the Peabody Hotel in Memphis. Statue of Elvis Presley unveiled at Elvis Presley Plaza.

Pilot Oil Co., which will become the nation's eighth-largest private company in 2015 with revenues of $31 billion, opens its first truck stop in Corbin, Kentucky.

Ronald Reagan elected President.

1981   Senator Baker elected majority leader in U.S. Senate.

Reagan inaugurated.

Iran frees fifty-two U.S. hostages held for 444 days.

Nissan breaks ground at Smyrna, Tennessee. Ceremonies disrupted by union protesters. The next day, Tennessee legislature passes resolution criticizing the demonstration and welcoming Nissan to Tennessee.

Jack C. Massey, co-founder of Hospital Corp. of America, and investor Lucius E. Burch form Massey Burch Investment Group. (The firm and its successor entities would eventually manage over $245 million and help grow more than eighty companies in many industries.)

Reagan appoints Brock U.S. trade representative. Julia Gibbons, appointed by Alexander, becomes the first woman to serve as judge of a Tennessee trial court.

Blanton convicted of extortion and conspiracy in connection with the illegal sale of a liquor store license. He would serve twenty-two months in prison.

Barbara Mandrell records "I Was Country When Country Wasn't Cool" (written by Kye Fleming and Dennis Morgan) in Nashville. It reaches number one on *Billboard* magazine's Hot Country Songs within three months.

Top country album is *9 to 5* by Dolly Parton.

Memphis's Peabody Hotel reopens.

U.S. Supreme Court, in the landmark *Citizens to Preserve Overton Park v. Volpe*, rules that Tennessee's Department of Transportation must redesign Interstate 40 to go around the popular Memphis park.

The Soviet Union, in retaliation for U.S. boycott of 1980 Olympic Games, announces cancelation of Soviet exhibit in the 1982 World's Fair. Knoxville organizers focus on recruitment of China to participate.

Sadat is assassinated in Cairo.

1982   World's Fair held in Knoxville. President Reagan attends the opening ceremonies. China provides major exhibit.

Megatrends by John Naisbitt is published.

Japan Center of Tennessee established in Murfreesboro on campus of Middle Tennessee State University.

Elvis Presley's Graceland opens to the public. MTSU's men's basketball team defeats the Kentucky Wildcats 50–44 in the first round of the NCAA tournament.

The HCA Foundation is established.

"Rocky Top," written by Felice and Boudleaux Bryant, named state song.

Task Force on Children and Youth appointed to study improvement and expansion of services for young Tennesseans.

Memphis Mayor Wyeth Chandler resigns to accept a judgeship. Bishop J.O. Patterson becomes the city's first black mayor.

FDIC bank examiners conduct a coordinated audit of the Butchers' East Tennessee banks on November 1.

Alexander re-elected to second term as governor, defeating Knoxville Mayor Randy Tyree, the Democratic nominee.

Willie Nelson's "Always on My Mind" is top country single.

Republican Don Sundquist elected to Congress from Tennessee's Seventh District, defeating Democrat Bob Clement.

Democrat Jim Cooper elected to Congress from Tennessee's Fourth District, defeating Republican Cissy Baker.

U.S. Senator Jim Sasser, Democrat, re-elected to a second term, defeating Representative Robin Beard.

Richard C. Hackett elected mayor of Memphis.

Soviet leader Leonid Brezhnev dies.

Top-grossing movie is *ET: The Extra-Terrestrial.*

1983   Baker announces he will not run for a fourth Senate term in 1984. Suggests he may run for president again in 1988.

Butcher banking empire collapses.

Chattanooga civic leaders form Chattanooga Venture, which will launch the Vision 2000 citywide visioning process.

A Nation At Risk is published by the U.S. Department of Education, urging higher standards for teaching and learning to prepare children for the future and make the U.S. more competitive.

Alexander proposes Better Schools Program with differential incentive pay for teachers, full funding for state college and university programs, and other reforms, to be funded by an increase in the state sales tax.

Nissan begins truck production at Smyrna, Tennessee.

Wilma Rudolph inducted into U.S. Olympic Hall of Fame.

TVA cancels the proposed Columbia Dam project on the Duck River over environmental issues.

Preparations begin for "Tennessee Homecoming '86" with designation of thirty-nine pilot communities.

The recording artist Prince releases *Purple Rain.*

Federal Express reports $1 billion in revenues, the first company to reach that milestone within ten years of startup without mergers or acquisitions.

The Honors Course, founded by John T. (Jack) Lupton, heir to the Coca-Cola bottling business, opens at Ooltewah, Tennessee, near Chattanooga.

Memphis's historic Beale Street is rededicated after remodeling is completed.

The *Memphis Press-Scimitar* evening newspaper publishes its final edition.

Bridgestone Tire Co. of Japan, the world's largest tire maker, acquires Firestone's U.S. manufacturing facility for truck tires in LaVergne, Tennessee.

The Healthy Children Initiative, chaired by First Lady Honey Alexander, begins four-year effort to emphasize health care for all children in Tennessee, pairing expectant mothers with pediatricians.

Legislature delays consideration of the Better Schools Program, referring the proposed reforms to a study committee chaired by State Senator Anna Belle Clement O'Brien, Democrat.

Memphis Jobs Conference recommends restoration of Beale Street and Orpheum Theatre, new funding for Agriculture Center, and a new Convention Center Hotel. State government provides capital funding support.

Reagan speaks at Knoxville's Farragut High School to advocate for merit pay for teachers and passage of the Better Schools Program.

Gaylord Broadcasting Co. of Oklahoma City completes its purchase of Nashville's WSM radio and the Opryland USA theme park. Gaylord launches The Nashville Network (TNN).

Dolly Parton and Kenny Rogers release the blockbuster duet "Islands in the Stream."

Publication of the book *Musical Instruments of the Southern Appalachian Mountains* by John Rice Irwin, founder the Museum of Appalachia at Clinton, Tennessee.

Gene Roberts elected mayor of Chattanooga.

Top pop single is "Thriller" by Michael Jackson. Top album is Jackson's *Thriller.*

Memphis State University's head football coach Rex Dockery and three others killed when their plane crashes near Lawrenceburg.

General Motors announces it will develop a new manufacturing concept—eventually called the Saturn program—to recapture car sales lost to Japanese imports.

1984   Blanton begins serving prison term at Maxwell Air Force Base, Alabama.

The University of Tennessee Lady Vols finish the 1983–84 NCAA women's basketball season with a record of 22 wins and 10 losses—Coach Pat Summitt's eighth consecutive twenty-win season.

Memphis's new four-hundred-room convention center hotel (initially a Crowne Plaza, later renamed Marriott and then Sheraton) opens, and the Orpheum Theater reopens.

William Leech departs as Tennessee's attorney general. Tennessee Supreme Court appoints W. J. Michael Cody of Memphis.

Alexander's Better Schools Program enacted by Tennessee legislature, including state sales tax increase for higher teacher pay and other improvements.

Chattanooga's Vision 2000 process identifies forty goals for the city's future, including improved air quality and enhancement of the riverfront.

Tracy Caulkins wins three Olympic gold medals in the 1984 Games at Los Angeles.

USA Women's Team, coached by Pat Summitt, wins Olympic gold medal.

NGA holds annual meeting in Nashville with thirty-one governors attending. Special guests include Baker; State Representative John T. Bragg of Murfreesboro, chair of the National Conference of State Legislatures; and country music stars Minnie Pearl, Brenda Lee, Charlie Daniels, Ray Stevens, and Lee Greenwood.

The movie *Marie* based on the story of the Blanton administration scandal, starring Cissy Spacek and Fred D. Thompson, is filmed in Nashville.

Federal Express begins intercontinental operations with service to Europe and Asia.

New York Representative Geraldine Ferraro becomes the first woman to be nominated for vice president, running with Democrat Walter Mondale.

Congressman Al Gore Jr. elected to U.S. Senate, succeeding Baker.

Reagan-Bush re-elected, carrying forty-eight states, defeating Mondale-Ferraro.

Kyle C. Testerman elected mayor of Knoxville.

State Representative Tommy Burnett re-elected to legislature while in federal prison on misdemeanor conviction unrelated to his legislative service.

Top pop single is Prince's "When Doves Cry."

Most popular TV show is the finale of *M.A.S.H.*

The Memphis Showboats, an expansion franchise of the United States Football League, begins play at Liberty Bowl Memorial Stadium. Cotton industrialist William Dunavant is owner/president, Pepper Rodgers head coach.

Nissan supplier Bridgestone Tire reports in December its production of truck tires increased by 60 percent from January levels, approaching two thousand tires per day.

1985   Baker retires from U.S. Senate.

Memphis Convention and Visitors Bureau launches the "Start Something Great in Memphis" ad campaign.

Fred Smith, founder of Federal Express, leads a local effort to recruit the NFL's Baltimore Colts to Memphis.

Memphis opens the new convention center hotel, later called the Marriott.

Alexander elected chairman of the National Governors Association.

Reagan appoints Bill Brock secretary of labor; Joe M. Rodgers the U.S. ambassador to France, and Alexander to chair the new President's Commission on Americans Outdoors.

McWherter holds first large fundraising event in anticipation of running for governor in 1986.

General Motors announces that its new operating subsidiary called Saturn Corp., with a new labor agreement with the UAW, will establish its manufacturing facility in Spring Hill, Tennessee.

The movie *Marie*, based on Tennessee's clemency-for-cash scandal is released.

Inmates at four Tennessee penitentiaries hold guards hostage and set fire to prison facilities, drawing national news coverage.

Jerry Lee Lewis, Roy Orbison, and Carl Perkins record "The Class of 1955," at Sun Studios in Memphis.

American Airlines announces it will establish a new hub in Nashville that will eventually serve sixty U.S. cities.

St. Jude's Hospital votes to stay in Memphis.

Alexander proposes a reform program for the state's prison system, then under federal court supervision, and calls an extraordinary session of the legislature to consider it.

Returning to Ft. Campbell, Kentucky, after a six-month peacekeeping mission in Egypt, 248 soldiers of the 101st Airborne Division die when their Arrow Air Flight 1285 crashes near Gander International Airport in Newfoundland.

Top pop recording is "Born in the U.S.A." by Bruce Springsteen.

1986   Alexander proposes a $3.3 billion Better Roads Program with a three-cent increase in the state's gasoline tax to be phased in over three years, recommending six interstate-type parkways, fifteen priority projects, and a general acceleration of the existing highway program. Speaker McWherter embraces the plan, and the Democratic-controlled legislature adopts it.

Space shuttle *Challenger* explodes.

McWherter announces he is running for governor.

Tennessee's "Homecoming '86" celebration, with Alex Haley and Minnie Pearl serving as honorary co-chairs. Special "Homecoming Train" travels from Bristol to Memphis, making nineteen stops along the way.

National Geographic profiles Tennessee under the headline "Rising, Shining Tennessee."

Chattanooga's Jack Lupton sells JTL Corporation, the family business, for $1.4 billion.

Bredesen sells HealthAmerica, the company he founded.

Southwest Airlines begins regular service to Nashville.

FBI and Tennessee Bureau of Investigation launch "Operation Rocky Top" probing illegal activities connected to Tennessee's regulation of charity bingo, including the illegal sale of bingo licenses.

Dollywood theme park, owned by songwriter-singer Dolly Parton, opens in Pigeon Forge, Tennessee.

Hamilton Place, the largest shopping mall in Tennessee, opens in Chattanooga.

Top-selling pop album is *Whitney Houston*. Top-grossing movie is *Top Gun*, starring Tom Cruise and featuring Fred Thompson.

Blanton released from prison.

Federal Express becomes the title sponsor of the St. Jude Classic golf tournament in Memphis.

Toyota announces it will build its third U.S. manufacturing plant in Lexington, Kentucky, not East Tennessee. Executives tell Alexander they will, as a consolation prize, place their Nippondenso supplier plant in Maryville. Nippondenso, renamed Denso, eventually hires four thousand.

USFL's anti-trust suit against the NFL fails. Memphis Showboats team folds, along with all other USFL franchises.

McWherter elected governor, defeating former Governor Dunn in the November general election.

Consolidation of the Knoxville and Knox County school systems is approved by referendum of city voters.

President Reagan appoints Baker his White House Chief of Staff, succeeding Donald Regan.

Memphis opens its "Ramses the Great" exhibit—first blockbuster installation in what will later be called the Wonder Series.

Democrat Bob Clement elected to Congress from Tennessee's Fifth District, defeating businessman Phil Bredesen in the August primary.

Victor Ashe elected Mayor of Knoxville.

1987   McWherter inaugurated governor, succeeding Alexander.

State Representative Ed Murray elected speaker of the state House, succeeding McWherter.

Wilder re-elected speaker of the state Senate and lieutenant governor.

Coach Pat Summitt leads the University of Tennessee Lady Vols to their first (of eight) NCAA women's basketball national championships, defeating Louisiana Tech 67–44.

Dr. Bill Frist and surgical team perform Tennessee's first heart-lung transplant, at Vanderbilt University Medical Center.

General Motors opens its Saturn Corp. auto plant in Spring Hill.

Hospital Corp. of America, now owning or managing 463 hospitals, spins off 104 hospitals to form HealthTrust. HCA President and COO R. Clayton McWhorter to be chairman, president, and CEO of the new company.

Donald J. Trump's *Trump: The Art of the Deal*, written with Tony Schwartz, is published.

Nashville bids to host the 1996 Summer Olympic Games to coincide with Tennessee's bicentennial.

Congressman Bill Boner elected mayor of Nashville, defeating Bredesen in a run-off election.

Nashville's new international airport opens.

Randy Travis' *Storms of Life* is the best-selling country album.

1988   A coalition of smaller school systems sues the State of Tennessee, claiming that funding decisions have deprived poor areas of their right to equal protection. Lewis Donelson, Alexander's former finance commissioner, is the coalition's attorney. The dispute will not be resolved for five years.

Alexander named President of the University of Tennessee system.

Lorraine Motel in Memphis is closed to be renovated into the National Civil Rights Museum.

Sara Lee Classic becomes a regular tournament on the Ladies Professional Golf Association tour. Held first at Hermitage Golf Club in Old Hickory and, in 2000, Legends Club at Franklin, Tennessee.

Rush Limbaugh's weekday radio program is syndicated by the ABC Radio Network.

Sasser re-elected to third term in U.S. Senate, defeating challenger Bill Anderson.

Bridgestone buys Firestone Tire and Rubber Co., headquartered in Akron, Ohio.

The movie *Great Balls of Fire*, about the life of Jerry Lee Lewis, is filmed in Memphis.

Blanton runs for Congress in Tennessee's Eighth District, losing in the Democratic primary to six-term State Representative John Tanner, a McWherter ally in the Tennessee House.

Tanner, defeating Ed Bryant in the general election, is elected to first of eleven terms.

Bridgestone relocates its sales staff of two hundred from California to Nashville.

Baker resigns as White House chief of staff.

Rain Man is the top-grossing movie.

HCA, believing its stock to be undervalued, completes a $5.1 billion leveraged buyout, taking the company private.

1989   Sasser becomes chairman of the Senate Budget Committee.

Bridgestone announces it will build a $350 million truck tire manufacturing plant in Warren County, Tennessee.

Operation Rocky Top becomes public when W. D. Walker, formerly the state's chief bingo inspector, pleads guilty to attempted bribery of a state legislator.

State Representative Ted Ray Miller, chairman of the House State and Local Government Committee, commits suicide after being charged with bribery.

Secretary of State Gentry Crowell, Walker's former boss, also implicated in the Operation Rocky Top scandal, commits suicide ahead of his scheduled third appearance before a federal grand jury.

John Rice Irwin is named a MacArthur Fellow for his work as "curator and cultural preservationist" in establishing the Museum of Appalachia.

Ground broken in Memphis for the Great American Pyramid.

Clint Black's "A Better Man" is the top country single.

Federal Express purchases Flying Tigers and becomes the world's largest full-service all-cargo airline, offering routes to twenty-one countries.

Nashville Area Chamber of Commerce launches Partnership 2000 economic development initiative.

Construction begins on Chattanooga's Riverwalk.

Fall of the Berlin Wall.

The Cosby Show is the most popular TV show for the fourth consecutive season.

1990   Tracy Caulkins inducted into the International Swimming Hall of Fame.

Jack Massey dies in Palm Beach, Florida.

General Motors Chairman Roger B. Smith drives the first Saturn car off assembly line at Spring Hill. Smith retires the next day.

The Silence of the Lambs, starring Jodie Foster and Anthony Hopkins, is filmed in Memphis.

Martha Craig Daughtrey becomes the first woman to serve on the Tennessee Supreme Court.

Bridgestone/Firestone and the Tennessee State Museum present "Masterworks," a major exhibition of sixty European paintings on loan from the Bridgestone Museum of Art in Tokyo—the first time this collection of the Ishibashi Foundation had left Japan since 1961. Show includes works by Picasso, Monet, Renoir, Cezanne, Matisse, Modigliani, and Van Gogh.

South Africa frees Nelson Mandela.

The top-grossing movie is *Home Alone.*

1991   State Representative Jimmy Naifeh, longtime ally of McWherter, becomes speaker of the Tennessee House of Representatives, succeeding Murray.

Daily newspaper the *Knoxville Journal* ceases operations.

National Civil Rights Museum opens in Memphis.

Danny Thomas, actor and founder of St. Jude's Hospital, dies. He is buried on the grounds of the Memphis hospital.

The National Football League announces it will add two franchises, the first league expansion since 1976. Memphis civic leaders mount a campaign for one of the new teams.

Alexander appointed U.S. Secretary of Education by President George H. W. Bush

Willie W. Herenton elected mayor of Memphis. The city's first elected African American mayor, he will serve five terms.

Breakup of the Soviet Union.

Bridgestone/Firestone Inc. announces it will relocate its corporate headquarters from Akron to Nashville.

National Civil Rights Museum opens in Memphis.

Memphis's Pyramid Arena opens. Memphis State University hosts DePaul.

Golf Club of Tennessee founded in Cheatham County by E. Bronson Ingram, George Gillett, and Toby Wilt.

Nashville Mayor Bill Boner appears on NBC's *The Phil Donahue Show* with his girlfriend, singer Traci Peel.

Alan Jackson's "Don't Rock the Jukebox" is the top country single.

In Memphis, initiative to replace the Liberty Bowl with a new stadium to attract NFL franchise falls through. The expansion teams are awarded to Jacksonville and Charlotte.

Phil Bredesen elected mayor of Nashville.

1992   Alexander announces he is running for president.

Benjamin L. Hooks, Memphis attorney, judge, and civil rights leader, resigns his position as executive director of the NAACP after serving fifteen years.

South Central Bell (later BellSouth) begins construction of its new Tennessee headquarters in Nashville.

Garth Brooks's *Ropin' the Wind* is the top-selling country album.

Senator Al Gore's book *Earth in the Balance: Ecology and the Human Spirit* published.

Governor McWherter signs the Education Improvement Act into law, together with a half-cent increase in the state sales tax, enacting the Better Education Plan in response to the successful legal challenge brought by Tennessee's smaller school systems to the existing funding scheme for local schools.

Al and Tipper Gore host the first Family Re-Union conference in Nashville. It becomes an annual event.

Former Arkansas governor Bill Clinton and Tennessee senator Al Gore elected president and vice president. Gore resigns from the Senate. McWherter appoints Deputy Governor Harlan Mathews to complete the unexpired Senate term.

HCA re-emerges as a public company.

Tennessee Aquarium opens in Chattanooga.

Bridgestone/Firestone, now the largest tire and rubber company in the world, completes its corporate relocation to Nashville.

Alex Haley dies in Seattle. Buried in Henning, Tennessee.

1993   President Clinton nominates Martha Craig Daughtrey to the U.S. Court of Appeals for the Sixth Circuit.

Nashville's Agenda, the citywide visioning process, publishes "21 Goals for the 21st Century." Recommendations include a new housing fund, a downtown art museum, and recruitment of professional sports.

Mayor Bredesen proposes a downtown Nashville arena for entertainment and sports. Design work begins.

The McWherter administration, responding to escalating costs in the state's Medicaid program, begins design of a replacement program. It will be called TennCare.

Two motion pictures based on John Grisham novels, *The Firm* and *The Client*, are filmed in Memphis.

Coach Pat Summitt achieves her five-hundredth win as the Lady Vols defeat Ohio State 80–45.

Whitney Houston's recording of Dolly Parton's "I Will Always Love You" is the top-selling pop recording.

1994   McWherter implements the TennCare program after receiving a federal government waiver for deviations from the standard Medicaid rules.

HCA merges with Columbia, a rival hospital company headquartered in Louisville, Kentucky.

Michael Ramirez, editorial cartoonist for the Memphis *Commercial Appeal* newspaper, wins the Pulitzer Prize.

Nashville's Agenda action teams begin planning for what will become the Nashville Housing Fund, the Frist Center for the Visual Arts, and other initiatives inspired by the citywide visioning process of 1993.

Amazon.com founded in Bellevue, Washington.

Death of State Senator Avon N. Williams Jr.

BellSouth opens its Tennessee headquarters tower, the state's tallest building, in downtown Nashville.

BellSouth Senior Classic launched at Gaylord's Springhouse Golf Club. Lee Trevino wins the first tournament. (The event will occur annually on the PGA's Champions Tour through 2003.)

Dr. Bill Frist elected to U.S. Senate, defeating Bob Corker in the Republican primary and incumbent Jim Sasser in the general election.

Fred Thompson elected to full term in U.S. Senate, defeating Democrat Jim Cooper in a special election.

Republicans seize majority control of Congress for the first time since 1954.

Republican Don Sundquist elected governor, defeating Nashville mayor Phil Bredesen. Sundquist appoints Bob Corker to be commissioner of finance and administration.

Former Olympic athlete and sports icon Wilma Rudolph dies.

Disney's *The Lion King* is the top-grossing movie.

1995   Columbia/HCA and Mayor Bredesen announce the company will move its headquarters from Louisville back to Nashville, the city of HCA's founding. Clayton McWhorter becomes Chairman of the Board of Columbia/HCA.

Sundquist inaugurated governor.

Bredesen develops a $20 million package of incentives to attract a pro team (either NBA or NHL) to Nashville's arena (under construction). Bredesen authorizes Gaylord exec Dick Evans to use it as a "hunting license" to find the team.

State legislature abolishes the Tennessee Public Service Commission, replacing it with a new Tennessee Regulatory Authority appointed by the governor and the legislature's two speakers.

New Jersey Devils owner John McMullen says he may relocate franchise if he cannot get a better deal at the Byrne Meadowlands. Evans offers Nashville's $20 million package. New Jersey's Sports and Exposition Authority counters next day. Team remains in Newark.

Domestic-terrorist bombing of the Alfred Murrah Federal Building in Oklahoma City kills 168 people.

Murder trial of O.J. Simpson.

Nashville industrialist Bronson Ingram dies.

Saturn produces its one-millionth car.

Gaylord's Evans introduces Craig Leipold to Bredesen.

Dolly Parton launches the Imagination Library, providing free books to pre-school children. (By 2015, the program will distribute over 700,000 books per month to 1,500 communities in the U.S. and Canada.)

Contact by NFL's Houston Oilers with Nashville officials. Bredesen and Oilers owner Bud Adams begin negotiations. Adams announces his intention to move the Oilers from Houston to Nashville.

American Airlines discontinues its Nashville hub operations. Cost-cutting over two years has reduced daily flights from 140 to 73.

Seinfeld is the most popular TV show.

1996   Tennessee's Bicentennial, the statewide celebration of statehood. Bicentennial Mall State Park opens.

Alexander runs for president a second time.

Governor Sundquist's Families First welfare reform program adopted
by the Democratic-majority Tennessee General Assembly.

NFL owners approve the Oilers relocation to Nashville.

Mayor Bredesen proposes a new NFL-caliber stadium, to cost $292
million, to secure relocation of Houston Oilers to Nashville. Opponents collect 43,600 signatures forcing a local referendum. Supporters launch "NFL Yes!" campaign. Stadium referendum passes with 58
percent of voters approving. Nashville's Gateway Partnership proposes
development design for seventeen acres around city's new downtown
arena.

Bombing at the Summer Olympics, in Atlanta's Centennial Olympic
Park, kills one and injures 111.

Tiger Woods, representing Arizona State University, wins the NCAA
Division 1 Men's Golf Championship on the Honors Course near
Chattanooga.

William Leech, the former state attorney general, dies at his home in
Santa Fe, Tennessee.

Clinton-Gore re-elected to second term.

Fred Thompson re-elected to a full Senate term.

Jim Sasser appointed U.S. ambassador to China.

"My Maria" by Brooks and Dunn is the top country single.

Former governor Ray Blanton dies in Jackson, Tennessee, while in hospital awaiting a liver transplant.

Nashville's new arena opens without a sports tenant. First event is
Amy Grant's "Tennessee Christmas."

1997   U.S. Figure Skating Championships held in Nashville, the first sports
event at the city's new arena.

Houston Oilers complete the team's relocation to Tennessee. With the
city's new NFL stadium under construction, the Tennessee Oilers play
one season in Memphis at the Liberty Bowl.

Dr. Thomas F. Frist Jr., a founder of HCA, returns as chairman and
CEO of Columbia/HCA, announcing plans to restructure the company. (HCA will become a privately held company in 2006. In 2011,
returns as a public company again on the New York Stock Exchange.)

Saturn begins selling right-hand drive cars in Japan.

Inaugural season of the Women's National Basketball Association.

NHL Expansion Committee meets in Nashville. Civic leaders hoping for a new NHL franchise stage a large public event at the new arena welcoming NHL Commissioner Gary Bettman to the city.

Jon Kinsey elected mayor of Chattanooga.

Leipold is granted a conditional franchise by the NHL Board of Governors and forms Powers Management Corp. to manage the arena. Kicks off season ticket sales with the "Ice Breaker Bash" and more than twelve thousand fans attend in three hours.

Titanic is the top-grossing movie.

1998   Nashville's Music City Bowl inaugurated. Virginia Tech defeats Alabama.

In college football, the University of Tennessee Volunteers win the Fiesta Bowl, defeating Florida State University 23–16 for the national championship title.

James Earl Ray dies.

Two Chattanooga newspapers, the *Chattanooga Times* and the *Chattanooga Free Press* are merged. The *Times* ceases publication.

Peyton Manning is the NFL's number one draft pick, signed by the Indianapolis Colts.

Statue of author Alex Haley unveiled in Knoxville.

Murder of state Senator Tommy Burks at his home in Monterey, Tennessee. His political opponent Byron Looper arrested a week later and convicted in 2000.

UT Lady Vols finish the 1997–98 season undefeated (39–0) and win third consecutive national championship.

Coach Pat Summitt featured on the cover of *Sports Illustrated* with the headline "The Wizard of Knoxville."

Lady Vols standout Chamique Holdsclaw drafted by Washington Mystics of the WNBA.

Tammy Wynnette, the "Queen of Country Music," dies in Nashville.

Saving Private Ryan is the top-grossing movie.

National Hockey League announces the Nashville Predators as the twenty-seventh franchise in league history. Team hosts Florida Panthers for first NHL game before a sellout crowd of 17,298.

Tennessee Oilers, after poor attendance in Memphis, shift to Nashville to play second Tennessee season at Vanderbilt's Dudley Field.

Workers at GM's Saturn plant authorize union leaders to call a strike.

Governor Sundquist re-elected.

The afternoon daily *Nashville Banner* ceases publication.

Former Senator Albert Gore Sr. dies in Carthage, Tennessee.

1999   Nissan/Renault CEO Carlos Ghosn initiates the "Nissan Revival Plan" to return the automaker to profitability.

Nashville's NFL stadium, called Adelphia Coliseum, opens.

Sundquist proposes adoption of a state income tax, triggering protests at the State Capitol.

Al Gore Jr. opens campaign for president, with national headquarters in Nashville.

Bill Purcell elected mayor of Nashville.

Two teenage students murder thirteen other students and teachers at Columbine High School in Colorado.

Women's Basketball Hall of Fame opens in Knoxville.

Soviet president Mikhail Gorbachev announces his resignation, and the final collapse of the U.S.S.R.

Fears of the "Y2K bug" trigger crisis planning by business, government, and universities to avert widespread computer failures.

2000   Tennessee Titans lose Super Bowl XXXIV to St. Louis Rams.

The Japan-America Society of Tennessee established.

USS Cole bombed near Yemen, killing seventeen U.S. sailors.

Rock 'n' Soul Museum opens in Memphis.

Tennessee Sports Hall of Fame and Museum establishes new home at Nashville Arena.

Byron "Low Tax" Looper convicted in the murder of state Senator Tommy Burks and sentenced to life in prison.

Texas Governor George W. Bush elected president, defeating Gore in a close election. Supreme Court rules in Bush's favor over disputed results in Florida.

Senator Frist re-elected.

Top country single is "Breathe" by Faith Hill.

2001   President George W. Bush inaugurated.

Two new cultural institutions—the Frist Center for the Visual Arts and the Country Music Hall of Fame and Museum—open in downtown Nashville.

Baker appointed U.S. ambassador to Japan.

Guitar virtuoso Chet Atkins dies.

Sundquist begins effort to attract Nissan's North American headquarters to Tennessee.

NBA Relocation Committee approves move of Vancouver Grizzlies to Memphis. Rookie camp established at Rhodes College.

Tennessee Valley Authority donates thirteen thousand acres along the Duck River, originally planned for the canceled Columbia Dam project, to the state for public use.

September 11 terrorist attacks in New York City and Washington, D.C.

U.S. invades Afghanistan.

Bob Corker elected mayor of Chattanooga.

2002   Tennessee legislature rejects Sundquist's income tax proposal and fails to pass a balanced budget, triggering a partial government shutdown. Solution is another increase in state sales tax.

Bonnaroo music festival begins in Manchester, Tennessee.

Conexion Americas founded in Nashville.

Senator Thompson announces he will not run for re-election. Alexander announces he will run.

Spider-Man is the top-grossing movie of the year.

Alexander elected to U.S. Senate.

Bredesen elected governor, defeating the Republican congressman Van Hilleary.

Sundquist, Bredesen, Frist, Alexander, and Purcell meet with Nissan CEO Carlos Ghosn in Washington about the automaker's U.S. headquarters location.

Frist elected Senate majority leader after Senator Trent Lott steps down.

The Interviews

My own understanding of what happened in the in-between time—of the politicians and how they worked, and of the policies and progress that arose because they crossed the aisle—has come from many sources. In addition to my own personal experiences and observations in that time, I have benefitted from the shared perspectives I have learned from hundreds of interviews and conversations with other Tennesseans who were in a position to know. I am especially grateful to these 384 women and men listed below who helped me know the stories.

A
Gerald Adams
Darrell Akins
Honey Alexander
Lamar Alexander
Tim Amos
Betty Anderson
Victor Ashe
Phil Ashford
Vicki Hunter Askew
Ben Atchley
Tom Atkinson

B
Gordon Ball
Joe Barker
George Barrett
Megan Barry
Tom Beasley
Gordon Belt
Andy Bennett
Tom Benson
Lady Bird
Pete Bird
Steve Bivens
Peaches G. Blank
Mark Bloom

Charles W. Bone
Gordon Bonnyman
Robert Booker
Denny Bottorff
Randy Boyd
Mark Braden
John A. Bradley
Leonard K. Bradley
Tommy Bragg
Dan Brawner
Phil Bredesen
John A. Bridges
Bill Brock
Pat Brock
James W. (Woody) Brosnan
George H. Brown Jr.
Wayne Brown
Joyce Broyles
Stuart Brunson
Gene Bryant
Walter Bussart

C
Ham Carey
Anne Carr
Richard L. Chapman
Cavit Cheshier

Fred Harris
Thelma Harper
Larry Harrington
Dana Hart
Terry (Max) Haston
Aubrey Harwell
Beth Harwell
Bill Haslam
James Haslam II
Jimmy Haslam
Warner Hassell
Sam Hatcher
Diane Hayes
Peter Heidenreich
Gerry Helper
Douglas Henry Jr.
Jim Henry
Tom Hensley
Mike Herron
Roy Herron
Waymon Hickman
Jim Hill
Kem Hinton
Jimmy Holt
Robin Hood
James Hoobler
John Jay Hooker
Ryland Hoskins
Ashley Brown Howell
Tom Humphrey
Marsha Mason Hunt
Shannon Hunt
Zach Hunt

I
Martha R. Ingram
Orrin H. Ingram
Tom Ingram
Gordon Inman
John Rice Irwin
Bill Ivey

J
Peter Jenkins
Carolyn Carter Jensen
Tom Jensen
Bill Johnson
Carl Johnson

Dr. Joe Johnson
R. Milton Johnson
Bob Jones
George Jones
Tiny Jones
D. Bryan Jordan
Tom Jurkovich

K
Tracy D. Kane
Christine Karbowiak
Dale R. Kelley
Mike Kelly
Sam Kennedy
Ben S. Kimbrough
John King
Jon Kinsey
Matt Kisber
Randy Knight
John Knowles
Laura Lea Knox
Debby Patterson Koch
William C. Koch
Teresa Rotier Koeberlein
Marguerite Sallee Kondracke
Mike Kopp
Walter C. Kurtz

L
Edith Taylor Langster
Martha Brown Larkin
Elizabeth P. Latt
Kevin Lavender
C. Lewis Lavine
Marc Lavine
Tom Lee
Craig Leipold
Richard Locker
J. Richard Lodge
J.W. Luna
Billy Lynch

M
James Mackler
Beth Fletcher Maddin
Margaret Major
Cynthia Floyd Manley
David Manning

Larry B. Martin
Phil Martin
R. Brad Martin
Janice Mashburn
Steven Mason
Harlan Mathews
Patsy Mathews
Hardy Mays
Derl McCloud
Hubert McCullough
Bob McDonald
Angus McEachran
Ann McGauran
Mike McGehee
Robert M. McKay Jr.
Randy McNally
Mark McNeely
Nancy Hickman McNulty
Mike McWherter
Clayton McWhorter
Jon Meacham
Keith Miles
Teresa Miller
David Minnigan
Rick Montague
Richard Montgomery
Carl R. Moore
Dana Moore
Wendell Moore
Bob Mueller
Wade Munday

N
Jimmy Naifeh
Roy M. Neel
James G. Neeley
Donna M. Nicely
Gerald F. Nicely
Roy S. Nicks
Betty C. Nixon
Pat Nolan
Stephen H. Norris

O
Jim O'Hara
Cynthia Oliphant
Doug Overbey
Russ Overby

P
E. J. Parker
John L. Parish
Courtney N. Pearre
Philip M. Pfeffer
Bill Phillips
George Plaster
Dan Pomeroy
Anne B. Pope
Jerry Preston
Keith C. Preston
Jane M. Pullum
Bill Purcell
Cabot Pyle

R
Claude Ramsey
Scott Ramsey
Randy Rayburn
Colin Reed
Gerald G. Reed
Rick Regen
Linda Rendtorff
Emily Reynolds
Milton P. Rice
Don Ridgeway
Nathan Ridley
Rich Riebeling
Lois Riggins-Ezzell
Bo Roberts
Kenneth L. Roberts
Sandra Roberts
David Rogers
Alice Rolli
Mike Rollins
Carol Rose
Mickey Rose
Mike Rose
Nancy Russell
Phil Ryan
John L. Ryder

S
Buddy Sadler
Chip Saltsman
Ronald L. Samuels
Otis Sanford
W. Keith Sanford

Bill Sansom
Jim Sasser
Linda Peek Schacht
Ralph Schulz
John L. Seigenthaler
David Seivers
Tom Sherrard
Parker Sherrill
Mike Shmerling
Jim Shulman
Russ Simons
Susan Simons
Gary Sisco
Herbert H. Slatery III
Charles Smith
David Smith
Frederick W. Smith
M. Lee Smith
Butch Spyridon
James D. Squires
Billy Stair
Don Stansberry
Ronnie Steine
Anne Stringham
Paul G. Summers
Don Sundquist
Frank Sutherland

T
Paul Tagliabue
John S. Tanner
Ray Tarkington
Debi Taylor Tate
Ron Terry
Jennie Carter Thomas
Jon R. Thomas
Raymond Thomasson
Fred Thompson
Byron Trauger
Charles Trost
Charles T. Tuggle Jr.
Mike Turner
Steve Turner
Randy Tyree

V
Alan D. Valentine
Karl VanDevender, M.D.
John Van Mol
Carroll Van West
Katy Varney
Ted vonCannon

W
Irene Ward
Michael D. Warren, M.D.
Teresa Wasson
Beth Waters
John B. Waters Jr.
J. Stroud Watson
Bob Weaver
Colleen Conway Welch
David H. Welles
Harry Wellford
E.W. (Bud) Wendell
Janice Wendell
Frank Wentworth
AC Wharton Jr.
Weldon B. White Jr.
Leigh Wieland
Sharon Sinclair Wiggs
Susan Richardson Williams
Jeff Wilson
Justin P. Wilson
William M. Wilson
Jerry Winters
Betty Wiseman
Tom Wiseman
Brenda Wynn

Y
Jeff Yarbro
Kyle Young

Z
Nicholas S. Zeppos

Bibliography and Recommended Reading

Much of America's political history and how government works today have been shaped by Tennesseans—from the rise of Jacksonian democracy in the middle nineteenth century to the rebalancing of our democracy that *Baker v. Carr* brought about in the middle twentieth.

The listing below is more than a standard bibliography. Each of these documents, most of them by or about Tennesseans, have been valuable to my understanding of the in-between time and will tell you more about what happened as the twenty-first century approached.

Abramson, Rudy, and Jean Haskell, Editors. *Encyclopedia of Appalachia*. The University of Tennessee Press, 2006.

Alexander, Lamar. *Friends. Japanese and Tennesseans. A Model of U.S.-Japan Cooperation. Photographs by Robin Hood.* Harper and Row, 1986.

———. *Steps Along The Way: A Governor's Scrapbook*. Thomas Nelson Publishers, 1986.

———. "What in the World is Tennessee Doing?" Governor Lamar Alexander's Farewell Address, January 14, 1987.

———. *Six Months Off: An American Family's Australian Adventure*. Wm. Morrow and Co., 1988.

———. "Find The Good And Praise It," *Parade Magazine*, January 24, 1993.

———. "Honoring Governor Clement and the Clinton 12," Weekly Column, August 24, 2008.

———. Eulogy of Senator Howard Baker Jr. at Huntsville, Tennessee, July 1, 2014.

———. Eulogy of Governor Ned McWherter at U.S. Senate, Washington, D.C. April 4, 2011. Find at: *www.youtube.com/watch?v=L1LjrzD2ykE*

———. "Remarks at the Unveiling of Sam Houston's Statue in Maryville," March 19, 2016. Find in "Speeches and Floor Statements, Office of Senator Alexander. Also at: *www.alexander.senate.gov/public/index.cfm/2016/3/alexand er-speaks-at-sam -houston-statue-unveiling-in-maryville*

———, Secretary, U.S. Department of Education, in *Parents Speak Out for America's Children*, Report of the Surgeon General's Conference on "Healthy Children, Ready to Learn," February 9–12, 1992, page 105.

Anderson, Dave. "A Move to Nashville? Devils' Lemaire Is Not So Sure He Would Go," *The New York Times*, June 4, 1995.

Annis, James Lee Jr. *Howard Baker: Conciliator in an Age of Crisis*. University of Tennessee Press, 2007.

———. "Howard H. Baker Jr.: A Life in Public Service," *Baker Center Journal of Applied Public Policy*, Volume IV, No. II (Fall, 2012).

Ansolabehere, Stephen, and James M. Snyder Jr. *The End of Inequality: One Person, One Vote and the Transformation of American Politics*. W.W. Norton and Company, Inc., 2008.

Applebome, Peter. *Dixie Rising: How the South Is Shaping American Values, Politics, and Culture*. Mariner Books, 1997.

Arnold, Dean W. *Old Money, New South: The Spirit of Chattanooga*. Chattanooga Historical Foundation, 2006.

Associated Press, "Teacher Union Head Near Favoring Merit Pay," *Nashua Telegraph*, July 7, 1983.

———. "Grizzlies Officially Moving to Memphis," July 3, 2001.

Avery, Sally, Jeremy Stiles and Robert Suttles. *Foreign Direct Investment in Tennessee*, Center for Economic Research in Tennessee, Tennessee Department of Economic and Community Development, 2016.

Badger, Anthony J. *New Deal / New South*. University of Arkansas Press, 2007.

Baker, Jackson. "How Tennessee Turned Red," *Memphis Flyer*, July 31, 2014. *m.memphisflyer.com/memphis/how-tennessee-turned-red/Content?oid=3713764*

Ball, Gordon. "Jim Steiner Interview, Butcher Banking Trial," *Gordon Ball Memoirs*, McCamish Media, May 27, 2016. Videotaped interview provided to the author by Mr. Ball.

Balz, Dan. "In Tennessee, consensus politics makes a last stand," *The Washington Post*, July 29, 2014. *www.washingtonpost.com/politics/for-tennessee-gop-its-the-tea -party-vs-the-legacy-of-howard-baker/2014/07/29/53403502–12a6–11e4–9285 -4243a40ddc97_story.html?wpisrc=nl_politics*

Bass, Jack, and Walter De Vries, *The Transformation of Southern Politics: Social Change and Political Consequence Since 1945*. See chapter 12: "Tennessee: Genuine Two-Party Politics." The University of Georgia Press, 1995.

Behle, Thad, editor. *Gubernatorial Transitions: The 1983 and 1984 Elections*. Duke University Press, 1989.

Beifuss, John. "Documentary explores 'Boss' Crump's stranglehold on Memphis Politics," *The Commercial Appeal*, April 20, 2010.

Bloom, Allan. *The Closing of the American Mind, How Higher Education Has Failed Democracy and Impoverished the Souls of Today's Students*, Simon and Schuster, 1987.

Bradford, Justin B. *Nashville Predators, The Making of Smashville*. The History Press, Charleston, South Carolina, 2015.

Branston, John. "From Memphis, With Envy," *Nashville Scene*, November30, 1995.

Broder, David S. *Changing of the Guard: Power and Leadership in America*. Simon and Schuster, 1980.

Bunnell, Gene. *Making Places Special, Stories of Real Places Made Better by Planning*, American Planning Association, 2003.

Byrnes, Mark Eaton. *Lobbying Effectiveness in the Tennessee General Assembly* (master's thesis, Vanderbilt University), 1986.

Calkins, Geoff. "Twenty years ago, Memphis told the NFL and the Oilers (now the Titans) to stick it," Memphis *Commercial Appeal* (USA TODAY Network), August 29, 2017.

Carey, Bill. *Fortunes Fiddles and Fried Chicken, A Nashville Business History*. Hillsboro Press/Providence House Publishers, 2000.

Caster, Shawn, and Russ Overby. *Reaching TANF Recipients with the Greatest Barriers to Work: Tennessee's Family Services Counseling Program*. Tennessee Justice Center, 2006.

Chappell, Lindsay. "Morton rises in Nissan power vacuum," *Automotive News*, May 1, 2006.

Charlier, Tom. "Chattanooga emerges from smog as leader in ecology," *The Commercial Appeal*, November 20, 1995.

Clement, Bob. "Lessons from My Aunt," *The Wilson Post*, September2013. *www .wilsonpost.com/lessons-from-my-aunt-cms-80545*

———. *Presidents, Kings, and Convicts*. Archway Publishing, 2016. Clinton, Bill. *My Life*. Alfred A. Knopf (Random House), 2004.

Clymer, Adam. "Detroit Chosen by G.O.P. For Its Convention in 1980," *The New York Times*, January 24, 1979.

———. "The GOP Bid for Majority Control," *The New York Times*, June 14, 1981. *www.nytimes.com/1981/06/14/magazine/the-gop-bid-for-majority-control. html?pagewanted=all*

Cody, W.J. Michael, and Richardson R. Lynn. *Honest Government, An Ethics Guide for Public Service*. Foreword by Senator Howard Baker. Praeger Publishers, 1992.

Cohn, David L. *God Shakes Creation*. Harper and Brothers, 1935.

———. *Where I Was Born and Raised*. University of Notre Dame Press, 1967.

Comptroller of the Treasury. *Mothers and Babies: The Health of Tennessee's Future*. Report No. R-04–06, Office of Research and Education Accountability, Comptroller of the Treasury, State of Tennessee, 2006.

———. *Special Report, Select Oversight Committee on Corrections*, April, 2008.

Connolly, Ceci. "Gore in His Element at Celebration of Wonks," *The Washington Post*," June 23, 1999.

Cooper, William H. "U.S.-Japan Economic Relations: Significance, Prospects, and Policy Options," Congressional Research Service, February 18, 2014, p. 11.

Cotter, Patrick R. "Alabama, From One Party to Competition, and Maybe Back Again," chapter 3 in *The New Politics of the Old South: An Introduction to Southern Politics*, edited by Charles S. Bullock III, Mark J. Rozell. Rowman and Littlefield, 2014.

Crandlemere, Cynthia. "Edward Hull Crump: A Political History," *Bridgewater Review*, Volume 7, Issue 2, Bridgewater State University, November 1987.

Crawford, Charles W. *An Oral History of the Winfield Dunn Administration: Interviews with Eugene W. Fowinkle, August 1, 1985*, Oral History Research Office, Memphis State University.

———. *An Oral History of the Winfield Dunn Administration: Interview with Mr. Dan Kuykendall, May 17, 1976*, Oral History Research Office, Memphis State University.

———. *An Oral History of the Winfield Dunn Administration: Interviews with M. Lee Smith, March 29, 1975, and December 31, 1979*, Oral History Research Office, Memphis State University.

Creamer, Colleen. "Tennessee roads named best by U.S. truckers," *Nashville City Paper*, December 20, 2001.

Cromer, Ed. "Master Teacher Battle Rages," *The Tennessean*, April 9, 1983.

Cromer, Ed, and Jim O'Hara. "At Issue: Master Teacher and Its Funding," *The Tennessean*, January 8, 1984.

Cronan, Joan. *Sport Is Life with the Volume Turned Up, Lessons Learned that Apply to Business and Life*. The University of Tennessee Press, 2015.

Daughtrey, Larry, et al. *Borrowed Money, Borrowed Time: The Fall of the House of Butcher*, 1983. (This was a series of eighteen news articles, appearing in *The Tennessean* and *Knoxville Journal* between October 24 and November 12, 1983, and later bound in tabloid format.)

Davis, Lincoln. "Anna Belle Clement O'Brien Presented With 2009 Humanitarian Leadership Award," *Congressional Record*, March 4, 2009.

Dedman, Bill. "Jack Lupton talks about a city and its destiny," *The Chattanooga Times*, January 1986.

Degges, Paul, P.E. *The 1986 Road Program, The Comprehensive Tax Restructure Act of 1986*, Tennessee Department of Transportation, July 1, 2015.

Dennis, G. Michael. *The People's Governor, Ned Ray McWherter, Democratic Tennessee Governor, 1930–2011*. Video documentary. Courtesy of Mike McWherter.

DeParle, Jason. "The First Primary," *The New York Times*, April 16, 1995.

Dickson, Paul, and William D. Hickman, edited by Nelson Eddy. *Firestone: A Legend. A Century. A Celebration.* Bridgestone/Firestone, Inc., 2000.

Dobie, Bruce. "In the Huddle: The Inside Story of the Oilers, the Mayor and Operation Cherokee," *Nashville Scene*, City Press LLC, February 29, 1996.

———, "Watauga," *Nashville Scene*, May 9, 2002.

——— and Liz Murray Garrigan. "Switch Play. Gaylord moves into the arena," *Nashville Scene*, July 25, 1996.

Donelson, Lewis R., III. *Lewie*. Rhodes College, 2012.

Dunn, Winfield. *From a Standing Start: My Tennessee Political Odyssey*. Magellan Press, 2007.

Eblen, Tom. "Datsun Builder Stands Firm," Associated Press, *Daily News*, Bowling Green, Kentucky, February 6, 1981.

Eichenthal, David, and Tracy Windeknecht. "Chattanooga, Tennessee—A Restoring Prosperity Case Study," Metropolitan Policy Program at Brookings, The Brookings Institution, September, 2008. *www.brookings.edu/~/media/research/files/papers /2008/9/17-chattanooga-eichenthal-windeknecht/200809_chattanooga.pdf*

Ely, James W. Jr. ed., with Thomas Brown Jr. et al. *A History of the Tennessee Supreme Court*. The University of Tennessee Press, 2002.

Evanoff, Ted. "Make Way for the New Guard in Memphis," *Commercial Appeal*, December 15, 2013.

Finn, Chester E. Jr. *Troublemaker: A Personal History of School Reform since Sputnik*. Princeton University Press, 2008.

Flegenheimer, Matt. "Back Home, a Unanimous Verdict on Corker vs. Trump: That's Just Bob," *The New York Times*, October 14, 2017.

Flessner, David. "40 years after bank failure, First Tennessee grows into region's biggest bank," *Chattanooga Times Free Press*, February 21, 2016. *www.timesfreepress .com/news/business/aroundregion/story/2016/feb/21/40-years-after-bank-failure-first -tennessee-g/350855/*

———. "In 25 years, Tennessee Aquarium helps reshape Chattanooga downtown," *Chattanooga Times Free Press*, April 23, 2017. *www.timesfreepress.com/news/local /story/2017/apr/23/aquarium-attraction25-years-tennessee-aquariu/424265/*

Flood, Heather, "Chaos in Clinton," master's thesis, chapter 4 ("A Tumultuous Season"), pp. 40–61, Department of History, East Tennessee State University, December 2007.

Fowler, Ed. *Loser Takes All: Bud Adams, Bad Football, and Big Business*. Longstreet Press, 1997.

Frank, Judy, and Richard Mullins. "$15 million community 'wish list' gets approval of Venture board," *The Chattanooga Times*, October 31, 1985.

Frank, Judy. "9 million put in state budget for Riverpark," *The Chattanooga Times*, December 25, 1985.

Freeland, Dennis. "Six Years Later," *Memphis Flyer*, May 22–28, 1997.

Frenay, Robert. "Chattanooga Turnaround," *Audubon*, January-February, 1996.

French, Rose, The Associated Press. "Nissan Moving North American Headquarters," *The Washington Post*, November 10, 2005.

Frist, Thomas F. Jr. "Tommy Frist Jr.—A Legacy of Philanthropy," Earnhardt Films, August 18, 2015.

Frist, Senator William H., with J. Lee Annis Jr. *Tennessee Senators, 1911–2001, Portraits of Leadership in a Century of Change.* Madison Books, 1999.

Frist, William H. Frist, MD. *A Heart to Serve: The Passion to Bring Health, Hope and Healing.* Center Street, Hachette Book Group, 2009.

Fulton, Mayor Richard H. *'96 Olympics, Shine On, Nashville, Getting into the Game*, cover letter and bid proposal book, addressed to Larry McCollum, United States Olympic Committee, August 28, 1987.

Garber, Kim M. "Thomas F Frist Jr., M.D. In First Person: An Oral History." American Hospital Association, 2013.

Garrigan, Liz Murray. "Bid High, Bid Low. Gaylord and the mayor cut a deal," *Nashville Scene*, August 1, 1996.

———. "What Would Daddy Say? As Bob Clement Ponders the Governorship, He Could Use His Father's Advice," *Nashville Scene*, May 29, 1997.

Gaventa, John, Barbara E. Smith, Alex W. Willingham, eds. *Communities in Economic Crisis: Appalachia and the South.* Temple University Press, 1990.

Gelman, Andrew, Boris Shor, Joseph Bafumi, David Park. "Rich State, Poor State, Red State, Blue State: What's the Matter with Connecticut?" *Quarterly Journal of Political Science*, Vol. 2, Issue 4, (2007), pp. 345–367.

George, Thomas. "N.F.L. Owners Approve Move To Nashville by the Oilers," *The New York Times*, May 1, 1996.

Gibbons, Julia, "A Tribute to The Honorable Harry W. Wellford," *The University of Memphis Law Review*, Spring, 2000.

Gibson, Frank. "State's money could be the clincher," *The Tennessean*, August 12, 1995.

Goodman, Peter S. "John T. Lupton, Creator of a Coke-Bottling Empire, Dies at 83," *The New York Times*, May 19, 2010.

Gose, Daris Anne. *The Development of the Better Schools Program in Tennessee from 1981 to 1986*, (doctoral dissertation, East Tennessee State University Department of Educational Leadership and Policy Analysis), 1994.

Goto, Mitsuya. "The Tennessee Waltz, Truckin' Down to Nashville," Remarks delivered at the Japan-America Society of Chicago, July 21, 1982, published in *Speaking of Japan*, Speakers' Bureau, Keizai Hoho Center, Japan Institute for Social and Economic Affairs (Vol. 3, Number 23), November, 1982.

Graham, David A. "Red State, Blue City," *The Atlantic*, March, 2017.

Graham, Gene. *One Man One Vote: Baker v. Carr and the American Levellers.* Little, Brown and Company, 1972.

Green, Joshua. "Birth of the Southern Strategy," *Bloomberg Businessweek*, December 4, 2014.

Greene, Lee Seifert. *Lead Me On: Frank Goad Clement and Tennessee Politics.* University of Tennessee Press, 1982.

Greene, Lee Seifert; David H. Grubbs and Victor C. Hobday, *Government in Tennessee.* University of Tennessee Press, 1982.

Greenhaw, Wayne. *Elephants in the Cottonfields, Ronald Reagan and the New Republican South.* Macmillan, 1982.

Greimel, Hans. "Takashi Ishihara," *Automotive News,* May 19, 2008. *www.autonew s.com/article/20080519/OEM02/305199935/takashi-ishihara*

Gutman, Amy. "Rucker Rips TEA Leaders for Teachers' Low Morale," *The Tennessean,* February 14, 1986.

Haile, John. "A Butcher Profile: Political Banker," *The Tennessean,* July 23, 1978.

Halberstam, David. *The Reckoning.* William Morrow and Co., 1986.

Hall, Doug. "How the Candidates Spend Their Money," *The Tennessean,* July 23, 1978.

Haltom, William H. Jr. *The Other Fellow May Be Right, The Civility of Howard Baker.* Keith Publications, LLC, 2014.

———. "Pat Summitt's Full Court Press, Cape vs. Tennessee Secondary School Athletic Associations," *Tennessee Bar Journal,* August 2016, pp. 33–35.

Harrison, Scott. "When it comes to making cars, Tennessee is the best in the nation," *Nashville Business Journal,* July 30, 2015.

Havighurst, Craig. *Air Castle of the South: WSM and the Making of Music City.* University of Illinois Press, 2007.

Hawthorne, Ann. "Alex Haley at Home in the Hills of East Tennessee," *Appalachia* (Winter, 1992). Appalachian Regional Commission.

Henry, Joe W. Letter to Governor Winfield Dunn, November 18, 1971. Courtesy of William C. Koch.

Herron, Roy, and L.H. "Cotton" Ivy. *Tennessee Political Humor.* The University of Tennessee Press, 2000.

Hickerson, Justin R. "Judicial Influence and the United States Federal District Courts: A Case Study," (Honors Thesis, University of Tennessee, Knoxville), 2014.

Hinton, Kem G. *A Long Path: The Search for a Tennessee Bicentennial Landmark.* Hillsboro Press, 1997.

Hirsley, Michael. "Tennessee Prisons Bursting At Seams," *Chicago Tribune,* July 7, 1985.

———. "Tennessee Tempted By Prison Plan," *Chicago Tribune,* November 17, 1985.

Hobson, Jeremy. "A Conversation With Memphis Mayor A.C. Wharton," Here and Now With Robin Young and Jeremy Hobson, WBUR-FM Boston, December 23, 2014. Interview available at *hereandnow.wbur.org/2014/12/23/conversation-memphis -mayor*

Hofstadter, Richard. *Anti-Intellectualism in American Life,* Alfred A. Knopf, 1963.

Houston, Benjamin. *The Nashville Way: Racial Etiquette and the Struggle for Social Justice in a Southern City.* University of Georgia Press, 2012.

Howard, Jessica. "11th Family Re-Union focuses on youth," *The Daily Register,* Vanderbilt University, October 21, 2002.

Humphrey, Tom. "Waltz—Don't leave with those who bribed you," *Knoxville News Sentinel,* July 22, 2007.

Hunt, Keel. *Coup, The Day the Democrats Ousted Their Governor, Put Republican Lamar Alexander in Office Early, and Stopped a Pardon Scandal.* Vanderbilt University Press, 2013.

Hurst, Jack. "Tennessee Homecoming '86, Tennessee Looking for Native Volunteers To Come Home," *Chicago Tribune,* June 22, 1986.

Ingram, Martha Rivers. *E. Bronson Ingram: Complete These Unfinished Tasks of Mine.* Hillsboro Press, Providence Publishing Corp., 2001.

Ingrassia, Paul, and Joseph B. White. "Roger Smith Reflects on Role at GM," *The Wall Street Journal*, July 31, 1990.

Irwin, John Rice. *The Unlikely Story of the Museum of Appalachia and How It Came To Be.* Schiffer Publishing Ltd., 2012.

Jarrard, David. "Prof to direct Japan Center," MTSU *Sidelines*, February9, 1982.

Karoff, H. Peter and Jane Maddox. *The World We Want: New Dimensions in Philanthropy and Social Change.* Rowman Altamira, 2007.

Katz, Bruce. "An innovation district grows in Chattanooga," Metropolitan Policy Program, The Brookings Institution, Sept. 9, 2015.

Kelley, Dale R. *Honoring Our Heritage, Shaping Our Future.* Published by the author, 2015.

Key, V.O. Jr. *Southern Politics.* Vintage Books (Alfred A. Knopf and Random House), 1949.

Kreyling, Christine, with Keel Hunt et al. *From Post Office to Art Center, A Nashville Landmark in Transition.* Frist Center for the Visual Arts, 2001.

Lakin, Matt. "Carnival and Collapse: 1980s brought World's Fair and Butcher bank failure," *Knoxville News Sentinel*, September 30, 2012. *www.knoxnews.com/news /local-news/carnival-and-collapse-1980s-brought-worlds-fair*

——, " 'Ugliest city' insult prompts beautification efforts in Knoxville," *Knoxville News Sentinel*, May 27, 2012.

Langsdon, Phillip. *Tennessee, A Political History.* Hillsboro Press/Providence House Publishers, 2000.

Lawson, Richard, and Bush Bernard. "2 Governors, a timely pitch and lots of legwork landed HQ," *The Tennessean*, November 11, 2005.

Lay, Nancy E. *The Summitt Season: An Inside Look at Pat Head Summitt and the Lady Vols.* Leisure Press (copyright Nancy Lay and Pat Head Summitt), 1989.

Lea, Sandra. *Whirlwind: The Butcher Banking Scandal*, J. Lord (Oak Ridge, Tennessee), 2000.

Lee, David D. *Tennessee in Turmoil: Politics in the Volunteer State, 1920–1932*, Memphis State University Press, 1979.

Legal History Project (selected interviews), Tennessee Bar Foundation, Massey Library, Vanderbilt University Law School, and Tennessee State Library and Archives, Nashville, 2013.

Leipold, Craig, and Richard W. Oliver. *Hockey Tonk, The Amazing Story of the Nashville Predators.* Thomas Nelson Publishers, Nashville, 2000.

Longman, Jere. "Tennessee Redefining the Women's Game," *The New York Times*, March 26, 1998.

Lovett, Bobby L. *The Civil Rights Movement in Tennessee: A Narrative History.* The University of Tennessee Press, 2005.

Lyons, William, John M. Scheb II and Billy Stair. *Government and Politics in Tennessee.* University of Tennessee Press, 2001.

Martin, Tim. "City adjusts to American cuts," *The Tennessean*, January26, 1995.

Mathews, Harlan. *One Day At A Time, Five Decades with Six Tennessee Governors* (unpublished manuscript), 2014. Courtesy of Patsy Mathews.

Melton, Courtnee, and Mandy Pellegrin, "Medicaid Work Requirements: TN's Welfare-to-Work Experience," Policy Brief 2017–17 of The Sycamore Institute, Nashville, December 6, 2017.*Metropolitan Life Survey of State Actions to Upgrade Teachers and Education*, Metropolitan Life Insurance Co., March, 1985.

McClain, Joan G., and Joy L. Smith. "The Lost Way, The Lost Chapters of the Chattanooga Story," *Chattanooga Times Free Press*, September 24, 2017.

McGinnis, J. Michael, Pamela Williams-Russo and James R. Knickman. "The Case For More Active Policy Attention To Health Promotion," *Health Affairs*, Project HOPE: The People-to-People Health Foundation, Inc., February, 1978.

Miller, Stephen. "GM Chief Tried to Transform Auto Maker But Couldn't Halt Its Decline," *The Wall Street Journal*, December 1, 2007.

Morgan, Jon. *Glory for Sale: Fans, Dollars and the New NFL*, Bancroft Press (Baltimore, MD), 1997.

Muro, Mark, et al. *Drive! Moving Tennessee's Automotive Sector Up The Value Chain*, Brookings Advanced Industries Series, The Brookings Institution Metropolitan Policy Program, 2013.

Murphy, Reg, and Hall Gulliver. *The Southern Strategy*, Charles Scribner's Sons, 1971Murray, Ken. "NFL pass is batted down in Memphis, St. Louis, too," *Baltimore Sun*, February 22, 1991.

Nelson, Michael, and John Lyman Mason. *How the South Joined the Gambling Nation: The Politics of State Policy Innovation*. Louisiana State University Press, 2007.

Naisbitt, John. *Megatrends: Ten New Directions Transforming Our Lives*. Warner Books, 1982

National Commission on Excellence in Education, *A Nation At Risk: The Imperative for Educational Reform*. A Report to the Nation and the Secretary of Education, United States Department of Education, April, 1983.

Nelson, Michael. *Resilient America: Electing Nixon in 1968, Channeling Dissent, and Dividing Government*. University of Kansas Press, 2014.

———. "Tennessee, From Bluish to Reddish to Red," chapter 8 in *The New Politics of the Old South: An Introduction to Southern Politics*, edited by Charles S. Bullock III, Mark J. Rozell. Rowman and Littlefield, 2014.

Nissan in Tennessee. Commemorative book produced by Nissan Motor Manufacturing Corporation U.S.A. on the occasion of the formal dedication of its new facility at Smyrna, Tennessee, October 21, 1983.

Norrell, Robert J. *Alex Haley and the Books that Changed a Nation*. St. Martin's Press, 2015.

O'Shea, Jennifer L. "10 Things You Didn't Know About Fred Smith," *U.S. News and World Report*, July 24, 2008.

Parish, John. *You Should Write a Book* (unpublished manuscript).Courtesy of Janice Mashburn.

Partners for Livable Communities, "The City of Chattanooga, Tennessee," Washington, D.C., 2010. *livable.org/livability-resources/best-practices/447-the -city-of-chattanooga-tennessee*

Peirce, Neal. Column on Memphis, *The Peirce Reports*, April 11, 1987.

Perlstein, Rick. *Nixonland: The Rise of a President and the Fracturing of America*. Scribner, 2009.

Peters, Jeremy W. "Nissan to Move American Base to Tennessee," *The New York Times*, November 11, 2005.

———. "Nissan Set to Relocate; a Sales Chief Will Retire," *The New York Times*, March 9, 2006.

Pew Research Center. *Political Polarization in the American Public: How Increasing*

Ideological Uniformity and Partisan Antipathy Affect Politics, Compromise and Everyday Life, June 2014.

Phillips, Kevin P. *The Emerging Republican Majority*. Princeton University Press, 2015. (Original edition published by Arlington House, New York, 1969.)

Powell, Prater Lee. *The Influence of the Tennessee Secondary School Athletic Association on the Development of Girls' Basketball in Tennessee, 1925–1993* (doctoral dissertation, Middle Tennessee State University), 1994.

Rawlins, Bill. *The McWherter Years, Tennessee Comes of Age*. Red Desert Publishers, 2001.

Rawls, Wendell Jr. "Knoxville Unveils Its World's Fair," *The New York Times*, April 25, 1982.

Reagan, Ronald. Executive Order 12503—"Presidential Commission on Outdoor Recreation Resources Review," Reagan Library, January 28, 1985.

———. Executive Order 12529—"President's Commission on Americans Outdoors," Reagan Library, August 14, 1985.

Reich, Robert B. *The Common Good*. Alfred A. Knopf, 2018.

Roberts, Steven V. "We Must Not Be Enemies: Howard Baker Jr. and the Role of Civility in Politics," *Baker Center Journal of Applied Public Policy*, Volume IV, No. II (Fall, 2012).

Reddy, Patrick. "Did megatrends pan out? A look back at societal predictions, 30 years later," *The Buffalo News*, June 24, 2012.

Reid, T. R. "Detroit Chosen by GOP As '80 Convention Site," *TheWashington Post*, January 24, 1979.

Riggs, Kathy M. "HCI-IFU: Infant Follow-Up Services Offered by the Tennessee Department of Health and Environment," 1985.

Robinson, Kenneth S., M.D. Letter to Ethel Detch, Director, Office of Research, Comptroller of the Treasury, State of Tennessee, February17, 2006.

Rudolph, Linda, and Michael O'Hara. *Families First: Landmark Transition*. Tennessee Department of Human Services and Bureau of Business and Economic Research/Center for Manpower Studies, The University of Memphis, December 2002.

Russell, Ryan, and Karie A. Barbour. "Welfare Reform in Tennessee: A Summary of *Families First* Policy," Center for Business and Economic Research, College of Business Administration, The University of Tennessee Knoxville, October, 2000.

Russo, John. "Saturn's Rings: What GM's Saturn Project Is Really About," *Labor Research Review*, Cornell University, Vol. 1, No. 9 (1986). *digitalcommons.ilr.cornell.edu/cgi/viewcontent.cgi?arti cle=1084andcontext=lrr*

Rothfeder, Jeffrey. *Driving Honda: Inside the World's Most Innovative Car Company*. Penguin Portfolio, 2014.

Sabato, Larry. *Goodbye to Good-time Charlie, The American Governorship Transformed*, 2nd Edition. CQ Press, Congressional Quarterly Inc., 1983.

Sandomir, Richard. "New Jersey Makes an Offer to the Devils," *The New York Times*, May 18, 1995. www.nytimes.com/1995/05/18/sports/1995-nhl-playoffs-new-jersey-makes-an-offer-to-the-devils.html

Saunders, Robert L. "Efforts to Reform Teacher Education in Tennessee: A Ten Year Analysis," National Commission on Excellence in Teacher Education, Washington, D.C., 1984.

Sciolino, Elaine, and Jeff Gerth. "Lamar Alexander: Behind the Flannel Shirt, Deep Washington Roots," *The New York Times*, February 26, 1996.

Seigenthaler, John L. "Son of the South," essay in the collection *When Race Becomes Real: Black and White Writers Confront Their Personal Histories*, ed. Bernestine Singley. Southern Illinois University Press, September 2008.

Shear, Michael D., and Richard Perez-Pena. "Obama, in Tennessee, Begins Selling His Community College Tuition Plan," *The New York Times*, January 9, 2015.

Sherbourne, Robert. "Nissan Work Starting Today After Tradesmen Jeer Owners," *The Tennessean*, February 4, 1981.

Sherman, Joe. *In the Rings of Saturn*. Oxford University Press, 1993.

Smith, Melissa J., Ethel R. Detch, and Jason Walton. *The Education Improvement Act, A Progress Report*. Office of Education Accountability, John G. Morgan, Comptroller of the Treasury, State of Tennessee, April 2004.

Smothers, Ronald. "Tennessee Republicans See an Election Weapon in State's Bingo Scandal," *The New York Times*, January 28, 1990.

Stair, Billy. *McWherter: The Life and Career of Ned McWherter*. Stair Public Affairs, 2011.

Stephens, Bret. "The Dying Art of Disagreement" (text of lecture in Sydney, Australia, on September 23, 2017), *The New York Times*, September 24, 2017.

Summitt, Pat, with Sally Jenkins. *Reach for the Summit, The* Definite Dozen *System for Succeeding at Whatever You Do*. Broadway Books, 1998.

———. *Raise the Roof: The Inspiring Inside Story of the Tennessee Lady Vols' Historic 1997–98 Threepeat Season*. Three Rivers Press, 1999.

———. *Sum It Up: A Thousand and Ninety-Eight Victories, a Couple of Irrelevant Losses, and a Life in Perspective*. Three Rivers Press, 2014.

Tamburin, Adam. "Obama: Republicans, Democrats can work together on free college plan," *The Tennessean*, January 9, 2015.

The Tennessean. "Promise and problems of state welfare plan" (editorial), November 12, 1995.

Tennessee Bar Foundation Legal History Project, Interview of William L. (Dick) Barry. Conducted by Barri E. Bernstein, May 10, 2011, Lexington, Tennessee.

Tennessee Blue Book, 1979–1980. Secretary of State, State of Tennessee, 1979.

Tennessee Blue Book, 2013–2014. Dedicated to Coach Pat Summitt by Secretary of State Tre Hargett, State of Tennessee, 2013.

Thomas, Jennie Carter. *How Three Governors Involved the Public in Passing Their Education Reform Programs* (doctoral thesis, Peabody College for Teachers of Vanderbilt University), 1992.

———. "Lessons from the Kids at Hanging Limb," *Now and Then*, Vol. 4, Number 1, Center for Appalachian Studies and Services / Institute for Appalachian Affairs, East Tennessee State University, Spring, 1987.

Thompson, Fred. *Teaching the Pig to Dance*. Crown Forum, 2010.

Tidwell, Mary Louise Lea. *Luke Lea of Tennessee*. Bowling Green State University Popular Press, 1993.

Tillman, Judith. "Ted Ray Miller remembered as 'a champion,'" United Press International, July 20, 1989.

Tollerson, Ernest. "Alexander Seizes Role of Political Outsider," *The New York Times*, December 29, 1995.

Travis, Fred. "The Butcher Boys Buy Banks," *The New York Times*, May 9, 1976.

Trimble, Vance. *Overnight Success: Federal Express and Frederick Smith, Its Renegade Creator*. Crown, 1993.

Tucker, David. "Edward Hull 'Boss' Crump," *The Tennessee Encyclopedia of History and Culture*, Tennessee Historical Society, The University of Tennessee Press, 2016.

Tucker, David M. *Lieutenant Lee of Beale Street*, Vanderbilt University Press, 1971.

United Press International. "GM's Saturn Plan Gives Tennessee New Luster as an Industrial Power," *Los Angeles Times*, September 8, 1985.

———. "Butcher Gets 20 Years in $790-Million Bank Failure," June 3, 1985.

Vesilind, Priit. "Rising, Shining Tennessee." *National Geographic*, The National Geographic Society, Vol. 169, No. 5 (May, 1986).

Vile, John R., and Mark E. Byrnes. *Tennessee Government and Politics: Democracy in the Volunteer State.* Vanderbilt University Press, 1998.

Vise, David A. "Private Company Asks for Control of Tenn. Prisons," *The Washington Post*, September 22, 1985.

Vinovskis, Maris. *From a Nation at Risk to No Child Left Behind: National Education Goals and the Creation of Federal Education* Policy. Teachers College Press, 2008.

Vowell, Michele. "Fatal Gander Crash: 1985 tragedy impacts Fort Campbell, Army-wide procedures to present day," *The Fort Campbell Courier*, August 9, 2012.

Vlasic, Bill, Hiroko Tabuchi and Charles Duhigg. "In Pursuit of Nissan, a Jobs Lesson for the Tech Industry?" *The New York Times*, August 4, 2012.

Waters, John B. Jr. *Downbound: From Jaybird on the Little Pigeon River to Chairman of the Tennessee Valley Authority. The Memoirs of John B. Waters Jr.* The Nexus Company LLC, 2000.

West, Carroll Van. "Nissan Motor Manufacturing Corporation, U.S.A." *The Tennessee Encyclopedia of History and Culture*, Rutledge Hill Press and The Tennessee Historical Society, 1998. p. 692.

Wheeler, William Bruce. *Knoxville, Tennessee: A Mountain City in the New South* (second edition), The University of Tennessee Press, 2005.

White, Connie, Mary Ziegler, and Beth Bingman. "Families First: Implications of Welfare Reform for Tennessee Adult Basic Education," Center for Literacy Studies, University of Tennessee, NCSALL REPORTS #10C, April 1999.

Witt, Gerald. Videotape interview with John L. Seigenthaler for *Knoxville News Sentinel*, January 16, 2014. *www.youtube.com/watch?v=ppgiyfSZhxk*

Wood, E. Thomas. "Nashville now and then: Quenching a civic thirst," NashvillePost .com, October 26, 2007.

Woody, Larry. "Tennessee strikes oil," *The Tennessean*, August 12, 1995.

Acknowledgments

First, as always, to Marsha and all the members of my family who put up with my disappearances into the writing room. Also to my friends who have tolerated, with great patience, my endless digressions into these stories as I learned them.

My thanks to some dear friends for reading portions of the manuscript to help ensure accuracy in my telling of particular stories, especially Charles W. Bone, David Ewing, Kem Hinton, Emily Reynolds, J. Houston Gordon, Sam Hatcher, Bill Koch, Teresa Koeberlein, Lewis Lavine, and Ron Terry. If errors remain, they are my own.

For helping me locate relatives, former colleagues, and in some cases special memoirs, my special thanks to David Benson, Tom Cone, Aubrey Harwell, Joe Henry Jr., Janice Mashburn, Ken Maynard, Gray Sasser, and Beth Horne Waters.

To Patsy Mathews for sharing with me the manuscript written by her husband, Harlan Mathews, recounting his career over five decades working with six different governors of Tennessee.

To John L. Parish for sharing not only his memories of recruiting Bridgestone's U.S. headquarters to Tennessee but also photographs in his personal collection from the early trade missions to Japan.

To Ronnie Steine for access to his collection of historical buttons and posters from Tennessee political campaigns.

To the Appeals Court Judge Andy Bennett for sharing a special find: an extraordinary set of four photograph albums he acquired at the estate sale of the late John M. Parish, containing the press secretary's photos of Alexander's early visits in Tokyo with Nissan officials including Takashi Ishihara, and with U.S. ambassador Mike Mansfield.

To James W. (Woody) Brosnan, who kindly shared news articles and columns from his career with the *Commercial Appeal*.

To Anne Stringham for her research skills and also her own memories of the in-between time. And to Theresa Burson for her faithful transcriptions of many interviews.

To Michael Ames, Betsy Phillips, and Zachary Gresham of the Vanderbilt University Press.

And to the following institutions and their leaders for many kindnesses in sharing their knowledge, expertise, and special archives:

East Tennessee State University,
Charles C. Sherrod Library
Celia Szarejko

Nashville Public Library
Kent Oliver, Director
Beth Odle, Nashville Room
Debbie May, Nashville Room

Rhodes College
Michael Nelson

The University of Memphis
Otis Sanford

The University of Tennessee
Dr. Joe Johnson

The University of Tennessee,
Chattanooga—UTC Library
Theresa Liedtka, Dean of the Library
Carolyn Runyon

Vanderbilt University
Nicholas S. Zeppos
Beth Fortune
Elizabeth P. Latt
Ann Marie Deer Owens
Dawn T. Turton
Department of Political Science
John G. Geer
Tracey E. George
Andrew Michael Engelhardt
Vanderbilt University
Libraries—Special Collections
Connie Vinita Dowell
Karen Smith
Juanita G. Murray
Teresa Gray
Molly Dohrmann
John L. Seigenthaler First Amendment
Center
Gay Campbell

Chattanooga Times Free Press
Bruce Hartmann
Alison Gerber

Tennessee Bar Foundation
Barri E. Bernstein

The Tennessean
Michael Anastasi
Maria DeVarenne
Beverly Burnett
Ricky Rogers

Office of Senator Lamar Alexander
David Cleary
Allison Martin
Ashton Davies
Sarah Fairchild
Patrick Jaynes
Faye Head
Kay Durham
Jane Chedester

Office of Senator Bob Corker
Todd Womack
Brent Wiles

Office of Representative Jim Cooper
Lisa Quigley
Haley Davidson
Chris Cooper

Office of Representative Jimmy
Duncan
Don Walker
Alexa Williams

Office of Governor Lamar Alexander
Tom Ingram
Lewis Lavine
William C. Koch
Debby Patterson Koch
Janice Mashburn

Jennifer Barker Graham
Beth Fletcher Madden

Office of Governor Ned McWherter
Billy Stair
James Hall
Katy Varney
Betty Anderson
Ken Renner

Office of Governor Don Sundquist
Peaches G. Blank
Leonard K. Bradley
Justin Wilson
Beth Fortune
Hardy Mays
Wendell Moore

Office of Governor Phil Bredesen
Stuart Brunson
Janie Conyers
Shannon Hunt

Office of Mayor Phil Bredesen
Dave Cooley
Joe Huddleston, Director of
    Finance
Phil Ashford
Tam Gordon
Shannon Hunt

Office of Governor Bill Haslam
Jim Henry
Janet McGaha
Beth Tipps

**Office of Lieutenant Governor
    Randy McNally**
Adam Kleinheider

**Office of House Speaker Beth
    Harwell**
Lisa Falkenbach

Office of the Chief Clerk
Tammy Letzler
Callie Nobles
Eddie Weeks

Office of Senator Douglas Henry
Diane Majors

Office of Senator Jeff Yarbro
Julie Quinn

Office of the Secretary of State
Tre Hargett, Secretary of State
Tennessee State Library and Archives
Charles A. Sherrill, State Librarian and
    Archivist
Wayne Moore
Gordon Belt
Vincent McGrath

Tennessee State Museum
Ashley Brown Howell
Lois Riggins-Ezzell
Jim Hoobler
Dan Pomeroy
Chris Grisham

**Tennessee Department of Finance
    and Administration**
Commissioner Larry B. Martin
Emily Mitchell
Ann McGauran, State Architect

**Tennessee Department of
    Economic and Community
    Development**
Commissioner Randy Boyd
Commissioner Bill Hagerty
Alice Rolli, Assistant Commissioner
Jed DeKalb, Chief of Photographic
    Services
Jennifer Birdwell
Janet Plumlee

Center for Economic Research in Tennessee
Sally Avery, Director
Tecora Duckett
Robert Suttles

Tennessee Department of Transportation
Lyndsay Botts
Paul Degges
B. J. Doughty

Bridgestone Americas, USA
Christine Karbowiak
Emily Richard

Country Music Hall of Fame and Museum
Steve Turner
E. W. (Bud) Wendell
Kyle Young
Bill Ivey
Jay Orr
Haley Houser

Nissan Motor Manufacturing USA
Jere Benefield
Justin P. Saia

Nashville Predators
Gerry Helper

Tuck Hinton Architects Nashville
Kem Hinton
Seab Tuck

WTVF-TV Nashville
Michael Rose

Crisp Communications, Nashville
John Crisp

Derryberry Public Relations, Chattanooga
Robin Derryberry

The Ingram Group Nashville
Tom Ingram
Lewis Lavine
Greg Hinote
Beecher Frazier
Janet Murphy
Rachel Albright
Emily Brzozowicz
Elizabeth McPherson
Sarah Currey

The Strategy Group, Nashville
Zach Hunt
Elizabeth Fielding

Nashville Convention and Visitors Corp.
Butch Spyridon
Terry Clements
Meghan Moore

Nashville Sports Council
Scott Ramsey
Brandon Cox

INDEX